Multiculturalism and American Democracy

Symposium on Science, Reason, and Modern Democracy

MICHIGAN STATE UNIVERSITY

Multiculturalism and American Democracy

Edited by

Arthur M. Melzer
Jerry Weinberger
M. Richard Zinman

University Press of Kansas

© 1998 by the University Press of Kansas
All rights reserved

Published by the University Press of Kansas (Lawrence, Kansas 66049), which was organized by the Kansas Board of Regents and is operated and funded by Emporia State University, Fort Hays State University, Kansas State University, Pittsburg State University, the University of Kansas, and Wichita State University

Library of Congress Cataloging-in-Publication Data

Multiculturalism and American democracy / edited by Arthur M. Melzer,
  Jerry Weinberger, and M. Richard Zinman.
      p.   cm.
  Essays collected here were delivered as papers at a conference
sponsored by the body Symposium on Science, Reason, and Modern
Democracy, held in April 1993 at Michigan State University.
  Includes bibliographical references and index.
  ISBN 0-7006-0881-8 (cloth : alk. paper). — ISBN 0-7006-0882-6
(pbk. : alk. paper)
    1. Democracy—United States—Congresses.   2. Multiculturalism-
-United States—Congresses.   3. Pluralism (Social sciences)—United
States—Congresses.   I. Melzer, Arthur M.   II. Weinberger, J.
III. Zinman, M. Richard.   IV. Symposium on Science, Reason, and
Modern Democracy.
JK1726.M77   1998
305.8'00973—dc21   97-45707

British Library Cataloguing in Publication Data is available.

Printed in the United States of America

10 9 8 7 6 5 4 3 2 1

The paper used in this publication meets the minimum requirements of
the American National Standard for Permanence of Paper for Printed Library
Materials Z39.48-1984.

CONTENTS

Acknowledgments   *vii*

Introduction   1
Arthur M. Melzer, Jerry Weinberger, and M. Richard Zinman

PART I. FROM PLURALISM TO MULTICULTURALISM

1. Is Assimilation Dead?   15
   Nathan Glazer

2. The Limits of Pluralism   37
   K. Anthony Appiah

3. Meanings for Multiculturalism   55
   C. Vann Woodward

4. Boutique Multiculturalism   69
   Stanley Fish

PART II. MULTICULTURALISM AND THE PRINCIPLES OF DEMOCRACY

5. Constitutionalism and Multiculturalism   91
   Walter Berns

6. Majoritarian Democracy and Cultural Minorities   112
   Bernard Boxill

7. Democratic Multiculturalism   120
   Wilson Carey McWilliams

8. The Virtues of Multiculturalism   130
   Anne Norton

9. Multiculturalism and American Liberal Democracy   139
   James Ceaser

10. Liberal Democracy, Universalism, and Multiculturalism   157
   Marc F. Plattner

PART III. MULTICULTURALISM AND CIVIC EDUCATION

11. Civic Education in a Changing Society   165
   Linda Chavez

12. Multiculturalism and Civic Education   173
   Lorraine Pangle

PART IV. MULTICULTURALISM AND THE ARTS

13. What Is a Classic?   199
   J. M. Coetzee

14. Fiction: The Power of Lies   216
   Mario Vargas Llosa

List of Contributors   227

Index   231

ACKNOWLEDGMENTS

This is the third volume of essays to be published by the Symposium on Science, Reason, and Modern Democracy. Established in 1989 in the Department of Political Science at Michigan State University, the symposium sponsors teaching, research, and public lectures on the relationship between liberal democracy and the great issues of contemporary life. This volume grew from the symposium's fourth annual program: a lecture series that ran from September 1992 through March 1993 and a three-day conference held in April 1993. All the essays presented here, with the exception of Mario Vargas Llosa's, were originally written for the program or especially for this volume. Stanley Fish's essay appeared later in *Critical Inquiry* 23 (Winter 1997), as did J. M. Coetzee's in *Current Writing* 5 (October 1993). Later versions of Nathan Glazer's essay were published in the *Annals* 530 (November 1993) and in his book *We Are All Multiculturalists Now* (Cambridge: Harvard University Press, 1997). An earlier version of Vargas Llosa's essay appeared in the *New York Times Book Review* (October 7, 1984). We thank Sage Publications and Harvard University Press for permission to reprint Professor Glazer's essay and the University of Chicago Press for permission to reprint Professor Fish's.

The symposium's 1992–93 program, and indeed all of its activities, was made possible by grants from the Lynde and Harry Bradley Foundation of Milwaukee, Wisconsin, the Carthage Foundation of Pittsburgh, Pennsylvania, and the Earhart Foundation of Ann Arbor, Michigan. We are grateful for their continuing support.

Michigan State's Department of Political Science has provided a congenial and lively home for the symposium. The Office of the Provost, the College of Social Science, and James Madison College have provided valuable encouragement and assistance. We thank our colleagues in each of these institutions. In particular, we thank Lou Anna K. Simon, provost and vice president for academic affairs; Kenneth E. Corey, dean of the College of

Social Science; Brian Silver, former chair of the Department of Political Science; William Allen, dean of James Madison College; Kenneth Waltzer, former acting dean of James Madison College; Joshua Parens, the symposium's post-doctoral fellow for 1992–93; Patrick Jackson, our undergraduate assistant; and Patricia Thompson, Michigan State's art librarian, for their special contributions during our fourth year. We are grateful for the stellar support provided by Karen Battin, Rhonda Burns, Iris Dunn, and Elaine Eschtruth, the administrative staff of the Department of Political Science. Ms. Battin, the symposium's administrative coordinator, played a crucial role in the preparation of this volume. We thank her for her excellent work.

In addition to the authors whose essays are included in this volume, the following individuals took part in the symposium's 1992–93 program: Richard Delgado, Richard Flathman, Michael S. Greve, Michael W. McConnell, David K. Scott, Jean Stefancic, Rogers M. Smith, Ronald Takaki, and Kenneth Waltzer. We thank them for their important contributions.

Finally, we thank Fred M. Woodward, director of the University Press of Kansas, for his faith in this project.

Introduction

Arthur M. Melzer, Jerry Weinberger, and M. Richard Zinman

After more than a decade of discussion, the subject of multiculturalism still remains bitterly controversial. This is a fact we have learned at first hand. Among the many people who have seen or heard these essays prior to publication, including four official readers, there was, in a sense, complete agreement: some of the essays are outstanding in their penetration, clarity, and fair-mindedness, while others are essentially useless and beside the point. There was almost total disagreement, however, as to which essays belonged in which category.

Partisan passion alone cannot account for this curious phenomenon. Equally important would seem to be the fact that multiculturalism, for all its influence and ubiquity, remains an unusually ill-defined movement. Some social movements, of which Marxism is the classic example, strive for precision and unanimity in their self-definition. The usual consequence, of course, is sectarianism. Multiculturalism, by contrast, is and seems content to remain quite amorphous. It has no recognized leader, no authoritative ideologist, no fundamental text, no official history. It is, of course, quite consistent, perhaps inevitable, that this particular movement should resist any single, monocultural formulation. But as a result, participants in this ideological debate, perhaps more than in any other, tend to experience their opponents as completely missing the point or as engaging in willful distortion.

With all of this in mind, we offer these essays to the public in the chastened hope that they will find some of them interesting.

Much as we might like to leave it at that, however, it is impossible, in a work of this kind, to escape the need for at least a working definition of multiculturalism. We will attempt to supply one, as well as to place this movement in some political and philosophical context. But we acknowledge from the start, because we know for a fact, that the remarks to follow are not acceptable to all the participants in this volume.

1

If one considers the positive goals of multiculturalism, while ignoring for the moment all that it says and does in the struggle to achieve them, it can sound very much like traditional American liberalism. Both hold that discrimination and insensitivity are bad, toleration and cultural diversity are good, and we should all strive to treat each other with open-mindedness and respect. Amid all the boasts and fears about the subversion of Western civilization, it is not useless to spend a moment reflecting on the kinship of positive ends between the multicultural and liberal camps. Indeed, there are those, particularly on the left, who profess to see in multiculturalism only a repackaging of liberal pluralism. It is pluralism with added urgency and a new rhetoric, stemming from the theoretical insight that all cultures are necessarily constructed of multiple sources.

Doubtless, many people who now call themselves multiculturalists are indeed nothing but old liberals who have embraced this fresher and apparently more powerful rhetoric. But they do not form the core of the movement—or, at any rate, the core of what makes it new, important, and controversial. To do justice to multiculturalism, one must acknowledge the serious challenge it means to pose to traditional liberalism. To view it properly, one must place it in the context of the "radical tradition" of American politics, especially the various liberation movements of the sixties. Like these earlier movements, multiculturalism is *radical* because it holds that precisely the *liberal* goal of toleration and diversity cannot be achieved through *liberal* practices and modes of thought, but only through a fundamental transformation of institutions and consciousness.

Yet, despite this important kinship, the multicultural movement is also quite different from the liberation movements of thirty years ago. Indeed, the most distinctive features of the former come to light most clearly, we believe, through a contrast with the latter. What is the difference, let us then ask, between the multiculturalism of the nineties and the counterculture of the sixties?

Many of the differences are merely circumstantial, arising from the great changes that have occurred in this country over the last thirty years. Thus, the counterculture was fueled, in large part, by the kinds of discontents that arise within a nation at war, both hot and cold; whereas multiculturalism springs more from the kinds of long-repressed domestic discontents that burgeon in a nation suddenly at peace and without serious enemies. Perhaps for the same reason, as well as others, the counterculture was essentially a youth movement, whereas multiculturalism is not.

But the most fundamental differences between the two movements, we believe, concern their ideological or theoretical differences. Generally speaking, the intellectual roots of sixties radicalism ultimately trace back, through Marcuse and the Frankfurt School, to Marx; whereas contemporary multi-culturalism draws its most important concepts from postmodernist thought, which in turn ultimately stems from Marx's great antagonist, Nietzsche. This is not to claim, of course, that the two movements followed these two thinkers in any close, programmatic, or even conscious way. But each movement was decisively shaped by theoretical presuppositions and paradigms that received their first or most influential formulations in the two philosophers. The concrete meaning of this polar shift from Marx to Nietzsche can be seen in four fundamental changes that would seem to characterize or define multiculturalism, at least as we are given to see it.

First, as heirs of Marx, the sixties radicals were still the heirs of Enlightenment rationalism. To be sure, much of what made the New Left "new" was its concern for cultural and sexual liberation and a growing tendency to question rationalism—anticipations of contemporary multiculturalism. But in its leading political documents and strategies the New Left continued to embrace the idea of universal truth. In particular, it fought for the rights of women and minorities precisely by claiming that these rights were grounded in some objective and universal notion of truth and justice.

Multiculturalism, by contrast, tends to accept and build upon the Nietzschean rejection of rationalism. There *is no* universal truth or justice. Thus, multiculturalism fights for the rights of women and minorities in a new way: by subverting the truth-claims of all who would exclude them. Multiculturalists fight indirectly, not by claiming to have the truth themselves, but by denying that anyone else does. The premise is: where there is no truth, there can be no intolerance. The denial of truth will make us free.

Second, sixties radicalism, for all its emphasis on personal growth, remained primarily focused, in good Marxian fashion, on economic matters: on poverty, exploitation, and imperialism and on the *economic* deprivations of women and minorities. But in opposition to Marx, Nietzsche argued that the defining characteristic of human beings is the need not for material goods but for dignity and self-esteem. If we have our own "why" of life, he proclaimed, we can get along with almost any "how."

Multiculturalism largely accepts this Nietzschean premise. Therefore, the fundamental concern of the multicultural movement is no longer economics but esteem, not income but identity, and thus not Western capitalism but Western culture. For this reason, the main battleground has moved from "the system" to the school; and the main antagonists are understood not as economic classes, but as ethnic and racial groups. There has been a shift, in a word, from political economy to identity politics.

Third, the New Left, like Marx before it, focused ultimately on the welfare of the individual as opposed to that of larger groups or of the state: revolution would abolish social class and, with it, the state and nation as well. By contrast, multiculturalism, in the tradition of earlier nationalist thinkers including (in a complicated way) Nietzsche, tends to focus on the welfare of peoples or cultural groupings, which are seen as the source of the socially constructed identities of individuals. It emphasizes group over individual rights. Multiculturalism could in fact be called "left-wing nationalism": it seeks not indeed the unity and exaltation of the nation-state under the banner of the majority culture, but rather the loosening of the nation-state to protect the identity and self-confidence of the multiple subcultures.

Finally, Marx and the New Left saw the root of human oppression in the economic structure; and, although they regarded the *liberal* state's proclamation of freedom and equality as so much propaganda, they did look forward to the final elimination of oppression in a better economic order. Among multiculturalists, however, there is at least a strong tendency to view oppression as a relatively permanent feature of human life, stemming directly from a psychological drive for esteem and cultural hegemony or something like Nietzsche's "will to power." From this perspective, all claims to impartiality come to light as deceitful, all claims to objective truth as assertions of power. Consequently, multiculturalists tend to be more skeptical and grim than sixties radicals, to lack the latter's visionary idealism and sentimental one-worldism, and to advocate solutions that are consciously anti-utopian, involving separatism and other forms of permanently controlled conflict.

In sum, and with all due trepidation, we suggest the following working definition for multiculturalism: it is a movement that radicalizes and Nietzscheanizes the liberal ideal of tolerance—thus turning that ideal against liberalism—by tending to deny the possibility of universal truth as well as of nonoppressive power and by seeking, through this very denial, a comprehensive redistribution, not so much of wealth as of self-esteem, and not so much to individuals as to various marginalized groups.

Part I of this work presents disparate views of the stakes involved as older notions of pluralism and assimilation give way to multiculturalism. Nathan

Glazer opens with a remarkable observation. While on the level of ideology the ideal of assimilation has been completely discredited in recent years, on the level of practice its power continues to grow, eroding once fixed boundaries of race, color, and religion. Assimilation and its logical result, intermarriage, proceed apace for Asians, Jews, Mestizo Latinos, and all other nonwhite newcomers. But one significant exception has persisted throughout the course of assimilation, "Americanization," and absorption of immigrant minorities: African Americans. For Glazer, this tragic black exceptionalism is the real source of multiculturalism, which blinds us to the great mixing taking place at the very time that we clamor for more separate and autonomous cultural identities.

Next, the call for such identities is examined by K. Anthony Appiah, but with a political perspective from beyond our shores. For Appiah, there is a crucial difference between multiculturalism in the strong sense that one finds in Africa—where racial and tribal differences threaten the integrity of the state as well as the pan-African identity that is still under construction—and the comparatively smoother and more easygoing pluralism that has been typical in the United States. The United States has always been multicultural in a weak sense, discouraging separate cultures—in the strong, anthropological sense of an exclusive way of life—while encouraging a plurality of cultures in the "high culture" sense of the interpretive and artistic expression of group experience. In Appiah's view, this is as it should be. But in an odd twist, America's universalistic exceptionalism still inclines us to ignorance of the ways of others, which in turn leads us to ignore the different high cultures that grow up in our largely European midst. Multiculturalism properly understood will encourage knowledge across high cultural boundaries and thus help cement the common bonds that unite us as a nation. Healthy multiculturalism is thus a corrective—but not an essential rival—to the older pluralism that was just never quite pluralistic enough.

C. Vann Woodward continues the discussion of these themes, but with a somewhat more skeptical outlook on recent calls for cultural diversity. In much the same vein as Glazer, Woodward argues that multiculturalism actually reflects white guilt at the one exception to an otherwise successful historical policy of assimilation. Given the vast number and diversity of America's immigrants, there was really no alternative to a policy of assimilation. African Americans were excluded from this policy and its good effects, but in spite of this tragic fact they too aimed for assimilation and integration—until recently. For Woodward, the cultural and political separatism now in the air are the results of legitimate and unanswered grievances, but that fact does not lessen the dangers posed by the more strident forms of multiculturalism that in his view have made alarming progress in the polity at large and especially in the universities. To the claims of Afrocentrists, Woodward responds that the idea of a common African culture is largely a myth hiding a dangerous multiculturalism, where tribalism and religious and ethnic divisions give rise to bloody conflict. Although it would be obtuse to ignore the grievances that fuel contemporary multiculturalism in America, Woodward warns against too much romanticism, especially in the universities, where it is even more likely than in the wider polity to do serious harm.

To these warnings, Stanley Fish essentially responds: "Relax, this is America." What Americans mean by "multiculturalism" is really a typical and largely harmless version of that old impossibility: having one's cake and eating it too. "Boutique multiculturalism" honors cultures in only their most superficial aspects, such as food and dress. Its very superficiality is rooted in a deeper loyalty to the principle of individual rational choice ("let's eat ethnic tonight") and is thus not real multiculturalism at all. "Strong multiculturalism" takes diversity much more seriously, but not so far as to accept the possible intolerance embedded in a given culture—for example, the death sentence declared against Salman Rushdie. Thus even strong multiculturalism is not *real* multiculturalism. But real multiculturalism—one that accepts the threat to Rushdie—is in fact monoculturalism and thus not multiculturalism at all. Those who fret about multiculturalism can stop worrying. Far from being a powerful idea opposed to liberalism, multiculturalism as a doctrine is in fact incoherent.

But liberals should not think this fact leaves their own principles as the only consistent game in town. For the inconsistency of multiculturalism has its counterpart in liberalism, especially when it comes to dealing with verbal assaults suffered by minorities. Fish argues that no consistent liberal policy is possible for preventing the harms of hate speech, so we must sometimes, perforce, use illiberal actions (the prohibition of some forms of speech) for the sake of liberal ends. For Fish, multiculturalism properly understood is not a doctrine, but an attitude governing the compassionate use of "inspired adhoccery" to address minority grievances.

In Part II of this work, the chapters turn to examine multiculturalism in its relation to the principles of democracy. Walter Berns leads off by arguing that multiculturalism is incompatible with the one thing that makes democracy possible: constitutionalism. In effect, Berns argues that the American founders addressed something like the multiculturalism of Fish's monocultural variety: they took multiculturalism as the mutually exclusive teachings of different religions. To avoid the danger of religious conflict, the Constitution banished multiculturalism to the sphere of private life, stripping it of all public power or recognition. But for Berns, this does not mean that the Constitution is merely neutral as regards all ways of life and especially as regards religion. It is clearly incompatible with some religions and hence some cultures (i.e., any culture that would claim the right to kill Salman Rushdie). For Berns, this fact shows how dangerous it is for multiculturalists to denounce the Constitution as the tool of white male hegemony. When we realize how divisive religion can be outside of our constitutional order, the moderate hegemony of constitutional norms makes perfect democratic and even multicultural sense.

Bernard Boxill then makes the case for multiculturalism as a means for preserving the fundamental goal of constitutional democracy: preventing majority tyranny. In our present situation of increasing diversity, constitutional rules as we know them seem able to preserve minorities' most basic interests. But these rules are not sufficient to allow for the flourishing of minorities and thus do not encourage the contributions, both cultural and political, that minorities might otherwise provide to the polity as a whole. Universal enfranchisement does not ensure actual representation for minorities, at least not without confining them to isolated electoral districts. Following J. S. Mill, Boxill argues that the actual representation of minorities is good both for minorities and for the democratic polity as a whole, which stands to learn from perspectives and ideas that are not otherwise available. Since the Constitution is notoriously silent about the rules for voting, Boxill, again following Mill, suggests that we take seriously Thomas Hare's system based on the single transferable vote. For Boxill, both the Constitution and constitutionalism will be enhanced by reforms that put brakes on majoritarian democracy and empower minorities, whose political voices tend to get lost in the larger majority crowd.

Wilson Carey McWilliams thinks liberal democracy can come to terms with multiculturalism, as it did earlier in the case of religion, but he is more concerned than is Boxill about the moral conditions for any possible accommodation. According to McWilliams, democracy is a "hard school," in which the forms and laws protecting inalienable individual *rights* often require that our individual and group *interests* be calculated and even bargained away. As a result, all cultures and faiths in America become involved in a process of "learning, forgetting, and selective memory that lays down boundaries of community and the civil meaning of the term 'American.'" McWilliams warns contemporary multiculturalists not to forget this hard fact. In a democracy, a subculture must adhere to the central tenets of democracy, which more often than not involve the dilution or compromise of that subculture's central beliefs. In particular, the current multicultural doctrine of the equality of all cultures is especially problematic. Such a view not only disdains the actual practice of cultures, which themselves regularly judge the relative merits of other cultures; it also denies the principle of equality as such. For as both Berns and Fish imply, if all cultures are equal, then we must accept the castes, racism, domination, sexism, and other forms of inequality embraced by some cultures.

Anne Norton then defends multiculturalism by appealing to the principles of its critics. In her eyes, multiculturalism fosters responsibility, inventiveness, and a generally critical spirit—all virtues necessary for a robust democracy. Moreover, multiculturalism contributes to the constitutional end of preventing majority tyranny, while at the same time combating the tendency toward mediocrity that always threatens the culture of an egalitarian democracy like our own. Thus Norton argues that multiculturalism actually fosters virtues more associated with aristocracy than with democracy—virtues such as magnanimity, friendship, and the love of learning. Invoking the spirit of Tocqueville, Norton argues that multiculturalism combats the leveling that stalks democratic culture and endangers democratic liberty.

James Ceaser breaks this sanguine mood with a hard-hitting argument that multiculturalism is conceptually and morally incoherent and at once parasitically dependent on and yet politically dangerous for liberal democracy. Multiculturalism claims to take seriously the diversity and multiplicity of cultures. But in fact there is nothing "multi" about it. Rather, multiculturalism divides the whole of human kind into two categories: "Hegemon" and "Other." The Hegemon is the white male European wrapped protectively in the liberal political order; the Other is composed of all the cultures he suppresses. But the dichotomy really makes no sense. First, its philosophical provenance consists solely of the thought of dead white European males. Second, the multicultural political agenda depends on liberal white guilt (pretty wimpy hegemons, those WASPS). And finally, it completely distorts the phenomenon of culture in America. Thus there are no separate cultures within the Hegemon—as if the Irish, the Italians, and Michigan's Finns are all the same, experienced no neglect, and hence can claim no compensation on multicultural grounds. These groups do have one thing in common: they are all white; and, for Ceaser, herein lies the ugly secret of multiculturalism. For all of its talk about the social construction of group identity, in practice multi-culturalism recognizes only nature—biology, race, and color.

In its ham-handed distortion of cultural reality—not just of the Hegemon, but also of the Other, which it describes with such racialist and culturally inaccurate categories as "Asian" and "Latino"—multiculturalism obscures the lessons that can be learned from the actual history of cultural and group politics in our liberal order. The liberal ideal of culture-free individualism was always something of a fiction, says Ceaser. Especially in big city politics and the national parties, group identities and interests indeed played major roles in the past. But these identities and interests were always informal and were never embodied in law or administrative rules. As a result, group identity ebbed and flowed: to be Irish or Italian in America no longer means today what it did sixty years ago. The color-blind individualism of the civil rights movement helped to erode many of the informal institutions once used by ethnic groups. At a later time, the ironic result has been the replacement of these informal institutions by a legal regime of preferences based solely on race. This fact, buttressed by the legitimizing theory of multiculturalism, cannot bode well for liberal democracy. For we can no longer be sure that group identity will be fluid, as it must be in a liberal order. It is now more likely that the really nasty aspects of culture will take advantage of the current multicultural regime. And no wonder, for the upshot of multiculturalism is racialism and biologism—the really great vices of Europe—which our founders sought to escape and which have done such harm to us to the extent that we did not.

In an equally hard-hitting essay, Marc Plattner ends the second part by arguing that when viewed from the international perspective, the whole multiculturalism debate appears strikingly "Amerocentric." The American multiculturalist, eager to press some political and cultural claim, insists that all universal principles are mere rationales for the domination of one group over others. But for the struggling dissidents who risk life and limb for freedom in faraway lands, the universal principles of human rights are life's very blood. And so while the rest of the world increasingly appeals to universal principles of rights and democracy, we treat that universalism with increasing contempt and disregard.

From politics, Part III turns to the question of multiculturalism and civic education. According to Linda Chavez, it is a mistake to think that the multicultural aspects of civic education should focus on the preservation of the many distinctive cultures associated with racial and ethnic groups. Groups have every right to pursue such interests; indeed, it is healthy that they should do so. But education along these lines must be carried out in private—in families and in communal organizations. To be sure, our civic education, if it lacked a multicultural dimension, would distort the reality of American experience and history, which is in large part the story of ethnic pluralism. But healthy multiculturalism should aim to show the common elements in American culture—those mores and institutions, shared by all, that make it possible for different groups to express their cultural lives in private and as they, not the government, see fit.

Lorraine Pangle next argues that the new multicultural thrust in civic education actually reproduces the vices of the old monocultural education it criticizes. It merely replaces one narrow, parochial, and shallow view of our history and civic culture with a variety of equally narrow, parochial, and shallow views, with each group exhorted—as a matter of therapeutic necessity—to take pride in what is simply its own. But therapy and group pride are no substitutes for genuine education of mind and character. What we need, says Pangle, is a really serious multiculturalism, one that encourages the student to look both above and beyond the limitations of any given culture. We must get beyond the stultifying categories of "absolutism" and "relativism"—both of which serve to encourage the lazy satisfaction with what is most familiar. For Pangle, genuine multiculturalism will transform civic education into liberal education. And well it should, for no civic education worth its salt should take civic concerns as the sole horizon for the mind or spirit. A proper multiculturalism, then, takes humanity as its ultimate theme.

A radical multiculturalist might respond, however, that Pangle's conclusion begs the fundamental question: Is there such a thing as universal humanity—discoverable by the humanities—that transcends particular political memberships and group identities? Or is such humanity an ideological fiction that hides the political hegemony of Western culture? Is there a real difference between the supposedly universal experience reflected in a Bach fugue and the particular function of the Papuan war dance? Is the culture that produced Bach properly called high and the Papuans' low? Are Shakespeare and the King James Bible genuine windows to the essence of human life, or might comic books be just as revelatory of the human condition that, in truth, has no real essence and is determined by cultural construction?

A moderate multiculturalist would reject these extreme alternatives, but might nevertheless find our genuine humanity too complex and elusive—

and too filtered through cultural experience—to be captured by any rigid list of classics or "great books." The issue is not high and low culture, but good and bad works of art, and the latter come in many forms and from many and diverse cultural experiences. We must be careful not to deify certain authors and works, however great they may be, lest we restrict our horizons and miss pictures of the human condition that are as rich and revealing as the ones we associate with the traditional curriculum.

These questions—so familiar from the "canon" wars—go to the heart of multiculturalism, and precisely because the latter as a political movement blurs the old distinction between material and cultural goods. The political stakes are identities, and identity involves culture. Small wonder, then, that multicultural debates about the arts, and especially about the university curriculum and great books, are so heated and so easily distorted by passion, ideological commitment, and interests that seem extrinsic to the arts themselves.

To get a fresh perspective on these questions, we wanted them discussed by accomplished writers from multicultural societies other than America. J. M. Coetzee and Mario Vargas Llosa were especially appropriate because both had at first declined our invitation, on the grounds that the discussion of multiculturalism and the arts was, in America, mired in our unique national preoccupations: race and the underclass, feminism, immigration and assimilation. They appear here, in Part IV, because we encouraged them to speak from above our local frays.

In "What Is a Classic?" J. M. Coetzee considers what classical perfection means at a time when historicism is the reigning frame of mind. After a subtle discussion of T. S. Eliot and J. S. Bach, Coetzee concludes that "the classic defines itself by surviving" in the course of regular testing by those professionals who teach and learn the various creative arts. The classic work emerges from the simple fact that such professionals—who would not struggle with a work whose "life functions have been terminated"—continue to repair to it. If shielded from critical attack, the classic "can never prove itself" in this professional way and thus become the broader social phenomenon we commonly mean by the term "classic." Thus, criticism, even of the most skeptical and multicultural kind, is not the foe of the classic, but its unwitting savior.

Finally, in "Fiction: The Power of Lies," Mario Vargas Llosa tells us that all good fiction lies, but not in the way commonly suggested by more radical multiculturalism, that is, by covering up and legitimizing existing power relations or by creating the "constructions" that establish cultural identity.

Rather, fiction responds to the simple fact that all human beings, regardless of their station or culture, long for lives they do not have. The lies of fiction reflect this unchanging truth of the human condition. Great fiction creates a world in which the reader can live with an impunity not granted by real life. For Vargas Llosa, the open deceptiveness of literature marks it off from mere propaganda; and a sure sign of totalitarianism is a blurring of the distinctions among fiction, politics, and history. Great fiction is an indictment of life under any regime or ideology. It thus demonstrates the permanent inadequacy of any merely civic culture—however narrow, pluralistic, or multicultural it may be.

Part I

From Pluralism to Multiculturalism

Chapter 1

Is Assimilation Dead?

Nathan Glazer

"Assimilation" is not today a popular term. Recently I asked a group of Harvard students taking a class on race and ethnicity in the United States what their attitude to the term "assimilation" was. The large majority had a negative reaction to it. Had I asked what they thought of the term "Americanization," the reaction I am sure would have been even more hostile. The "melting pot" is no longer a uniformly praised metaphor for American society, as it once was. It suggests too much a forced conformity, and reminds people today not of the welcome in American society of so many groups and races, but rather of American society's demands on those it allows to enter. Indeed, in recent years it has been taken for granted that assimilation, either as an expectation of how different ethnic and racial groups would respond to their common presence in one society, or as an ideal as to how the society should evolve, or as the expected result of a sober social scientific analysis of the ultimate consequence of the meeting of people and races, is to be rejected. Our ethnic and racial reality, we are told, does not exhibit the effects of assimilation; our social science should not expect it; and as an ideal it is somewhat disreputable, opposed to the reality of both individual and group difference and to the claims that such differences should be recognized and celebrated.

One might think there is nothing left to say. The idea that it would happen, that it should happen, has simply been discredited, and we live with a new reality. It was once called cultural pluralism, it is now called multiculturalism, and whatever the complications created by the term for educational policy, or for public policy in various other realms, that is what we must live with, and all of us seem to be ranged along a spectrum of greater or lesser enthusiasm for and acceptance of the new reality. Even critics of the new multiculturalism take their places within this spectrum. Those who truly stand against it, the true advocates and prophets of a full assimilationism, are so minuscule in American public and intellectual life that they can

15

scarcely be discerned in public discussion. One can point to the journal *Chronicles,* and scarcely anything else. Neither liberals nor neoliberals, conservatives nor neoconservatives, have much good to say about assimilation, and only a branch of paleoconservatism can now be mustered in its defense. It is only adherents of this hardly potent branch of conservatism who would argue that even if assimilation has not yet happened, it is something that, despite the reverses of the past thirty years, should have happened, and should still happen.

Yet assimilation, properly understood, is neither a dead hope nor a demeaning concept: It is rather, I will argue, still the most powerful force affecting the ethnic and racial elements of the United States. Our problem in recognizing this has to do with one great failure of assimilation in American life, the incorporation of the African American, a failure that has led in its turn to a more general counterattack on the ideology of assimilation.

But to go back: What was assimilation? It was the expectation that a new man would be born, was being born, in the United States. We can go back to that much quoted comment on what was the American, in Crèvecoeur's *Letters from an American Farmer* of 1782: "What then is the American, this new man? He is either a European or the descendant of a European, hence that strange mixture of blood, which you will find in no other country. I could point out to you a family whose grandfather was an Englishman, whose wife was Dutch, whose son married a French woman, and whose present four sons have four wives of four different nations. *He* is an American, who, leaving behind him all his ancient prejudices and manners, receives new ones from the new mode of life he has embraced, the new government he obeys, and the new rank he holds."[1]

This passage, which Philip Gleason tells us "has probably been quoted more than any other in the history of immigration," has of course been generally cited to celebrate American diversity and the general acceptance of this diversity as forming the basis of a new nation, a new national identity. But today we will look at it with more critical eyes, and note what it does not include as well as what it does: There is no reference to Negroes or blacks or Africans, who then made up a fifth of the American population, or to American Indians, who then were still a vivid and meaningful, on occasion menacing, presence in the colonies. In the course of an examination of the idea of assimilation in American history, we will find many other passages that to our contemporary eyes will express a similarly surprising unconsciousness, or hypocrisy, or unawareness: Today we would cry out, "There are others there you are not talking about! What about them, and what place will they have in the making of the new American?"

The concept of assimilation looked toward Europe: It referred to the expected experience and fate of the stream of immigrants who were a permanent part of American life and consciousness from the time of the first settlements on the Atlantic seaboard to the 1920s, when it was thought (incorrectly) that we were now done with mass immigration of people of varied backgrounds to the United States.

There has been a good deal of discussion of the significance of one major characteristic of the emerging American national consciousness, or, we would say today, the emerging American identity: In many authoritative formulations, from the Declaration of Independence on, the American, the new nationality being formed here, is not defined ethnically, as deriving from an ancient common stock or stocks, as almost all other major modern nations define themselves. I point out as an aside that while the term "identity" is almost essential in any discussion of this emerging American national character, it is a relative latecomer to the discussion. Philip Gleason tells us:

> The term "identity" has become indispensable in the discussion of ethnic affairs. Yet it was hardly used at all until the 1950's. The father of the concept, Erik H. Erikson, remarked on its novelty in . . . *Childhood and Society* (1950): "We begin to conceptualize matters of identity . . . in a country which attempts to make a super-identity of all the identities imported by its constituent immigrants." In an autobiographical account published 20 years later, Erikson . . . quoted this passage and added that the terms "identity" and "identity crisis" seemed to grow out of "the experience of emigration, immigration, and Americanization."[2]

Many could be quoted on this surprising characteristic of American identity and on the avoidance or very limited presence of explicit ethnic reference in the founding documents and in the debates on the revolution and the formation of the union. Despite the facts that the American revolution was fought almost exclusively by men who traced their origins to the British Isles, and primarily to England and that the signers of the Declaration of Independence and the framers of the Constitution were exclusively of this stock, they did not define their Americanness as an ethnic characteristic: They emphasized its dependence on adherence to ideals, to universal principles. Perhaps, as Gleason points out, it was because it was necessary for the rebels and revolutionaries to distinguish themselves from the ethnically almost identical country against which they were rebelling.

But in any case, the preference for an ideological formulation of the definition of the American was there at the beginning. Years ago I quoted Hans Kohn, Yehoshua Arieli, and S. M. Lipset on this characteristic of American identity.[3] One could add other voices. As Gleason writes:

> The ideological quality of American national identity was of decisive importance, vis-à-vis the question of immigration and ethnicity. To become an American a person did not have to be of any particular national, linguistic, religious, or ethnic background. All he had to do was to commit himself to the political ideology centered on the abstract ideals of liberty, equality, and republicanism. Thus the universalist ideological character of American nationality meant that it was open to anyone who willed to become an American.[4]

As anyone writing in 1980 must be, he is aware of the exclusions, not remarked on by the writers of those early ringing documents (perhaps exclusions of which they were not conscious) of blacks and Indians, and later, other groups not present at the beginning of the new United States. Even if they were not not specifically excluded, they were not intended to be included in these ringing affirmations of universality.

One could find here and there before the 1940s a few voices of significance who seem to make no exclusion: There was Emerson in 1845: "in this continent—asylum of all nations,—the energy of Irish, Germans, Swedes, Poles, and Cossacks, and all the European tribes,—of the Africans, and of the Polynesians,—will construct a new race, a new religion, a new state, a new literature, which will be as vigorous as the new Europe which came out of the smelting-pot of the Dark Ages."[5] There was Whitman. But one can ask even of Emerson, did he mean it? What did he know of Polynesians, after all? And one can ask of the term he introduced to characterize the assimilation of the different elements, the "smelting pot"—later to achieve fame in this discussion in the form of the "melting pot"—was that not too brutal, too strong, a metaphor for what was to be lost, to disappear, in order to make this new race? In the metaphor, the groups were to be more than melted, but rather smelted, as in two or more metals becoming one (the Emerson passage begins with a reference to "Corinthian brass"). But for the moment ignoring the question of whether assimilation was too strong a demand, it is necessary to focus on who was to be assimilated.

If we look back toward the nineteenth century from the perspective of the present, we can only be surprised at how unconcerned Americans were over the problem of assimilation until the 1890s or so. John Higham has pointed to this oddity, but notes that this unconcern was possible only because other races simply didn't enter into the consideration of the issue. As he writes:

> To speak of assimilation as a problem in nineteenth-century America is, in an important sense, to indulge in anachronism. That is because nineteenth-century Americans seemed for the most part curiously undaunted by, and generally insensitive to, the numerous and sometimes tragic divisions in their society along racial and ethnic lines. . . . Assimilation was either taken for granted or viewed as inconceivable. For European peoples it was thought to be the natural, almost inevitable, outcome of life in America. For other races assimilation was believed to be largely unattainable and therefore not a source of concern. Only at the end of the century did ethnic mixing arouse a sustained and urgent sense of danger. Only then did large numbers of white Americans come to fear that assimilation was *not* occurring among major European groups and that it was going too far among other minorities, notably blacks, Orientals, and Jews.[6]

The Americanization Movement

In almost all the discussions of Americanization or assimilation until about World War II, the participants have only Europeans in mind. This is true whether they favored or opposed assimilation and Americanization efforts. Today's reader of the documents of the great Americanization drive of the second decade of this century will find no reference to blacks, then as now our largest minority. It is as if the turmoil of abolitionism, slavery, the Civil War, Reconstruction, did not exist. All concern was with the "new" immigrants, that is, the mass immigration from Eastern and Southern Europe that brought enormous numbers of different kinds of Europeans from those the nation had become accustomed to. Admittedly one could make the argument that "Americanization," the name of the assimilation movement of the time, could address only those who were not Americans, and were not blacks American-born, and formally citizens? So, one could argue, this was the reason they were ignored in the great debate that finally degenerated into a resurgent Ku Klux Klan and the closing of the gates to the new immigrants.

how to make immigrant bold or American?

Yet when one looks at the aims of the Americanization movement one may well ask, and why not blacks too? The aims of the movement, in its earlier, benign form, were to make the newcomers citizens and encourage them to participate as individuals in politics (as against their domination by urban bosses), to teach them English (and here one main argument was to make them better and safer workers, in view of the huge toll of industrial accidents), to break up immigrant colonies ("distribution," it was called), to teach American customs, which to the Americanizers seemed to mean primarily sanitation and hygiene. All this would make the immigrants better Americans.

One major motivation was concern that the new immigrants would not become good Americans, owing to lack of English, citizenship, and knowledge of American customs. With World War I, to this motivation was added fear of lack of patriotism or disloyalty. But the vigorous advocates of Americanization—social workers and businessmen, a strange mix that nevertheless characterized much of the progressivism of the time—were also trying to plead the case of the new immigrants against those of their countrymen who increasingly favored immigration restriction. The social workers, we know, pled this case out of understanding and sympathy for the new immigrants. The businessmen, we may assume, took the same position primarily out of self-interest, much as the *Wall Street Journal* of today argues for free immigration. But if these were the aims of the Americanization movement, why were not the blacks included?

Their exclusion is even more striking to the current reader in view of the language of the time, in which ethnic groups are referred to as "races." But the first group that comes to mind today when we speak of "race" was not in the minds of these earnest and energetic advocates of assimilation and Americanization.

Consider one of the most authoritative statements of what was hoped for from Americanization, from a progressive woman social worker who was the heart and soul of the movement, indefatigably organizing committees, conventions, statements, and programs, Frances Kellor:

> Americanization is the science of racial relations in America, dealing with the assimilation and amalgamation of diverse races in equity into an integral part of the national life. By "assimilation" is meant the indistinguishable incorporation of the races into the substance of American life. By "amalgamation" is meant so perfect a blend that the absence or imperfection of any of the vital racial elements available, will impair the compound. By "an integral part" is

meant that, once fused, separation of units is thereafter impossible. By "in equity" is meant impartiality among the races accepted into the blend with no imputations of inferiority and no bestowed favors.[7]

This is a late statement, made when the movement was taking on a harsher tone, and rather stronger than we would find from most advocates of Americanization (in particular in its emphasis on "amalgamation," which can only mean intermarriage to the point of the indistinguishability of any distinct group), but the point in quoting this statement is that we may take it for granted, in the light of the attitude toward black-white intermarriage that then prevailed, that Frances Kellor simply did not have blacks in mind, despite the continual emphasis on the word "race."

One of the early climaxes of the movement was a great meeting in Philadelphia on May 10, 1915. Woodrow Wilson addressed a huge throng— five thousand newly naturalized citizens, eight thousand previously naturalized, with a chorus of five thousand voices, and the like. He does not use the term "race" in his paean to the all-inclusiveness of America; but all races are clearly implied in his term "the people of the world":

> This is the only country in the world which experiences this constant and repeated rebirth. Other countries depend upon the multiplication of their own native people. This country is constantly drinking strength out of new sources by the voluntary association with it of great bodies of strong men and forward-looking women out of other lands. . . . It is as if humanity had determined to see to it that this great Nation, founded for the benefit of humankind, should not lack for the allegiance of the people of the world.[8]

But we might again ask, where were the blacks? Clearly Wilson did not have them in mind.

This great meeting was the prelude to "Americanization Day" on July 4, 1915, when many mass meetings to welcome new citizens were held all over the country. One of them was in Faneuil Hall in Boston, addressed by Justice Brandeis. He asserted that what was distinctly American is "inclusive brotherhood." America, as against other nations, "has always declared herself for equality of nationalities as well as for equality of individuals. It recognizes racial equality as an essential of full human liberty and true brotherhood. . . . It has, therefore, given like welcome to all the peoples of Europe."[9] "The peoples of Europe" is what he has in mind, not blacks.

Most ironically, we find that one of the most active of the postwar Americanization groups was the "Inter-Racial Council." We know what that term would have meant had it been used twenty years later. But in 1919 it struck no one as odd, apparently, that it did not refer to blacks at all and it did not include blacks. Among a host of names of leading businessmen and bankers and political dignitaries we find some prominent immigrant names (Dr. Antonio Stella, M. I. Pupin, Gutzon Borglum, Jacob Schiff), but no blacks.[10]

As the Americanization movement began to shift from one befriending the immigrant, bringing him closer together to Americans, to one that seemed increasingly hostile, in which the generous offer of citizenship and full participation became the compulsory demand that the immigrant must learn English and American government, the Carnegie Corporation, trying to defend the earlier openness toward the immigrant, the spirit expressed by Jane Addams and Lillian Wald, sponsored a series of "Americanization Studies." Once again the language in these studies will surprise us in its unconsciousness of the fact that "race" might include other than Europeans.

In James A. Gavit's book, *Americans by Choice,* on the issue of naturalization, we find again the argument with which we are familiar: The American is not defined ethnically, he is defined by allegiance to an ideology. "The American Has No Racial Marks," one subtitle asserts:

> This absence of exclusive racial marks is the distinguishing physical characteristic of the American. True of him as of no other now or ever in the past is the fact that he is, broadly speaking, the product of *all* races. . . .
>
> We are in the midst of the making of the "American." He does not yet appear what he shall be but one thing is certain, he is not to be of any particular racial type now distinguishable. Saxon, Teuton, Kelt, Latin and Slav— to say nothing of any appreciable contribution by yellow and brown races as yet negligible. . . . —each of the races that we now know on this soil will have its share of "ancestorial" responsibility for the "typical American" that is to be.

The next heading reads, "Not Racial, But Cultural."[11]

Dealing as he does with naturalization, Gavit cannot, as more celebratory advocates of Americanization can, totally ignore the racial aspect: Naturalization was racially limited. Only whites (and Africans!) could become citizens. He does write:

> It is not yet true—perhaps it will be very long before it can be true—that there is absolutely no bar to any person on account of race; for the law and its interpretations exclude from citizenship Chinese, Japanese, and certain people of India not regarded as "white"—although the blacks of Africa are

expressly admitted. Nevertheless, it may be said broadly that regardless of race, the immigrant can come to America and win his way upon his own merits into the fellowship all the world calls "Americans".[12]

There is no comment on the fact that despite their formal equality as citizens, blacks were not allowed to participate in politics in the South.

We will find a similar liberal and welcoming tone in another volume of the Carnegie Corporation's Americanization series, *The Schooling of the Immigrant,* by Frank V. Thompson, then superintendent of Boston's public schools. It is mostly concerned with the teaching of English and of American ideals and habits, which are left rather unspecified and vague. The students he has in mind in most of the book are adults who he hopes will become naturalized. When it comes to schoolchildren, the children of immigrants, nothing much is proposed: The author has confidence in the assimilatory powers of the American public school, and while he commends some contemporary distinctive programs for immigrant children (not sufficiently specified to give any clear impression of what they do), he feels Americanization requires little in the way of special adaptation, and what little is required is the teaching of knowledge of American government. He writes: "An astonishing fact about the work of the common school is that Americanization has scarcely been a conscious motive. Americanization has taken place through the schools but it has been an unconscious by-product; . . . specifically the teacher has been concerned with the fundamental processes of education and with the fine and industrial arts." He thinks more attention should be paid specifically to "training in citizenship," and notes that teachers receive a good deal of training, and fulfill various requirements for promotion, "but nowhere among these is there a test of acquaintanceship with the problem of Americanization."[13]

So as regards school children he expresses no great concern; despite the lack of specific attention,

> Americanization and citizenship are usual resultants of all school training. The child receives impressions, inspirations, and impulses from the pictures he sees in the classroom, from the stories he reads in his history, from the exercises he attends in the assembly hall, from the celebration of patriotic anniversaries and the salute of the flag. We furnish special classes sometimes for non-English speaking children, but we do so merely for the purpose of enabling these children to enter the regular grades without delay.[14]

All this is very far from what we later came to know as intercultural education, which emphasized education in tolerance, and even farther from the present varieties of multiculturalism. There is supreme confidence in the assimilatory powers of American society and its distinctive agent, the public school. No special programs are required aside from the teaching of English and the strengthening of the rather puerile civics courses of the day. Thompson pays no attention to the distinctive culture of European children of different ethnic groups or religions. He does consider whether *any* distinctive variation for immigrant children in the public education generally provided is necessary, and he is doubtful. As he writes: "It is to our credit that in our schools we have never made invidious comparisons with respect to the children of the immigrant; we have received them on a basis of equality and made them feel that there were no distinctions on account of accidents of birth and circumstance."[15]

Nevertheless he does recommend that just as we make special provision for various kinds of "atypical" children, there should be some special provision to take account of the fact that "the majority of immigrant children, while normal with respect to range of mental capacities, do differ in social and economic condition from the children of families settled here for generations. The immigrant child . . . frequently suffers from the handicap of a foreign language in the household, and often from the inexperience of his parents in the American environment." What he seems to have in mind is the "steamer classes," common then for newly arrived immigrant children in some large cities. These did not characteristically last for more than a few months.[16]

We see here the characteristic assumption of the period that the assimilation of European children is no very difficult matter and the characteristic silence in regard to black children. Nor is there any reference to Asian children, and yet the question of separate schools for Japanese-American children had been and was an issue in California. Even when Thompson has a section titled "The South Awakened to Illiteracy," his main point is that there are few immigrants in the Deep South and the problem there is the substantial degree of illiteracy among the native population. He may have had blacks as well as whites in mind, though there is no reference to blacks. What centrally concerned him was to encourage tolerance and welcome, and appropriate kinds of assistance, for the European immigrant, adult or child.

As we know, the Americanization movement lost its aspect of welcome and inclusion in the midst of the passions aroused by World War I and the postwar fear of Bolshevism and radicalism. It turned into something harsh and oppressive, in which the issue became less the opportunity to learn English than the insistence that nothing but English be learned; less the generous offer of citizenship than the widespread fear of subversion from aliens and naturalized citizens. Americanization developed a bad name among liberals. Insofar as there was still concern for the living and working conditions of immigrants, this became encompassed in a larger liberal movement for improving the conditions of workingmen, a movement that was easily capable of reconciling commitment to the cause of working people with opposition to further immigration. If the word "assimilation" now makes us suspicious, and "Americanization" even more so, it is in part because of the excesses of the 1920s.

The Critics of Assimilationism

The term "Americanization" is no longer to be found in encyclopedias of the social sciences,[17] but it does appear in the first great *Encyclopedia of the Social Sciences* of 1930, and the comment we find there on the fate of Americanization will to some extent explain to us why we do not hear much about it today:

> This emphasis on the learning of English and naturalization, together with the unfortunate atmosphere of coercion and condescension in which so many wartime Americanization efforts were conceived, had the effect of bringing the word into a disrepute from which it has never fully recovered. Contributing to the same result, in the period following the war, were the widely expressed fear and suspicion of the immigrant, his frequent indictment as a radical, attempts to suppress his newspapers and organizations, the ignoring of his own culture and aspirations, the charge that certain nationalities and races were inferior and unassimilable, and the use of intimidating slogans. Americanization work too frequently made the assumption that American culture was something already complete which the newcomer must adopt in its entirety. Such attitudes and activities were important factors in promoting restriction of immigration, but they did not advance the assimilation of the immigrants who were already in America.[18]

My point in reciting episodes in the history of Americanization is not to add to the extensive literature that explores the neglect of the key question of the treatment of blacks in American society; nor to argue—which is true—that immigrants were better treated and taken more seriously than blacks from the point of view of their inclusion in American society; nor to attack the Americanization movement for its excesses—all legitimate responses to it. It is to set the stage for something that has also received little attention: that the *critics* of Americanization and assimilation also had nothing or little to say about blacks. However passionate their defense of the contribution to American economy, culture, politics, of immigrants and immigrant groups, however strong their resistance to the demand for assimilation, whatever the arguments they raised against the value of assimilation, the critics of Americanization and assimilation—we can call them for convenience the "cultural pluralists"—had little to say, indeed nothing to say, about adding blacks to the groups who they felt had every right to maintain their separate identity. Maybe they believed blacks should preserve their separate identity, maybe they never thought about the matter: Blacks just never entered into the argument.

There were critics of Americanization, fewer in its earlier more benign form, more when it evolved under the pressures of war into an attack on "hyphenated Americanism," even more when it further evolved into the repression of the postwar years. Thus Americanization became associated with laws restricting immigration, limiting the rights of aliens, and banning teaching in foreign languages (and on occasion even teaching foreign languages) and with harsh administrative actions expelling aliens. A powerful wave of nativist public opinion led to the sharp restriction of further immigration from Europe, and the nation experienced the mass hysteria of the Ku Klux Klan and similar organizations. But it is interesting to note that the few voices critical of extreme Americanization and defensive of cultural pluralism that were then raised, and that we have in recent decades disinterred, had almost nothing to say about blacks. This was true of Randolph Bourne in his advocacy of "Transnational America." It was true of Horace Kallen in his insistence that each group, each "race" in the language of the time, had an inherent genius or character that should not be suppressed but allowed to flower. We search this modest literature in vain for any reference to black Americans.[19]

Thus, when John Dewey spoke to the National Education Association in 1916 to defend the value of cultural pluralism, he did not seem to have blacks in mind. Of course, he was speaking in the context of an attack on the loyalty of European Americans, in the language of the time "hyphenated Americans." Nevertheless, one would have thought America's largest minority might have entered into the discussion. Many groups were mentioned in his talk. The American, Dewey asserts, "is international and interracial in his make-up. He is not American plus Pole or German. But the American is himself Pole-German-English-French-Spanish-Italian-Greek-Irish-Scandinavian-Bohemian-Jew—and so on."[20]

One searches Horace M. Kallen's *Culture and Democracy in the United States,* the fullest statement of the cultural pluralist view of the time, almost in vain for any reference to blacks. They cannot be fully escaped: After all, the introductory chapter is titled "Culture and the Ku Klux Klan," and Negroes are listed as among its targets. There are two other slightly fuller references. In speaking of the spirit of Know-Nothingism, he writes: "What differs from ourselves we spontaneously set upon a different level of value. If it seems to be strong it is called wicked and is feared; if it is regarded as weak, it is called brutish and exploited. Sometimes, as in the attitude toward the negro [sic], the emotions interpenetrate and become a sentiment focalizing the worst qualities of each." In the other passage, he is concerned with whether the current hysteria will wane, the integration of immigrants into American life under a liberal regime will continue (here "integration" clearly does not mean "assimilation"). But it may not happen. The immigrant may be fixed in the inferior economic position he now holds: "One need only cast an eye over the negro-white relations in the South to realize the limit that such a condition would, unchecked, engender."[21] Perhaps it is reading too much into very little, but one detects in this passage no expectation that there will be much change in the condition of the Negro.

The significance of this episode in the history of American thinking about race and ethnicity is that the argument over assimilation and Americanization evoked by the mass immigration of the period 1880–1924 and by the pressures of World War I simply did not take blacks, let alone Mexican Americans or Asians, into account.

Pluralism and World War II

When the issue of the relation of the immigrant and immigrant groups to American society emerged again in the late 1930s, matters were very different. Now the initiating historical circumstance was the rise of Hitler, his racism, and his threat to world peace. In World War I the objective of American leaders who favored the allied powers was to have the immigrant forget the country he came from: Memory and allegiance to one's past country among our largest immigrant groups (Germans, Irish) would not lead to sympathy for the Western Allies, but quite the reverse. If immigrants thought of themselves only as Americans, they would more likely accept alliance with England, the country that was the enemy of their homelands. In the run-up to our entry into World War II, matters were somewhat different. While patriotism and Americanism were hardly slighted, it generally served the interests of our national leaders that immigrant groups should remember their pasts and their homelands: So many of them were suffering under Nazi oppression.

But the opposition to Hitler involved considerably more than the strategy of using ethnic background to mobilize Americans against a foreign enemy. Hitler was an ideologist as well as a German nationalist, and his ideology was racism and anti-Semitism. Race now meant—in large measure because of Hitler and his racism—what we today understand as race: physical difference. If we were to fight racism, of course blacks could not be ignored. Mobilization in World War I meant a forceful assimilation and Americanization. Mobilization in World War II meant accentuating our tolerance, our diversity, against the racism and intolerance of Hitler. I do not mean to suggest that it was only the logic involved in the fight against Hitler that made it impossible to ignore blacks in considering the relationship of groups of different ethnic and racial background to American society. Many other changes that had taken place in the America of the New Deal and Franklin D. Roosevelt had brought blacks and their plight to public attention more sharply than in the America of Theodore Roosevelt and Woodrow Wilson, but certainly one factor was that American political and educational leaders wanted to emphasize our tolerance and inclusiveness against Hitler's intolerance and exclusiveness.

Thus as something like "cultural pluralism" began to raise its head again with the coming of Hitler and the fear of a future war, the growing concern was no longer with European immigrants alone, as it was in the buildup to World War I. Americans generally were not much concerned with the loyalty of German Americans, or Italian Americans. Security agencies were worried about German-American adherents of Nazism, about Italian-American adherents of Italian Fascism (much fewer), and most about Japanese Americans, who were the only group to be affected by a World War I–style popular hysteria. So there was a reprise to some extent of World War I concern with immigrant loyalty. Indeed, we even had a revival of something like the Americanization Day spectacles of the earlier period in the creation and brief history of "I am an American Day." But the tone of the new movement was different in some key respects.

First, mass immigration had come to an end, and no one expected it to revive, whatever the needs of persecuted Jews and other groups harried by the Nazis. European immigrant groups were already well on the way to assimilation. There was no particular need for a movement to emphasize the learning of English or to speed naturalization. Perhaps this explains the rather benign patriotism of World War II as compared with World War I.

But second, blacks and Hispanic Americans and Asians were now definitely part of the story. Because we were fighting Hitler and his ideology of racial superiority, we had to take into account our own groups of racially defined second-class citizens, all suffering under a weight of legal as well as informal segregation, discrimination, and prejudice. Cultural pluralism, which had been in World War I and its aftermath only the evanescent hope of a few philosophers and journalists, became a sturdy growth, under a new name: intercultural education. The focus of concern began to shift, from European immigrant groups to minorities of color. And in fighting the ideology of race—physical race, biological race—how could we not be concerned with how we treated our racial minorities?

What was to be the fate of assimilation in this new dispensation? Whatever the new degree of tolerance for diversity, it was generally expected assimilation would continue. "Intercultural education," the modest movement of the late 1930s and 1940s that taught tolerance of other groups in the schools, was a far cry from a full-bodied cultural pluralism and presented no resistance to assimilation. It stood for tolerance, not for the maintenance of cultural difference and identity. Indeed, even if the term was not used, assimilation was what the advocates for our largest and most oppressed minority also wanted.[22]

Assimilation and the Sociologists

The term "assimilation" was a key concept in the thinking of our most important sociologist of race and ethnicity, Robert E. Park, who established at the University of Chicago a strong commitment to questions of race and ethnicity. Park and his colleagues had participated in the Carnegie Americanization studies after World War I that I have referred to. Opponents of forceful Americanization, they nevertheless believed social trends were bringing an inevitable assimilation. They did not decry this: This was the inevitable result, in time, of the meeting of peoples. Park saw that the great problem in the way of assimilation was the blacks.

His 1930 article on assimilation in the *Encyclopedia of the Social Sciences* perceptively points to this as the stumbling block in the way of assimilation:

In a vast, varied and cosmopolitan society such as exists in America, the chief obstacle to assimilation seems to be not cultural differences but physical traits.... The Negro, during his three hundred years in this country, has not been assimilated. This is not because he has preserved in America a foreign culture and alien tradition.... No man is so entirely native to the soil.... To say the Negro is not assimilated means no more than to say that he is still regarded in some sense a stranger, a representative of an alien race.... This distinction which sets him apart from the rest of the population is real, but is not based upon cultural traits but upon physical and racial characteristics.

As for Europeans:

The ease and rapidity with which aliens have been able to take over American customs and manners have enabled the United States to digest every sort of normal human difference, with the exception of the purely external ones like that of the color of the skin.[23]

Park saw the key problem for assimilation: it was race. Black intellectuals and leaders were of course also aware that assimilation, as process or ideal, was leaving them out. They were not even participants in the debate over assimilation and Americanization. Nevertheless, in striving for the rights that would make them equal to white Americans, in aiming at a condition in which no distinction would be made between white and black Americans, they in effect were lined up with those who wanted to assimilate or integrate the immigrant. They saw no good reason for the maintenance of group distinctiveness in America. What Americanizers considered ideal for immigrants was what blacks considered ideal for themselves. Black leaders were not asking to be part of that orchestra of difference that Horace Kallen envisaged as the ideal for America. (In fact, black culture was sturdily established and maintained its distinctiveness with no widespread intentional effort or intention to do so, but this came naturally, so to speak, and owed nothing to the demands and hopes of black leaders.) American liberals in general, who supported black aims, also saw no good argument in principle against assimilation for all groups.

Park had set forth a scheme that became quite influential in sociology: Groups in contact moved through various phases, such as conflict and accommodation, ending in assimilation. Despite the growing attention to the plight of blacks during the 1930s and 1940s, an attention encouraged by white and black liberal scholars' important foundation-sponsored research and by key legal cases, there was little challenge to the expectation that assimilation or something like it—the term "integration" became popular—was the desirable solution to the American dilemma. Certainly no liberal and no black leader favored the continuation of segregation. No significant black leader favored separatism. Garvey's "Back to Africa" was an exotic oddity, and the American Communists' temporary advocacy of a separate black state in the South an even greater oddity. Garveyism reflected more the deep frustration of the American black over exclusion from American society than any positive commitment to the maintenance of a separate black culture. Until the late 1960s, there was no challenge to the assimilationist stance of sociologists who studied race and ethnicity and of black scholars and leaders.

Park and his leading students, while they did not put their preferences forth sharply, assumed assimilation not only was inevitable but would be all for the best. Thus, Louis Wirth, who was the chief successor to Park, made clear in his book on American Jews, *The Ghetto,* that his preference was for assimilation: The Jew continued to exist only because of prejudice and discrimination; all the reactions of the Jew to this antagonism were humanly limiting; and assimilation, which to be sure required lowering the barriers others placed in the way of assimilation, was the desirable end result of the interaction of Jews and non-Jews in contemporary society.[24]

The central work on the black condition in the United States in the 1940s, Gunnar Myrdal's *An American Dilemma,*[25] which expressed not only his views but to some degree those of his black collaborators, major black scholars and intellectuals of the times, could also be described as assimilationist. A number of these collaborators were Marxists (Myrdal of course was not) and as such saw racial and ethnic difference as a survival, something that would in time be overcome by the development of class consciousness, bringing together blacks and whites on the basis of class interest.[26]

The major works of E. Franklin Frazier on the black family could also be described as assimilationist. Insofar as the black family was stable and puritanical it was good—that was unquestioned. There was no hint that it was desirable that any distinctive cultural feature should survive as specifically Negro or black, or that there should be any effort to seek such features.

The best-informed, most liberal, and most sympathetic analysts of the ethnic and racial scene in the 1930s and 1940s saw assimilation as a desirable consequence of the reduction of prejudice and discrimination. Blacks wanted to live under circumstances no different from those whites lived under, and under these circumstances they would not be different from other Americans. It was rare to find among black intellectuals and political leaders any notion that some distinctive black culture or social practices must be protected and retained. In the face of the overwhelming task of dealing with white prejudice and discrimination, the issue of a distinctive black culture could not take a high place on any black agenda.

Although it was clear that blacks could never because of race be indistinguishable from whites, it was desirable that they become culturally, socially, economically, and politically assimilated, that they be simply Americans with dark skins. Until the 1960s, scarcely any black leader or intellectual diverged from this view. Their demand was that all public bodies, agencies of government, schools, and colleges and all private agencies that affected individual circumstances, including banks, businesses, housing producers, and landlords, be color-blind.

Among the white immigrant groups, or, to label them more properly, ethnic groups, for such they became as they maintained some degree of group cohesion and identity with the reduction in the numbers of the foreign-born, one could find the upholders of the ethnic conscience and consciousness, those who established and maintained schools, churches, philanthropic and civic organizations, insurance societies, social groups. But except among those whose direct interest was in maintaining this organizational network and the jobs it offered, these were regarded by the members of ethnic groups themselves as survivals, fated to fall away as acculturation and assimilation progressed. There was no more 100-percent American than the children of immigrants, the second generation.

Acculturation and assimilation, if not the cruder "Americanization," was thus generally accepted as the way America was going and should go. This prospect was favored by old Americans, regardless of their attitudes to the newer Americans, and by the immigrants of the great migration of the end of the nineteenth and beginning of the twentieth centuries and their children. Nativists as well as liberals most sympathetic to the newer Americans accepted the inevitability and desirability of assimilation.

Of course, as we know, we are now very far from all this. The voices of opposition to assimilation burst out in the late 1960s and have gone through many permutations since. Bland "intercultural education" has succumbed to the rather more forceful "multicultural education"—though that too comes in all brands, from the mildest recognition of differences to a rather hysterical and irrational Afrocentrism. We even had, in the late 1960s and 1970s, a brief explosion of revived ethnic assertiveness among white European ethnic groups, the heirs of the immigrants of the early decades of the century. It could not survive; assimilation had gone too far. We have a few modest programs in Italian-American studies, and a sturdier growth of Jewish programs, sturdier because Jewish programs are able to draw not only on ethnic attachments that tend to be stronger than those of most white Europeans, but also on religion, which creates a robust body of institutions to parallel the purely ethnic, and which has greater prestige and receives more tolerance in the American setting.

We come now to our question: Is assimilation then dead? The word may be dead, the concept may be disreputable; the reality continues to flourish. As so many observers in the past have noted, assimilation in the United States is not dependent on public ideology, on school curricula, on public approbation: Factors in social and economic and cultural life foster it, and it proceeds apace. Read Lewis was right when, in his now more than sixty-years-old article on "Americanization" in the *Encyclopedia of the Social Sciences,* he wrote:

> Important as these conscious efforts are toward Americanization, they represent only a part of the social forces which play continuously upon the immigrant and determine the degree and rapidity of his assimilation. A conspicuous force which makes for adjustment is the urge to material success, which makes the immigrant adapt himself to American ways of work and business. This usually involves learning the English language as quickly as possible. Standardizing forces such as national advertisements, ten-cent store products, movies, radio and the tabloid press play also upon the immigrant.[27]

Correct for inflation, add television, baseball, football, basketball, and so on, and it is clear the forces pressing assimilation have not lost power.

Call it "acculturation" if you will. But assimilation in its least deniable and strongest form, what was once called "amalgamation," also proceeds apace. The rates of intermarriage among all European ethnic groups are very high.[28] Even Jews, who have a strong cultural and religious bar against intermarriage, and who maintained a rather low rate of intermarriage until the last two or three decades, now show very high rates for individuals marrying outside the group. With such high rates, it is hardly clear to any individual what his or her ethnic group is and how it is to be defined. In answer to the question "What is this person's ancestry," asked in the census, most Americans give multiple ancestries.[29] Mary Waters, in *Ethnic Options,* shows how thin any sense of ethnicity among Americans of European origin has become.[30]

But there is the great exception. If intermarriage is taken as key evidence for powerful assimilatory forces, then blacks are not subject to these forces to the same degree as others. Hispanic groups and Asian groups, despite the recency of immigration of so many of them, and thus the greater power of family and group attachment, show rates of intermarriage approaching the levels of Europeans.[31] Blacks stand apart, with very low rates of intermarriage, rising slowly. They stand apart too in the degree of residential segregation.[32] Thirty years of effort, public and private, assisted by antidiscrimination law and a substantial rise in black earnings, have made little impact on this pattern.

Whatever the causes, the apartness is real. And it is this that feeds multiculturalism. For one group, assimilation, by some key measures, has certainly failed. For others, multicultural education may be a matter of sentiment. But most black children do attend black-majority schools. Most live in black neighborhoods. Why should not multiculturalism, in the form of the examination of group history, characteristics, problems, become compelling as one way of understanding one's situation, perhaps overcoming it? The large statements asserting that the American national ideal is inclusion, assimilation, understandably will ring false to many, despite the commitment of most black intellectuals and political leaders to integration.

For Hispanics and Asian Americans, marked in varying degree by race, it is in large measure a matter of choice, their choice, just how they will define their place in American society. We see elements in these groups who, in their support of bilingual education and other foreign-language rights, want to establish or preserve an institutional base for a separate identity that may maintain some resistance to the forces of assimilation. For blacks too there are choices—we see the existence of choices in the writings of black intellectuals who oppose the stronger tendencies of multiculturalism. But the difference that separates blacks from whites, and even from other groups "of color" that have undergone a history of discrimination and prejudice in this country, is not to be denied. This is the most powerful force arguing for multiculturalism and for resistance to the assimilatory trends of American education and of American society.

Notes

1. J. Hector St. John [Michel-Guillaume-Jean de] Crèvecoeur, *Letters from an American Farmer,* as quoted in Philip Gleason, "American Identity and Americanization," in

Harvard Encyclopedia of American Ethnic Groups (Cambridge, Mass.: Harvard University Press, 1980), 33.

2. Gleason, 31.

3. Nathan Glazer, *Affirmative Discrimination* (New York: Basic Books, 1975).

4. Gleason, 32.

5. Harold J. Abramson, "Assimilation and Pluralism," in *Harvard Encyclopedia of American Ethnic Groups,* 152.

6. John Higham, *Send These to Me: Immigrants in Urban America,* revised edition (Baltimore: Johns Hopkins University Press, 1984), 175.

7. Frances A. Kellor, "What is Americanization?" *Yale Review,* January 1919, as reprinted in Philip Davis, *Immigration and Americanization; Selected Readings* (Boston: Ginn, 1920), 625–26.

8. Davis, 612; for a description of the meeting, see Edward George Hartman, *The Movement to Americanize the Immigrant* (New York: AMS Press, 1967), 11 n.

9. Davis, 642–43.

10. Hartman, 220–21.

11. James A. Gavit, *Americans by Choice* (New York: Harper, 1922), 10, 11–12.

12. Gavit, 7–8.

13. Frank V. Thompson, *Schooling of the Immigrant* (New York, Harper and Brothers, 1920), 15–16.

14. Thompson, 16.

15. Thompson, 73.

16. Thompson, 74, 118.

17. Nor can we find what was once a key sociological concept, "assimilation," among the entries in the recent four-volume *Encyclopedia of Sociology* by C. F. and M. L. Borgatta (New York: Macmillan, l992).

18. Read Lewis, "Americanization," *Encyclopedia of the Social Sciences,* vol. 2 (New York: Macmillan, 1930), 33.

19. John Higham was perhaps the first to forcefully note the "fatal elision" of blacks from Horace Kallen's American orchestra of diverse ethnic and racial voices. See *Send These to Me,* 1st ed. (New York, Atheneum, 1975), 208.

20. John Dewey, as quoted in Horace Kallen, *Culture and Democracy in the United States* (New York: Boni and Liveright, 1924), 131–32.

21. Kallen, 127, 165.

22. For a characterization of the movement, see Nathan Glazer, *Ethnic Dilemmas, 1964–1982* (Cambridge, Mass.: Harvard University Press, 1983), 104–8.

23. Robert E. Park, "Assimilation," *Encyclopedia of the Social Sciences,* 282.

24. Louis Wirth, *The Ghetto* (Chicago, Ill.: University of Chicago Press, 1928).

25. Gunnar Myrdal, *An American Dilemma* (New York: Harper, 1944).

26. See, for example, Brian Urquhart, *Ralph Bunche: An American Life* (New York: W. W. Norton, 1993), 57, and elsewhere for a mainline black leader's position on this matter.

27. Lewis, 34.

28. Stanley Lieberson and Mary Waters, *From Many Strands: Ethnic and Racial Groups in Contemporary America* (New York: Russell Sage Press, 1988), ch. 6.

29. Lieberson and Waters, 45.

30. Mary Waters, *Ethnic Options* (Berkeley, California: California University Press, 1990).

31. Lieberson and Waters, 182.

32. Douglas S. Massey and Nancy A. Denton, *American Apartheid* (Cambridge, Mass.: Harvard University Press, 1993).

Chapter 2

The Limits of Pluralism

K. Anthony Appiah

It is, of course, true that the African identity is still in the making. There isn't a final identity that is African. But, at the same time, there is an identity coming into existence. And it has a certain context and a certain meaning. Because if somebody meets me, say, in a shop in Cambridge, he says "Are you from Africa?" Which means that Africa means something to some people. Each of these tags has a meaning, and a penalty and a responsibility.
— Chinua Achebe (1982)

There is an Akan proverb, from my home in Asante in Ghana, that says: Aban begu a, efiri yam. Proverbs are notoriously difficult to interpret, and thus also to translate. But this one means, roughly, that if the state is going to collapse, it will be from the belly.[1] The idea, of course, is that states collapse from within; and the proverb is used to express the sentiment that people suffer as a result of their own weaknesses, not from the attacks of others. It is a rhetoric familiar enough, these days, here in the United States. In the latest episodes of American jeremiad—truly the longest-running series in our history—it is being suggested that having "won the cold war," we have set out to destroy ourselves from within. American society is being destroyed not by drugs and poverty and political bungling but by multiculturalists intent on schism: here, then, is a society collapsing from the belly.

Naturally, I do not believe it. In a world that contains Bosnia-Herzegovina and Belfast and Beirut and East Timor and Sri Lanka, events such as the Los Angeles riots (multicultural riots, if ever there were any) do not convince me that the United States is being destroyed by an excess of ethnicity.[2] I am not of Arthur Schlesinger's party.

Those of us born and raised elsewhere, but happy to be living here in the United States, often find one thing above all odd in our adopted home, a tradition as old in America as American jeremiad, as old in the world as

37

nationalism, namely, this country's imagination of itself as so new a creature on God's earth that it cannot learn from others. This exceptionalism flows, in part, from a general ignorance of others that it is the aim of one part of the multicultural movement to correct. So I begin by talking about pluralism and identity in Africa in order to draw some lessons (both positive and negative) about the way we have dealt with our ethno-regional complications.

The cultural life of most of black Africa remained largely unaffected by European ideas until the last years of the nineteenth century; and most cultures began our own century with ways of life formed very little by direct contact with Europe. As a result, European cultural influence in Africa before the twentieth century was extremely limited. Deliberate attempts at change— through missionary activity or the establishment of Western schools—and unintended influence—through contact with explorers and colonizers in the interior and trading posts on the coasts—produced small enclaves of Europeanized Africans; but the major cultural impact of Europe is largely a product of the period since the First World War.

To understand the variety of Africa's contemporary cultures, therefore, we need first to recall the variety of the precolonial cultures. Differences in colonial experience have also played their part in shaping the continent's diversities; but even identical colonial policies identically implemented working on the very different cultural materials would surely have produced widely varying results.

No doubt at a certain abstract level we can find generalizations that hold true of most of black Africa before European conquest. It is a familiar idea in African historiography that Africa was the last continent in the Old World with an "uncaptured" peasantry, largely able to use land without the supervision of feudal overlords and able, if they chose, to market their products through a complex system of trading networks.[3] While European ruling classes were living off the surplus of peasants and the newly developing industrial working class, African rulers were essentially living off taxes on trade. But if we could have traveled through Africa's many cultures in those years—from the small groups of Bushman hunter-gatherers, with their Stone Age materials, to the Hausa kingdoms, rich in worked metal—we should have felt in every place profoundly different impulses, ideas, and forms of life. To speak of an African identity in the nineteenth century—if an identity is a coalescence of mutually responsive (if sometimes conflicting) modes of conduct, habits of thought, and patterns of evaluation; in short, a coherent kind of human social psychology—would have been "to give to aery nothing a local habitation and a name."

Yet there is no doubt that now, a century later, an African identity is coming into being. I have argued elsewhere[4] that this identity is a new thing; that it is, in part, the product of a colonial history; and that the bases through which it has largely so far been theorized—race, a common historical experience, a shared metaphysics—presuppose falsehoods too serious for us to ignore.

Now, every human identity is constructed, historical; every one has its share of false presuppositions, of the errors and inaccuracies that courtesy calls "myth," religion "heresy," and science "magic." Invented histories, invented biologies, invented cultural affinities come with every identity; each is a kind of role that has to be scripted, structured by conventions of narrative to which the world never quite manages to conform.

Often those who say this—who deny the biological reality of races or the literal truth of our national fictions—are treated by nationalists and "racemen" as if they are proposing genocide or the destruction of nations, as if in saying that there is literally no Negro race, one were obliterating all those who claim to be Negroes, in doubting the story of Okomfo Anokye one were repudiating the Asante nation.[5] This is an unhelpful hyperbole; but it is certainly true that there must be contexts in which a statement of these truths is politically inopportune. I am enough of a scholar to feel drawn to truth telling, though the heavens fall; enough of a political animal to recognize that there are places where the truth does more harm than good.

But, so far as I can see, we do not have to choose between these impulses: there is no reason to believe that racism is always—or even usually—advanced by denying the existence of races; and, though there is some reason to suspect that those who resist legal remedies for the history of racism might use the nonexistence of races to argue in the United States, for example, against affirmative action, that strategy is, as a matter of logic, easily opposed. For the existence of racism does not require the existence of races; and, we can add, nations are real enough, however invented their traditions.[6]

To raise the issue of whether these truths are truths to be uttered is to be forced, however, to face squarely the real political question, itself as old as political philosophy, of when we should endorse the noble lie. In the real world of practical politics, of everyday alliances and popular mobilizations, a rejection of races and nations in theory can be part of a program for coherent political practice only if we can show more than that the Black race—or the Shona tribe or any of the other modes of self-invention that Africa has inherited—fits the common pattern of relying on less than the literal truth. We would need to show not that race and national history are falsehoods, but that they are useless falsehoods at best or dangerous ones at worst: that another set of stories will build us identities through which we can make more productive alliances.

The problem, of course, is that group identity seems to work best when it is seen by its members as natural, as "real." Pan-Africanism, black solidarity, can be an important force with real political benefits; but it doesn't work without its attendant mystifications. (Nor, to turn to the other obvious example, is feminism without its occasional risks and mystifications either.) Recognizing the constructedness of the history of identities has seemed to many incompatible with taking these new identities with the seriousness they have for those who invent—or, as they would no doubt rather say, discover—and possess them.[7] In sum, the demands of agency seem always—in the real world of politics—to entail a misrecognition of its genesis; you cannot build alliances without mystifications and mythologies. And so I would like to explore the ways in which what is productive in African forms of identity politics can be fruitfully understood by those of us whose positions as intellectuals—as searchers after truth—make it impossible for us to live through the falsehoods of race and tribe and nation; and whose understanding of history makes us skeptical, at the same time, that nationalism and racial solidarity can do the good that they can do without the attendant evils of racism—and other particularisms; without the warring of nations.

I have argued often against the forms of racism implicit in much Pan-Africanist talk.[8] But such objections to a biologically rooted conception of race may still seem all too theoretical: if Africans can get together around the idea of the Black Person, if they can create through this notion productive alliances with African Americans and people of African descent in Europe and the Caribbean, surely these theoretical objections should pale in the light of the practical value of these alliances. But there is every reason to doubt that they can. Within Africa—in the Organization of African Unity (OAU), in the Sudan, in Mauritania[9]—racialization has produced arbitrary boundaries and exacerbated tensions; in the diaspora alliances with other peoples of color, *as* victims of racism—people of South Asian descent in England, Hispanics in the United States, "Arabs" in France, Turks in Germany—have proved essential.

In short, I think it is clear enough that a biologically rooted conception of race is both dangerous in practice and misleading in theory: African unity, African identity, need securer foundations than race.

The passage from Achebe with which I began continues in these words: "All these tags, unfortunately for the black man, are tags of disability." But it seems to me that they are not so much labels of disability as disabling labels; which is, in essence, my complaint against Africa as a racial mythology—the identity of Alexander Crummell and W. E. B. Du Bois and the older Pan-Africanists; against Africa as a shared metaphysics or a fancied past of shared glories—the identity of the "Afrocentrists." These complaints can be briskly summarized.

"Race" disables us because it proposes as a basis for common action the illusion that black (and white and yellow) people are fundamentally allied by nature and, thus, without effort; it leaves us unprepared, therefore, to handle the "intraracial" conflicts that arise from the very different situations of black (and white and yellow) people in different parts of the economy and of the world.

A retreat to African metaphysical traditions (exemplified, for example, in the powerful rhetoric of Wole Soyinka[10]) disables us because it founds our unity in gods who have not served us well in our dealings with the world— Soyinka never defends what he calls the "African World" against the charge made by the Ghanaian philosopher Kwasi Wiredu, that since people die daily in Ghana because they prefer traditional herbal remedies to Western medicines, "Any inclination to glorify the unanalytical [i.e., the traditional] cast of mind is not just retrograde; it is tragic."[11] Soyinka has proved the Yoruba pantheon a powerful literary resource: but he cannot explain why Christianity and Islam have so widely displaced the old gods or why an image of the West has so powerful a hold on the contemporary Yoruba imagination; nor can his myth making offer us the resources for creating economies and polities adequate to our various places in the world.

And the Afrocentrists—like all who have chosen to root Africa's modern identity in an imaginary history—require us to see the past as the moment of wholeness and unity; tie us to the values and beliefs of the past; and thus divert us from the problems of the present and the hopes of the future.

If an African identity is to empower us, so it seems to me, what is required is not so much that we throw out falsehood but that we acknowledge first of all that race and history and metaphysics do not enforce an identity: that we must choose, within broad limits set by ecological, political, and economic realities, what it will mean to be African in the coming years.

I do not want to be misunderstood. We are Africans already. And we can give numerous examples from multiple domains of what our being African means. We have, for example, in the OAU and the African Development Bank, and in such regional organizations as the Southern African Development Coordination Conference (SADCC) and the Economic Community of West African States (ECOWAS), as well as in the African caucuses of the agencies of the United Nations and the World Bank, African institutions. At the Olympics and the Commonwealth games, athletes from African countries are seen as Africans by the world—and, perhaps more importantly, by each other. Being African already has "a certain context and a certain meaning."

But, as Achebe suggests, that meaning is not always one we can be happy with; and that identity is one we must continue to reshape. And in thinking about how we are to reshape it, we would do well to remember that the African identity is, for its bearers, only one among many. Like all identities, institutionalized before anyone has permanently fixed a single meaning for them—like the German identity at the beginning of this century, or the American in the latter eighteenth century, or the Indian identity at independence so few years ago—being African is, for its bearers, one among other salient modes of being, all of which have to be constantly fought for and rethought. And indeed, in Africa, it is another of these identities that provides one of the most useful models for such rethinking; it is a model that draws on other identities central to contemporary life in the subcontinent: namely, the constantly shifting redefinition of "tribal" identities to meet the economic and political exigencies of the modern world.

Once more, let me quote Achebe:

The duration of awareness, of consciousness of an identity, has really very little to do with how deep it is. You can suddenly become aware of an identity which you have been suffering from for a long time without knowing. For instance, take the Igbo people. In my area, historically, they did not see themselves as Igbo. They saw themselves as people from this village or that village. In fact in some places "Igbo" was a word of abuse; they were the "other" people, down in the bush. And yet, after the experience of the Biafran War, during a period of two years, it became a very powerful consciousness. But it was *real* all the time. They spoke the same language, called "Igbo", even though they were not using that identity in any way. But the moment came when this identity became very very powerful . . . and over a very short period.[12]

A short period it was; and also a tragic one. The Nigerian Civil War defined an Igbo identity: it did so in complex ways, which grew out of the development of a common Igbo identity in colonial Nigeria, an identity that created the Igbo traders in the cities of northern Nigeria as an identifiable object of assault in the period that led up to the invention of Biafra.

Recognizing Igbo identity as a new thing is not a way of privileging other Nigerian identities: each of the three central ethnic identities of modern political life—Hausa-Fulani, Yoruba, Igbo—is a product of the rough-and-tumble of the transition through colonial to postcolonial status. David Laitin has pointed out that "the idea that there was a single Hausa-Fulani tribe . . . was largely a political claim of the NPC [Northern Peoples' Congress] in their battle against the South" while "many elders intimately involved in rural Yoruba society today recall that, as late as the 1930s, 'Yoruba' was not a common form of political identification."[13] Nnamdi Azikiwe—one of the key figures in the construction of Nigerian nationalism—was extremely popular (as Laitin also points out) in Yoruba Lagos, where "he edited his nationalist newspaper, the *West African Pilot*. It was only subsequent events that led him to be defined in Nigeria as an *Igbo* leader."[14] Yet Nigerian politics—and the more everyday economy of ordinary personal relations—is oriented along such axes; and only very occasionally does the fact float into view that even these three problematic identities account for at most seven out of ten Nigerians.

And the story is repeated, even in places where it was not drawn in lines of blood. As Johannes Fabian has observed, the powerful Lingala and Swahili-speaking identities of modern Zaire exist "because spheres of political and economic interest were established before the Belgians took full control, and continued to inform relations between regions under colonial rule."[15] Modern Ghana witnesses the development of an Akan identity, as speakers of the three major regional dialects of Twi—Asante, Fante, Akuapem—organize themselves into a corporation against an (equally novel) Ewe unity.[16]

When it is not the "tribe" that is invested with new uses and meanings, it is religion. Yet the idea that Nigeria is composed of a Muslim north, a Christian south, and a mosaic of "pagan" holdovers is as inaccurate as the picture of three historic tribal identities. Two out of every five southern Yoruba people are Muslim; and, as Laitin tells us:

Many northern groups, especially in what are today Benue, Plateau, Gongola, and Kwara states, are largely Christian. When the leaders of Biafra tried to convince the world that they were oppressed by northern Muslims, ignorant foreigners (including the pope) believed them. . . . But the Nigerian army . . . was led by a northern Christian.[17]

It is as useless here, as in the case of race, to point out in each case that the tribe or the religion is, like all social identities, based on an idealizing fiction, for life in Nigeria or in Zaire has come to be lived through that idealization; the Igbo identity is real because Nigerians believe in it, the Shona identity because Zimbabweans have given it meaning. The rhetoric of a Muslim north and a Christian south structured political discussions in the period before Nigerian independence; but it was equally important in the debates about instituting a Muslim court of appeals in the draft constitution of 1976; and it could be found, for example, in many an article in the Nigerian press as electoral registration for a new civilian era began in July 1989.

There are, I think, three crucial lessons for us in the United States in these cases. First, identities are complex and multiple and grow out of a history of changing responses to economic, political, and cultural forces, almost always in opposition to other identities. Second, they flourish despite what I earlier called our "misrecognition" of their origins; despite, that is, their roots in myths and in lies. And third, there is, in consequence, no large place for reason in the construction—as opposed to the study and the management—of identities. One temptation, then, for those who see the centrality of these fictions in our lives, is to leave reason behind: to celebrate and endorse those identities that seem at the moment to offer the best hope of advancing our other goals, and to keep silence about the lies and the myths. But, as I said earlier, intellectuals do not easily neglect the truth, and, all things considered, our societies profit, in my view, from the institutionalization of this imperative in the academy. So it is important for us to continue trying to tell our truths. But the facts I have been rehearsing should imbue us all with a strong sense of the marginality of such work to the central issue of the resistance to racism and ethnic violence—and to sexism, and to the other structures of difference that shape the world of power; and they should force upon us the clear realization that the real battle is not being fought in the academy. As the fires raged in Los Angeles, it seemed oddly irrelevant to fuss about racial ideologies: the solutions are the conquest of drugs and despair, new jobs, better education, more credit, and so many other more practical steps. And yet, as we all know, the shape of our world (the shape of modern

Africa) is in large part the product, often the unintended and unanticipated product, of theories; even the most vulgar of Marxists will have to admit that economic interests operate *through* ideologies. We cannot change the world simply by evidence and reasoning, but we surely cannot change it without them either.

What we in the academy *can* contribute—even if only slowly and marginally—is a disruption of the discourse of "racial" and "tribal" differences. For, in my perfectly unoriginal opinion, the reality of these many competing identities in Africa today plays into the hands of the very exploiters whose shackles we are trying to escape. "Race" in Europe and "tribe" in Africa are central to the way in which the objective interests of the worst-off are distorted. The analogous point for African Americans was recognized long ago by Du Bois.[18] Du Bois argued in *Black Reconstruction* that racist ideology had essentially blocked the formation of a significant labor movement in the United States; for such a movement would have required the collaboration of the nine million ex-slave and white peasant workers of the South.[19] It is, in other words, because the categories of difference often cut across our economic interests that they operate to blind us to them. What binds the middle-class African American to dark-skinned fellow citizens downtown is not economic interest, but racism and the cultural products of resistance to it that are shared across (much of) African-American culture.

I have been arguing, in effect, that the political meanings of identities are historically and geographically relative. Because the value of identities is thus relative, we must argue for and against them case by case. And given the current situation in Africa, I think it remains true that Pan-Africanism—as the project of a continental fraternity and sorority, *not* as the project of a racialized Negro nationalism—however false or muddled its theoretical roots, can be a progressive force. It is as fellow Africans that Ghanaian diplomats (my father among them) interceded between the warring nationalist parties in Rhodesia under the Unilateral Declaration of Independence; as fellow Africans that OAU teams can mediate regional conflicts; as fellow Africans that the human rights assessors organized under the OAU's Banjul Declaration can intercede for citizens of African states against the excesses of our governments. If there is to be hope, too, for a Pan-Africanism of the African diaspora once it, too, is released from bondage to racial ideologies (alongside the many bases of alliance available to Africa's peoples in their political and cultural struggles), it is crucial that we recognize the independence, once "Negro" nationalism is gone, of the Pan-Africanism of the diaspora and the

Pan-Africanism of the continent. It is, I believe, in the exploration of these issues, these possibilities, that the future of an intellectually reinvigorated Pan-Africanism lies.

Informed by these African histories, I am impressed by a simple point of contrast: ethnic variety in the United States is simply not the real resource for resistance to the state and its processes of unification that it can be in my homeland of Ghana and most other parts of Africa and Asia. Africa's societies are multicultural in a much stronger sense than the United States is, and that makes it interesting to compare the reality of Africa with the rhetoric of American multiculturalism.

I am not much one for "isms"; and talk of multiculturalism makes me as nervous as much of the other talk of "isms" that surrounds us. Multicultural-*ism* sounds like the name of an ideology, a single agenda, a unified political vision. If there *is* such a unified ideology out there, I certainly don't know what it is. What I *do* know is that—in at least one sense of the much-abused word "culture"—we live in a society of many cultures, a multicultural society.

The idea of "culture" is much abused because it is so elastic. But we can reduce it to some kind of order by identifying a spectrum that begins with the most basic sense of the term—the anthropologist's sense—in which culture means all the ideas and practices that are shared by a social group, and ends with what we call "high" culture—the critical notion of culture—which picks from among those ideas and practices a subset that requires in both producers and consumers the greatest training or the most individual skill. The habit of shaking hands at meetings belongs to culture in the anthropologist's sense; Sandro Botticelli and Martin Buber and Count Basie belong to culture in the critical sense.

No one is likely to make much fuss about the fact that a society is multicultural in the critic's sense. For, in this sense, most large-scale societies have been multicultural. Once you have division of labor and social stratification, there will be people who do and people who don't know about music and literature and pottery and painting; if we call all these specialized spheres together "high" culture, then everyone will participate in the high culture to varying degrees, and there are likely to be subgroups (opera lovers, say, or dedicated movie-goers, or lovers of poetry or rap) who share significant practices and ideas with each other that are not shared with everyone else.

If being multicultural is a problem, it is because societies are multicultural in the anthropological sense, *pace* those who seem preoccupied with stopping multiculturalism at the National Endowment for the Humanities or National Endowment for the Arts, but the problems created by our many cultures largely lie elsewhere.

Culture in the anthropologist's sense is what a social group has socially in common: it is what we teach our children; and in teaching them, we make them members of our social group. By definition, therefore, culture in this sense is shared; it is the social bottom line. It includes language and table manners, religious ideas, moral values. With this idea of culture goes the idea of a subculture: people who share not just the common ideas and practices of the whole social group, but also more specific other practices and values as well.

I say "social group" because a single society, a group of persons living together in a common state, under common authorities, need not have a common culture. There is no single shared body of ideas and practices in most contemporary African states: there is, as we have learned so sadly in recent months, no such shared culture in Bosnia and Herzegovina. And I think it is fair to say that there is not now and there has never been such a shared culture in the United States.

The reason is simple: the United States has always been multilingual, and has always had minorities who did not speak or understand English. It has always had a plurality of religious traditions; beginning with Native American religions and Puritans and Catholics and including now many varieties of Judaism, Islam, Buddhism, Jainism, Taoism, Bahai . . . and so on. And Americans have always differed significantly even among those who do speak English, from North to South and East to West, and from country to city, in customs of greeting, notions of civility, and a whole host of other ways.

At the same time, it has also always been true that there was a dominant culture in these United States. It was Christian, it spoke English, and it identified with the high cultural traditions of Europe, and more particularly of England. And, until recently, when people spoke approvingly of American culture, this is what they meant. (When they spoke disapprovingly of American culture, especially in Europe, they meant the popular culture of Hollywood, Coca-Cola, and bubble gum.)

As public education has expanded in the United States, America's citizens, and especially those citizens educated in public elementary schools in this country, have come to share a body of historical knowledge and an understanding of the American political system. And it is increasingly true that whatever other languages children in this country speak, they speak and understand English, and they watch many of the same television programs and listen to much of the same music. In that sense, most young Americans have a shared culture based in a whole variety of kinds of English; but it is no longer that older Christian, Anglo-Saxon tradition that used to be called American culture.

The outlines of this common culture, to which only very few Americans are external, are somewhat blurry. But it includes, for example, in its practices, baseball; in its ideas, democracy; in its arts, rap music and music videos and many movies. This culture is to a large extent, as I have implied, the product of schools and of the media. But even those who share this common culture—the shared cultural literacy of E. D. Hirsch, let us say—live in subcultures of language, religion, family organization, and political assumptions. And, more than this, most who are black and Hispanic have, irrespective of their incomes, radically different experiences and expectations of the state. If anyone did not believe this before, surely every sane person recognizes this after the Rodney King and O. J. Simpson verdicts and the racially divided responses to each.

Now I take it that multiculturalism is meant to be the name of a response to these familiar facts: that it is meant to be an approach to education and to public culture that acknowledges the diversity of cultures and subcultures in the United States and that proposes to deal with that diversity in some other way than by imposing the values and ideas of the hitherto dominant Anglo-Saxon cultural tradition. That, I think, is the common core of all the things that have been called multiculturalism.

I think this common idea is a good one. It is a good idea for a number of reasons. It is a good idea, first, because the old practice of imposing Christian, Anglo-Saxon tradition was rooted in—and to that extent expresses—racism and anti-Semitism (and sexism and heterosexism . . . but that is another story). But it is a good idea, second, because making the culture of *one* subculture the official culture of a state privileges the members of that subculture—gives them advantages in public life—in ways that are profoundly antiegalitarian and, thus, antidemocratic.

Yet agreeing to this idea does not tell you much about what you should do in schools and in public culture. It tells you that you mustn't impose certain practices and ideas, but it doesn't tell you what you should do affirmatively. I want to suggest that one affirmative strategy in this area is a *bad* idea for public education and that there are other strategies that are better. And then, in closing, I want to say something about why living together in a multicultural society is bound to turn out to be difficult.

Many multiculturalists seems to think that the way to deal with the fact of our many cultures in the public education system is to teach each child the culture of its group. This is the strategy of many Afrocentrists and of some (but by no means all) of those who have favored bilingual education for Hispanics.

This is the strategy I oppose.

To explain my first basis for objection, I need to elicit a paradox in this approach, which we can do by considering the Afrocentric answer to the question: Why should we teach African American children something different from what we teach other children? The Afrocentric answer comes in two parts: the first part says that we should do so because they already come from a different culture; the second part says we should do so because we should teach *all* people about their own traditions.

It's the first answer that is paradoxical. It is paradoxical because it proposes to solve the problems created by the fact that children have different cultures by emphasizing and entrenching those differences, not by trying to reduce them.[20] I should make it plain that I have no problem with the argument that children's home cultures need to be taken into account in deciding how to teach them: there's no point in talking to kids in languages or dialects they don't understand or punishing them for behavior that they are being taught at home. But to admit *that* is to admit only that culture may sometimes make a difference to *how* you should teach, not that it should make a difference to *what* you should teach. And defending teaching children different histories (Afrocentric history) or different forms of speech or writing (Black English) on the grounds that this is *already* their culture simply begs the question: if we teach African-American children different histories from other children, then, indeed, it will become true that knowing that history and not knowing any other history will be part of the culture of African Americans. But the fact is that if we don't enforce cultural differences of this kind in the schools, surely they will largely disappear.

The contrast here with the multicultural realities of a country like Ghana could not be more striking. For there substantial differences in language and culture are created outside the state, independently of the media and the schools. There it is really true that schools need to work hard to create a shared culture, here it is increasingly true that schools are central in articulating cultural differences.

And what that means is that the *only* serious argument for Afrocentricity that survives is the second answer I considered earlier: the claim that we must teach each child the culture of "its" group, because that is the right thing to do, because we should.

That idea is much more powerful. It is presumably at the basis of the thought that many nonobservant Jews share with observant Jews (who have other reasons for believing this), namely, that it is good to teach their children Jewish history and customs because they are Jewish children. It is the argument—"we have Plato to our father"—that led to the sense of exclusion that many African Americans felt when the history and culture of the United States was taught to them as the continuation of a white Western tradition, the argument against which so much Afrocentrism is a reaction. I myself am skeptical of all arguments of this form: I think that traditions are worth teaching because they are beautiful and good and true, never because they are ours or yours, mine or thine. After my first Seder, it struck me that this was a tradition worth teaching to *every*body, Jew or Gentile; and I have always valued the experience of family community among my Muslim cousins at Ramadan. But this is not the place to pursue this argument. Because all I need to point out here is that even if teaching children "their" history is good, it is not something that it would be practical for American public schools to do. For if carried to its ultimate, this policy would require segregation into cultural groups either within or between public schools, in ways that would be plainly unconstitutional in the United States. And if we did have unsegregated classes teaching Jewish history, and African-American history, and Anglo history, and Hispanic history, and Chinese history in our schools, by what right would we forbid children from going to the "wrong" classes?

Of course there are things that we surely all believe that we should teach all American children: in particular, we should teach them something of the history of the American political system. And here too is another reason why we cannot hope to teach each child only "its" cultural tradition: for understanding the American constitutional system and its history requires us to know about slavery and immigration, about the Civil War and Reconstruction, the Underground Railroad and Ellis Island. If there is a sense in which each of these belongs more to the history of some social groups than others, there is also a clear sense in which they belong to us all.

And it is *that* idea that motivates the approach to dealing with our multicultural society that I favor, that undergirds my multiculturalism, a multiculturalism whose affinities with an older pluralism will, I hope, be obvious.

For it seems to me that what is ideal in a multicultural society, whose multicultural character is created outside the state in the sphere of civil society, is that the state should seek in its educational systems to make these multiple subcultures known to each other. A multicultural education, in my view, should be one that leaves you not only knowing and loving what is good in the traditions of your subculture but also understanding and appreciating the traditions of others (and, yes, critically rejecting the worst of *all* traditions). This approach has its practical problems also: a curriculum filled with the history of Korean Americans and African Americans and Anglo Americans and Jewish Americans and so on risks being a curriculum with a shallow appreciation of all of them. But the principle of selection is clear: we should try to teach about those many world traditions that have come to be important at different stages of American history. This means that we begin with Native American and Protestant Dutch and English and African and Iberian cultures, adding voices to the story as they were added to the nation. Because different elements are important to different degrees in different places today, we can assume that the balance will be and should be differently struck in different places.[21]

I have a final argument against Afrocentricity and suchlike movements. It is that they are dangerous, for reasons that have to do with the final point I want to make, which is about the difficulty of managing multicultural—plural—societies.

I said earlier that no one is likely to be troubled by the variety of subcultures in high culture. Why is this? Because however important our participation in high culture is, it is unlikely to be at the heart of our ethnicity. High culture crosses ethnic boundaries to an extraordinary degree. (The boundaries that it crosses with less ease are those of class.) The result is that subdivisions of high culture are not so likely to become central to the organization of political life. The United States is not threatened by the cultural autonomy of the American Philosophical Association (to which I have the privilege of belonging) or (even) the American Medical Association (to which I have the privilege of not belonging). In this respect the associations of high culture are like many elements of popular culture: the next New York mayoral election is not going to be between followers of the Mets and of the Yankees.

But differences in subcultures—in the anthropologist's sense of culture—are rather different. We pass on our language to the next generation because we care to communicate with them; we pass on religion because we care for its vision and endorse its values; we pass on our folkways because we value people with those folkways. Even when these values are not explicitly articulated, they lie at the heart of our self-conceptions and our conceptions of community. Culture in this sense is the home of what we care about most. If other people organize their solidarity around cultures different from ours, this makes them, to that extent, different from us in ways that matter to us deeply. The result, of course, is not just that we have difficulty understanding across cultures—this is an inevitable result of cultural difference, for much of culture consists of language and other shared modes of understanding—but that we end up preferring our own kind: and if we prefer our own kind, it is easy enough to slip into preferring to vote for our own kind, to employ our own kind, and so on. In sum: Culture undergirds loyalties. To the extent that these loyalties matter they will be mobilized in politics, *except to the extent that a civic culture can be created that explicitly seeks to exclude them.* And that is why my multiculturalism is so necessary: it is the only way to reduce the misunderstandings across subcultures, the only way to build bridges of loyalty across the ethnicities that have so often divided us. Multiculturalism of this sort—pluralism, to use an older word—is the only way of making sure we care enough about people across ethnic divides to keep those ethnic divides from destroying us.

The task is not to replace one ethnocentrism with many, not to reject old ideals of truth and impartiality as intrinsically biased. Rather it is to recognize that those ideals have yet to be fully lived up to in our scholarship, that the bias has derived not from scholars who took Western standards (which often turn out to be everybody's standards) of truth for granted, but that they didn't take them seriously enough.

The old way of dealing with the problem of many cultures was to make us *e pluribus unum*. Out of many cultures, to mold one. Anyone who appreciates the vibrancy of American popular culture and high culture, the splendid variety of our literatures and musics and cuisines, is likely to balk at such a project. And anyone who has looked at our history and seen how often the one into which we were to be made was white and Anglo-Saxon and Protestant will be skeptical that the one into which we are to be made could be anything other than the cover for the domination of one of our sectional cultures. These are, in my view, legitimate skepticisms. And the only alternative, so far as I can see, that doesn't threaten perpetual schism is the hard work of a multiculturalism that accepts America's diversity while teaching each of us the ways and the worth of others.

Notes

Pages 38–41 of this chapter are based on chapter 9 of Kwame Appiah, *In My Father's House: Africa in the Philosophy of Culture* (New York: Oxford University Press, 1992). Some passages cited in the text are from my own unpublished transcription of an interview edited and published as "Interview with Anthony Appiah, D. A. N. Jones, and John Ryle," *Times Literary Supplement,* 26 February 1982.

1. My father would never have forgiven the solecism of trying to explain a proverb!

2. About half of those arrested in the Los Angeles riots were Latino; a little over a third were black. This is unlikely to be a "fair" representation of rates of participation in the unrest, since there is some evidence that the police were more likely to arrest Latinos. But the point is that these figures do show what many people will have seen on their televisions, namely, that the riots were not monoracial.

3. See, for example, Robert Harms, *Times Literary Supplement,* 29 November 1985, 1343.

4. See Kwame Appiah, *In My Fathers House: Africa in the Philosophy of Culture* (New York: Oxford University Press, 1992), chs. 1, 2, and 9.

5. Okomfo Anokye is the name of the priest who helped the first of the Asante kings, Osei Tutu, form the nation from the various Akan kingdoms that it united. He is said to have brought the Golden Stool, symbol of Asante kingship, down from heaven.

6. Tzvetan Todorov, " 'Race,' Writing and Culture" in *"Race," Writing and Difference,* ed. Henry Louis Gates, Jr. (Chicago: University of Chicago Press, 1986), 370–80. You don't have to believe in witchcraft, after all, to believe that women were persecuted as witches in colonial Massachusetts.

7. Gayatri Spivak recognizes these problems when she speaks of "strategic essentialisms." See Spivak, *In Other Worlds: Essays in Cultural Politics* (New York: Routledge, 1988), 205.

8. See, for example, K. Anthony Appiah, "The Uncompleted Argument: Du Bois and the Illusion of Race," in Gates, 21–37; and K. Anthony Appiah, "Alexander Crummell and the Invention of Africa," *Massachusetts Review* 31 (Autumn 1990): 385–406.

9. The violence between Senegalese and Mauritanians in spring 1989 can be understood only when we recall that the legal abolition of racial slavery of "Negroes" owned by "Moorish" masters occurred in the early 1980s.

10. See Wole Soyinka, *Myth, Literature and the African World* (New York: Cambridge University Press, 1976).

11. Kwasi Wiredu, *Philosophy and an African Culture* (New York: Cambridge University Press, 1980), 38.

12. "Interview with Anthony Appiah, D. A. N. Jones, and John Ryle," *Times Literary Supplement,* 26 February 1982.

13. David Laitin, *Hegemony and Culture: Politics and Religious Change among the Yoruba* (Chicago: Chicago University Press, 1986), 7–8.

14. Laitin, 8.

15. This passage continues: "Increasingly also Lingala and Swahili came to divide functions between them. Lingala served the military and much of the administration in the capital of the lower Congo; Swahili became the language of the workers in the mines of Katanga. This created cultural connotations which began to emerge very early and which remained prevalent in Mobutu's Zaire. From the point of view of Katanga/Shaba, Lingala has been the undignified jargon of unproductive soldiers, government clerks, entertainers, and, recently, of a power clique, all of them designated as *batoka chini,* people from down-river, i.e. from Kinshasa. Swahili as spoken in Katanga was a symbol of regionalism, even for those colonials who spoke it badly." Johannes Fabian, *Language and Colonial Power* (New York: Cambridge University Press, 1986), 42–43. The dominance of Swahili in certain areas is already itself a colonial product (Fabian, 6).

16. Similarly Shona and Ndebele identities in modern Zimbabwe became associated with political parties at independence, even though Shona-speaking peoples had spent much of the late precolonial period in military confrontations with each other.

17. Laitin, 8. I need hardly add that religious identities are equally salient and equally mythological in Lebanon or in Ireland.

18. That "race" operates this way has been clear to many other African Americans: so, for example, it shows up in a fictional context as a central theme of George Schuyler's *Black No More* (New York: Macaulay, 1931); see, for example, p. 59. Du Bois (as usual) provides in *Black Reconstruction: An Essay Toward a History of the Part which Black People Played in America 1860–1880* (New York: Russell and Russell, 1935) a body of evidence that remains relevant. As Cedric Robinson writes: "Once the industrial class emerged as dominant in the nation, it possessed not only its own basis of power and the social relations historically related to that power, but it also had available to it the instruments of repression created by the now subordinate Southern ruling class. In its struggle with labour, it could activate racism to divide the labour movement into antagonistic forces. Moreover, the permutations of the instrument appeared endless: Black against white; Anglo-Saxon against southern and eastern European; domestic against immigrant; proletariat against share-cropper; white American against Asian, Black, Latin American, etc." Cedric Robinson, *Black Marxism: The Making of the Black Radical Tradition* (London: Zed Press, 1983), 286.

19. See Robinson, 313.

20. I think of this as the "WASPS have Christmas, Jews have Hanukkah, so Blacks should have Kwanzaa" approach.

21. All of this presupposes a general improvement, I should add, in the quality of American elementary and secondary education.

Chapter 3

Meanings for Multiculturalism

C. Vann Woodward

Before we get very far in the discussion of multiculturalism in the university, it might be well to agree, if possible, on what it is we are talking about and on how we define and use the word "culture." We need not pause over the prefix "multi" or the suffix "ism," but the key word "culture" requires close attention. Starting from the Latin root word *cultus*, to till, the word in English has taken on usages not only in agriculture but also in education, religion, and art. Historians once spoke of "high culture." The usage most commonly involved in our present discussion, however, is the one developed by anthropologists. They are not entirely consistent in their usage of the word, but "culture" for them usually means the sum total of behavior patterns, arts, values, beliefs, institutions, and other products of work and thought characteristic of a people and socially transmitted.

If we accept as a working definition the latter usage of "culture," we clarify the confusion by narrowing the definition in some degree. For one thing we remove some groups of the academic community mistakenly described as "cultural" from the cultural category. For example, every culture influences the restraints, discriminations, and status imposed on its female members, but these impositions are part of the culture in which women live, and do not constitute a separate culture for women. The same is true of homosexuals and the members of classes that divide any culture. This is in no way intended to dismiss or diminish the injustices they suffer, but these are results of conflicts within a culture, not between separate cultures. With regard to racial, ethnic, and national minorities, categories less clearly defined, it is not so easy to deny separate cultural identity. For each of them that much of separate identity has been claimed at one time or another, and their claims should be fairly assessed.

Americans of African descent have been especially insistent in claims of a separate culture based upon race; and these claims in the academy have been, if anything, increasing over the last decade. Proponents of the black

55

culture movement often turn to the mother continent for "roots," for bonds of unity, for cultural origins, and for the heritage of an ancient past. In so doing they are attempting to identify race with culture. They are also attributing to African history and Africans characteristics that have to be critically examined before we can accept them as foundations for African-American unity and cultural identity.

Of the three extant human types completely indigenous to Africa, only one is visibly represented among African Americans. That is the tallest, darkest, most dominant, and most numerous type, the type with which the history of human development south of the Sahara has been almost exclusively concerned. They were the Africans known elsewhere as "Negroes," a term not used on the continent itself, nor by present-day scholars save in quotation marks. For one thing the term has acquired derogatory connotations, but scholars reject it primarily because it is so unsatisfactory when used to describe people of such wide differences in culture as well as in physical appearance. Scholars list 60, some over 160, different ethnic groups, from the Asanti to the Zulu. These people south of the Sahara have developed at least a thousand distinct languages, including fifty major ones (each spoken by a million or more people), and a multitude of dialects in addition. That is far more languages than can be found in any other continent, making Africa the one of greatest linguistic complexity. African languages have little relevance to national boundaries, and most of the postcolonial nations retain a major European language as the official tongue, even though it is not spoken by many of their citizens.

Turning to other cultural diversities, those of religion are less marked than those of language, with Christian and Muslim forms predominating. Christianity of the Coptic order gained footing in Egypt in the first century and Ethiopia in the fourth, well in advance of West European foundings. But the large-scale Christian gains in Africa did not come until the nineteenth century, when Christian denominations made great strides. Recent estimates are some sixty-four million Roman Catholics, sixty million Protestants, and thirty-four million Independent Protestants and Coptics. The pattern of these religions is similar to that in Europe and America. The largest number of Christians are in South Africa, Zaire, Nigeria, and Uganda. Islam entered Egypt in the year 640 and reached the Atlantic by the end of the century, but did not gain hold south of the Sahara except along the eastern coast until the eleventh century, and, like Christianity, waited until the nineteenth century for its greatest expansion in Africa. Muslims' numbers, how-

ever, never rivaled those of the Christians. In addition to the major organized religions are numerous preliterate traditional religions, which coexist
with both Christianity and Islam, often within the same individual, and frequently dominate them.

In addition to language and religion, the creative arts are important components and expressions of a culture. And in sub-Saharan Africa all the
familiar forms are found—sculpture, painting, architecture, music, dance,
drama and poetry, textiles and other fabrics, along with costume and jew-
elry. Knowledge of sub-Saharan arts is still fragmentary, but the earliest
known sculpture goes back to 500 B.C. Old and modern art of the continent,
rich and fascinating as it is, comes in such a bewildering variety of styles,
however, that it is little help to call them "African." While there are a few
themes in common, each style was developed in its own particular historical, ecological, and social circumstances. Christianity did not serve to uni-
versalize art as it did in Europe, and Islam frowned upon the use of images.
Traditional religions, on the other hand, favored artistic particularism, while
language and ethnic barriers did not promote exchange of influence and
ideas among the artists. The American minorities who look to Africa for the
foundation of the cultural unity to which they aspire will look in vain. Africa
itself is multicultural—extravagantly, even disastrously, so. Yet romantic
black Americans imagine it to be a single culture.

If color and race have not served to unify African cultures, neither has
color or ethnicity served to unify Africans. That was true of precolonial
Africa, and it has remained true throughout the European intrusions and
aggressions of modern history. The Atlantic slave trade failed to bring about
unified black resistance, in part because Africans were themselves slaveholders of a milder sort, and in part because some African chiefdoms accepted partnerships with Europeans and Americans in the trade, providing
the enslaved and profiting thereby. Prominent among such partners, incidentally, were the Swahili, whose language black American students in the
1960s, then wearing their dashikis, eagerly studied—but not for very long.
Unilingual students with multicultural enthusiasms are quite common.

European imperial powers, in colonial control and exploitation of African peoples after the 1880s, though differing in particulars from one colony
to another, all used the ancient strategy of divide-and-rule. But they did not
have to do all the dividing themselves, since their preliterate and preindus-
trial subjects were already divided in numerous ways. Politically they were
divided into a few kingdoms, a large number of small chiefdoms, and many

who lived without any central authority at all. None of them were strong enough to prevent colonization. Their experience as colonial subjects under seven separate European powers differed greatly. The worst horrors were those suffered in the Congo Free State under Belgian rule, but the lives of many Africans were little affected by colonialism.

After the end of colonial rule, beginning in the 1950s, the newly independent nation-states gained some measure of independence but little unity, either between nations or within their rather arbitrarily drawn borders. Partly to blame was continuation or renewal of foreign economic control and interventions by the two major parties to the Cold War. In addition to foreign meddling and the heritage of colonial bureaucracy, the Africans were cursed with wretched poverty. Of its 160 members, the United Nations reports recently that 32 of the 40 most impoverished are in Africa.

The prevailing political system following "liberation" of the African colonies was heavily authoritarian—dictatorship in one form or another. In its annual classification of nations in 1987 Freedom House rated only three of the fifty-two African nations as "free," fifteen as partly free, and thirty-four as not free. The next two years saw a turn for the better and promise of more democracy, with eight states rated free, twenty-three as partly free, and a decline of highly authoritarian states to twenty-one. To some this seemed a "second liberation," but to others these years spelled retrogression, as in Algeria, Angola, Liberia, Nigeria, Zaire, and others. By 1996, nothing much had changed: nine free, twenty partly free, and twenty-four not free. Dictators and their regimes were as harshly brutal and totally corrupt as ever.

Ethnic differences, illiteracy, and droughts add other miseries to the wretchedness of poverty and dictatorship. But with those misfortunes came civil wars and anarchy that disgraced many African states during the last three decades of independence. In fifteen nations south of the Sahara, civil wars raged in 1993 along ethnic lines. None of these conflicts has yet been resolved. One has only to think of the endless mayhem following the dissolution of the Ethiopian empire, or the horrors in Uganda, the Sudan, Tanzania, Mozambique, Nigeria, Angola, Somalia, Rwanda, Burundi, and Zaire, to mention only a few examples. Even in the midst of struggles to bring to terms or end lingering white minority regimes and apartheid in Zimbabwe and South Africa, blacks could not put a stop to the slaughter of blacks by blacks. And in famine- and drought-ridden Somalia, warring factions could not suspend the civil strife resulting in 300,000 deaths long enough to permit the Red Cross to bring temporary relief to their starving millions.

If by any chance my sad account of events in Africa should bring to mind developments not entirely dissimilar taking place to the north and north-east of the "dark continent," then I must admit that this coincidence had also occurred to me. In fact, I have not been wholly innocent of deliberate intention of provoking this analogy. I believe it could prove useful in our reflections upon culture wars and multiculturalism. The *New York Times* goes so far as to say that "today's true dark continent begins in the Balkans and extends eastward."

It is naturally the similarities and correspondences that come to mind first, for they are the more striking and unavoidable. To think of the pathetic pictures from Somalia is to think of those from Bosnia appearing in the same edition of our newspapers and news broadcasts. Dissimilarities between the ferocity and destructiveness of cultural and ethnic wars on the two continents are in large part due to disparities in the firepower and effectiveness of weapons available. With the more modern and superior armaments at their disposal, warriors of cultural hatred to the north have far outstripped those of underdeveloped Africa. No horror of Africa equals that of Europe's Holocaust. Hate conflict has torn the Near East and Middle East to shreds, turned Lebanon into a no-man's-land, and left Beirut in ruins. The tragedy of culture conflict and its ancient hatreds and feuds has subjected Croatia and Bosnia-Herzegovina to the ravages of what is called "ethnic cleansing" and turned many inhabited cities and architectural treasures into rubble. From the Balkans in the south to the Baltic in the north of Europe, cultural and ethnic differences disturb the peace of the world in one degree or another, and they are more in evidence than ever to the east and west of that region. It would seem, indeed, that multiculturalism and its consequences have become an obsessive preoccupation, a spreading fever of tribalism, in large parts of the world.

One of the several ironies in the recent spread of this fever is the part played by what was otherwise regarded as a boon to the cause of world peace. That is the collapse of communist power over vast areas and the substitution of democracy or at least attempts at democratic self-rule. But this also meant an end to the iron discipline that had held united the multicultured republics of Eastern Europe that were cobbled together after the First and Second World Wars and left under control of Russia. Some of these, for example, Czechoslovakia, began to come apart, and others to suffer internal strife of one ethnic or cultural group against another. The dissolution of Tito's variation of the Russian dictatorship in Yugoslavia was also in part the result of the collapse of that regime. More ominous was the dissolution of the Soviet Union itself and the consequent emergence of new nation-states and revival of suppressed nations.

But the now defunct Soviet Union embraced more cultures than it did nations. It has been compared with a state that united a Norway and a Pakistan—and one might throw in an Afghanistan. But it was more complex than that, for in addition to glaring disparities in economic development, several of these nations were divided culturally against themselves, divided by language, by religion, by history, and some by age-old hatreds. The Soviet state had attempted to create a melting pot, based on Soviet Russian culture, for these multicultural multitudes. The policy failed. The pot did not melt. When the force imposing the policy was removed, the unrest of repressed cultural minorities and majority hatreds of them broke into conflict and violence in many areas, earliest in Kazakhstan and Yakutiva, most violently against minorities in the Central Asian republics. Pogroms in Uzbekistan against Meshketian Turks were so ugly that they forced an evacuation from the Uzbek republic. Christian Armenians and Muslim Turks continued their century-long strife. In the Caucasus, Russia brutalized Chechnya; Georgia abused the human rights of its minorities: Armenians, Russians, Azerbaijani, Greeks, Jews, Ukrainians, and Kurds.

And so it goes, with cultural, ethnic, and religious conflict producing thousands of casualties and hundreds of thousands of exiles and refugees. Boris Yeltsin fears ending up in a neo-Balkan abyss. But the presence of 25 million Russian inhabitants in the new non-Russian states and their appeal for Russian military intervention to protect their rights, supported at home by Russian nationalists, threatens to undermine the Yeltsin policy. Gloomy predictions of the new order turning out to be another Weimar prelude to new varieties of fascism are often heard. It is too early to say what all this portends for the future of the fifteen new states of the former Soviet Union or its former satellite countries to the west. But it is not too early to conclude that multiculturalism is not the ideal foundation for national peace, unity, and stability, and that such of these achievements as now exist are haunted by terrible fragility.

European nations to the west of the old Iron Curtain and Berlin Wall are not without their own varieties of what the Germans call the *Kulturkampf.* The dividing line, or zone, between Eastern and Western European multicultures runs north and south all the way across the continent, a wandering line defined by religion and history. To the east is the Europe of Orthodox or Greek Christianity and Islam; to the west, the Europe of Roman or Latin Catholicism and Protestantism. On the one side are nations formed by the collapse of the Ottoman and Hapsburg empires, while on the other side are those shaped by Renaissance, Reformation, Enlightenment, and Revolution. The line roughly sets off Poland from Ukraine; claims the Baltic republics, the Czechs, and most Hungarians for the West; splits Romania; and divides Yugoslavia. These ancient cleavages of the spirit and culture can surface with startling force in modern times. "We have been waiting for this moment for eight centuries," said the defense minister of independent Croatia in 1991.

The manifestations of multiculturalism in Western Europe have in recent centuries proved somewhat less bloody and more manageable than those of the East. But the West was populated by migrations from the East, and few nations can claim ethnic purity. Even the English are plagued by explosions of Celts in Ireland, the French by Celts of Breton, the Spanish by Basque Celts, and Portugal by Celts of her own. In addition to the western fringe of Celts, these nations have other, if more dormant, minorities. England before the Roman conquest had the Danish invaders and afterward the Normans, and is now by way of being colonized by those it once colonized in Asia and the West Indies. France copes with Vikings, Gauls, Catalans, and Provençals of older times in addition to modern Polish and Russian Jewish migrants and recent immigrants from her former colonies in Asia and Africa. Spain contains older immigrants, Iberian, Visigoth, Vandal, Catalan, Castilian, Greek, and Arab. And surely the two nations populating Belgium, the Walloon and the Flemish, must not be overlooked.

It is of some comfort to find in Western Europe movements now under way to counter the divisive effects of these cultural and national enmities, not only in the West but in other parts of the world. In the West we have the hesitant and stumbling struggles for unity expressed by the European Community. And beyond that exists a growing bond between democracies or would-be democracies of West and East that are seeking ways to head off ethnic conflicts and force negotiation. These efforts have involved the United Nations, the European Community, and the Conference on Security and Coöperation in Europe. Their attempts have so far failed in Yugoslavia and in Soviet successor states and are likely to meet with other failures for a long time to come, but they do continue their efforts.

And now what has all this to do with our transatlantic New World? Well, before we turn to the United States, we might spare a moment for a glance at our neighbor—or perhaps I should say neighbors—to the north. For the

Canadian territory, rather like Belgium with its Walloons and Flemings, is inhabited by two nationalities. In addition to the more recent influx of immigrants from all over, Canada has for centuries consisted of two populations, the British and the French. And we to the south have watched with anxiety while they periodically threaten to tear themselves apart.

The population of the United States is in the vast diversity of its origins perhaps the most multicultural in the world. That made assimilation a matter of necessity, a matter of national survival, and helps explain the extremes of American nationalism as a means to that end. Immigrants poured across the Atlantic from all countries and cultures of Europe in tidal waves and human hordes. In the single century from 1815 to 1914 over 35 million came across, largely as individuals, and in the twenty-five years of greatest intensity in that century 17 million crossed over. That overshadows all other population movements in human history up to that time, dwarfing the barbarian invasions of the late Roman Empire into numerical insignificance.

By 1890 one in every four Philadelphians was foreign-born, and in Boston and Chicago one out of three. Greater New York City, with four out of five foreign-born or of foreign parentage, had half as many Italians as Naples and two and a half times as many Irish as Dublin. To those new immigrants were to be added increasing numbers coming in on the other side of the continent from Asiatic countries and cultures. All Americans are descended from immigrants of the last four centuries except the native Indians—with enormous tribal diversities of their own—whose immigrant ancestors are a bit more remote.

The great majority of the immigrants came to America to better their lot or to escape worse abroad. Few of them came to preserve, perpetuate, or spread their Old World culture in the New World. Rather their urge was to shed their foreign ways, looks, and accents and take on the new ways, looks, and speech as quickly as possible—to Americanize, to assimilate. Prominent Europeans of the last century and more—Alexis de Tocqueville, James Bryce, Gunnar Myrdal—marveled at and admired the success of the American policy of assimilation, what Lord Bryce called "the amazing solvent power which American institutions, habits, and ideas exercise upon newcomers of all races."

But what about the oldest and largest American minority of all—in terms of the percentage of the race whose ancestors arrived in the seventeenth and eighteenth centuries? I mean the African Americans, whom I have so far rarely mentioned. Neither did J. Hector St. John de Crèvecoeur in 1782 when he defined the American as "either an European or the descendant of an European"—thus silently defining blacks and others of non-European descent out of American identity. In so doing he had the support of the majority of white Americans and their government. For it was the glaring failure and disgrace of the American promise of assimilation and equality to all comers that it was denied to African Americans and continued to be withheld long after their liberation from slavery. Yet they, among the oldest of the immigrants, as much as the latest, continued to demand and struggle for assimilation, integration, and equality in the American system.

It is true that an occasional back-to-Africa movement attracted a few followers; and with the help of whites who wanted to rid the country of free blacks, Liberia was founded in 1847 to receive them. But the outstanding leaders of African Americans, from David Walker in 1829 to Martin Luther King, Jr., in the 1960s, have resisted that romantic appeal of Africa and called instead for assimilation and integration and equality in American society. When King declared unequivocally, "The Negro is American. We know nothing of Africa," he was echoing W. E. B. DuBois, who in his early career had said his black associates "felt themselves Americans, not Africans," and who noted among NAACP members, "a fierce repugnance toward anything African." I am aware, of course, that DuBois later underwent a change of view on cultural separatism.

DuBois, in fact, later pointed the way for other American minorities—whether black, brown, yellow, red, or white—that in recent years have suddenly renounced long-cherished goals of integration and assimilation and joined movements of cultural separatism. Each of these has its own separatist slogans, myths, and programs of ethnicity, and they are often at odds with one another. For example Hispanic Americans reject "Black English" but promote bilingualism, which African Americans reject. Both of them are potential sources of cultural fragmentation and separatism, though mutually antagonistic. What these various culturally separatist groups have in common is the cult of victimization, inflammable sensitivity, and a passion for "roots" and recovery of an ancestral culture, however remote. That does not bring them together, but instead encourages self-segregation. Whereas Chief Justice Warren held in the *Brown* school-segregation decision of 1954 that segregation "generates a feeling of inferiority," the multiculturalists with political ends now contend that it is integration that generates such feelings and that segregation is the cure instead of the cause.

It would at first seem ironic that the oldest of the American minorities should be the one to take the lead in these neosegregation movements. Yet it is the one that has suffered most from exclusion, injustice, discrimination, and denial of assimilation. And before we weigh criticisms of American multicultural separatism, we should acknowledge certain positive contributions. Most important has been to force long overdue recognition of the contributions that racial minorities and women have made to national achievement and American civilization. This in turn has resulted in admission of the long unchallenged dominance by white male Anglo-Saxons and their casual habit of claiming credit for everything and collecting most of the honors and rewards.

But the cost of these gains threatens to be excessive. One of the threats is to the long-standing and peculiarly American tradition that has been the envy of all countries torn by multicultural conflict—the remarkable success, despite failures noted, it has enjoyed with its policy of assimilation and integration of all cultures. I agree with Arthur M. Schlesinger, Jr., who in *The Disuniting of America* says we are facing "a struggle to redefine the national identity" and an effort to change it from "a transformative nation with an identity all its own" to a nation that preserves or revives old identities, that thinks and acts in groups, in "a quarrelsome sputter of enclaves, ghettos and tribes," one that cherishes *pluribus* over *unum* and abandons the national ideal of *e pluribus unum.*

Few adherents of these culturally separatist movements joined them with such direful intentions in mind. But extremists often influence and sometimes dominate the members and are permitted to speak for them. Extremists among the Afrocentrists, for example, denounce or trivialize Western or European culture while at the same time claiming that Africa was schoolmaster to Greece and Rome and "the mother of Western civilization." Another divides humankind into the cold, materialistic "ice people" of the North and the warm, humanist "sun people" of the South, the former bringing death and destruction, the latter joy and happiness. Still another, a black psychiatrist, attributes white racial inferiority to lack of the skin pigmentation melanin. A black psychologist contends that the mind of the black student works in distinctive ways in learning and thinking, thus accounting for their difficulties under the present educational system and the need for racially separate classes to teach "Black English" and for black professors for black students. The black Nation of Islam has published a massive volume of anti-Semitism, hate literature blaming Jews for leading responsibility in the Atlantic slave trade. And from another quarter we hear black supremacy proclaimed in terms as bigoted as those once used by white supremacists.

Shall we then discourage or exclude the study of multiculturalism from the university curriculum? By no means! Not when an understanding of the long and bloody history of multicultural societies and their conflicts is so urgently relevant to events of our own time—at home as well as abroad. I fondly believe that had the last two or three generations of American college students been exposed to the sort of history I outlined in the first half of my paper, particularly the multicultural history of sub-Saharan Africa, they might have been spared many of their current misadventures in cultural separatism and romanticism. No, what the academy needs is more rather than less attention and curriculum time devoted to the history and consequences of multiculturalism—using the term as I have used it here.

Which reminds me of the title I chose for this essay: "Meanings for Multiculturalism." The term has quite a different meaning and connotation in the current language of cultural separatists in American universities. There it is commonly used to mean the courses taught, the faculty appointed, the living and dining arrangements provided, and the codes of conduct passed in order to promote the separatism and political ends of various organized groups, whether racial, sexual, national, or whatever. This strikes me as a misuse of the university, a political use, and a misconception of the purpose, the mission, and the very idea of the university. Unlike the study of multicultural history I advocated, the political multiculturalism of the separatist cults is, I think, harmful.

I do not mean to include as harmful scholarly courses in racial, sexual, or national history and literature. Had black students been exposed to courses of this sort, for example, they would have been aware of what such distinguished fellow citizens as Frederick Douglass, W. E. B. DuBois, James Baldwin, Richard Wright, Horace Mann Bond, Ralph Bunche, and John Hope Franklin have had to say about looking back three hundred years to Africa for cultural roots, rituals, and colorful costumes to wear in public. Propaganda-free courses of high quality and standards on the history and literature of minorities are still offered, and more are needed to do justice to the rich contributions minorities have made that have been neglected or ignored in our curriculum for the humanities.

But these are not the objectives that multicultural separatists have primarily in mind. The history for their new curriculum is inventive and exculpatory, purposive history to shape group identity, unity, and pride of self-esteem. Their mission is not to enrich or add to the existing culture and university curriculum, but rather to replace them, often by denigrating and demeaning the prevailing system and its originators. The Afrocentric teachings I offered as examples a bit earlier—"ice people" versus "sun people," skin pigmentation as the secret of racial superiority, racial differences in the learning process, black teachers and separate departments for black students—may have struck some as extremist. And so they are; but the perpetrators of all these doctrines cited, with the exception of the Nation of Islam, have tenure in faculties of reputable colleges and universities.

Preferences, wishes, and demands of separatist groups and organizations have met with little resistance from some university administrations and with eager compliance from a few in faculty appointments and promotions and student admissions. University presidents have on some occasions applauded and extravagantly financed segregated student unions, dormitories, and dining halls and approved or condoned segregated clubs, fraternities, and sororities. There exists at least one instance of a separate yearbook for the senior class. Athletic teams have universally resisted segregation and adhered rather strictly to standards of merit and achievement. Alumni notoriously prefer victory to virtue.

The elaborate pains taken to accommodate segregation have been explained in part as a means of avoiding tensions, insults, and conflicts. As things turned out, however, the more segregation flourished and other precautions were taken, the more instances of harassment, slurs, and insults occurred. The University of Michigan desperately developed scores of programs for "consciousness raising" and "sensitivity training" for whites and covered the campus with posters condemning racial and sexual harassments. When black students denounced these efforts as racist, the university finally resorted to adopting an elaborate code of racial and sexual etiquette and penalties for speech that violated it. This example of speech censorship was followed by numerous universities all over the country until the American Civil Liberties Union filed a suit and U.S. District Judge Avern Cohen declared the Michigan code unconstitutional. Judge Cohen pointed out that "statutes punishing speech or conduct solely on the grounds they are unseemly or offensive are unconstitutionally overbroad."

It is good to hear some voices among champions of black studies calling for moderation and compromise, even if not always consistently. One such voice, for example, is that of Professor Henry Louis Gates, Jr., of Harvard University. It is reassuring to read his forthright denunciation of the violent anti-Semitism of the Nation of Islam, his admission that some of the hundreds of black studies programs are intellectually "bogus" for inventing an African past that never was, and his acknowledgment that irrationality, racism, and victimization are not all on one side. On the other hand he finds occasion to write that "now we must at last don the empowering mask of blackness and talk *that* talk, the language of black difference." Only thus, it seems, can we "know and test the dark secrets of a black discursive universe that awaits its disclosure through the black arts of interpretation." Dark secrets and black arts at Harvard?

The real clue to the power of multiculturalism in universities is not political correctness but moral correctness. In almost any group of separatists we are dealing with here we are confronted with moral issues, some older and deeper than others to be sure, but all involving injustice, neglect, and abuse, including inhuman brutality, a record at odds with the most cherished principles of American democracy. It would be morally obtuse for us to remain indifferent to these grievances and for a society to do nothing to correct them. The question is whether the university is the place to do this. Given the amount of white guilt endemic to current-day university circles, it is not surprising to find many eager to assume the entire responsibility.

On this difficult question I find wisdom in the views held by my colleague Professor Jaroslav Pelikan of Yale. In his book *The Idea of the University: A Reexamination,* he writes that "the university urgently needs to find new ways of protecting the freedom of inquiry without allowing itself to become the tool of the polarities of nation, race, class, and gender that will continue to shape the ideological climate both outside and inside the academy." He also observes that the university "can run the danger of debasing the educational currency in the very process of redistributing it."

It remains to account for the degree to which university administrations and faculties have yielded to the demands of extremists among the cultural separatists. First a word of sympathy for hard-pressed administrators, whom faculties often give a hard time. No doubt some have proved weak and compliant. But what is one to do when all the complaints and demands come from one side, and the faculty eggs them on? As for the faculty, their alignments are often attributed to radicalism: "tenured radicals," they are called.

I think radicalism in faculties has been much exaggerated. I would hesitate to call all of them tenured conformists, but "conformity" better describes their characteristic response than "radicalism." Radicalism made conformity more difficult for the majority of faculty members, who were liberals or conservatives. The genuine Marxist program calls for *class* conflict and frowns upon conflict between cultures and races. With the decline of ideological radicalism and Marxism everywhere, including universities, moral correctness appeared as a welcome substitute for political correctness, and was surely more comfortable for conformists. Many faculty members, of course, support the multiculturalist movements out of sincere if misguided conviction rather than conformity. That does not make them radicals, however, any more than it does the pure conformists. Nor, I might add, does it turn their critics and opponents into conservatives.

Chapter 4

Boutique Multiculturalism

Stanley Fish

Multiculturalism Does Not Exist

Multiculturalism comes in at least two versions, boutique multiculturalism and strong multiculturalism. Boutique multiculturalism is the multiculturalism of ethnic restaurants, weekend festivals, and high-profile flirtations with the "other" in the manner satirized by Tom Wolfe under the rubric of "radical chic."[1]

Boutique multiculturalism is characterized by its superficial or cosmetic relationship to the objects of its affection. Boutique multiculturalists admire or appreciate or enjoy or sympathize with or (at the very most) "recognize the legitimacy of" the traditions of cultures other than their own; but boutique multiculturalists will always stop short of approving other cultures at a point where some value at those cultures' center generates an act that offends against the canons of civilized decency, as they have been either declared or assumed. The death sentence under which Salman Rushdie now lives is an obvious and perspicuous example, although it is an example so extreme that it might be better to begin with a few that are less dramatic. A boutique multiculturalist may find something of value in rap music and patronize (pun intended) soul-food restaurants, but he will be uneasy about affirmative action and downright hostile to an Afrocentrist curriculum. A boutique multiculturalist may enjoy watching Native American religious ceremonies and insist that they be freely allowed to occur, but he will balk if those ceremonies include animal sacrifice or the use of a controlled substance.[2] A boutique multiculturalist may acknowledge the diversity of opinions about abortion, but he is likely to find something illegitimate in the actions of abortion opponents who block the entrance to clinics and subject the women who approach them to verbal assaults. A boutique multiculturalist may honor the tenets of religions other than his own, but he will draw the line when the adherents of a religion engage in the practice of polygamy.

69

In each of these cases (and in the many analogous cases that could be instanced) the boutique multiculturalist resists the force of the appreciated culture at precisely the point at which it matters most to its strongly committed members: the point at which the African American tries to make the content of his culture the content of his children's education, the point at which a Native American wants to practice his religion as its ancient rituals direct him to, the point at which antiabortionists directly confront the evil that they believe is destroying the moral fiber of the country, the point at which Mormons seek to be faithful to the word and practices of their prophets and elders.

Another way to put this is to say that a boutique multiculturalist does not and cannot take seriously the core values of the cultures he tolerates. The reason he cannot is that he does not see those values as truly "core" but as overlays on a substratum of essential humanity. That is the true core, and the differences that mark us externally—differences in language, clothing, religious practices, race, gender, class, and so on—are for the boutique multiculturalist no more than what Milton calls in his *Areopagitica* "moderat varieties and brotherly dissimilitudes that are not vastly disproportionale."[3] We may dress differently, speak differently, woo differently, worship or not worship differently, but underneath (or so the argument goes) there is something we all share (or that shares us) and that something constitutes the core of our identities. Those who follow the practices of their local culture to the point of failing to respect the practices of other cultures—by calling for the death of an author whose writings denigrate a religion or by seeking to suppress pornography because it is offensive to a gender—have simply mistaken who they are by identifying with what is finally only an *accidental* aspect of their beings.

The essential boutique multiculturalist point is articulated concisely by Steven C. Rockefeller: "Our universal identity as human beings is our primary identity and is more fundamental than any particular identity, whether it be a matter of citizenship, gender, race, or ethnic origin."[4] Taking pleasure in one's "particular identity" is perfectly all right so long as when the pinch comes, and a question of basic allegiance arises, it is one's universal identity that is affirmed, for as "important as respect for diversity is in multicultural democratic societies, ethnic identity is not the foundation of recognition of equal value and the related idea of equal rights."[5] That is to say, we have rights not as men or women or Jews or Christians or blacks or Asians, but as human beings, and what makes a human being a human being is not the particular choices he or she makes, but the capacity for choice itself; and it is this capacity rather than any of its actualizations that must be protected.

It follows then that while any particular choice can be pursued at the individual's pleasure, it cannot be pursued to the point at which it interferes with or prescribes or proscribes the choices of other individuals. (This is of course a reformulation of J. S. Mill's "harm principle" in *On Liberty*.) One may practice one's religion, even if it is devil worship, in any manner one likes; but one may not practice one's religion to the extent of seeking to prevent others from practicing theirs, for example, by suppressing their sacred texts or jailing their ministers. Women may rightly insist that they receive equal pay for equal work, but they cannot rightfully insist that they be given extra compensation or preferential treatment just because they are women. One may choose either to read or to disdain pornography; but one who believes in pornography's liberatory effects cannot compel others to read it, and one who believes that pornography corrupts cannot forbid others to publish it.

Of course it is just those two actions (or some versions of them) that pro- and antipornography forces will most want to take, since they flow logically from the beliefs of the respective parties and will be seen by those parties as positive moral requirements. This is what I meant earlier when I pointed out that the boutique multiculturalist will withhold approval of a particular culture's practices at the point at which they matter most to its strongly committed members: a deeply religious person is precisely that, *deeply* religious; and the survival and propagation of his faith is not for him an incidental (and bracketable) matter, but an essential matter, and essential too in his view for those who have fallen under the sway of false faiths. To tell such a person that while his convictions may be held he must stop short of fully implementing them is to tell him that his vision of the good is either something he must keep to himself or something he must offer with a diffidence that might characterize his offer of canapés at a cocktail party.[6] Rockefeller might say that "respect for the individual is understood to involve not only respect for . . . universal human potential . . . but also respect for . . . the different cultural forms in and through which individuals actualize their humanity," but it is clear from his commentary that the latter respect will be superficial precisely in the measure that the cultural forms that are its object have themselves been judged to be superficial, that is, not intrinsic to universal identity.[7]

The politics generated by views like Rockefeller's has been called by Charles Taylor "a politics of equal dignity." The politics of equal dignity, Taylor explains, ascribes to everyone "an identical basket of rights and immunities," identical because it is limited to that aspect of everyone that is assumed to be universally the same, namely, "our status as rational agents," agents defined by a shared potential for deliberative reason.[8] The idea is that so long as that potential is protected by law, particular forms of its realization—cultural traditions, religious dogmas, ethnic allegiances—can be left to make their way or fail to make their way in the to-and-fro of marketplace debate. A tradition may die, a religion may languish, an ethnic community may fail to secure representation in the classroom or the boardroom; but these consequences are of less moment and concern than the integrity of the process that generates them, a process that values deliberation over the results of deliberation, results that are, from the perspective of this politics, indifferent.[9]

Results or outcomes are not at all indifferent in another politics, named by Taylor the "politics of difference."[10] The politics of difference, as Taylor explains it, does not merely allow traditions a run for their money; it is committed to their flourishing. If the politics of equal dignity subordinates local cultural values to the universal value of free rational choice, the politics of difference names as its preferred value the active fostering of the unique distinctiveness of particular cultures. It is that distinctiveness rather than any general capacity of which it is an actualization that is cherished and protected by this politics. Whereas the politics of equal dignity "focuses on what is the same in all" and regards particularity as icing on a basically homogeneous cake, the politics of difference asks us "to recognize and even foster particularity" as a first principle.[11]

In practical terms, fostering particularity requires that we make special adjustments to the special requirements of distinctive groups, for if we refuse such adjustments in the name of some baseline measure of rational potential, we weaken the distinctiveness whose recognition is our chief obligation. "Where the politics of universal dignity fought for forms of nondiscrimination that were quite 'blind' to the ways in which citizens differ, the politics of difference often redefines nondiscrimination as requiring that we make those distinctions the basis of differential treatment."[12] It is the politics of difference that gives us campus speech codes (like Stanford's before it was struck down) that judicialize racist epithets directed against minorities but do not consider epithets directed against Caucasian males (honkey, redneck, whitey) a form of racism (on the reasoning that racism is defined as hostility plus power rather than as mere hostility). It is the politics of difference that leads to the establishment of schools for young black males in our inner cities (on the reasoning that the maintenance of cultural and gender homogeneity will bolster confidence and stimulate learning). It is the politics of difference that produces demands by blacks, Asians, and Native Americans that they be portrayed in films and plays by actors who are themselves blacks, Asians, and Native Americans. It is the politics of difference that asks for proportional representation of various cultural traditions in the classroom and in faculty hiring. The politics of difference is the equivalent of an endangered species act for human beings, where the species to be protected are not owls and snail darters, but Arabs, Jews, homosexuals, Chicanos, Italian Americans, and on and on and on.

The politics of difference is what I mean by strong multiculturalism. It is strong because it values difference in and for itself rather than as a manifestation of something more basically constitutive. Whereas the boutique multiculturalist will accord a superficial respect to cultures other than his own, a respect he will withdraw when he finds the practices of a culture irrational or inhumane, a strong multiculturalist will want to accord a *deep* respect to all cultures at their core, for he believes that each has the right to form its own identity and nourish its own sense of what is rational and humane. For the strong multiculturalist the first principle is not rationality or some other supracultural universal, but tolerance.

But the trouble with stipulating tolerance as your first principle is that you cannot possibly be faithful to it because sooner or later the culture whose core values you are tolerating will reveal itself to be intolerant at that same core; that is, the distinctiveness that marks it as unique and self-defining will resist the appeal of moderation or incorporation into a larger whole. Confronted with a demand that it surrender its viewpoint or enlarge it to include the practices of its natural enemies—other religions, other races, other genders, other classes—a beleaguered culture will fight back with everything from discriminatory legislation to violence.

At this point the strong multiculturalist faces a dilemma: either he stretches his toleration so that it extends to the intolerance residing at the heart of a culture he would honor, in which case tolerance is no longer his guiding principle, or he condemns the core intolerance of that culture (recoiling in horror when Khomeini calls for the death of Rushdie), in which case he is no longer according it respect at the point where its distinctiveness is most obviously at stake. Typically, the strong multiculturalist will grab the second handle of this dilemma (usually in the name of some supracultural universal now seen to have been hiding up his sleeve from the beginning) and thereby reveal himself not to be a strong multiculturalist at all. Indeed it turns out that strong multiculturalism is not a distinct position, but a somewhat deeper instance of the shallow category of boutique multiculturalism.

To be sure, there will still be a difference, but it will be a difference in degree. When the novelist Paul Theroux encounters a Pakistani with an advanced degree in science who nevertheless declares "Rushdie must die," he responds in true boutique multiculturalist fashion by setting him "straight" and informing him (as if he were a child) that his "are ignorant and barbarous sentiments."[13] (I bet that really convinced him!) Contrast this with M. M. Slaughter, a strong multiculturalist who, in the place of name calling, offers an explanation of why an educated Muslim whose sense of identity "is inseparable from the community of believers" might think himself mortally wounded by something written in a book. For Slaughter, the issue is properly understood not as a simple contrast between civilization and barbarity, but as a tension between "essentialist ideologies that inevitably and irreconcilably conflict: . . . The concept of the autonomous self requires the free speech principle; the socially situated self of Islamic society necessarily rejects free speech in favor of prohibitions against insult and defamation." Yet even while she elaborates the point, Slaughter declines to extend her act of sympathetic understanding into a statement of approval, and she is careful to declare at the beginning of her essay that "the placing of a bounty on Rushdie's head" is "a terroristic act."[14] Slaughter's judgment, in short, is finally not all that different from Theroux's, although it comes accompanied by an analysis the novelist has no interest in making. Both Theroux and Slaughter—one of whom sees the *fatwa* as an instance of fanaticism bordering on insanity, while the other pushes through to a comprehension of the system of thought in which the *fatwa* might constitute a moral obligation—stop far short of going all the way, that is, of saying, with Theroux's Pakistani, "Rushdie must die."

In the end neither the boutique multiculturalist nor the strong multiculturalist is able to come to terms with difference, although their inabilities are asymmetrical. The boutique multiculturalist does not take difference seriously because its marks (quaint clothing, atonal music, curious table manners) are for him matters of lifestyle, and as such they should not be allowed to overwhelm the substratum of rationality that makes us all brothers under the skin. The strong multiculturalist takes difference so seriously as a general principle that he cannot take any *particular* difference seriously, cannot allow its imperatives their full realization in a political program, for their full realization would inevitably involve the suppression of difference. The only way out for the would-be strong multiculturalist is to speak not for difference in general, but for *a* difference, that is, for the imperatives of a distinctive culture even when they impinge on the freedom of some other distinctive culture.

But if he did that the strong multiculturalist would no longer be faithful to his general principle. Instead he would have become a "really strong" multiculturalist, someone whose commitment to respecting a culture was so strong that he would stay its course no matter what; but that would mean that he wasn't a multiculturalist at all, since if he stuck with the distinctiveness of a culture even at the point where it expressed itself in a determination to stamp out the distinctiveness of some other culture, he would have become (what I think every one of us always is) a uniculturalist. It may at first seem counterintuitive, but given the alternative modes of multiculturalism—boutique multiculturalism, which honors diversity only in its most superficial aspects because its deeper loyalty is to a universal potential for rational choice; strong multiculturalism, which honors diversity in general, but cannot honor a particular instance of diversity insofar as it refuses (as it always will) to be generous in its turn; and really strong multiculturalism, which goes to the wall with a particular instance of diversity and is therefore not multiculturalism at all—no one could possibly *be* a multiculturalist in any interesting and coherent sense.[15]

Multiculturalism as Demographic Fact

The reason that this will sound counterintuitive is that multiculturalism and its discontents are all people are talking about these days. Is everyone arguing about something that doesn't exist? An answer to that question will require a fresh beginning to our analysis and the introduction of a new distinction between multiculturalism as a philosophical problem and multiculturalism as a demographic fact. Multiculturalism as a philosophical problem is what we've been wrestling with in the preceding passages, with results not unlike those achieved (if that is the word) by Milton's fallen angels who try to reason about fate, foreknowledge, and free will and find themselves "in wandering mazes lost."[16] We too become lost in mazes if we think of multiculturalism as an abstract concept that we are called upon to either affirm or reject. But if we think of multiculturalism as a demographic fact—the fact that in the United States today many cultural traditions flourish and make claims on those who identify with them—the impulse to either affirm or reject it begins to look rather silly; saying yes or no to multiculturalism seems to make about as much sense as saying yes or no to history, which will keep on rolling along irrespective of the judgment you pass on it.

Not that there is nothing to say once you have recognized that multiculturalism is a demographic fact; it is just that what you say will have more to do with the defusing of potential crises than the solving of conceptual puzzles. We may never be able to reconcile the claims of difference and community in a satisfactory formula, but we may be able to figure out a way for *these* differences to occupy the civic and political space of *this* community without coming to blows. "All societies," Taylor observes, "are becoming increasingly multicultural"; as a result "substantial numbers of people who are citizens" of a particular country are also members of a culture "that calls into question" that country's "philosophical boundaries."[17] What we "are going to need . . . in years to come," Taylor predicts, is some "inspired adhoccery."[18]

I want to take the phrase "inspired adhoccery" seriously. What it means is that the solutions to particular problems will be found by regarding each situation-of-crisis as an opportunity for improvisation and not as an occasion for the application of rules and principles (although the invoking and the recharacterizing of rules and principles will often be components of the improvisation). Any solution devised in this manner is likely to be temporary—that is what *ad hoc* means—and when a new set of problems has outstripped the solution's efficacy, it will be time to improvise again. It follows then that definitions of multiculturalism will be beside the point, for multiculturalism will not be one thing, but many things; and the many things it will be will weigh differently in different sectors of the society. In some sectors multiculturalism will take care of itself, in others its problematic will hardly register, and in others it will be a "problem" that must be confronted.

It will not, however, typically be a philosophical or theoretical problem. Multiculturalism in the workforce? Projections of demographic patterns indicate that in the forseeable future the workforce will be largely made up of women and minorities; accordingly, corporations have already begun to change their recruiting patterns. It is clear, Corning CEO James Houghton has said, that no company can afford a predominantly white, male workforce. Neither can a company afford a workplace driven by racial and ethnic tensions; and therefore the same bottom-line consideration that is altering hiring and promotion policies is also mandating sensitivity programs, a more consultative organizational structure, and decentered management. In short, for the business world it's multiculturalism or die.

The same formula applies, for different reasons, to colleges and universities. When the college population was relatively small and homogeneous it was a matter of neither concern nor surprise that the range of cultural materials studied was restricted to the books produced by earlier generations of that same homogeneous population. But when the GI bill brought many to college who would otherwise not have thought to go, and when some of those newly introduced to the academy found that they liked it and decided to stay on as faculty members, and when the rising tide of feminist consciousness led women to no longer be willing to sacrifice their careers to the ambitions of their husbands, and when a college degree became a prerequisite for employment opportunities previously open to high-school graduates, and when immigration after the Korean and Vietnam wars added large numbers of motivated students to a growing cultural mix, and when pride in ethnic traditions (stimulated in part by the extraordinary impact of the television series *Roots*) weakened the appeal of the "melting pot" ideal, the pressures to include new materials in the classroom and to ask that they be taught by members of the cultures or subcultures from which they were drawn seemed to come from all directions. Although multiculturalism is sometimes characterized as a conscious strategy devised by insurgent political groups desirous of capturing America's cultural space so that it can be turned over to alien ideas, in fact it is a development that was planned by no one. As an effect it was decidedly overdetermined; and now that it is here, those who wish to turn the clock back will find themselves increasingly frustrated.

To be sure there will always remain a few colleges (like Hillsdale in Michigan) that set themselves up as the brave defenders of the beachheads others have ignominiously abandoned; but by and large, at least in the world of education, multiculturalism is a baseline condition rather than an option one can be either for or against. Indeed, in many facets of American life there is no multiculturalism issue despite the fact that it is endlessly debated by pundits who pronounce on the meaning of democracy, the content of universal rights, the nature of community, the primacy of the individual, and so on. These mind-numbing abstractions may be the official currency of academic discussion, but they do not point us to what is really at stake in the large social and economic dislocations to which they are an inadequate (and even irrelevant) response. In and of themselves they do no genuine work, and insofar as they do any work it is in the service of the adhoccery to which they are rhetorically opposed.

I would not be misunderstood as recommending adhoccery; my point, rather, is that adhoccery will be what is going on despite the fact that the issues will be framed as if they were matters of principle and were available to a principled resolution. As we have seen, there are principles aplenty—autonomy, respect, toleration, equality—but when they are put into play by sophisticated intelligences the result is not resolution but a sharpened sense of the blind alleys into which they lead us. Here, for example, is Amy Gutmann asking a series of questions to which she apparently thinks there are answers:

> Should a liberal democratic society respect those cultures whose attitudes of ethnic or racial superiority . . . are antagonistic to other cultures? If so, how can respect for a culture of ethnic or racial superiority be reconciled with the commitment to treating all people as equals? If a liberal democracy need not or should not respect such "supremacist" cultures, even if those cultures are highly valued by many among the disadvantaged, what precisely are the moral limits on the legitimate demand for political recognition of particular cultures?[19]

You will recognize in these questions the interlocking quandaries that led me to conclude that multiculturalism is an incoherent concept, which cannot be meaningfully either affirmed or rejected. But this is not Gutmann's conclusion. In good liberal-rationalist fashion, she regards the difficulties she uncovers as spurs to a greater conceptual effort; and she sets herself the task of coming up with a formulation that will rescue us from a world of entrenched "political battlefields" and point the way to "mutually respectful communities of substantial, sometimes even fundamental, intellectual disagreement."[20] What is remarkable about this statement is its reproduction of the dilemmas it claims to resolve and the determined (if unintentional) evasion of the difficulties these dilemmas present. The vocabulary will not stand up to even the most obvious lines of interrogation. How respectful can one be of "fundamental" differences? If the difference is fundamental—that is, touches basic beliefs and commitments—how can you respect it without *dis*-respecting your own beliefs and commitments? And on the other side, do you really show respect for a view by tolerating it, as you might tolerate the buzzing of a fly? Or do you show respect when you take it seriously enough to oppose it, root and branch?

It is these and related questions that Gutmann begs and even hides from herself by inserting the word "intellectual" between "fundamental" and "disagreement." What "intellectual" does is limit disagreement to matters that can be debated within the decorums of Enlightenment rationalism. Fiercer disagreements, disagreements marked by the refusal of either party to listen to reason, are placed beyond the pale, where, presumably, they occupy the status of monstrosities, both above and below our notice (above our notice when they are disagreements over matters of religion, below our notice when they are disagreements between groups that want not to talk to one another but to exterminate one another). As a result, the category of the fundamental has been reconfigured—indeed, stood on its head—so as to exclude conflicts between deeply antithetical positions; that is, to exclude conflicts that are, in fact, fundamental.

The sleight of hand involved here is nicely illustrated by Gutmann's example of a disagreement that she says can be pursued in the context of mutual respect, the disagreement between the pro-choice and pro-life parties in the abortion debate. It is an example that tells against the principle it supposedly supports; for as everyone knows, strong pro-life advocates regard pro-choicers as either murderers or supporters of murderers, while in the eyes of pro-choicers, pro-life advocates are determined to deprive women of the right to control their own bodies. The disagreement between them is anything but intellectual because it is so obviously fundamental. In an intellectual disagreement the parties can talk to one another because they share a set of basic assumptions; but in a fundamental disagreement, basic assumptions are precisely what is in dispute. Either you can have "fundamental" or you can have "intellectual," but you can't have both; and if, like Gutmann, you privilege "intellectual," you have not honored the level of fundamental disagreement but evaded it.

Hate Speech

Gutmann does it again when she turns to the vexed issue of campus hate speech. Here the question is, How can we have a community of mutually respectful cultures when it is a practice in some cultures to vilify the members of others?[21] It looks like an intractable problem; but Gutmann solves it, she thinks, by distinguishing between differences one merely tolerates and differences one respects. You respect a difference when you see it as a candidate for serious moral debate; it has a point even though it is not your point.

But some differences are asserted so irrationally that debate is foreclosed; and those differences, while they must be tolerated in a free society, must also be denounced by all right-thinking persons. Hate speech—speech directed against women, Jews, blacks, and gays—falls into the second category; it is "indefensible on moral and empirical grounds."[22]

This seems neat and satisfying until one realizes that the "moral and empirical grounds" on the basis of which the arguments of certain speakers are judged "indefensible" have not been elaborated. Rather, they are simply presupposed, and presupposed too is their normative status. In effect Gutmann is saying, "Well, everybody knows that some assertions just aren't worth taking seriously." This is the result of withdrawing the offending opinions from the circle of rationality: one turns a blind eye toward the impact they might have on the world by assuming—without any empirical evidence whatsoever—that they will have none, that only crazy people will listen to crazy talk. With that assumption in place—and it is in place before she begins—the community of mutually respectful disputants has been safely constituted by the simple strategy of exiling anything that might disturb it. No wonder that within its confines disputants exercise mutual respect, since mutuality (of an extremely pallid kind) has been guaranteed in advance, as problems are "solved" by being defined out of existence.[23] Once hate speech—a designation its producers would resist—has been labeled "radically implausible"[24] (and "plausibility" added to the abstractions whose essentialist shape Gutmann blithely assumes), it is no more threatening than a belch or a fart: something disagreeable, to be sure, but something we can live with, especially since the category of the "we" has been restricted to those who already see things as Gutmann does.

In the end, the distinction between what is to be respected and what is tolerated turns out to be a device for elevating the decorum of academic dinner parties to the status of discourse universals while consigning alternate decorums to the dustbin of the hopelessly vulgar. In the expanded edition of the volume she edits, Gutmann is joined by Jürgen Habermas, who declines to admit religious fundamentalists into his constitutional republic because they "claim *exclusiveness* for a privileged way of life" and are therefore unfit for entry into "a civilized debate . . . in which one party can recognize the other parties as co-combatants in the search for authentic truths."[25] Of course, religious fundamentalists begin with the conclusion that the truths they hold are already authentic, but that is precisely why they will be denied entry to the "ideal speech" seminar when it is convened. (I hear you knocking but you can't come in.) Fundamentalists and hate speakers might seem an odd couple; what links them and makes them candidates for peremptory exclusion is a refusal to respect the boundaries between what one can and cannot say in the liberal public forum. (You can't say "kike" and you can't say "God.") Although the enemies named by Gutmann and Habermas are different, they are dispatched in the same way, not by being defeated in combat but by being declared ineligible before the fight begins.

The result is the kind of "civilized" conversation dear to the hearts of academic liberals who believe, on the model of the world-as-philosophy-seminar, that any differences between "rational" persons can be talked through. It is finally a faith in talk—in what liberals call "open and inclusive dialogue"—that underwrites a program like Gutmann's. But the dialogue is not really open at all, as we can see when she sets down the requirements for entry: "Mutual respect requires a widespread willingness and ability to articulate our disagreements, to defend them before people with whom we disagree, to discern the difference between respectable and disrespectable disagreement, and to be open to changing our own minds when faced with well-reasoned criticism."[26] Words like "widespread" and "open" suggest a forensic table to which all are invited, but between them is the clause that gives the lie to the apparent liberality—"to discern the difference between respectable and disrespectable disagreement"—which means of course to decide in advance which views will be heard and which will be dismissed. It is a strange openness indeed that is defined by what it peremptorily excludes.

It is not my intention, however, to fault Gutmann for not being open enough. Quite the reverse. It is her desire to be open that is the problem because it prevents her from taking the true measure of what she recognizes as an evil. If you wish to strike a blow against beliefs you think pernicious and "fraught with death" (the phrase is Oliver Wendell Holmes's in *Abrams v. United States*),[27] you will have to do something more than exclaim, "I exclude you from my community of mutual respect." That kind of exclusion will be no blow to an agenda whose proponents are not interested in being respected but in triumphing. Banishing hate speakers from your little conversation leaves them all the freer to pursue their deadly work in the dark corners from which you have averted your fastidious eyes. Gutmann's instinct to exclude is the right one; it is just that her gesture of exclusion is too tame—it amounts to little more than holding her nose in disgust—and falls far short of wounding the enemy at its heart. A deeper wound will only be inflicted by methods and weapons her liberalism disdains: by acts of ungenerosity, intolerance, perhaps even repression, by acts that respond to evil not by tolerating it—in the hope that its energies will simply dissipate in the face of scorn—but by trying to stamp it out. This is a lesson liberalism will never learn; it is the lesson liberalism is *pledged* never to learn because underlying liberal thought is the assumption that, given world enough and time (and so long as embarrassing "outlaws" have been discounted in advance), difference and conflict can always be resolved by rational deliberation, defined of course without consulting those who have been excluded from it.

I remarked earlier that producers of what is called hate speech would not accept that description of their words, words that they would hear as both rational and true. In arguments like Gutmann's and Habermas's, rationality is a single thing whose protocols can be recognized and accepted by persons of varying and opposing beliefs. In this model (as in Rockefeller's) differences are superficial, and those who base political and social judgments on them are labeled irrational. But if rationality is always differential, always an engine of exclusion and boundary making, the opposition is never between the rational and the irrational, but between opposing rationalities, each of which is equally, but differently, intolerant. This leads to the perhaps startling but inevitable conclusion that hate speech is rational and that its nature as a problem must be rethought. Indeed, it is only when hate speech is characterized as irrational that the label "problem" seems appropriate to it, and also comforting, because a problem is something that can be "treated," either by benign neglect (don't worry, it's a fringe phenomenon that will never catch on), by education and dialogue (the answer to hate speech is more speech: remember Theroux and the Pakistani), or, in a darker view of the matter, by quarantine and excommunication (you have a disease and while we won't exterminate you, neither will we have anything to do with you). This is the entire spectrum of remedies in the liberal pharmacy, which can only regard hate speech as something we can live with or something we can cure or something we can't cure but can avoid by refusing to join a militia.

It is in relation to this spectrum that speech codes seem obviously counterproductive, either because they are an overly strong response to a minor irritant, because they stand in the way of the dialogue that will lead to health, or because they will only reinforce the paranoia that produced the problem in the first place. Everything changes, however, once hate speech is seen not as evidence of some cognitive confusion or as a moral anomaly, but as the expression of a morality you despise, that is, as what *your* enemy (not the universal enemy) says.[28] If you think of hate speech as evidence of moral or cognitive confusion, you will try to clean the confusion up by the application of good reasons; but if you think that hate speakers rather than being confused are simply wrong—they reason well enough, but their reasons are anchored in beliefs (about racial characteristics, sexual norms, and so on) you abhor—you will not place your faith in argument but look for something stronger.[29] The difference between seeing hate speech as a problem and seeing it as what your enemy says is that in response to a "problem" you think in terms of therapy and ask of any proposal, "Will it eliminate the pathology?"; whereas in response to what your enemy says, you think in terms of strategy and ask of any proposal, "Will it retard the growth of the evil I loath and fear?"

The advantage of this shift is that it asks a real question to which there can be a variety of nuanced answers. When you ask, as liberals always do, "Will speech codes dispel racism and remove prejudice from the hearts of those who now display it?" the answer can only be "no," which I would say points not to the inadequacy of speech codes, but to the inadequacy of the question. The demand that speech codes dispel racism trades on the knowledge (which I share with antiregulation liberals) that racism cannot be altered by external forces; it is not that kind of thing. But the fact that it is not that kind of thing does not mean that there is nothing to be done; it merely means that whatever we do will stop short of rooting out racism at its source (as we might succeed in doing if it were a disease and not a way of thinking) and that the best we can hope for is a succession of tactical victories in which the enemy is weakened, discomforted, embarrassed, deprived of political power, and on occasion routed. (My phrase "the enemy" might suggest that I was referring to everyone's enemy and slipping back into a liberal univeralism, in which anomalous monsters are clearly labeled and known to everyone; but my use of the phrase marks the point at which I come out from behind the arras of analysis and declare my own position, which rests not on the judgment that racism doesn't make any sense [it makes perfect sense if that's the way you think] but that it makes a sense I despise. I am now reaching out to readers who are on my side and saying if you want to win—and who doesn't?—do this.)

This, however, is not a small basket of hopes, and what's more, the hopes are realizable. If you think of speech codes not as a magic bullet capable of definitive resolution, but as a possible component of a provisional strategy, you no longer have to debate them in all-or-nothing terms. You can ask if in this situation, at this time and in this place, it would be reasonable to deploy them in the service of your agenda (which, again, is not to eliminate racism, but to harrass and discomfort racists). The answer will often be "no," and, in fact, that is my usual answer. In most cases speech codes will cause more problems than they solve; and, all things considered, it will often be the better part of wisdom to tolerate the sound of hate and murmur something about sticks and stones and the value of free expression. At that moment you will be talking like a liberal, but there's nothing wrong with that as long as you don't take your liberalism too seriously and hew to it as a matter of principle.[30] Just as speech codes become thinkable once they are no longer asked to do impossible things, so do liberal platitudes become usable when all you want from them is a way of marking time between the battles you think you can win. Switching back and forth between talking like a liberal and engaging in distinctly illiberal actions is something we all do anyway; it is the essence of adhoccery. Perhaps if we did it with less anxiety, we might do it better. We might even be inspired.

Notes

1. See Tom Wolfe, *Radical Chic and Mau-Mauing the Flak Catchers* (New York: Farrar, Straus and Giroux, 1970).

2. See *Employment Div., Dept. of Human Resources of Oregon et al., v. Smith et al.*, 494 U.S. 872 (1990), in which Native Americans were denied exception for the religious use of peyote.

3. John Milton, "Areopagitica," in *The Prose of John Milton*, ed. J. Max Patrick (Garden City, N.Y.: Doubleday, 1967), 322.

4. Steven C. Rockefeller, "Comment," in *Multiculturalism and "The Politics of Recognition": An Essay by Charles Taylor, with Commentary by Amy Gutmann, Steven C. Rockefeller, Michael Walzer, and Susan Wolf*, ed. Amy Gutmann (Princeton: Princeton University Press, 1992), 88.

5. Rockefeller, 88.

6. Some political theorists go so far as to insist not merely that religious reasons be disallowed in the public forum, but that citizens should not advocate or vote for any position unless their motives are "adequately secular." Robert Audi, "The Separation of Church and State and the Obligations of Citizenship," *Philosophy and Public Affairs* 18 (Summer 1989): 280. See also the full discussion of the question in Kent Greenawalt, *Private Consciences and Public Reasons* (Oxford: Oxford University Press, 1995).

7. Rockefeller, 87.

8. Charles Taylor, "The Politics of Recognition," in *Multiculturalism and "The Politics of Recognition,"* 38, 41.

9. John Rawls puts it this way: "The state is not to do anything that makes it more likely that individuals accept any particular conception rather than another." John Rawls, *Political Liberalism* (New York: Columbia University Press, 1993), 193. Rawls acknowledges that "some conceptions will die out and others survive only barely," but this, he says, is inevitable because "no society can include within itself all forms of life" (a statement made with all the complacency of someone who knows that his form of life will certainly be included in his society). Rawls, 197.

10. Taylor, "Politics," 38.

11. Taylor, "Politics," 43.

12. Taylor, "Politics," 39.

13. Paul Theroux, letter to Salman Rushdie, in *The Rushdie Letters: Freedom to Speak, Freedom to Write,* ed. Steve MacDonogh (Lincoln, Nebr.: University of Nebraska Press, 1993), 33.

14. M. M. Slaughter, "The Salman Rushdie Affair: Apostasy, Honor, and Freedom of Speech," *Virginia Law Review* 79 (February 1993): 198, 156, 155, 154.

15. For evidence I might point to *Multiculturalism: A Critical Reader,* ed. David Theo Goldberg (Cambridge, Mass.: Blackwell, 1994), a volume in which the contributors wrestle unsuccessfully with the conundrums I have been explicating. Some of the essays urge something called critical multiculturalism, which Peter McLaren glosses as the "task of transforming the social, cultural, and institutional relations in which meanings are generated" (Peter McLaren, "White Terror and Oppositional Agency: Toward a Critical Multiculturalism," 53). This is to be done in the service and name of heterogeneity (see Goldberg, "Introduction: Multicultural Conditions," 25–31), but just where is heterogeneity to be located? Whose heterogeneity (read "difference") is it? If it is located somewhere, then it is not heterogeneity. If it is located everywhere, then it is universalist liberalism all over again, and the supposed enemy has been embraced.

The Chicago Cultural Studies Group tries to finesse this dilemma by urging full disclosure. One should "indicate the goal of one's knowledge production" and thereby "disrupt one's claim to academic authority and authorial self-mastery." Chicago Cultural Studies Group, "Critical Multiculturalism," *Critical Inquiry* 18 (Spring 1992): 549; report in *Multiculturalism,* 114–391. But by now this gesture *is* a claim to authority and signifies mastery and control even as they are disowned in search of a "better standpoint for substantive critique" (Chicago Cultural Studies Group, 549). The authors can only conclude that "a genuinely critical multiculturalism cannot be brought about by good will or by theory, but requires institutions, genres, and media that do not yet exist" (Chicago Cultural Studies Group, 553). They never will.

16. John Milton, *Paradise Lost,* in *John Milton,* ed. Stephen Orgel and Jonathan Goldberg (Oxford: Oxford University Press, 1990), bk. 2, 1.561, p. 389.

17. Taylor, "Politics," 63.

18. Charles Taylor, "The Rushdie Controversy," *Public Culture* 2 (Fall 1989): 121.

19. Amy Gutmann, "Introduction," *Multiculturalism and "The Politics of Recognition,"* 5.

20. Gutman, 20.

21. This is a standard question in discussions of multiculturalism from a liberal perspective. Will Kymlicka asks it in *Multicultural Citizenship* (Oxford: Clarendon Press, 1995), 94: "How should liberals respond to illiberal cultures?" His answer is that since liberals should eschew illiberal practices, they "should not prevent illiberal nations from maintaining their societal culture, but should promote the liberalization of these cultures" (Kymlicka, 94–95). In other words, respect the culture by trying to change it. In his inability to see the contradiction between maintaining a tradition and setting out to soften it and blur its edges, Kymlicka enacts the dilemmas traced out in the first part of this essay. He is trying to be a strong multiculturalist, but turns boutique when the going gets tough. He would reply that by "promote" he means persuade rather than impose and that rational persuasion is always an appropriate decorum. "Hence liberal reformers inside the culture should seek to promote their liberal principles through reason or example, and liberals outside should lend their support to any efforts the group makes to liberalize their culture" (Kymlicka, 168). The key word is "reason," which for Kymlicka, as for Rockefeller, is a standard that crosses cultural boundaries and will be recognized by all parties (except those that are nuts). But reasons of the kind liberals recognize— abstract, universal, transhistorical—are precisely what the members of many so-called illiberal cultures reject. The application of "reason" in an effort to persuade is not the opposite of imposition, but a version of it.

22. Gutman, 23.

23. Rawls makes essentially the same move in *Political Liberalism* when he acknowledges that "prejudice and bias, self and group interest, blindness and willfulness, play their all too familiar part in political life," but he insists that these "sources of unreasonable disagreement stand in marked contrast to those compatible with everyone's being fully reasonable" (Rawls, 58). One must ask, how does the contrast get marked? And the answer is, from the perspective of a predecision to confine reasonable disagreements to those engaged in by coolly deliberative persons. The irony is that "prejudice," "bias," "blindness," and "willfulness" are instances of name calling, just the kind of activity Rawls wants to avoid. These words stigmatize certain kinds of argument in advance and remove them peremptorily from the arena of appropriate conversation. Susan Mendus neatly illustrates the strategy in a single brief sentence: "Prejudice and bigotry, not moral disapproval, are the hallmarks of racism." Susan Mendus, *Toleration and the Limits of Liberalism* (Atlantic Highlands, N.J.: Humanities Press International, 1989), 15. The assertion is that racists (another instance of name calling) have no arguments, only primitive biases. The assertion works if you accept its first (unstated) premise: only arguments that are abstract and universal are really arguments; all others are mere prejudice. This leaves the field of "moral disputation" to those who have already rejected as accidental or regrettable any affiliations or commitments based on race or ethnicity. Moral dispute will then go on in the same sanitized forum marked out by Gutmann's distinction between views you tolerate (but don't deign to argue with) and views you respect. The alternative would

be to see that prejudice—that is, partiality—is a feature of any moral position, including the liberal one championed by Gutmann, Rawls, and Mendus, and that what you want to say about those who devalue persons on the basis of race is not that they are outside the arena of moral debate but that theirs is a morality you think wrong, evil, and dangerous (provided of course that is what you think).

24. Gutman, 22.

25. Jürgen Habermas, "Struggles for Recognition in the Democratic Constitutional State," in *Multiculturalism: Examining the Politics of Recognition,* ed. Amy Gutmann (Princeton, N.J.: Princeton University Press, 1994), 133; emphasis mine. As Larry Alexander points out, "An actual dialogue test is, in effect, a requirement of unanimity." That is, participants must already agree as to what is appropriate and what is not; but agreement is supposedly the goal of the dialogue, and if it is made a requirement for entry (in the manner of Gutmann and Habermas) the goal has been reached in advance by rigging the context. Success is then assured; but it is empty because impediments to it have been exiled in advance, even though they surely exist in the world. Larry Alexander, "Liberalism, Religion, and the Unity of Epistemology," *San Diego Law Review* 30 (Fall 1993): 782.

26. Gutman, 24.

27. *Abrams v. United States,* 250 U.S. 616 (1919).

28. Liberalism requires a universal enemy so that its procedures of inclusion and exclusion can be implemented in the name of everyone. If, however, there is no universal enemy but only enemies (mine or yours), procedures will always be invoked in the name of some and against some others. The unavailability of a universal enemy is something liberal thinkers are always running up against. They respond typically either by just stipulating someone's enemy as universal (as Gutmann does) or by giving up the attempt to identify an enemy and regarding everyone as potentially persuadable to the appropriate liberal views. (This might be thought of as sentimental or sappy multiculturalism.) See on these points Ellen Rooney's *Seductive Reasoning: Pluralism as the Problematic of Contemporary Literary Theory* (Ithaca, N.Y.: Cornell University Press, 1989), especially her discussion of the theoretical dream of general persuasion.

29. Since Gutmann identifies virtue with the capacity for rational deliberation, she will assume that hate speakers are deficient reasoners; but in fact they will often have cognitive abilities as strong as anyone's, and they will be able to answer reason with reason. As Richard Rorty has put it in the context of the familiar demand that we be able to prove to a Nazi that he is wrong: "Attempts at showing the philosophically sophisticated Nazi that he is caught in a logical . . . self-contradiction will simply impel him to construct . . . redescriptions of the presuppositions of the charge of contradiction." Richard Rorty, "Truth and Freedom: A Reply to Thomas McCarthy," *Critical Inquiry* 16 (Spring 1990): 637.

30. One way of characterizing this essay would be as an attack on principle, or, more precisely, "neutral principle" as it is commonly sought in legal and social contexts. A neutral principle is one you would be willing to apply no matter what the circumstances or

the interests involved. The trouble with a neutral principle is either that so much content has been eliminated on the way to formulating it that it is empty or that it retains the content of an agenda that will now be able to present itself politically and rhetorically as universal. Liberalism of the kind urged by Gutmann, Rawls, Kymlicka, Rockefeller, and Mendus displays both these liabilities, liabilities that are really advantages to a position that will not or cannot face its contradictions.

The alternative to the neutral principle is a real principle, a principle rooted in a moral conviction (of which racism, sexism, and homophobia would be examples) that you either accept or reject. From the vantage point of a real principle, you don't say to your enemy, "You're not respecting the decorum of enlightened argument"; you say, "You are wrong." Lauren Berlant and Michael Warner complain that there is "no rhetoric available in the national media to throw the right into a . . . defensive ambivalence." Lauren Berlant and Michael Warner, "Introduction to 'Critical Multiculturalism,'" in *Multiculturalism: A Critical Reader,* 111. If this is true it is because Berlant and Warner, like other liberals and leftists, agree to play in the arena of principle marked out by universals like "free inquiry, open intellectual discussion, and respect for individuals" (Berlant and Warner, 111). In this arena they will always lose because those words, as currently deployed, rule out in advance the agendas they might wish to promote. What they should do is not fight over title to that vocabulary, but just drop it and say that those who currently wrap themselves in it are wrong and dangerous.

On the question of principle and what I term its immorality, see Stanley Fish, "At the Federalist Society," *Howard Law Journal* 39 (Spring 1996), and the excellent discussion in Larry Alexander and Ken Kress, "Against Legal Principles," *Law and Interpretation: Essays in Legal Philosophy,* ed. Andrei Marmor (Oxford: Oxford University Press, 1995), 279–327. See especially page 325, where the authors observe that since arguments of principle require officials systematically to disregard both their own moral convictions and the moral convictions of those they disagree with, "they must do what is unjust from everyone's perspective." Their conclusion is mine: "Surely this is a perverse requirement."

Part II

Multiculturalism and the Principles
of Democracy

Chapter 5

Constitutionalism and Multiculturalism

Walter Berns

Hath not a Jew eyes? hath not a Jew hands, organs, dementions, sences, affections, passions, fed with the same foode, hurt with the same weapons, subject to the same diseases, healed by the same meanes, warmed and cooled by the same Winter and Sommer as a Christian is; if you pricke us doe we not bleede? If you tickle us, doe we not laugh? if you poison us doe we not die? and if you wrong us shall we not revenge? if we are like you in the rest, we will resemble you in that.
— William Shakespeare, *The Merchant of Venice*

Alexis de Tocqueville, writing in the 1830s, very much feared that liberty and equality would be at war with each other; today there is a tendency among some intellectuals to think that peace between them can be achieved by combining them under the label cultural pluralism. Cultural pluralism implies equality, we are told, and equality implies freedom for the various elements (mainly religious opinions and ethnic groups) being combined. It also implies—indeed, it is said to require—a "nonideological state," or an ideologically neutral state; and it is only a short step from this to say that such a state is obliged to promote "multiculturalism" by making it a part, in fact the organizing principle, of the public school curriculum, for example. In such a curriculum all "cultures" are to be treated as equal, or as equally deserving of respect. But there is a question as to whether multiculturalism is compatible with the principles of the Constitution and, therefore, capable of providing a foundation for what is said to be the cultural pluralism we have long enjoyed in this country. Whether it is compatible depends on what is meant by culture.

Although not the first to use the term in its modern sense, Thomas Carlyle (in the 1860s) spoke of culture as the body of arts and learning separate from the "work" of society. This definition has the merit of reflecting (and that very clearly) the problem that gave rise to the idea of culture and the attempt to define it in the early nineteenth century. Carlyle was preceded by Coleridge, Keats, Shelley, and Wordsworth, who, in his role as poet, saw himself as an "upholder of culture" in a world that disdained it; and by John Stuart Mill, for whom culture meant the qualities and faculties that characterize our humanity, or those aspects of humanity that he foresaw would be missing in a utilitarian society. Carlyle was followed by Matthew Arnold, for whom culture meant not only literary pursuits but—in a sentence that became familiar if not famous—the pursuit of "the best which has been thought and said in the world."[1]

What these critics had in common was a concern for the sublime (or the aesthetic) and a complaint against the modern democratic and commercial society in which it had no firm place. The founders of this modern society—say, John Locke and Adam Smith—promised to provide for the needs of the body (and in this they surely succeeded); culture was intended to provide for the needs of the soul—Coleridge, for example, made this the business of his "clerisy." As Allan Bloom put it, "only when the true ends of society have nothing to do with the sublime does 'culture' become necessary as a veneer to cover the void."[2]

The proponents of multiculturalism have something different in mind when they speak of culture. Introducing Charles Taylor's essay on the subject, political scientist Amy Gutmann says that public institutions, "including government agencies, schools, and liberal arts colleges and universities, have come under severe criticism these days for failing to recognize or respect the particular cultural identities of citizens." She mentions specifically African Americans, Asian Americans, Native Americans, and women.[3] Culture here seems to mean not "the best which has been thought or said in the world," which, as such, might serve (as Shakespeare's plays and poems have served) to civilize and, in some way, even to unify peoples; rather, culture here seems to mean the different customs, ways, mores, or morals/manners—*moeurs,* as Tocqueville called them—of peoples, groups, and (if we are to believe Amy Gutmann) even the sexes. Thus, in the body of his essay, Taylor refers specifically to the French Canadians, whose *moeurs* are not those of the English Canadians and for which the former demand recognition. Demand it and apparently deserve it, not because their culture is superior in Matthew Arnold's sense to that of the English Canadians but simply because it is theirs.

No country has done more to recognize the diversity of morals/manners than Canada; it even has a (federal) Department of Multiculturalism and

Citizenship and provides generous subsidies for "'ethnic' music, painting, dance, drama, museums, etc." Initiated in the 1970s by Prime Minister Pierre Elliott Trudeau, the department had the purpose "to add to the cultural richness of Canadian life by assisting the smaller ethnic groups [that is, groups other than the English and French Canadians] to maintain certain of their traditional cultural forms and a distinct sense of identity, if such was their desire."[4] These diverse groups were to form the Canadian "mosaic." But it is one thing to provide subsidies for folk-dancing groups and ethnic cooking and quite another to allow these groups, without exception, to retain their "cultural identities." The feasibility of the latter program would surely depend on what it is in their culture that they want to retain. After all, to the extent that they allow some groups to retain their cultural identities, they will inherit some nasty ethnic rivalries.

Nevertheless, Canadians speak of multiculturalism as a form of Canadian nationalism "that will convert ethnic rivalries from one of the problems or weaknesses of a society into one of its strengths."[5] But success here will depend, to some extent at least, on a strengthening of national identity and a corresponding weakening of ethnic identity, a subject I'll have more to say about in due course. But how does a government intend to go about converting its Serbs and Croats, for example, into Canadians? Not, surely, by policies designed to refurbish and strengthen their memories or otherwise preserve their traditions. Better that they forget their history, lest they be led to repeat it in Canada.[6] And they can be led to forget it only by being taught that Canada is something more than the sum of its diverse parts and something better than any of its parts. This, of course, is what the United States set out to do in 1787, except that its "parts" were understood to be individuals with rights, not groups making up a "mosaic."

The framers of our Constitution never spoke of multiculturalism, cultural pluralism, or, for that matter, even of pluralism. Such terms were not part of their political vocabulary.[7] Nor were they sanguine about the possibility of combining cultures. Instead, as the following passage from *Federalist* 2 indicates, they were sanguine about our prospects only because we were (or were said to be) united in all essential respects:

> Providence has been pleased to give this one connected country to one united people—a people descended from the same ancestors, speaking the same language, professing the same religion, attached to the same principles

of government, very similar in their manners and customs, and who, by their joint counsels, arms, and efforts, fighting side by side throughout a long and bloody war, have nobly established their general liberty and independence.

The same concern for unity, or a similarity of manners, customs, and, above all, opinion concerning the principles of government is reflected in the early statements and congressional debates having to do with immigration and naturalization. These debates took place in 1790 and 1794, and everyone who addressed the issue favored population growth and, to that end, a liberal immigration policy; but, at the same time, everyone recognized the importance of excluding the immigrant who, in Madison's words, could not readily "incorporate himself into our society," or, as Theodore Sedgwick put it, would not "mingle [here] in social affection with each other, or with us," or, finally, "would not be attached to the principles of the government of the United States."[8] As Jefferson said, "Every species of government has its specific principles [and] ours perhaps are more peculiar than those of any other in the universe." He, of course, knew nothing of those who would be of concern to later generations of politicians, the fascists and communists; he was concerned with monarchists and even the immigrants who had been ruled by monarchs. He was afraid that they would bring with them "the principles of the governments they leave, imbibed in their early youth; or, if able to throw them off, it [would] be in exchange for an unbounded licentiousness, passing, as is usual, from one extreme to another." Those principles, he continued, they might transmit to their children. "In proportion to their numbers, they will share with us the legislation [and] will infuse into it their spirit, warp and bias its directions, and render it a heterogeneous, incoherent, distracted mass."[9]

Thus, rather than seeing advantages of diversity, the framers wanted immigrants to be assimilated, incorporated into "our society," with a view to maintaining a population whose members would be attached to the same "principles of government." (As Jefferson put it, a "homogeneous" society would be "more peaceful [and] more durable."[10]) They had no idea of accommodating a variety of disparate "cultures." From all that appears, they would have thought that impossible.

What we see as cultural differences, they saw as religious differences. Indeed, they probably would have agreed with one of his critics that Horace Kallen (who was the first to use the term "cultural pluralism") did not take culture seriously precisely because he did not appreciate its religious foundations:

> If we think of culture not superficially in terms of graphic arts, music or literature, but as the firm cradle of custom in which the baby is laid and which inevitably forms his emotional life, his food habits, his language, his thoughts, his skills, his sexual life, his work, and his moral values, the envisioned fluid "cultural mobility" becomes rather incredible. One cannot be brought up in all languages, all family patterns, all religions.[11]

Since our constitutional principles are most evident in those provisions dealing with religion, for the purposes of this essay cultural pluralism, at least initially, will mean religious pluralism. Besides language (and political memories), what distinguishes the French from the English Canadians save religion? Is it possible that the culture in multiculturalism—especially when it is taken seriously—means religion, or at least has its ultimate source in religion? After all, as Shakespeare's Shylock indicates (see the epigraph above), we are *one* with respect to the body and its passions but *many* only with respect to our memories and our manners/morals, whose source is in our political and religious (or irreligious) beliefs. Understanding the conditions of our religious pluralism will shed some light on the possibility—or better, the impossibility—of multiculturalism.

In 1776, we declared ourselves a "new order of the ages," the first nation in all of history to build itself on the self-evident truth that all men are created equal insofar as they are equally endowed by Nature's God with the unalienable rights to life, liberty, and the pursuit of happiness. The purpose of government, we then said, was "to secure these rights." This was to be done—because, given our principles, it had to be done—only with the consent of the governed.

But it was understood by the framers of the Constitution that the governed would not always agree on the definition of rights, or on how rights were to be secured, or on whose rights deserved to be secured or, in the event of a conflict, preferred; in fact, the framers expected the people to have sharply different views on these matters. Thus, the "one people" that declared its independence in 1776 and the "we the people" that constituted a government in 1787–88 in order to secure those rights would, as a matter of course, thereafter be divided into factions, and unless steps were taken to avoid it, warring factions. According to James Madison (writing in number 10, the most frequently quoted and celebrated of the *Federalist Papers*), "the latent causes of faction are . . . sown in the nature of man," and by definition these factions have interests "adverse to the rights of other citizens, or to the permanent and aggregate interests of the community."

Given these conditions, the securing of equal rights would not be an easy matter; it would be especially difficult because Nature, so equitable in its endowment of rights, was by no means equitable in its endowment or distribution of talents or faculties, particularly, as Madison put it, the "faculties of acquiring property." Still, he did not hesitate to say that protecting these "different and unequal faculties"—naturally different and naturally unequal—was "the first object of government." The consequence of securing the equal rights of unequally endowed human beings would be a society divided between "those who hold and those who are without property." It followed for him that the regulation of these property factions—creditors, debtors, and landed, manufacturing, mercantile, moneyed, and "many lesser interests"—would be the "principal task of modern legislation." Unlike the others—for example, religious factions—these property factions could be regulated (and accommodated) because, although divided one from another, they shared a common interest in economic growth, and to promote this growth would be the task of modern legislation. America's business would be (as Calvin Coolidge many years later said it was) business.

Madison proved to be a poor prophet with respect to the "business" that occupied the country during the first half and more of the nineteenth century. From 1819—when Congress began to debate the Missouri question, through the years of the Mexican War (and the Wilmot Proviso it provoked), the compromise of 1850, the Kansas-Nebraska Act of 1854 (and the "Bloody Kansas" *it* provoked), and the *Dred Scott* decision of 1857, to the Civil War and Reconstruction—Congress, and indeed the entire country, was principally concerned with an issue that Madison neglected to mention in *Federalist* 10, namely, the slavery issue and the factions it aroused.

To judge from what he wrote in *Federalist* 56, he expected (or hoped) that time would resolve this "multicultural" issue. "At present," he wrote, some of the states, and especially the southern states, were little more than societies of husbandmen. Few of them, he went on, "have made much progress in those branches of industry which give a variety and complexity to the affairs of a nation." But he expected this would change in time; with time would come a diversification of the state economies, which, if true, would relieve the southern states of their dependence on slave labor, with the result that slavery would cease to be, or would not become, an issue in national politics. In fact, of course, it became *the* issue in national politics, and the Madisonian system proved incapable of resolving it. Had he foreseen this, Madison might have said in 1788 what Abraham Lincoln said in

1858 (and, of course, Lincoln was quoting the Bible), namely, that "a house divided against itself cannot stand," which, until proven otherwise, can stand as our definitive statement on the possibility of multiculturalism.

The question then arises as to why Madison was so confident that the other sorts of factions that he identified, particularly religious factions, would not require legislative "regulation." Or, to speak more plainly, why did he think this modern "civilized" nation would be able to avoid the religious problem? That had not been true in the past, especially in the Britain whose history he knew so well, and it is not true everywhere now. In the Britain he knew religion had given rise not only to factions but to civil war and revolution. Why was he confident that this would not be the case in America?

The answer is that the Constitution took religion out of politics, thereby making legislative regulation unnecessary. By separating church and state, specifically, by guaranteeing the free exercise of every religion while favoring none, the Constitution guarantees a proliferation of religious sects, a plurality or "multiplicity of sects," as Madison puts it in *Federalist* 51, none of them capable of constituting a legislative majority. The various sects will have to live with each other; more to the point, as merely one among many, each sect will be required to forgo any attempt to impose its views on the others. The government itself will be neutral in religious matters, and this makes it possible to say that almost anybody, and of any religious persuasion—or, at least, nominally of any religious persuasion—can become an American. All we require is a pledge of allegiance "to the flag of the United States and to the republic for which it stands," implying (especially nowadays) that anybody can make the promise and that no one will have difficulty keeping it.

In saying this, however, we tend to forget the restrictions we used to impose—on Chinese immigration, for example—or the limits we in fact used to enforce. Until recently, that pledge of allegiance was understood to imply a renunciation even of certain political opinions—for example, the advocacy of the overthrow of government by force or violence. It was only in 1974 that the Supreme Court held that members of the Communist party could not be kept off the ballot for refusing to take an oath renouncing such advocacy.[12] Nor was our record much different with respect to religious opinion, and this despite the First Amendment. For example, our toleration did not extend so far as to embrace the Mormons and their practice of plural marriages. "To call [the advocacy of bigamy and polygamy] a tenet of religion is to offend the common sense of mankind," the Supreme Court said in 1890.[13] When, a few years earlier, Abraham Lincoln was asked what he would do about the Mormons, he replied that he proposed "to let them alone"; but his Democratic adversary, Senator Stephen A. Douglas, campaigned to keep them out—by keeping Utah out—of our union.

But all this is history, a history that many of us would prefer to forget; today no one has reason to be concerned about the communists, and no one publicly advocates polygamy (to say nothing of slavery). It is, of course, true that the Constitution is not *altogether* neutral respecting religion. It counts the years in a Christian manner (see Article VII), and it recognizes, at least for one purpose, Sunday as the Sabbath (see Article I, section 7); but the non-Christians have learned to live with this. Speaking for a Supreme Court majority, Justice George Sutherland once said, "We are a Christian people";[14] but that was in 1931, and no one—at least, no one in an official capacity—would say that today. Instead, we are inclined to speak of "our Judeo-Christian tradition," and if there were to be, as there has been in Britain, a great increase in the number of Muslims among us, I have no doubt that our multiculturalists would happily adapt this to read "our Judeo-Islamic-Christian tradition."

The situation in Britain is worth describing because, while interesting in itself, it also serves to remind us of the persistence of the religious issue and the difficulties facing a multicultural society. Britain has a religious problem today, and not simply because, unlike us, they do not separate church and state. By law, the Church of England remains the established church: its archbishop of Canterbury retains his precedence, even over the prime minister, and only its doctrines are protected by the law of blasphemy. Despite this, the British might claim to be a pluralist society, in practice if not in principle. They began in 1689 by tolerating most Protestants, including the Quakers, and over the course of the years—which, in the event, proved to be centuries—have extended this privilege to Roman Catholics, Jews, and every variety of Protestant. In theory, there remains, as there was in 1689, a majority church, but only 2.3 percent of the population now attend its services on any given Sunday. The Queen, an Anglican in England and a Presbyterian in Scotland, might attend "chapel" services in Wales, a Roman Catholic mass in Liverpool—or, I suspect, even recite the Kaddish at a Jewish burial service—without arousing public comment.

Under the 1944 Education Act, religious minorities were permitted to invoke the "conscience clause" in order to exclude their children from participating in certain acts of worship or religious instruction programs in the state schools; more than that, Roman Catholics and Jews were entitled to public funding for their own denominational schools. For all these reasons, Britain might have thought that it had become, in the words of the Anglican Book of Common Prayer, a haven for "all sorts and conditions of men." Instead, as I said, it finds itself with a religious or cultural problem. And, faced with a similar situation, so might we.

The problem arose from the fact that there are now one and a half million Muslims in England alone, a total exceeding the number of Roman Catholics and Jews; and, to say the least, Muslims especially do not believe, because they cannot believe, in the separation of church and state. Bernard Lewis explained why this is so. "Muhammed," he said, "was not only a prophet and a teacher, like the founders of other religions; he was also the head of a polity and of a community, a ruler and a soldier."[15] It was this (and "a thousand other reasons") that led Tocqueville to say that Islam and democracy could not readily coexist.[16] The Salman Rushdie affair made the British very much aware of this; they learned, as we might come to learn, that Muslims do not believe in freedom of speech, for example.[17]

Freedom of speech is not the only problem for Muslims (to the extent they remain committed Muslims). The other is secularism; and Britain, having embarked on the path of toleration in 1689, has reached the point where it has become a secular society. In response to complaints made by various minority groups—not, we are told, only the Muslims—the British government decided to "celebrate diversity" by instituting a program of multicultural religious instruction in the state schools. Under the new program, all religions were, nominally at least, to be "taught"; in fact, however, each was to be taught as a "possible system of meaning and value," or, in the words of the Swann Report recommending the program, taught insofar as its doctrines were not in conflict with "rationally-shared values." Reasonably enough, the Muslims objected to the program (as well as to other elements of the curriculum: anthropomorphic art, sensual music, "progressive" sex education, and the Darwinian theory of evolution). They continue to cling to their "cultural identity" by taking their religion seriously, unlike the British majority. Because they do, they prefer the old system, under which the state schools taught Christian doctrine (or a watered-down version of Christian doctrine) but allowed Muslims to remove their children from the program by invoking the "conscience clause" on their behalf. As they see it, better a "benign uniformity," as one commentator put it, than a "compulsory 'diversity.'" At least under the old system they were not compelled to subscribe to opinions contrary to their articles of religion.

As one writer suggested, the problem might be resolved by providing public funding of denominational schools without exception:

> British Muslims, and for that matter British Hindus, Sikhs, and even its conservative Protestants continue to be denied the denominational status that their numbers and popularity demand. They resent this. They point out, correctly enough, that they pay taxes like everyone else, and should accordingly be granted the same privilege as any other religious minority. They conclude, reasonably enough, that they are denied those privileges because the central authorities fear that, if granted them, they might actually use them for something other than the pursuit of "rationally-shared values."[18]

Rather than accommodating its Muslims, Hindus, and Sikhs by providing public funding of denominational schools without exception, the British majority insists on imposing its policy of not taking religion seriously on minorities that do take it seriously. As a result, Britain has a serious cultural problem.

Unlike the British, we confine religion to the private sphere, and there is much to be said for that policy. Moreover, we protect it there. Thus, in 1925 the Supreme Court held that no state may compel students to attend public, rather than private, or parochial, schools.[19] As Jefferson once said, "Our civil rights have no dependence on our religious opinions, any more than our opinions in physics or geometry."[20]

Still, contrary to Madison's expectations, the religious problem abides. Try as we might, there are certain to be times in the life of a nation, even a nation devoted to business and its regulation, when men's religious opinions will carry more political weight than their opinions in physics or geometry—or, as the abortion issue should remind us, than their opinions in genetics, ontology, sociology, or whatever. Of course, Madison would have said that abortion did not belong on the national political agenda, and that it was only because of the Supreme Court's improper intervention that it was put there. On the whole, however, our policy of separating church and state has served us well, which is why it is important to understand what it requires of us.

Separation of society and state; separation of the private and the public; separation of church and state—these distinctions are major stones in the foundation on which American constitutionalism is built, and all of them rest on the constitutional distinction between soul and body. If not the first to make these distinctions, John Locke was the first to persuade Americans of their necessity in politics; and, in his (Virginia) Bill for Religious Freedom, Jefferson was the first to propose that the last of them be embodied in legislation. He had made a careful study of Locke's *Letter on Toleration,* and in so many words repeated Locke's statements concerning the care of body and soul respectively. According to Locke, the commonwealth is "a society of men constituted only for the procuring, preserving, and advancing . . . life, liberty, health, and indolency of body; and the possession of outward things, such as money, lands, houses, furniture, and the like"; whereas the care "of each man's soul belongs to himself."[21] Or, in Jefferson's words, "the operations of the mind, [as opposed to] the acts of the body, are [not] subject to the coercion of the laws."[22] Accordingly, the framers of the Constitution separated church and state, thereby making religion a wholly private matter.

Keeping it private is another matter. As I have pointed out in another place,[23] because the biblical religions especially—Judaism, Christianity, and Islam alike—teach that souls belong to God and that, whether through the agency of Moses, Jesus, or the Archangel Gabriel (or Jibral), God has revealed His will or His law respecting the care of souls, there is always the possibility (if not a clear and present danger) that someone, someone not attached to our constitutional principles, will claim to know God's will and try to enforce it on his neighbors. Indeed, as we are reminded almost daily by the events in Algeria, Iran, Iraq, Nagorno-Karabakh, Tajikistan, India, Israel, and what used to be known as Yugoslavia, to say nothing of Northern Ireland, there are people who, when given the chance, will do just that. Such people prefer to fight religious wars rather than accept cultural pluralism; as such, they cannot be "attached to the principles of the government of the United States," and, to recall Madison's words, they cannot readily be incorporated "into our society."

We cannot tolerate *them* (at least, not in any numbers) because *they* are not tolerant; more precisely, we must insist that they disclaim the authority on the basis of which one might *be* intolerant.[24] This means that, in their capacity as citizens, they must recognize the right of liberty of conscience. For example, just as the Constitution expects us to forget that we were English (Irish, German, or whatever), it expects Episcopalians, for example, to forget the eighteenth of their thirty-nine Articles of Religion, which reads: "They also are to be [held] accursed that presume to say, that every man shall be saved by the Law or Sect which he professeth, [so long as] he be diligent to frame his life according to that Law, and the light of Nature." In their capacity as citizens, however, Episcopalians are required to be guided by that light of nature. They are expected to follow the example of a Reverend Mr. Shute in the Massachusetts Ratifying Convention of 30 January 1788: "Far from limiting my charity and confidence to men of my own denomination in religion, I suppose, sir, that there are worthy characters among men of every denomination—among the Quakers, the Baptists, the Church of England; and even among those who have no other guide, in the way to virtue and heaven, than the dictates of natural religion."[25]

In the light of nature (and according to the Constitution), nobody is "accursed." On the contrary, by nature everybody is endowed with the unalienable right to pursue happiness as he (and not his neighbor or the government) defines it.[26] As Locke put it, liberty of conscience is "every man's natural right," a principle echoed by Jefferson in the (Virginia) Bill for Religious Freedom, where we read that "the rights [of conscience] hereby asserted are of the natural rights of mankind." That principle is embodied in the Constitution—in fact, our constitutionalism rests on it—and we are all expected to acknowledge it when we act politically. The Constitution speaks not of Christian, Jew, or Muslim, but consistently only of undifferentiated "persons" (and, in one place, of "Indians, not taxed"). By so speaking, it seeks to discourage religious (and antireligious) parties in favor of secular political parties. It expects us—whatever our religion, and whatever our cultural "identity"—to be able to come together in those parties. But it is not easy to form a governing political majority with those whom, by their failure to subscribe to our particular articles of religion, we hold to be "accursed."

Thus, contrary to the multiculturalists, the Constitution is not ideologically neutral. If it were, all political issues would be properly resolved, one way or the other, by popular vote of the people or their elected representatives. Among these issues is, or was, the one that engaged Senator Stephen A. Douglas and Abraham Lincoln in the 1850s: the issue of slavery in the territories. Douglas called his slavery policy "popular sovereignty" and made it, thus dignified, the principle of his Kansas-Nebraska Act. But Lincoln insisted that the act was un-American precisely because it took no stand— which is to say, because it was neutral—on the question of whether slavery was good or bad. The act's moral neutrality contradicted the self-evident truth that all men are created equal.

So, too, with respect to religious issues. Of course, the Constitution is neutral with respect to religion, neutral insofar as it forbids any government policy favoring one religion over another; but this means that religious issues, like that of slavery in the territories, are not properly resolved by popular vote of the people or their elected representatives. Were it otherwise, no constitutional principle would stand in the way of a self-styled "moral majority" determined to impose its ways on those it regards as immoral minorities. Our religious pluralism depends not on ideological neutrality but on the continued vitality of the principles we held to be self-evident in 1776 and embodied in the Constitution in 1787–1788, and prominent among these truths is that the care of each man's soul belongs to himself alone. Not every "culture" recognizes these truths; those that do not cannot be regarded as equal to ours. Which is to say, in the light of the Constitution, all men are created equal, but not all "cultures."

As Amy Gutmann points out (as if it needed pointing out), we encounter problems with multiculturalism "once we look into the *content* of the various valued cultures." She wonders whether we can afford to respect, or "recognize," illiberal cultures or, as she puts it, "those cultures whose attitudes of ethnic or racial superiority . . . are antagonistic to other cultures."[27] She would surely agree that we cannot allow the successors to the Ayatollah Khomeini to send their agents among us to assassinate our "blasphemous" Salman Rushdies. Unlike Iranian law, under our Constitution there is no such thing as blasphemous speech. If, nevertheless, such assassins do appear among us and commence their vocation, and we apprehend them, as we have apparently apprehended the bombers of the World Trade Center, are they entitled to be tried by the sort of jury that sat in the case of El Sayyid A. Nosair, the accused assassin of Rabbi Meir Kahane? Which is to say, a jury prepared to help a group preserve its cultural identity? There are those who say so. Nosair was represented by the redoubtable William M. Kunstler, who demanded a jury of "third world people"; and, having gotten it, he got an acquittal on the murder charge.

The Sixth Amendment to the Constitution provides that in "all criminal prosecutions, the accused shall enjoy the right to a speedy and public trial, by an impartial jury of the State and district wherein the crime shall have been committed." Now black Americans—whether on trial themselves or as the victims of alleged crimes committed by others—have begun to insist that juries cannot be impartial unless they are representative. In response, several state legislatures, including Florida's, have proposed laws guaranteeing racially balanced juries. This may be in violation of the Sixth Amendment, which, the Supreme Court said recently, requires "impartial" juries, but does not require, and may even forbid, "representative" juries.[28]

This jury issue is not new; in fact, it is at least nine hundred years old. In 1255, King Henry III ordered the arrest of some ninety-two Jews on charges of ritual murder. On being indicted and sent to London for trial, eighteen of them, "regarding conviction as a foregone conclusion unless they were allowed a mixed jury, refused to put themselves upon the country." This was construed as a confession of guilt, and the eighteen were summarily executed.

The privilege of being tried by a mixed jury—or, in the official language of the time, by a panel *de medietate,* which, in this case, meant half Jewish, half Christian—was sometimes denied, and, upon Edward I's accession to the throne in 1272, was revoked for a time; but, when honored, it served as some protection for this particular "cultural" community. That protection came to an end on—and surely not by chance—All Saints Day, November 1, 1290, when Edward "issued a decree consigning the Jewry of England to perpetual banishment."[29] And with the banishment ended this early experiment in multiculturalism.

Then there is the more recent British practice, the one adopted to deal with the multicultural situation in Northern Ireland. (To paraphrase W. S. Gilbert, Northern Ireland is the very model of a modern multiculturalism.) The current problem is a variation of the one the British faced earlier when they governed the whole of Ireland. Not surprisingly, at that time, trial by jury did not function in Ireland as it did in England. Too often, Irish juries simply refused to convict the guilty; even so, we are told, "that most hallowed right of English law, trial by common jury, was preserved even in Ireland" for most of the nineteenth century. Not so in Northern Ireland today. Faced with unacceptable differences in the way Protestant and Catholic defendants were treated, the British Parliament, in 1973, abolished trial by jury for defendants accused of violent crimes.[30] So much, then, for that "most hallowed right of English law, trial by common jury."

Banishment is one way to deal with a multicultural problem and abolishing trial by jury is another, but neither is permitted to any government of the United States; our Constitution based on the rights of man forbids it. Do we, then, adopt different rules of justice for our different groups? Amy Gutmann says that "recognizing and treating members of some groups as equals now seems to require public institutions to acknowledge rather than ignore cultural peculiarities, at least for those people whose self-understanding depends on the vitality of their culture."[31] But instead of recognizing their "cultural peculiarities," especially their peculiar or different rules of justice, do we not owe it to ourselves to persuade them of the superiority of ours: trial by impartial jury and the other elements making up due process of law; government by the consent of the governed; freedom of speech, press, and conscience; in a word, government designed to secure the unalienable rights not of groups or "cultures" but of man? Indeed, does not our system of constitutional government itself presuppose *one* people—in the words of *Federalist* 2, a people "attached to the same principles of government"? To pose the jury question bluntly, does not the criminal justice system presuppose that African American, Hispanic American, Asian American, and Jewish American defendants can receive a fair trial by "impartial" juries and judges? And that it will be a sorry day for this country if they cannot?

The jury problem pales almost to insignificance when weighed with the problem facing many liberal democracies today, especially those of Western Europe, that of accommodating the refugees from the east and south. The problem is new, but its seeds were sown in religious conflicts five hundred and more years ago. Speaking in Washington a few years ago, political scientist Samuel P. Huntington said that "the most significant dividing line in Europe may well be the eastern boundary of Western Christianity in the year 1500."

> The peoples to the north and west of this line are Protestant or Catholic; they share the common experience of European history; they are generally better off than the peoples to the east. The peoples to the east and south are Orthodox or Muslim; they historically belonged to the Ottoman or tsarist empires; they were only lightly touched by events shaping the rest of Europe. Conflict along the fault line between Western and Islamic civilizations has been a seesaw for 1,300 years, and it is unlikely to cease.[32]

The movement of peoples today—sometimes almost entire populations—illustrates not only the enduring strength of these religious and ethnic hatreds but the extent of the problem facing liberal regimes today. It is sufficient to mention Germany, where the influx of refugees from Eastern Europe has given rise to a resurgence of nationalist sentiments of the nastiest kind; or Italy, which turned back entire shiploads of people fleeing Albania; or France and its treatment of North Africans; or, for that matter, President Clinton's tergiversation respecting Haitian refugees.

In this situation, it is easy to sympathize with Prime Minister Trudeau's multicultural policy; generous, tolerant, and seemingly liberal, it was supposed to provide an example to a world sorely in need of what it had to offer. It was to make Canada "a special place, and a stronger place," stronger than the United States, a multicultural "mosaic" rather than a "melting pot," "a brilliant prototype for the moulding of tomorrow's civilization."[33]

At his urging, Canada officially became a bilingual country. In order to become the master of its own fate, it arranged to have the British North American Act of 1867 converted into the Canadian constitution, or, in the word at the time, it "patriated" its constitution from Britain. To guarantee the rights of all its people, in whatever province they might reside, in 1982 it attached to that "patriated" constitution a Charter of Rights and Freedoms. Since then the country has been engaged in what might be described as a perpetual and itinerant constitutional debate, moving from Ottawa, to Meech Lake, to Charlottetown, with frequent stops in all the provincial capitals, most frequently and persistently Quebec. At issue was (and is) Canadian unity.

The first Ottawa round—commentators have adopted the parlance of prize fighting to describe this debate—ended when Trudeau's nation-building effort, with its emphasis on the equal rights of Canadian citizens at the expense of the powers of the provinces, went down to defeat at the hands of the Quebecois. In round two, the western provinces, reacting to Trudeau's language and energy policies, began to demand a restructuring of the Senate in order to check the power of populous Ontario and Quebec. This was followed by the election of a separatist government, under Rene Levesque, in Quebec. Round three began in 1980 with Trudeau's effort to bypass the provincial governments by appealing to the people directly; but, failing in this, he was forced to make the concessions demanded by the provincial governments in order to get the constitution "patriated"; even so, Quebec refused to go along. Round four engaged the aboriginal peoples who, dissatisfied with a constitutional provision guaranteeing their "existing rights," renewed their demand for self-government; at the same time, Ottawa (now represented by Brian Mulroney) and Quebec (now represented by Robert Bourassa) began a series of negotiations with the various provincial premiers, leading to the Meech Lake Accord of April 30, 1987. Under this agreement, all the provinces would gain the powers demanded by Quebec, although Quebec was to be recognized as a "distinct society." Under its terms, the accord had to be ratified by the federal parliament and all ten provincial legislatures. This requirement proved to be its undoing because by involving the legislatures it involved the people, if only indirectly; and, as the public opinion polls indicated, a majority of the people were strongly opposed to it. Round five came to an end in October 1992, when a majority of Canadians, in a majority of provinces, and in a national referendum, rejected the Charlottetown Accord. It was rejected largely because, in order to win equal representation in the Senate, the polygenetic western provinces had to agree to allow largely French Quebec, regardless of the size of its population, to have 25 percent of the seats in the House of Commons. One commentator described the process as "a deal-maker but a referendum-breaker."[34] Then, in October 1995, a proposal to make Quebec a sovereign nation was defeated 49.4 to 50.6 percent in a popular referendum. The leader of the separatist Bloc Quebecois, Lucien Bouchard, said that "the next time will be the right time, and the next time may come sooner than people think."

From this brief account it is possible to draw several conclusions bearing on multiculturalism: the effort to accord recognition and its attendant privileges to one group, cultural or otherwise, will provoke either similar demands from other groups or, especially when the people are brought into the process, a stubborn refusal to make the accommodation. The "Ukrainians" of Manitoba are less likely than their political leaders (at least those at Meech Lake) to indulge the "French" of Quebec. Like other "peoples," especially in a regime that recognizes "peoples," they have pride too. Thus, although the Meech Lake politicians saw the proposed constitutional recognition of Quebec's "distinct society" as merely symbolic and understood that what really mattered was the extent of the powers granted to the provinces, the "people" stamped their feet and said no.

Comparisons with the United States are surely unfair to Canadians; but, if we would avoid its problems, comparison with Canada can be useful to us. Canada began as two societies and remained two largely separated societies for the better part of its history; and its efforts to build one multicultural society have ended, for the time at least, with a country more divided than ever. Whereas, if (but only for the time being) we ignore the black-white division (which was resolved, to the extent that it was resolved, only by a civil war), America began as one people; and its policy of assimilating, rather than accommodating, its immigrants has allowed it (for the time, at least) to remain one. It was able to assimilate them because it was able to persuade them that its ways, its rules of justice, and its religious principles were superior to those they may have brought with them.

"All eyes are open, or opening, to the rights of man. The general spread of the light of science has already laid open to every view the palpable truth, that the mass of mankind has not been born with saddles on their backs, nor a favored few booted and spurred, ready to ride them legitimately, by the grace of God." So wrote Jefferson in the last of his many letters.[35] But too many eyes are closed, or closing, today. Today that abstract or palpable truth is too often seen as mere opinion, one opinion among many, and all of them equal; and if our multiculturalists have their way—and if all cultures are equal, why should they not have their way?—all of them are to be taught in the public schools. The idea of the rights of man will occupy no special place in such a curriculum. As one of many ideas, its authority is almost certain to be weakened, and with its weakening will come a weakening of the foundation on which we have built the pluralism—and the liberty—we have enjoyed from the beginning.

It is especially likely to be weakened when the loudest voices we hear today are contemptuous of the world built by Jefferson and his colleagues. His invocation of "the light of science" is seen by some as part of a plot, a way of justifying the continued hegemony of his kind, namely, white European males and their white American male coconspirators.

This contempt for things American—at its base a *self*-contempt—is nowhere better expressed than in the 1993 Bienniel Exhibition of American Art at New York's Whitney Museum. Intended to portray the "victims" of American civilization, the show (described in the catalogue as a "multicultural" exhibition) features videos and photographs of black gang members, Mexican hookers, battered women, transvestites; female self-portraits with dildos and prosthetic breasts; "installations" displaying a splat of simulated vomit; and, at the end, in cut-out letters two feet high, the statement "In the rich man's house the only place to spit is in his face." As evidence of their having paid the admissions fee, and by order of the museum's director (rich white David Ross), visitors are required to display a button bearing the words "I can't imagine ever wanting to be white."[36]

Leo Strauss had something like this Whitney exhibition in mind when, twenty-nine years ago, he wrote that every such accusation presupposes a law—in this case (so severe are the Whitney accusations) something like a holy law—against which political life is to be measured.[37] One might think that life in the United States could be heaven, or was supposed to be heaven; but the founders promised no such thing. What they promised was liberty, including the liberty to tend to the salvation of our own souls; and the country they established was the first in all of history to make, and to keep, that promise. By keeping it—here I quote Werner J. Dannhauser—they made "corruption voluntary to an appreciable degree."[38]

The proponents of multiculturalism fail to appreciate what has been accomplished in and by the United States, and their project, when taken seriously, would have the effect—and, in the case of the Whitney people, the intended effect—of undermining its foundation. The future of constitutionalism depends, in part, on our ability to understand this.

Notes

1. For an account of the attempt to define culture, see Raymond Williams, *Culture and Society* (New York: Columbia University Press, 1958).

2. Allan Bloom, "Commerce and Culture," in *Giants and Dwarfs* (New York: Simon & Schuster, 1990), 280.

3. Amy Gutmann, "Introduction," *Multiculturalism and "The Politics of Recognition": An Essay by Charles Taylor, with Commentary by Amy Gutmann, Steven C. Rockefeller, Michael Walzer, and Susan Wolf,* ed. Amy Gutmann (Princeton: Princeton University Press, 1992), 3.

4. H. D. Forbes, "Multiculturalism: The General Principles in the Canadian Case" (paper prepared for delivery at the 1990 Annual Meeting of the American Political Science Association), 2.

5. Forbes, 16.

6. A news item of some years ago illustrates the problem: "Gojko Susak, the Croatian defense minister who three years ago was running a chain of pizza parlors in Ottawa, Canada, says the U.N. complaints about Croatian deception are 'their excuse for not doing what they are supposed to do.' In his Zagreb office, where a bear skin rug that once belonged to former Yugoslavian strongman Josip Broz Tito covers the floor, Mr. Susak [insists] that the Croats have stopped [the Serbian] offensive." *Wall Street Journal,* 8 March 1993, A6.

7. In this connection, it is interesting to note that "pluralism" as a political term is a neologism, one that made its first appearance in the *Oxford English Dictionary* only with the publication of the *Supplement* in 1982. There we are told that "pluralism," meaning "the existence or toleration of diversity of ethnic groups within a society or state, of beliefs or attitudes within a body or institution, etc.," was first used in 1956 by Horace Kallen in his book *Cultural Pluralism and the American Idea.* Rogers Smith informs me, correctly, that Kallen used the term "cultural pluralism" in 1924 in his *Culture and Democracy.*

8. *Annals of Congress,* vol. 1 (Feb. 3, 1790), 1150; vol. 3 (Dec. 22, 1794), 1008.

9. Thomas Jefferson, *Notes on the State of Virginia,* Query VIII, in Jefferson, *Writings* (New York: The Library of America, 1984), 211.

10. Jefferson, *Notes,* 212.

11. Goodwin Watson, in Horace Kallen, *Cultural Pluralism and the American Idea* (Philadelphia: University of Pennsylvania Press, 1956), 166.

12. *Communist Party of Indiana v. Whitcomb,* 414 U.S. 441 (1974).

13. *Davis v. Beason,* 133 U.S. 334 (1890), 341–42.

14. *United States v. Macintosh,* 283 U.S. 605 (1931), 625.

15. Bernard Lewis, 19th Jefferson Lecture (Washington, D.C., May 1990).

16. Alexis de Tocqueville, *Democracy in America,* vol. 2 (New York: Vintage Books, 1990), book 1, ch. 5, p. 23.

17. The Ayatollah Khomeini ordered Rushdie to be assassinated for publishing what Khomeini said was a blasphemous book, *Satanic Verses.*

18. S. J. D. Green, "Religion and the Limits of Pluralism in Contemporary Britain," *Antioch Review* 49, no. 4 (Fall 1991): 581. I am indebted to this article for my account of the British situation.

19. *Pierce v. Society of Sisters,* 268 U.S. 510 (1925).

20. Thomas Jefferson, *A Bill for Establishing Religious Freedom,* in *Writings,* 346.

21. John Locke, *A Letter Concerning Toleration* (Indianapolis: The Library of Liberal Arts, 1955), paragraphs 6–7, 36, pp. 17, 30.

22. Jefferson, *Notes,* Query XVII, in *Writings,* 285.

23. See Walter Berns, *Taking the Constitution Seriously* (New York: Simon & Schuster, 1987; paperback ed., Madison Books, 1992), 162.

24. The difference between a policy of toleration and the American policy was well stated by George Washington in his famous letter of August 17, 1790, to the Hebrew Congregation of Newport, Rhode Island: "It is now no more that toleration is spoken of as if it were the indulgence of one class of people that another enjoyed the exercise of their inherent natural rights, for, happily, the Government of the United States, which gives to bigotry no sanction, to persecution no assistance, requires only that they who live under its protection should demean themselves as good citizens in giving it on all occasions their effectual support. . . .

"May the children of the stock of Abraham who dwell in this land continue to merit and enjoy the good will of the other inhabitants—while every one shall sit in safety under his own vine and fig tree and there shall be none to make him afraid." *The Writings of George Washington,* vol. 31, ed. John C. Fitzpatrick (Washington, D.C.: Government Printing Office, 1939), 93n.

25. Jonathan Elliot, ed., *The Debates in the Several State Conventions on the Adoption of the Federal Constitution,* vol. 2 (New York: Burt Franklin, n.d.), 118. The article being debated was the Article VI provision forbidding religious tests for office holders.

26. "The legitimate powers of government extend to such acts only as are injurious to

others. But it does me no injury for my neighbor to say there are twenty gods, or no god. It neither picks my pocket nor breaks my leg." Jefferson, *Notes,* Query XVII, in *Writings,* 285.

27. Gutmann, 5.

28. See *Holland v. Illinois,* 493 U.S. 474 (1990).

29. Selden Society, *Select Pleas, Starrs, and Other Records from the Rolls of the Exchequer of the Jews,* ed. J. M. Rigg (London: Bernard Quaritch, 1902), xxi, xl–xlii.

30. Kevin Boyle, Tom Hadden, and Paddy Hillyard, *Law and State: The Case of Northern Ireland* (London: Martin Robertson; Amherst: University of Massachusetts Press, 1975), 95–96, 174–75.

31. Gutmann, 5.

32. For an expanded version of Huntington's lecture, see his essay "Political Conflict after the Cold War," in *History and the Idea of Progress,* ed. Arthur M. Melzer, Jerry Weinberger, and M. Richard Zinman (Ithaca: Cornell University Press, 1995), 137–54.

33. Pierre Elliott Trudeau, *Federalism and the French Canadians* (Toronto: Macmillan, 1968), 178–79. As printed in Forbes, 16.

34. Peter H. Russell, "The End of Mega Constitutional Politics in Canada?" *PS* (March 1993), 33. I am indebted to Professor Russell for much of the above account.

35. Thomas Jefferson to Roger C. Weightman, June 24, 1826, in *Writings,* 1517.

36. *Washington Post,* 4 March 1993, C1, C4; *Wall Street Journal,* 5 March 1993, A7.

37. Leo Strauss, *Liberalism: Ancient and Modern* (New York: Basic Books, Inc., 1968), 262.

38. Werner J. Dannhauser, "Ancients, Moderns and Canadians," *Denver Quarterly* 4 (1969): 97.

Chapter 6

Majoritarian Democracy and Cultural Minorities

Bernard Boxill

The classic problem of majoritarian democracy is that it enables the majority to tyrannize minorities. This problem is less serious if different majorities tend to form on different issues, for in that case no minority is likely to be a permanent minority. It is more serious in culturally plural societies where one of the cultural groups is an absolute majority. The cultural ties binding the members of such a majority will incline them to stand together on many different issues, to use the principle of majority rule to secure their interests at the expense of the minority cultures, and to impose their values and way of life on them.

Members of the majority culture may claim that they should be free to impose their values and way of life on minorities. To support this claim they may appeal to the dangers of culturally plural societies and to the benefits of culturally homogeneous societies. Culturally plural societies are said to be prone to murderous conflict, and culturally homogeneous societies are said to contribute to community, fraternity, and a sense of belonging. But even if these claims are true, a cultural majority may act wrongly in imposing its values and way of life on cultural minorities. People may have rights to retain their culture and to pass it on to their children, which forbid their forcible acculturation, even if that would make the society culturally homogeneous and a better society.

Democracies have standardly tried to solve the problem of the tyranny of the majority by enshrining certain rights in a constitution that can be changed only by an overwhelming majority. This device can be applied to the particular problem of a majority culture trying to impose its values and way of life on minorities. But it is not altogether satisfactory. For one thing, even rights enshrined in a constitution can be revoked if the majority that wants them revoked is large and determined enough. More importantly, the device only forces the majority to tolerate minorities. It may prevent a majority from violating minorities' most basic interests, but it need not give minorities opportunity to flourish or to contribute to the society. In this essay I develop this objection to majoritarian democracy and suggest briefly one possible solution to the problem it points to.

I begin with the argument that the usual rights enshrined in the Constitution for the protection of minorities need not give them an opportunity to flourish. My argument is based on an argument proposed by Mill in *Representative Government*. In that book Mill argued that "true" democracy required provisions to ensure that minorities were represented in the legislative body. Since the usual systems of majoritarian rule keep minorities out of the legislative body, Mill called them "false" democracy and argued that their "inevitable consequence" was the "complete disfranchisement of minorities" even if they had the vote.[1] Mill's conclusion is too strong. Although he was right that the usual systems of majoritarian rule do not ensure that minorities are represented in legislative bodies, he was wrong to conclude that they lead to the disfranchisement of minorities. People are not disfranchised because their favorite candidate for office is not elected, they are disfranchised when their right to vote is violated; but the usual systems of majoritarian rule guarantee minorities the right to vote. Still, there is something to Mill's complaint about majoritarian democracy. Part of this, I argue, is that majoritarian democracy may not give cultural minorities an equal opportunity to flourish.

I assume that Mill's claim about majoritarian democracy and minorities in general implies a similar claim about majoritarian democracy and cultural minorities. That claim, that majoritarian democracy keeps members of cultural minorities out of legislative bodies, is the main premise of my argument. It does not imply by itself that majoritarian democracies do not give people of minority cultures an equal opportunity to flourish; arguably, to flourish in such democracies people must be represented by politicians who pass legislation to help them flourish, and such politicians may be drawn from the majority culture. My argument therefore appeals to two further considerations: first, that, given the usual assumptions of majoritarian democracy, politicians will normally be reluctant to pass legislation specifically to enable people of minority cultures to advance; second, that politicians who care about such people's interests and understand the kind of legislation necessary to enable them to thrive will probably share their culture.

Despite some utopian thinkers, it may not be possible to design policies that enable all cultural groups to advance and to do so at the same rate. In particular, legislation that enables people of minority cultures to advance may very well slow the advance of those of the majority culture. Further, because human beings usually seem to want to have others to feel superior to, people of the majority culture often feel threatened by legislation that would only enable people of minority cultures to gain on them. Since voters do not support politicians who introduce legislation they see as threatening and politicians want voters' support, politicians usually do not even discuss legislation that would obviously enable people of minority cultures to advance.

It is an invidious assumption that people from the majority culture cannot care about the interests of those in minority cultures and cannot possibly understand and devise the kind of legislation that would enable them to thrive. But two considerations suggest that, all else equal, people of minority cultures are more likely to be well represented by those who share their culture than by others. First, people who share their culture are more likely to identify with them, and consequently to love and care for them, than are outsiders. Supposing that this is usually the case, politicians from a minority culture are likely to be more strongly motivated to design and pass legislation aimed at helping their cultural group advance than are politicians from the majority culture.

The second argument that people of minority cultures are better represented by those who share their culture than by outsiders is that people who share their culture are likely to better understand their culture than outsiders, and consequently likely to better understand what legislation will help them to thrive. This may seem false on the ground that an outsider, standing outside a culture, may better understand a culture's strengths and weaknesses than does a cultural insider. I grant that one must be able to stand outside a culture in order to appreciate its strengths and weaknesses. But politicians from the minority culture will often be able to stand outside their own culture, because they live in a society dominated by the majority culture and are therefore often compelled to step outside their own culture and to operate in the majority culture. Consequently, they will be able to gain the perspective necessary to assessing its strengths and weaknesses. Assuming that they are likely to be among their culture's more mobile and energetic members, they will be especially able to have an informed outsider's view of it, although most members of the culture will enjoy this advantage to some degree. Further, standing outside a culture enables one to appreciate its strengths and weaknesses only if one knows the culture intimately. But politicians from the majority are not likely to know the minority culture intimately. Their culture dominates the society and they do not need to know much about minority cultures. Consequently, unlike politicians from minority cultures, they are unlikely to have an informed outsider's view of minority cultures.

It may be objected that minority cultures do not have to be represented by people who understand their peculiarities and who care about them specifically. I will be reminded of the Japanese and Jews, who have done remarkably well in the United States although they are usually represented by Caucasians and Christians who neither understand them nor particularly care for them. These cases, and others that could be cited, show that it is not a necessary condition that a cultural minority be represented by its members, or even those who understand and care about it, in order to thrive. The cultural minority may feel itself invisible or may believe that the majority will not take the trouble to devise legislation detrimental to it; or it may have qualities that enable it to advance, given the legislation that the politicians elected by the majority pass, even if this legislation is not passed in order to enable it to advance. Considerations such as these probably account for the success of the Japanese and Jews, though it is arguable that the Japanese might have avoided some disasters—I have in mind their internment during the Second World War—if they had not kept such a low political profile. But we cannot generalize from these exceptional cases and conclude that cultural minorities ordinarily do not need to represent themselves politically in order to flourish. In many cases a cultural minority's qualities will not enable it to advance given the legislation that the politicians elected by the majority pass. Normally, to thrive it must be represented by those who understand and care about it, and usually such people will come from its own ranks. This is the basic point about political life that the American revolutionaries learned, and that justified their separation from Great Britain; and it explains why cultural groups invariably seek political representation and power as soon as they become too numerous or too successful to be invisible.

My argument that the usual apparatus of democratic procedures need not give minority cultures opportunity to thrive assumes that members of minority cultures will not be elected to office. This is a reasonable assumption, given the principle of majoritarian democracy that the candidate elected to office gets the most votes and that people tend to vote for candidates from their own cultural group. But it is not always true. A cultural group can constitute a majority in several voting districts even if it is a small minority in the country as a whole. In these districts it will probably be represented by those who share its culture, precisely because people tend to vote for candidates of their own cultural groups, and the candidates elected to office are those who get the most votes.

Such representation is better than no representation. It gives the minority culture some measure of self-government and ensures that its representatives have an opportunity to urge policies for its advancement in legislatures made up of representatives of many voting districts, even if the policies they urge are unlikely to be adopted, given that the principle of majority rule holds in the legislature as well as in the competition for office. Nevertheless, requiring cultural groups to segregate themselves in particular voting districts in order to make themselves majorities in those districts has unacceptable consequences. The segregation involved is not likely to be only the innocent result of like-minded people freely choosing to live together. It will probably also require coercion. In order to remain, or to become, a majority in a voting district, a cultural group may have to prevent those of different cultures from moving into the district, or even compel them to leave if they are already there. Since this is unjust and likely to lead to conflict between cultural groups, representation achieved by cultural segregation probably comes at too high a price.

I now take up the argument that majoritarian democracies also fail to give people of minority cultures an equal opportunity to contribute to their societies by taking part directly in legislation. This does not mean, of course, that majoritarian democracies altogether prevent members of cultural minorities from contributing to their societies. There are ways to contribute to one's society besides being elected to office.

The argument that majoritarian democracies do not give members of minority cultures an equal opportunity to contribute directly to the legislation of their society is in a sense a trivial implication of the fact, already established, that majoritarian democracies give members of minority cultures little opportunity to be elected to office. But members of cultural minorities who are excluded from political office by the mechanisms of majoritarian democracy are not likely to feel that their exclusion is trivial. Elected officials design and pass legislation and consequently are able to contribute to their societies in peculiarly powerful and effective ways.

I also want to make the stronger point that members of minority cultures have something to contribute to legislation in their society that of the majority culture may not be able to contribute. It relies on the kind of considerations that John Stuart Mill used to justify his claim that society should value freethinkers, eccentrics, and intellectuals. Mill did not simply urge mechanisms and policies—like systems of entrenched rights—that would help to prevent the majority from overwhelming freethinkers, eccentrics, and intellectuals. More generally, he did not want the majority only to tolerate these minorities. He believed that it should *value* them because they could have something to teach it. His best-known argument is stated in *On Liberty*. In that work Mill maintains that unless people harm others they should be allowed to live as they decide. Some of his arguments for this claim justify only toleration. I have in mind where he argues that a person's "own mode of laying out his existence is best, not because it is best in itself, but because it is his own mode."[2] But other arguments stress that allowing others to live as they please can contribute to the discovery of ways to live that are objectively best. This is the well-known "experiments in living" argument. Mill's idea was that people who try unconventional ways of living may well hit on practices that the majority can learn from and adopt to its benefit. As he wrote, "It is important to give the freest scope possible to uncustomary things, in order that it may in time appear which of these are fit to be converted into customs."[3]

If Mill's argument is sound, valuable and useful ideas about how to live probably derive from all cultures, and consequently from minority cultures. I believe this to be the case because cultures are experiments in living.

People do not normally think of their own culture as an experiment in living. They do not suppose that their culture's mores and practices are hypotheses about how life should be lived and that in following these mores and practices they are behaving somewhat like scientists subjecting hypotheses to empirical tests. Normally they act as their culture dictates because they don't think about it, or because they believe that alternatives are wrong, or sometimes because they cannot conceive of alternatives. Still a culture is an experiment in living in the sense that things happen as a result of people following its mores and practices, and people do learn from how and why these things happen. This is why cultures change. People see what the consequences of living according to the mores and practices of their culture are, and as a result some of the more sensitive or imaginative or daring among them are moved from time to time to do things differently themselves or to urge their fellows to do things differently. When their example is followed, or their suggestions are accepted—and only rarely does either happen quickly—their culture slowly changes.

I say "changes" advisedly, and not "improves." An enterprising knave may hit on a way to circumvent an important cultural convention for his personal advantage. If others follow his example, the overall result could be retrogression. Of course, in time people will learn from that "experiment," and some of them may introduce reforms, though again we cannot conclude that these reforms will be altogether successful or that they will not have unforeseen and undesirable side effects. Still, if Mill is right that a majority may stand to learn from the experiments in living of freethinkers and eccentrics, it probably stands to learn much more from the experiments in living of minority cultures. The experiments in living of freethinkers and eccentrics are usually conducted on a small scale and for a short time. This should make a large society that wants to reproduce itself extremely wary of taking them seriously, however attractive they may seem. A culture, on the other hand, is always the result of an exceedingly long series of related experiments in living in which each experiment is designed in the light of what was learned in earlier experiments. More than that, it is also partly a series of interrelated reflections on the series of experiments in living. People do not only learn from their mores and practices; they also reflect on what they have learned, on the possibilities and impossibilities it reveals to them, and consequently on what they can and cannot reasonably hope to achieve. Each of these reflections is made in the light of previous reflections and influences the direction the series of experiments in living takes. As a result the experiments in living of a culture become an attempt to work out a point of view of how to live, and every culture contains a commentary on the difficulties and possibilities of working out that point of view. Now it is highly unlikely that every culture has the same point of view on how to live and the same commentary on the difficulties and possibilities of working it out. The protean nature of human inventiveness and the variety of circumstances in which cultures evolve ensure this. Assuming that the majority has not discovered all there is to know about how to live, and that minorities have not gotten it all wrong, I conclude that minority cultures may well contain moral and political ideas that would help legislatures make better laws if they were presented there.

The main conclusion of the preceding sections is that the classic problem of majoritarian democracy, the "tyranny of the majority," is likely to be especially pertinent and costly in culturally plural societies where one of the cultural groups is an absolute majority. In such societies, majoritarian democracy denies cultural minorities opportunities to flourish and to contribute directly to legislation. Since people feel alienated from their societies when they are denied such opportunities, it is hardly surprising that the standard democratic apparatus of measures and provisions often fails to foster a sense of community and belonging in culturally plural societies.

This suggests that culturally plural societies should begin to consider seriously alternatives to the standard procedures of majoritarian democracy. One alternative is especially attractive because it has much to recommend it apart from the fact that it seems a promising way to correct the tendency of majoritarian democracy to exclude cultural minorities from public office. This is Thomas Hare's system of the single transferable vote, which Mill hailed as "among the greatest improvements yet made in the theory and practice of governments."[4] Mill was enthusiastic about Hare's system because it ensured that his favorite minorities—freethinkers and intellectuals—would get represented in proportion to their numbers without having to live in any particular part of the country. But it would also ensure that cultural minorities were represented in proportion to their numbers without having to segregate themselves in particular voting districts.[5] Majoritarians have strongly criticized the single transferable vote system and have questioned Mill's motives for endorsing it.[6] These criticisms have to be taken seriously. But the single transferable vote system seems a good place to start the search for a way to avoid the weakness of majoritarian democracy in culturally plural societies.

Notes

1. John Stuart Mill, *Utilitarianism, On Liberty and Representative Government* (New York: Dutton, 1951), 345.

2. Mill, 167.

3. Mill, 167.

4. Mill, 354.

5. Arthur Lewis made this point when he recommended proportional representation to the culturally plural societies of West Africa. See his *Politics in West Africa* (New York: Oxford University Press, 1965).

6. See, for example, Paul B. Kern, "Universal Suffrage Without Democracy: Thomas Hare and John Stuart Mill," *Review of Politics* 34 (1972): 306–22; and Gideon Doron and Richard Kronick, "Single Transferable Vote: An Example of a Perverse Social Choice Function," *American Journal of Political Science* 21 (1977): 303–11.

Chapter 7

Democratic Multiculturalism

Wilson Carey McWilliams

Historically, multiculturalism has not often been associated with democracy; more often, it has been the practice of empires and hegemonies, the condition of a policy of divide and rule.[1] In fact, multiculturalism is not easily compatible with democracy, as any day's newspaper can tell us: Yugoslavia managed, more or less, as a one-party autocracy, but it proved unable to survive democratization, and it would be easy to add other painful examples.

Nor is this surprising: a grand tradition in political theory holds that democracy requires a high level of trust in one's fellow citizens, or at least a broad sphere of the taken-for-granted in civil life. As in the New England of Tocqueville's describing, an open *politics* presumes a more or less closed *society*.[2]

The Federalist's argument for a large and diverse republic, of course, reverses this order of things. It prescribes social openness of a fairly radical sort, making it a first principle to protect the differences in our faculties and opinions. The new order of the American republic, consequently, is not defined by usages and habits, but by forms and laws.[3] The framers' tolerance did have limits: they assumed and relied on a people who observed the decencies and for whom a word was a bond. At bottom, however, they afforded us a relatively open society on the basis of a *politics* that is closed in critical respects. The Constitution's constraints and barriers only follow the even stricter teaching of the Declaration of Independence, according to which we are allowed to calculate our interests and to bargain them away, but our rights are unalienable, immune to the discountings of interest or culture.[4]

It is worth remembering that there were serious conflicts of culture in eighteenth-century America, most evident in the problem of slavery—for slavery, as Anne Norton reminds us, did create a culture and a tenacious one—but also simmering in the relations between Europeans and aboriginal peoples, in the conflict between religion and secularism, and in the largely forgotten animosities among sects.[5] From the beginning, multiculturality has tested the Constitution and the laws, raising the question of

120

whether conflicts between cultures can be subordinated to and confined within democratic forms or whether "culture wars" will be fought with weapons other than words and votes.[6]

Slavery, of course, proved too much for democratic politics, and Tocqueville, who feared as much, was also too close to the mark in his pessimism about race. But Tocqueville was impressed by the American entente with religion, especially because the republic seemed on the way to an accommodation with Roman Catholicism; and his argument has a good deal to say about the conditions of successful multiculturality.

Tocqueville observed that any religious doctrine (and he might have added, any culture) has a political tendency that will assert itself if unchecked. Circumstances, however, can alter the *effects* of belief, its expression in day-to-day life. Thus, despite its aristocratic structure and historic affinities, Roman Catholicism in America had some sympathy for republican government, just as most Catholics supported the Democratic Party, if only because, en masse, American Catholics were poor.[7]

Confrontation with new circumstances unsettles authority and forces a belief or culture to abandon the habitual for the more or less conscious and chosen, separating those things that seem essential—that must be remembered and retained—from those that can be safely left behind.[8] The new world of Tocqueville's discerning, of course, challenges all ways and faiths to accommodate themselves to democratic principles. Prudence dictates that the majority not be opposed except in vital matters, and even then, with the foreknowledge that defeat is likely: "In ages of equality, kings may often command obedience, but the majority always commands belief."[9] That counsel is even more urgent in a country like the United States, where democracy has shaped the laws. Religions and cultures are fortunate, consequently, if their tenets are at least compatible with democratic doctrine. Without that consonance, they face political society on an implicit field of battle; and even those, like Tocqueville, who are confident that they can predict the winner may regret the war.

In Tocqueville's view, Catholics were among the lucky, because America imposed only a kind of purification on a faith already egalitarian at root. As Tocqueville explained it, amid the unequal societies of the feudal era, responding to a world of nations, castes, and classes, the Church—while clinging to the universal sovereignty of God—had "improperly enhanced" the importance of "divine agents."[10] America, Tocqueville claimed, had allowed and compelled the Church to return to first things, and especially to an emphasis on human unity. (By contrast, Tocqueville thought that any relation between democracy and Islam would be more troubled, because so much traditional legal and political teaching is included in the Koran, at the heart of the creed; and there is very little, so far, to suggest that he was not right.)[11]

Moreover, among Catholics, American laws were nurturing new political beliefs. Catholics had accepted a religiously neutral government partly from necessity and partly to protect themselves against old animosities, but Tocqueville found them increasingly positive in their support for a separation of church and state. Even the zealous Father Mullon told Tocqueville and Beaumont that state support for religion was harmful; and startlingly, the vicar general claimed that "enlightenment" was favorable to the "religious spirit."[12]

As Catholicism was "modified" in a democratic and republican direction, Tocqueville contended, there was a reciprocal growth of tolerance between Catholics and non-Catholics, a softening of the boundaries between communions. Not that Catholicism had dissolved into indistinction: its rites and beliefs still seemed bizarre to the Protestant majority. But, as Tocqueville saw it, the Church was winning a respected place in American life, with more promise for the future.[13]

Uncharacteristically, Tocqueville was overoptimistic: memories of the Reformation remained a fault line in American party politics at least until 1960, along with the even more tenacious legacy of slavery and the Civil War.[14] Yet partisan conflicts, as George Washington Plunkitt reminded us, mark democracy's ascendancy over cultures; and in the long term, Tocqueville seems to have been right in thinking that he had discerned a success story in the American politics of culture.[15]

What his argument shows us, however, is stern as well as sunny. Economic and social circumstances, especially well-being, can combine with cultural compatibility to make matters much less painful; but in the end, democracy can accommodate a culture only to the extent that it accepts the sovereignty of democratic laws, and hence the certainty of at least some cultural attenuation. In America, all cultures and faiths—the established as well as the excluded—are caught up in an ongoing redefinition in relation to the laws and to each other, a process of learning, forgetting, and selectively remembering that lays down both the boundaries of community and the civil meaning of the term "American."[16]

Since, as a general rule, the Constitution insists on an individual's right to leave faith or community behind, the hold of such cultures depends on persuasion and social sanctions, and especially on an early education capable of armoring the soul against the power of majority opinion. In critical respects, consequently, a multicultural politics is always a politics of schooling. As institutions, the schools are a proving ground, for there, if not before, the public can make itself heard. (These days, of course, the media inserts its "hidden curriculum" much earlier and more pervasively.)[17] In the dialogue between the public and the cultures, an element of multiculturalism is only good manners, an acknowledgement of one's audience that schools commonly have tried to practice. But contemporary multiculturalism goes farther: up to a point, it seeks to enlist public authority on the side of the cultures—though not, significantly, on the side of faith.

For most of its contemporary defenders, multiculturalism is only a means in the service of a generous, democratic end: their real goal is inclusion, the hope of drawing new groups and cultures into a respected place in a strengthened civic life. As multiculturalists observe, there are cracks in some of the old pillars of American civic education. In lean economic times, there are no guarantees of the assurance of work at socially adequate wages that Jefferson saw as the right bower in the game of civic dignity.[18] And multiculturalists are even more moved by the fact that the economy and the media are fragmenting communities and cultures, muting the second voice of America's grand dialogue in favor of an increasingly radical individualism on one hand and tyranny of the majority on the other.[19] Multiculturalism, in this view, is an attempt to check disintegration and to promote a political pluralism in the image of Randolph Bourne's celebrated essay, "Trans-National America."[20]

Notice at the outset, however, that this sort of multiculturalism regards a broadly democratic politics not as one culture among many, but as a superior standard entitled to rule. That assumption is reflected in the common tendency to slide over or suppress the nondemocratic aspects of the cultures being recognized, implicitly rejecting whatever is incompatible with a democratic life and creed. (I will have more to say about this later on.) And, of course, commitment to multiculturalism is ordinarily accompanied by the insistence that racism, sexism, homophobia, and the like are thoroughly unacceptable. Multiculturalism aspires to substitute a salad bowl for the melting pot, but—as the metaphor indicates—it still looks for a politics enclosed by a democratic orthodoxy.

Yet in their thinking about democracy, multiculturalists incline to focus on the social and the cultural, and to slight democratic *institutions*—a tendency that is especially unfortunate given the close relationship between the Constitution and the very idea of a multicultural republic. In fact, the multicultural persuasion is apt to stress the presence of slavery and the absence of women in the Constitution, or to argue that even the proclamation of natural equality in the Declaration of Independence refers only to "men," and implicitly only to white men, and to conclude that the Declaration and the Constitution reflect only the culture and interests of European males in the then-dominant class.

A good deal of this is simply silly. There is ample evidence, for example, that the Declaration's affirmation of equality was understood to refer to all races, and that the accommodation with slavery in the Constitution—made necessary, paradoxically, by the multicultural goal of including the South in the Union—was regarded as a violation of natural right. Consider the exchange in South Carolina, when one legislator asked that stock-in-trade Antifederalist question, "Why was not this Constitution ushered in with a bill of rights?" Charles Cotesworth Pinckney answered that, among other reasons, "Such bills generally begin with declaring that all men are by nature born free. Now, we should make that declaration with very bad grace, when a large part of our property consists in men who are actually born slaves."[21]

Even where the multiculturalist critique tells us something important about the Constitution, as it does by pointing to oppressions based on race and gender, it underrates the importance of constitutional forms. The norm of equality makes violations of that rule anomalous, things that have to be euphemized or explained. The exceptions are constantly criticized by the rule, which by setting a direction can become, as Harvey Mansfield observes, "the cause of going if not getting there."[22]

Democracy, moreover, is a hard school, and the culture of democracy depends on forms, especially in a large republic. Its cornerstone, majority rule, depends on the form by which every vote is treated as equal; similarly, the vast majority of us can have a voice in public councils only through the form of representation, determined in districts and by election. Even our efforts to acquire a more substantial voice through participation require the "art of association," and hence the discipline of Roberts' Rules or some other form of order.[23] At best, our politics involves frustrations and indignities, and rapid economic change and the resulting disorder of society weaken the compensations of private life. Americans are eager for a kind of strong government, but their support for democratic institutions is dangerously thin.[24] Multiculturalists, the champions of minorities, have very good reason to give more—and more serious—attention to the institutional frame of American democratic life.

It is a far more serious problem, however, that democratic multiculturalists are tempted to adopt, as a weapon of convenience against established America, the doctrine of the *equality of cultures,* forgetting that the enemy of my enemy is not necessarily my friend.[25] This philosophic multiculturalism holds that cultures are incommensurable, "separate realities" or "stories," so that there can be no ranking of cultures or of the comparative excellence of their parts. And for democratic multiculturalists, that teaching involves at least two towering problems.

In the first place, it disdains cultures themselves, for on their own terms, cultures engage in just this sort of comparison and ranking. When Marc Swartz studied Truk, early in his distinguished career, he expected the islanders to be ethnocentric, proclaiming their ways superior to all others. He found, however, that Trukese often expressed admiration for American technology and deprecated their own crafts. At the same time, the Trukese to whom Swartz talked were shocked by his accounts of family life in America, and especially by the fact that he was not expected, periodically, to work for his brother-in-law, reasoning that their own ways were more likely to unify families (a conclusion that seems tenable, to say the least). The Trukese, in other words, did not see cultures as monads, each locked into the island of its own uniqueness, but as more or less effective answers to human problems.[26] In the same way, Michael Herzfeld observes that the Cretan villagers he studied understand the world on the basis of a "folk theory," which includes ideas of what it means to be a good man (or to be more exact, to be good at *being* a man). The superiority of one's self, one's village, or one's nation, in these terms, is inseparable from excellence in fulfilling norms that are asserted as universals.[27] Even a culture that maintains that "our blood is superior to yours" thinks we can be measured by the same rule. Great cultures instruct and challenge us precisely because they ask, and offer compelling answers to, the questions, "What is human? And what is the best life?" To take cultures seriously is to recognize that such encounters lead to arguments and point toward philosophy, just as diversity is only humanity in masquerade.

Second, a belief in the equality of *cultures* is at odds with the principle of *equality.* Plenty of cultures, after all, include a hierarchy of castes or classes or teach a hankering after dominion, to say nothing of racism and sexism. To support democratic equality is to maintain that, in this respect, some creeds and cultures are better and others worse: even the secular spirits among the framers, for example, were inclined to find good words for

Christianity—whatever their quarrels with it—because of its devotion to egalitarian teaching in the realm of the spirit.[28] On its own terms, equality is a ruling standard, entitled to judge the cultures, weighing their customs in the scales of nature.

As I have observed, because most multiculturalists are democrats at bottom, they are tempted or disposed to discount any antidemocratic aspects they meet in a culture. But, the fostering of illusions aside, such "playful multiculturalism"—the term is David Carlin's—loses precisely what is best in a confrontation with a profound and unfamiliar teaching: its capacity to shake our complacency, to force us to articulate first principles, and in general to make us think more seriously about political things. Fuzzing the debate also obscures the likelihood that American citizenship is incompatible with at least some aspects of any ethnic tradition, with the consequence that such citizenship requires that a great deal of any heritage be left behind—a hard truth, but a necessary one for democratic life, and not only in such obvious cases as the Irish and the South Slavs.[29] G. K. Chesterton put democratic multiculturalism in perspective when, not altogether playfully, he likened the United States to the Spanish Inquisition, because while America is not entitled to exclude per se a Catholic or a Muslim, a Japanese or—pace Pat Buchanan—a Zulu, it has both a right and a duty to reject any challenge to equality as the ruling principle of public life.[30]

And while, unlike the Inquisitors, we are not allowed to burn the heterodox—the self-immolation of the Branch Davidians constrains me to add, at least not on purpose—it is incumbent on us to recognize that the "equality of cultures" is a rival principle, one that asserts its superiority over democracy, which it reduces to one culture among many. In fact, it regards *all* cultures as decisively inferior to the enlightened perspective that sees them as no more than a kind of entertaining storytelling. In the view of those Carlin calls "grave multiculturalists," the real title to rule rests with nihilists, happy or otherwise, who recognize that true ranking of human understanding.[31]

It is a troubled time for the republic, and we have every reason to draw on what is best in all our cultures and traditions—including, if it needs to be said, voices from the underside and from new or neglected corners of American life. (Among many possibilities, I am thinking of Maxine Hong Kingston's *The Woman Warrior* and Carlos Bulosan's remarkable *America Is from the Heart*.[32]) But when economic circumstances are not cheering and the compatibility of cultures is imperfect, even more than usual the possibilities of multicultural democracy depend on the framing strength of the Constitution and the laws. For democratic multiculturalists, no imperative is greater than the need to rebuild the institutions that connect citizens with their government, and with them, a politics guided by the proposition that all human beings are created equal.[33]

Notes

1. Among modern examples, British India comes to mind, especially because the British so often justified their rule as essential to multicultural peace. Ironically, those who are attracted to the language of "Hegemon" and "Other" tend to pass lightly over these connections between multiculturalism and elite rule, although, as I will be arguing, there is a sense in which it is not ironic after all.

2. Alexis de Tocqueville, *Democracy in America,* trans. Henry Reeve (New York: Knopf, 1980), 1:43. See also Joshua Miller, *The Rise and Fall of Democracy in Early America, 1630–1789* (University Park: Pennsylvania State University Press, 1991), 21–49.

3. Despite anxieties about immigrants, which found expression in the early naturalization laws, the Constitution's requirements for habituation are extremely modest. The debate in the Convention is instructive. See James Madison, *Notes of Debates in the Federal Convention of 1787* (Athens: Ohio University Press, 1966), 409–11.

4. Harvey C. Mansfield, Jr., *America's Constitutional Soul* (Baltimore: Johns Hopkins University Press, 1991), 82.

5. Anne Norton, *Alternative America: A Reading of Antebellum Political Culture* (Chicago: University of Chicago Press, 1986).

6. Part of the contemporary version of this test is discussed in James D. Hunter, *Culture Wars: The Struggle to Define America* (New York: Basic Books, 1991).

7. Alexis de Tocqueville, *Journey to America,* ed. J. P. Mayer (New Haven: Yale University Press, 1962), 150.

8. Tocqueville, *Democracy in America,* 2:25–26. Tocqueville noticed a tendency among Catholic clergy to emphasize the "spirit" rather than the "letter" of the law. Tocqueville, *Democracy in America,* 2:27.

9. Tocqueville, *Democracy in America,* 2:26.

10. Tocqueville, *Democracy in America,* 2:23-24.

11. Tocqueville, *Democracy in America,* 2:23. While Christianity includes political teachings, John Hallowell wrote, it "is not itself a political philosophy or an economic program." *Main Currents in Modern Political Thought* (New York: Holt, Rinehart and Winston, 1950), 692.

12. Tocqueville, *Journey to America,* 33, 206, 257.

13. Tocqueville, *Journey to America,* 59–60, 236–37; and Tocqueville, *Democracy in America,* 2:29–30.

14. Samuel P. Hays, "Political Parties and the Community-Society Continuum," in *The American Party System,* ed. William N. Chambers and Walter D. Burnham (New York: Oxford University Press, 1967), 152–81; V. O. Key, "The Future of the Democratic Party," *Virginia Quarterly* 28 (1952): 161–75; and John H. Schaar and Wilson C. McWilliams, "Uncle Sam Vanishes," *New University Thought* 1 (1961): 61–68.

15. William Riordon, *Plunkitt of Tammany Hall* (New York: Dutton, 1963), 13.

16. For example, in 1993, the Ancient Order of Hibernians won the right to exclude Irish gays and lesbians from the St. Patrick's Day parade in New York, arguing that the holiday is distinctively Catholic. Yet only a few Americans remember the conflict of Green and Orange, and to most of those who do, it seems curmudgeonly to wear Protestant colors—as I do—on March 17.

17. Uri Bronfenbrenner, "Contexts of Child Rearing," *American Psychologist* 34 (1979): 844–50. Of course, communities can create their own schools as supplements to public education or as alternatives to it. But the requirement of accreditation means that public doctrine cannot be altogether excluded.

18. Letter to John Adams, October 28, 1813, in *Life and Selected Writings of Jefferson,* ed. Adrienne Koch and William Peden (New York: Modern Library, 1944), 633.

19. Robert Bellah et al., *Habits of the Heart: Individualism and Commitment in American Life* (Berkeley and Los Angeles: University of California Press, 1985).

20. Randolph Bourne, "Trans-National America," *Atlantic Monthly* 118 (July 1916): 86–97.

21. Cited in Robert M. Weir, "South Carolina: Slavery and the Structure of the Union," in *Ratifying the Constitution,* ed. Michael Allen Gillespie and Michael Lienesch (Lawrence: University Press of Kansas, 1989), 222.

22. Mansfield, 12.

23. Tocqueville, *Democracy in America,* 2:102–5, 109–10.

24. See my essay "The Meaning of the Election," in Gerald M. Pomper et al., *The Election of 1992* (Chatham: Chatham House, 1993), 194–97.

25. This is an old temptation, to which—as Eric Goldman observed—the American reform tradition is particularly subject. *Rendezvous with Destiny* (New York: Knopf, 1952). It is, of course, not confined to reformers or to America: "Are you secretly, then," an anguished Demea asks belatedly, "a more dangerous enemy than Cleanthes himself?" David Hume, *Dialogues Concerning Natural Religion* in *Hume: Selections,* ed. Charles W. Hendel (New York: Scribner's, 1927), 382.

26. Marc Swartz, "Negative Ethnocentrism," *Journal of Conflict Resolution* 5 (1961): 79.

27. Michael Herzfeld, *The Poetics of Manhood* (Princeton: Princeton University Press, 1985).

28. For example, Jefferson's letter to Benjamin Rush, April 21, 1803, in *Life and Selected Writings of Jefferson,* 566–70.

29. Compare Tocqueville's prescription in *Democracy in America,* 1:7.

30. G. K. Chesterton, *What I Saw in America* (London: Hodder and Stoughton, 1922), 7.

31. David Carlin, "Let Them Eat Cake: A Love Letter to Multiculturalists," *Commonweal*, 23 April 1993, 9–10.

32. Maxine Hong Kingston, *The Woman Warrior* (New York: Vintage, 1975); Carlos Bulosan's *America Is from the Heart*, originally published in 1943, was reprinted by the University of Washington Press in 1973.

33. For some suggestions, see my essay "Tocqueville and Responsible Parties: Individualism, Partisanship and Citizenship in America," in *Challenges to Party Government*, ed. John K. White and Jerome Mileur (Carbondale: Southern Illinois University Press, 1992), 190–211.

Chapter 8

The Virtues of Multiculturalism

Anne Norton

If democracy is rule of the people, then we confront, in practice, not democracy but democracies: the rule of different peoples, each people ruling in its own way, each rule bearing the marks of particular pasts, particular conflicts, particular aspirations. We concern ourselves here not with Democracy, but with democracy in America.

When Edmund Burke, the defender of both English tradition and American revolution, looked to the future of America, he foresaw an English nation. "It is the English Constitution, which, infused through the mighty mass, pervades, feeds, unites, invigorates, vivifies every part of the empire, even down to the minutest member." "English privileges have made it all that it is; English privileges alone will make it all that it can be." America would grow, it would change, it might "put the full breast of its youthful exuberance to the mouth of its exhausted parent" but it would remain English, bound not only by adherence to "liberty according to English ideas and on English principles," but also by "the close affection which grows from common names, from kindred blood."[1]

For Burke, peoples were made on the land, in the habits of daily life. They shared a common experience in the flesh, a common ancestry, common roots. History was ancestry. History was a constitution written in the flesh. History was memory.[2]

> In America, the English may have
> . . . planted England with a stubborn trust.
> But the cleft dust was never English dust.[3]

"The land was ours before we were the land's," as Robert Frost wrote, and we have yet to grow into it. We are ruled not as Burke would have us, by habit and unconscious practice, but by the practiced conviction that change might be for the better and that, therefore, the unexamined life is not worth living. The Americans who bred and taught me, my friends and enemies, those I see on television and those I pass on the street, have uncommon names and well-mixed blood. We look not to an English past, but to a various and diverse future.

No people can mistake history for memory in the simplest sense. Little of what we remember as a nation lives in our separate memories. Most of what we take for our history is foreign to our private memories and personal experiences. The second birth into civility that, in Rousseau's words, "from a stupid and unimaginative animal makes an intelligent being and a man" also alters our being in time.[4] In becoming citizens we acquire a form of being that extends beyond the limits of our separate bodies. Our private memories are supplemented by public and political histories. Insofar as we are citizens, we take those histories for common memory.

For Americans, the taking of history for memory has required that we replace the pious fictions of ancestor-worship with acts of democratic imagination. In order to take history for memory, we have been obliged to turn from the dictatorship of the flesh to a thoughtful election of our pasts.

Most Americans cannot assimilate national histories to the memories of our ancestors. My ancestors, peasants from every backward corner of Europe, did not touch this land until the late nineteenth century. One would have to go nearly back to Adam to find any link between these and Washington, or "Plymouth Rock and all that inbred landlord stock."[5] Yet Washington and Winthrop, Mather and Williams, figure in my histories. These are my people. We are bound together by name, imagination, and desire. I have elected to have a history in common with these, to mark these, foreign to my ancestry in the flesh, as my progenitors.

The opponents of multiculturalism would have me confine my ideal ancestry, my imagined history, to Europe. Why? These alone are not adequate to the constitution of my nationality. My nationality is constituted in the works of W. E. B. Du Bois as well as those of James Madison, in the words of Langston Hughes as well as those of Walt Whitman, in the acts of Osceola as well as those of John Marshall. If I, as an American with no English ancestry, have a past in England, I see no reason why I should not have a past in Africa, a past in Asia.

After all, I do, like my country, have a past in Asia. My father was a naval officer who served two tours of duty in Vietnam. While he was in Vietnam, my family lived in a suburban neighborhood in Orange County. That neighborhood is now called "Little Vietnam." Between those two tours of duty, we lived in Bangkok. I learned the Ramayana, acquired a taste for mangoes and unripe coconut, and saw the workings of imperialism at school and on the streets. Like my country, I have a past in Asia.

What Hannah Arendt called "the Europe-determined world of the United States" is not large enough for Emerson, Whitman, or Longfellow, for the revelations of the Mormons or the cadences of Gullah speech.[6] Emerson and Thoreau gave themselves a past in India. The Randolphs prided themselves on their descent from the woman Vachel Lindsay called "Our Mother, Pocahontas."[7] Those who took it upon themselves to create not merely a new nation, but a new world order, refused the boundaries of a "Europe-determined world" for Locke's more expansive vision of America.

What we debate here is neither multiculturalism nor democracy: it is the constitution of democracy in America—not the geographic or demographic nation, but the ideal and temporal nation, the nation in history. We—we multiculturalists—do indeed aim at remaking those ideal and temporal boundaries. We have found elements of the American past in Africa, in Asia, and in American cultures preceding the arrival of the Europeans. We recognize that the histories and the canons that have occupied places of privilege in the American academy and in American popular culture do not do justice to America.

I argue—in terms that accord with the values the opponents of multiculturalism profess—that multiculturalism does more than justice to America. Multiculturalism does America good. It secures virtues we have at our best, and presents obstacles and correctives to vices we have at our worst. It offers us an invitation to reclaim ancient virtues.

Democracy in America has certain modern, bourgeois virtues that I would like to praise. The first is responsibility.

The pretense that history is the objective record of "what happened" is at best evidence of a naivete inappropriate to a scholar. When we write our histories we are engaged in a constitutional enterprise. We choose which aspects of the past we will regard as constitutional. We designate those historical moments when we (as a people) have been—and when we have failed to be—true to our word.

We multiculturalists take the second enterprise—the memory of our faults—to be as important to our constitution as the first. We cannot have the histories of our choosing. Honor forces us to acknowledge our sins and our failings as a people. Yet though we cannot have the histories of our choice, we do have a choice among histories. We choose what in the past we will remember, record, recall.

Justice may not end with paying one's debts, but assuredly it begins there. Insofar as it reminds us of the contributions and (let us not mince words here) the suffering of subaltern groups in America, multiculturalism holds us to an ethic of responsibility, it calls us to account. In doing so, we perform for the nation the service Socrates performed for the Athenian citizen. "I shall question and cross-examine him, and if I find that he does not possess virtue, but says he does, I shall rebuke him for scorning the things that are of most importance and caring more for what is of less worth."[8]

In calling ourselves to account, we bear witness to what we wish to become, what we have been, and the space between them. We engage in a democratic automachia, we become "self-made men." It is this enterprise that makes our culture more than "the dead hand of the past." It is this enterprise that makes us more than "the booby heirs," as Randolph said, of an illustrious lineage in decline. This activity makes us founders: authors of ourselves and our nation.

When we reduce our culture to an inheritance we diminish both the founders and ourselves. We deny the founders' ability to make a nation capable of overcoming itself. We deny their ability to surpass themselves. We refuse the authority the Constitution ascribes to us. We deny the possibility that we may constitute a new world order. When he lost faith with the republic, Herman Melville wrote:

> The Founders' dream will flee.
> Age after Age will be
> What Age after Age has been.
> (From man's changeless heart their way they win.)[9]

That is no democratic faith.

Democratic citizens place their faith in change. The democratic project entails faith in the capacity of citizens to put an end to the rule of history, to take upon themselves the work of providence, to become their own creators. They will not be what age after age has been. They will be the authors of a new world order. They have another bourgeois virtue. They are inventive.

Democratic citizens not only invent themselves, they endeavor to remake the world. Imagination and the capacity to invent oneself anew, to make a new world order on the foundations of the old, bottom the American constitutional enterprise. Those who would link democracy to capitalism should look to these virtues, for they link "the free market" to the commonplace practices of free peoples enlisted in the constitutional enterprise of self-overcoming.

Those who commend the competitive nature of "the free market" should not attempt to silence debates over the canon.

Opposition to multiculturalism attempts to limit our knowledge of alternatives, to constrain our writing of history, to constrain our reading, to impose upon us a cultural and canonical hierarchy that is not subject to question. This position is inconsistent with many works in the canon it purports to defend. It removes from "Western Political Thought" the very virtue that they errantly suppose unique to it: the capacity for critique.

The opponents of multiculturalism desire the illusion of a culture of consensus, without differences, without division. Cultures are constituted in debate as well as in consensus. Those who oppose themselves to multiculturalism, arguing for adherence to a traditional canon, desire the illusion of a culture that remains constant and unchanging. They are permitted to believe this possible only while they remain ignorant of the history they purportedly prize.

Those who study the canon learn early on that its content has changed with time and context. We see the Presocratics fall in and out of favor, we see Maimonides forgotten and remembered. We see Aristotle contend with Plato, and Aristophanes ridicule him. We see Pope mock Dryden. We forget Filmer. There are, in America, generations who read Calhoun and generations who neglect him. Winthrop and Mather, Henry and Taylor, Webster and Clay, Adams and Dewey, are sometimes read, sometimes honored, sometimes forgotten.

The opponents of multiculturalism do no more justice to the texts they profess to honor. The works within even the most hidebound conceptions of the canon direct their readers outside the boundaries the opponents of multiculturalism would have us observe. Those who read the *Symposium* or *The Bacchae* find in those works elements of an unfamiliar, often alien culture. Those elements they find familiar—men in drag, for example—may be no less disturbing to traditionalists. Neither Athens nor Jerusalem can be called a wholly Western place. Those who read those works as an inheritance, adhering to an imagined Greece as a remembered place, will find that Plato and Herodotus direct them beyond it, to a deference for Egypt and Minoan Crete. Weber and Hegel, Nietzsche and Kojève, would have their readers look to their future in China and Japan. The refusal of multiculturalism requires its followers to be deaf to the teachings of the texts they read.

If it were possible to isolate a body of works whose claims to greatness would remain unexamined—or whose greatness would remain unequalled—

we would have occasion for shame and sorrow. The belief that we can neither examine nor surpass the works that we venerate marks a lapse of faith, a failure of nerve. In it we declare that we cannot be, as a people, greater than we have been.

An unreflecting deference to an unexamined past entails a refusal of the duties of democracy. Rather than attempting to secure the blessings of liberty to ourselves and our posterity, we would endeavor to deprive our posterity of the qualities they require to rule themselves, to constitute themselves, in the most fundamental sense. That is no democratic education.

The opposition to multiculturalism not only stifles democratic virtues, it feeds—and feeds upon—democratic vices. The opponents of multiculturalism, in their disdain for the work of African Americans, Latinos, women, and others (many others), evince a primitive majoritarianism. They bow down to Randolph's "King Numbers."

A more demanding democracy requires that merit matter more than majorities. Unless you wish to make the argument that merit belongs only to the works of—whom? Europeans? whites? men? men writing before the twentieth century?—considerations of merit will produce . . . multiculturalism.

The opponents of multiculturalism are much given to charges that women and minorities are attempting to find a place in the canon (or the curriculum) without merit. These charges would be more just were they reversed. In assuming that politics alone could make a place for women and people of color in the canon, the opponents of multiculturalism assume that merit could not possibly belong to them. The refusal to reexamine the canon is the issue of either an ignorant complacency or a desire to maintain an unearned privilege.

Multiculturalism encourages the bourgeois virtues of responsibility and invention, the valued (and profitable) practices of competition and self-making. Multiculturalism requires that honors be earned, and distinctions given on the basis of merit.

Certain vices Tocqueville saw in the American democracy—a relentless tendency to mediocrity, the tyranny of the majority—may be ameliorated by multiculturalism. Those who fear that multiculturalism will exacerbate sectarian hostilities would do well to recall *Federalist* 10. Madison looked not to the muting but to the multiplication of sects and interests to diminish the hazards of faction and the tyrannical potential of the majority.

I have argued that multiculturalism tends to preserve democratic virtues and tends to diminish democratic vices. I would like to make another claim:

that multiculturalism may enable us to recover certain virtuous practices democracies have neglected: magnanimity, friendship, and learning.

In one form, often seen among the religious, magnanimity reveals itself in the generous excess of mercy and forgiveness. In the form of a martial patriotism, it sparks unnecessary, irrational heroism. In its constitutional form, magnanimity sets itself against the limits of history. This is the ambition that looked not to secure the once-established rights of British subjects, but rather to create a new world order. This is a virtue surpassing responsibility. From this virtue comes the desire for a polity where "justice rolls down like water, and righteousness like a mighty stream." This is a virtue of excess.

Aspects of multiculturalism cultivate this virtue. By drawing attention to the limits of history, by calling people to account and prompting them (in the well-used rhetoric of the jeremiad) to overcome themselves, multiculturalists enlist themselves in an admirably excessive project. The desire to include all, to comprehend all, has animated the projects of Lewis and Clark, NASA, the Library of Congress, and the land grant universities. Madison's vision of security in size and multiplicity, no less than Whitman's poetry, testifies to an American faith in the virtues of excess.

There are dangers in these excesses. Lockean universalism and a disposition to democratic evangelism have led to conquest and colonialism. An appetite for learning can become a passion for collection. Nietzsche saw this as one of the defects of modernity. "The modern man carries inside him an enormous heap of indigestible knowledge-stones that occasionally rattle together in his body."[10] Such people are always acquiring knowledge that they never make their own. The recognition that historical learning must be made one's own, however, leaves the question of what may be one's own unanswered. The example of those who are to be born posthumously and those who are nurslings of older ages suggests that neither nationalism nor a simple linear chronology can determine the limits of what may come to be one's own.

The second virtue we should cultivate more carefully is friendship. The ancients had a high regard for friendship; moderns have neglected it. In friendship, difference is understood not as in tension with community, but as the very basis for it. Common sense and experience apprise us of our inadequacies. We turn to others to supply our lack.

We should, however, be attracted to difference not only by need, but by desire. Friendships are formed in the desire for more knowledge: the knowledge possessed by a friend, or common desire for knowledge that surpasses them both. Friendships are formed from the desire for more beauty, more virtue, more instances of the sublime. Those who study difference—and the different—may be similarly moved. Neither friendship nor multiculturalism requires one to abandon one's peculiar virtues. What they offer is an invitation to recognize virtue for its own sake: because it is good, not because it is one's own.

Multiculturalists know that the study of difference is no simple undertaking. We have been among the sternest critics of the Enlightenment. Yet I think we who are critical of the Enlightenment tradition advance its project more loyally than its partisans. Multiculturalists do not pretend to an understanding of history that is definitive, comprehensive, singularly authentic, or entirely objective. (They thus have a greater claim to honesty than those academics whose startling hubris has made such claims commonplace.) Yet they approach these ends—whose impossibility they acknowledge—more nearly than previous histories. They present a more comprehensive recollection of the past. Theirs is a representation of the past less subject to the interests and preferences of the powerful, more fully representative of past conditions, events, and forms of life. Their histories acknowledge their incompletion. They invite those who read them to pursue what is missing. They invite alternative interpretations. They demand that the reader abandon the passivity of the disciple for the activity of the scholar.

The academy that multiculturalists advance is obliged to question the composition of its canons, the completeness and the objectivity of its histories, to look again at neglected—and venerated—works and question their merits. These are the ordinary duties of the scholar. The nation that multiculturalists advance is obliged to become mindful of its temporal and ideal boundaries, to consider what it has been, what it is, and what it wills itself to become. These are the practices of constitutional democracy.

What then prompts fears of multiculturalism? Is America so small that it cannot contain these differences? Is the canon's claim to merit so slight that it cannot withstand question or scrutiny? If so we need a greater nation, and a greater canon.

Notes

1. Edmund Burke, *Speech on Conciliation with the Colonies,* ed. Jeffrey Hart (Chicago: Henry Regnery, 1964), 139, 141, 57, 137. As the matter of Burke's speech suggests, however, much variety went into the making of that seemingly uniform England. One might also consider Daniel Defoe's poem "The True-born Englishman."

2. Burke recognized, however, that historians, politicians, and peoples choose between histories. In the *Reflections on the Revolution in France,* Burke castigated the French revolutionaries for choosing the wrong history.

3. Stephen Vincent Benet, "Invocation," in *John Brown's Body* (New York: Rinehart and Company, 1941). Benet writes of America:

> I think that I have seen you, not as one,
> But clad in diverse semblances and powers.

4. "D'un animal stupide et borne, fit un etre intelligent et un homme." Jean-Jacques Rousseau, *Du Contrat Social,* ed. Ronald Grimsley (Oxford: Oxford University Press, 1972), 119.

5. Vachel Lindsay, "Bryan, Bryan, Bryan, Bryan," in *Selected Poems of Vachel Lindsay,* ed. Mark Harris (New York: Macmillan, 1963), 124.

6. I have in mind Emerson's poem "Brahma" and his other references to Indian and Persian thought, Longfellow's poem "Hiawatha," and the scriptures of the Church of Latter Day Saints that give Jesus Christ a past in America. The quotation from Hannah Arendt comes from *The Origins of Totalitarianism* (New York: Harcourt Brace Jovanovich, 1979), 191.

7. Vachel Lindsay, "Our Mother, Pocahontas," in *Selected Poems,* 115–17. For Lindsay, in this poem, American identity entails a refusal of Europe.

> We here renounce our Saxon blood.
> Tomorrow's hopes, an April flood
> Come roaring in. The newest race
> Is born of her resilient grace.
> We here renounce our Teuton pride;
> Norse and Slavic boasts have died:
> Italian dreams are swept away,
> And Celtic feuds are lost today.

Robert Frost echoes this argument in "The Gift Outright," the poem he read at Kennedy's Inauguration.

8. Plato, *The Apology,* trans. Harold North Fowler (Cambridge: Harvard University Press, 1977), 109.

9. Herman Melville, "The Conflict of Convictions," in *Battle Pieces* (Amherst: University of Massachusetts Press, 1972), 17.

10. Friedrich Nietzsche, *The Use and Abuse of History* (Indianapolis: Bobbs Merrill, 1957), 23.

Chapter 9

Multiculturalism and American Liberal Democracy

James Ceaser

Practical inquiry in political science focuses on the question of how different causes contribute to the maintenance or destruction of various forms of government. These causes include such factors as the character of the economic system, the arrangement of political institutions, and the kinds of political and intellectual doctrines that prevail in society. The centrality of the concern about the form of government (or the regime) stems from the fact that the regime is the "house" or structure in which a people lives. As such, it helps account for the quality of life of any people and for the chances it may have to survive and prosper.

The "ism" at the end of multiculturalism suggests that, like certain other "ism" terms used to define a doctrine in political life, multiculturalism is a kind of ideology. A *political* analysis of multiculturalism, such as I propose here, should therefore explore the consequences of this ideology for the maintenance or destruction of liberal democratic government in the United States. Does multiculturalism function to support or undermine American liberal democracy? If multiculturalism works to undermine American liberal democracy, does it support some alternative form of government? What would that alternative be, would it be viable in the United States, and would it be preferable to a liberal democracy? To answer these questions, we must seek first to define the key terms, beginning with multiculturalism itself.

What Is Multiculturalism?

An older and perhaps literal meaning of a multicultural system refers to the situation in which a number of different "peoples" or "nationalities" live together under the same government. Under this conception, the question of establishing a viable multicultural state is that of how to accommodate

139

different peoples and secure for them—as one possible solution—a degree of recognition and autonomy while still providing for an adequate conception of national unity. This question has a long history in political science and was a subject of study in imperial Rome as well as in the Austro-Hungarian empire. It is of obvious concern in states today that contain identifiable national groups living in distinct territories. In some instances, schemes of federalism or regional government have been developed to provide varying degrees of autonomy for subnational groups, as in the cases, for example, of Switzerland, Belgium, Canada, and Spain. In other instances, governments have attempted to solve the challenge of a multiplicity of peoples by ignoring or repressing these differences. A survey of the different cases in this area would almost certainly demonstrate no single "best rule," as the character of each situation is so distinct.

This older question has little to do, however, with the intellectual doctrine known as "multiculturalism" in the United States. Oddly, this elementary point seems to have escaped many political theorists, who move from the older and more literal meaning of the term to its American case. Thus, in a recent and widely read book on multiculturalism entitled *Multiculturalism and "The Politics of Recognition,"* which consists of a long essay by the Canadian political theorist Charles Taylor followed by commentaries by a number of American scholars, the authors become so interested in their theoretical inquiries that they hardly pause to notice the vastly different political situations they are addressing in both countries.[1] Canada faces the traditional issue of two peoples in the same nation, while the problems in America are of an entirely different sort. The groups counted as "cultures" in the American context (according to the book's editor, Amy Gutmann) include "African Americans, Asian Americans, Native Americans, and women."[2] Excepting the case of a few Native American tribes, none of these "cultures" is seeking a separate region and government where it would exercise juridical sovereignty and live as a partially distinct political society. The inclusion of "women" on Gutmann's list of "cultures" renders any such notion highly impracticable: No traditional conception of "peoples" or "cultures" has ever divided men and women into distinct "peoples," and no society would be able to long survive if such peoples were physically separated.

The slogan of our day that American intellectuals have helped export to the rest of the world is "multiculturalism"—or, for those who prefer the more philosophical title, "the politics of difference." Multiculturalism is being addressed everywhere in the international republic of letters—in symposia, books, and in-depth essays. It has been identified by some as the major ideology of Western intellectuals in the wake of the collapse of communism. Yet inside America, where multiculturalism seems on the surface to be the strongest, it is also the most difficult to define or characterize. It has been used to designate policies as mild as those that would require students to learn more about nonmainline European groups and as controversial as plans to eliminate study of the "canon" of Western thought or schemes to transform the Constitution in order to guarantee political representation for various minority groups.

Multiculturalism in the United States, for the purposes of this essay, will be taken in one or another of its stronger senses. So let us remind ourselves—as if most in the arts or academia today need to be reminded!—what American multiculturalism means as an intellectual "ism." Citing some examples might prove instructive. On college campuses today, proponents of multiculturalism can regularly be found demanding that more women and "people of color" be hired on the faculty to overcome the "male, Eurocentric" bias of the current education system. Multiculturalism here refers to different biological groups reputed to hold different value systems. In the art world, in 1992 there was a major "multicultural" exhibit at the Whitney Museum in New York in which one requirement for inclusion was that the art focus on the experience of being "marginalized." White males who visited the museum were asked to wear buttons proclaiming their guilt. The exhibit included—as an example of art—a famous television videotape made by an observer at the scene (named Holiday) in which Rodney King (a black man) is shown being beaten by four white Los Angeles policemen. In the words of the museum's curator, "There's a long history of art showing us something about the world, and the Holiday tape adds a new dynamic to that tradition."[3]

If these examples reveal something of the character or "spirit" of multiculturalism in America, can we now give it a more precise definition? Unfortunately, this is difficult, as the term itself often hides or conceals its real meaning. Just as it was once said of the Holy Roman Empire that it was neither Holy nor Roman, nor in its later stages an empire, so it should be said of American multicultural theory that it is neither multi, nor cultural, nor at this stage genuinely theoretical.

1. Let me develop each of these points, starting with the claim that multiculturalism is not essentially "multi," or "plural." It is on the contrary binary, or dualistic. The main structure of the theory—the categorization schema under which it "constructs" the world—lays everything out on a binary grid based on the distinction between the Oppressor and the Oppressed, or (to use the current jargon) between the "Hegemon" and the "Other." This binary distinction lies at the core of high-brow multicultural discourse in America. If ordinary political scientists have not yet met the Other, they should get prepared to do so, for She will surely be making her debut in professional journals like the *American Political Science Review,* no doubt fortified by a panoply of regression equations.

The Hegemon-Other distinction has been aptly defined and sketched by Charles Taylor. Those with the "hegemonic power" possess above all the power to bestow or to fail to bestow recognition. The failure to recognize another culture "can inflict a grievous wound, saddling its victims with a crippling self-hatred."[4] The victim—misrecognized and marginalized—is the "Other," the "voice" that is submerged. This same distinction is made by Iris Marion Young, author of the influential *The Politics of Difference.* According to Young, the pervasive experience of America is that of "cultural imperialism," defined as a situation in which "the dominant meanings of society render the particular perspective of one's group invisible at the same time as they stereotype one's group and mark it out as the Other."[5]

Every ideology or discourse contains a standard for determining honor and distributing praise and blame ("valorizing" and "devalorizing," to use the current jargon). The system of honor in multicultural theory derives from this binary structure of thought. The "Other," as anyone who reads the literature in this field will appreciate, is more than a term of description; it is a term of distinction. Other is the one who, having had her "voice" silenced for so long, will now at last be heard, while Hegemon, having misrecognized her, should now be silent. The two chief passions that multiculturalism attempts to foster derive from this distinction. These passions are supine contrition (on the part of the Hegemon) and aggressive resentment (on the part of the Other). These are exactly the passions that the exhibition at the Whitney Museum was meant to stimulate.

Despite, therefore, its blistering critique of American society, multiculturalism is at heart a curiously upbeat and melioristic ideology. It is designed, somehow, to reverse the awful situation it describes. The discourse of multiculturalism is strangely dependent on contemporary "liberal" (i.e., mildly leftist) thought, or at any rate on the tolerance and compassion that this thought has tended to promote. This dependency is easily seen from the fact that if the hegemonic culture actually acted in the way it is depicted—if the Hegemon behaved with confidence as an oppressor—it would use its power to suppress the Other. But while the Hegemon frequently does act to maintain his power—which is what lends some plausibility to the discourse—one objective of multicultural discourse is to induce the Hegemon to act in just the opposite way and yield his stronger place—to "roll over" and to assume the (standard) academic position of apologizing first and asking permission second. (Hegemony should be made of sterner stuff!) Only, therefore, where one may presuppose a strong underlying sentiment of compassion or guilt, a characteristic sentiment of a powerful element inside of all liberal democratic societies, will multicultural discourse have the desired effect of eventually defeating the Hegemon. Multiculturalism thus has a symbiotic relationship to the compassionate strand of liberalism, which is why it fares so well on many university campuses.

Although the primary criterion of categorization in multiculturalism is binary and not multi, a multi or plural dimension does play a secondary role. *After* the societal pie has been divided into its two large pieces (the Hegemon and the Other), multicultural theory goes on to split the "Other" into a multiplicity of "cultures." In public discourse, proponents of multiculturalism often allow the binary distinction to fade into the background (it sounds too harsh), preferring instead to speak of tolerance among a variety of different cultures. It is by means of this rhetorical technique that proponents of multiculturalism succeed in leaving the impression that their discourse is fundamentally "multi." The subordination of the category of multiplicity to that of the binary distinction is nonetheless easily observed. Thus, the multiplicity of cultures (which is presented as a nice thing) is only admitted to exist in the category of the Other, not in the category of the Hegemon. The Other is always plural, a veritable cornucopia of skin pigmentations, linguistic groups, and alternative sex preferences: blacks, women, Asians, Latinos, Amerindians, gays, lesbians, and so on. Meanwhile, the Hegemon for all practical purposes is always an undifferentiated one: the white, or the white European, or the white European-descendant males, or the Anglo white European descendant males—or what have you. Lost, somewhere, in the category of the Hegemon are all those subtle shades of white that exist among Minnesotans of Norwegian, and Finnish, and Swedish origin, not to speak of the differences between the blond Aryans and the various groups whom the father of racist theory, Arthur de Gobineau, once classified as the "rubbish" *(détritus)* of Europe dumped on our shores: the Irish, Germans (mostly unpure), and Italians.

To allow the Hegemon to be plural might, of course, break down the whole structure of the ideology. For if the Hegemon were plural, then it too would contain a multiplicity of cultures, some of which would certainly have enjoyed the distinction of being oppressed and misrecognized. This admission would call into question the claim that only groups inside the marginalized Other are "cultures" that merit recompensation.

The primacy of the binary (Hegemon-Other) over the multi in multiculturalism can again be seen in instances when, for example, someone from a cultural category designated objectively as Other does not share the multicultural doctrine of marginalization. Multiculturalism then assigns such people to the status of nonbeing by the claim that such a person is not "really" what he or she is. Try, for example, to recommend a woman for a women's studies program who is not a feminist and see how quickly the concern for "diversity" is redefined to be understood in a "broader context." Or consider the racial status among multiculturalists of African-American Supreme Court Justice Clarence Thomas. Such persons, their gender or color notwithstanding, are considered as "inauthentic."

What is the source of this binary schema of Hegemon and Other? It seems doubtful that it reflects a natural division. No anthropologist to my knowledge has ever recorded indigenous peoples in their native habitat discoursing about "Hegemons and Others" (though they do frequently hold to some such distinctions as "one's own" and "foreign.") Multicultural categories are thus, in today's preferred language, "cultural constructs"—indeed, constructs of rather recent origin. Multiculturalism is the direct heir, transferred onto the American scene, of a species of modern philosophical thought. This is the view of proponents of multiculturalism itself. Turning once again to Iris Marion Young: She finds that the source of the idea of "difference" (or multiculturalism) lies in a powerful critique of rationalist enlightenment thought that was made by Theodore Adorno and Jacques Derrida (originally, in fact, by Martin Heidegger). This critique—the reader must forgive me the abstractions here—holds that "reason" or the "logic of identity" reflects an "urge to think things together [and] to reduce them to unity. . . . Reason seeks essence, a single formula that classifies concrete particulars as inside or outside a category." This way of thinking misses multiplicity ("denies or represses difference") and constructs a political field in which there is imperialism and marginalization. Cornel West, while not making the connection quite as exclusive, emphasizes "the oppressive deeds done under the ideological aegis of the notions" of "necessity, universality, rationality, objectivity, and transcendentality."[6]

Reason so conceived is the source of our deepest political problem today: repression and the marginalization of difference. Repression in liberal societies is all the more insidious for being "hidden" and done under the cover of universal principles. According to Young, "The irony of the logic of identity is that by seeking to reduce the differently similar to the same, it turns the merely different into the absolutely other." Translated into politics, rationalism results in the various "isms" of repression endemic to America, such as sexism and racism—in short, the very dichotomous or binary way of thinking that gives us the distinction between the Hegemon and the Other. Here then is the startling (and "ironic") conclusion. The universal ideas of American liberalism become the sources of modern repression. Enlightenment thought, including the thought of America's "republican fathers," "explicitly justified the restriction of citizenship to white men on the grounds that the unity of the nation depended on homogeneity and dispassionate reason."[7]

All this abstract talk—"essences," "categories," and the "universal versus the particular"—may perhaps serve to excite a few of the philosophically minded, but it is clearly too bloodless to move the mass of intellectuals. It requires a more concrete discourse, which is now being supplied by the fields of American studies and American history. In her recent presidential address to the Organization of American Historians, Joyce Appleby proclaimed that it is now time for American historians to adopt a new "narrative" that is faithful to the premises and methods of "multicultural history." The old narrative taught that the fundamental principles of liberty and natural rights were antidotes to oppression, and that slavery, racism, and unequal treatment derived from other parts of the American experience. Yet according to multicultural history, it is America's fundamental principles that cause or are inseparable from oppression. The ideals of liberty and equality, far from being antidotes to oppression and racism, are now more or less bound up with it. The core American creed, according to Richard Sennett, makes up a nationalist "myth," which "legitimates attacks on peoples whose lives are different."[8] Appleby, while not denying the "enviable freedoms we Americans enjoy," wants to help us see the "oppression exercised by [our] omnipresent cultural model." America's dedication to the "cultural artifact" of its revolutionary principles, she contends, has covered up our real experience and prevented us from appreciating our "authentic diversity."[9]

There is perhaps another source of multiculturalism. Charles Taylor has traced it to the ideology of third-worldism that was articulated by Franz Fanon.[10] Third-worldism is a racialist restatement of Lenin's theory of imperialism, which therefore makes multiculturalism a sort of Marxism with a cultural face. Some have accordingly sought to trace multiculturalism back to Marx and even further to the psychology of recognition as discussed by Hegel and ultimately Rousseau.[11] Whatever the source, however, multiculturalism is a pure artifact of dead white European male thinking, and it can be reconstructed from the works that appear on the multicultural Index, otherwise known as "the Canon."

It may be worthwhile to pause a moment to speculate about whether its binary schema manages to help us capture what is "out there" in the world, assuming one can speak of a social reality that is not merely constructed. In some measure, of course, the multicultural narrative has focused on an important reality. Without the fact of European colonialism, the fact that whites enslaved blacks purely on racial grounds, the fact that Europeans either conquered or exterminated the Amerindians, the fact that males have largely dominated females, and the fact that race (as distinct from intracaucasian ethnicity) has been used at one time or another as the basis for official (legal) discrimination in the United States—without all of these facts, it is almost inconceivable that so many well-educated people could find so powerful an appeal in multiculturalism.

These facts stand on their own. The question is whether they add up to the full-blown doctrine of multiculturalism. One may doubt whether they do. The binary schema of multiculturalism produces some remarkable distortions. It suffers, in fact, from all of the limitations of a schema that overlooks, if the term may be used, "difference." The dualistic approach leads multiculturalism to miss what a more supple and pragmatic theory could easily detect. There is almost no form of oppression said to occur between the Hegemon and the Other that has not occurred—and fairly recently—among groups within the category of the Hegemon (and, for that matter, among groups inside the category of the Other). White tribes have decimated each other with as much savagery and fury as they have "peoples of color"; and "peoples of color" have oppressed each other with no less vigor than have white people. Within this decade alone, there has been ethnic cleansing among whites in the former Yugoslavia and genocide among blacks in Rwanda. Within this century, white Europeans have visited upon other white Europeans a degree of savagery that probably knows no parallel in human history. If there is any one single indicator of a common human nature, is it not in the universal tendency of peoples of all colors and stripes to oppress and abuse one another?[12]

Distorting the record of history may be the least of the costs of this binary mode of categorization, for every sophisticated person today knows that one man's historical record is merely another woman's "narrative." Yet a distortion of experience may prevent us from dealing with the concrete reality with which we must deal in America today. The doctrinairism of multiculturalism stands in the way of examining the means by which various groups have been able to move in America from a marginalized status in the past to achieve a place of approximate equality today. Analyzing how such changes took place might then be compared with the current policy approaches advocated by proponents of multiculturalism today. Allowing, as one should, for the uniqueness of each political situation, one could then at least begin an informed discussion of which strategies offer the best prospects for improving the lot of burdened groups and for maintaining the stability of liberal democracy.

2. Multiculturalism, I also noted, is misnamed because the movement itself is not cultural. Cultures are not (usually) multicultural, and multiculturalism is not (quite) a culture.

On the first point, cultures are often proud of their superiority and hostile to other cultures. Cultures are, in a word, often intolerant, not only of other cultures, but of individual rights as well. They can be closed, dividing the world very clearly between an "us" and a "them," between the civilized and the barbarian.

As for multiculturalism itself, it hardly seems that it can qualify as a full or authentic culture. On what would such a culture be based? Multiculturalists have a jargon of their own, but scarcely a genuine language; they are filled with passionate convictions, but these are not quite the same as a common set of religious beliefs. The only possible basis on which multiculturalism could become a culture would be on the ground of a belief in the poles of the Hegemon and the Other. Yet not even multiculturalists, apparently, think that these abstract categories carry the "thickness" to be able to bear the weight of a culture. Cultures are almost always described as involving something deep-seated and rooted, something that evolves and is not formed overnight. (Still, a good part of modern feminist "culture" does take its direction from this kind of thought; the deepest element of this culture is the "experience" of victimization, which has been heightened by the philosophy of "difference.")

At most it appears that multiculturalism is a kind of add-on or overlay designed to modify other cultures. Each culture is to remain fully itself, but also (somehow) to slip on an outer jacket of multiculturalism. Thus, to qualify as a culture in the multicultural club, each culture must "take the pledge" and, if need be, change itself by agreeing to respect the worth of every other culture (as well, most add, as the rights of individuals). Thus, Chinese culture must give up its traditionally hostile views about women, Chicanos their traditionally hostile view of gays, and so forth. There is a slight difficulty here, however. Multiculturalism so conceived becomes almost a species of Eurocentric culture, for the "pledge" has grown out of a post-Enlightenment, Western intellectual movement. Why the various cultures should agree to abandon their own beliefs and accept the imperialism of the ideology of difference is never made clear. Nor are multiculturalists exactly in the best position to insist that submerged cultures really accept such pledges of tolerance, given their starting premise about the equal validity of all cultures.

One might even argue that multiculturalism dissolves any kind of genuine culture. If our only culture is the multiculture, that is, the common partaking by all Americans in all of our multiplicity of cultures—a kind of mixing in which, so to speak, you eat kosher one night, Italian the next, and Chinese (with pork fried rice) the next—what really remains of the idea of culture? In any case, is not this kind of constant "tasting" of cultures really the province of a cosmopolitan elite that is detached and sophisticated enough to delight in the customs of different peoples who themselves are not quite as sophisticated as those enjoying the diversity of customs? For if the masses were ever to adopt this mishmash as their "culture," rather than sticking predominantly to one culture, what sort of genuine or rooted cultures would remain? How far can one go in this direction without losing real cultural roots?

These alternatives represent three theoretical possibilities for the "culture" of multiculturalism. Yet the most likely result of this movement may well be none of these three, but instead the encouragement of "culturalism" pure and simple, that is, "tribalism" or "nationalism." Multiculturalism is a curious movement. If ever it becomes a mass movement, the *multi*culturalists (who preach the value of multiplicity or difference) are almost certain to be outnumbered by the culturalists (who are devoted to the beliefs of their own particular culture). The culturalists, moreover, invariably appear as more "authentic" than the multiculturalists, because the culturalists espouse their beliefs in full simplicity without the need of going through an elaborate exercise of intellectual consciousness raising. The culturalists, moreover, are "the peoples of color," as witness, for example, the Nation of Islam. Finally, the culturalists are likely to be more resolute. The multiculturalists are thus in danger of becoming the dupes of the culturalists. Many who march under the banner of multiculturalism do not believe in the "multi" at all, but merely recognize the tactical benefits to be had from joining a temporary coalition against the "Eurocentric" power structure.

The culture that comes closest to the (tolerant) multicultural idea is liberalism. Yet liberalism in its best statement is not the same thing as benign multiculturalism, however tolerant liberalism itself may be of the diversity of different cultures. American liberalism has assigned the primary public or legal identity to the individual, while it has accorded the culture or group a secondary and less formal status. Multiculturalism, while wandering all over the place in regard to its view of the individual, in the end assigns or consigns every individual to a "cultural" unit; it is finally a group philosophy. It thereby tries to raise the "cultural" unit to the first rank in our thinking about society and justice (as well, of course, as in the assignment of legal benefits). Even when it comes to rights, the multiculturalists who play the current Harvard Law School "trump" game prefer to play their card with group rights, not individual rights. They "privilege" group culture.

3. Finally, multicultural theory is not really theoretical. If it were theoretical, it would (as that word "theory" implies) examine the major categories or phenomena it claims to investigate. Yet multiculturalism is without much insight into its own central term: culture.

What is a culture? Does it refer to specific language communities, religious groups, ethnic groups, races, sexes, or what? Multiculturalism has no answer, beyond playing off various meanings of the term as they exist today. This is more of a problem in the case of the word "culture" than for almost any other word of which I am aware. For "culture" is a word that refers today to no clear "natural" phenomenon; it is not a term of common sense. Rather, it is a category with a complicated history—a term that different schools of thought have sought to capture to pursue different programs.

The imprecision that attaches today to the term allows those who use it to "play off" of all sorts of traditions without achieving any kind of coherence of thought.

There is something deeply disturbing in the existence of a whole school of thought ("multiculturalism") that is so imprecise about its own language. I offer only one example of the incoherence into which this leads many today. The use of the term "culture" in cultural anthropology was a kind of creation of Franz Boas. Boas adopted the term "culture" in an effort to argue that the primary human groupings were formed by different patterns of socialization rather than by different biological or racial characteristics. In other words, the concept of culture in anthropology was designed explicitly to replace race as that discipline's central organizing category. "Culture," Boas wrote, "is the result of innumerable interacting factors and there is no evidence that the differences between human races . . . have any direct influence upon the course of development of culture."[13]

Multiculturalists play off this idea, frequently claiming that they are speaking of different "cultural" groups in this sense. Yet to the extent they actually make use of the term for practical purposes (as in demands for cultural diversity), culture, for multiculturalism, is invariably expressed in terms of certain racial and/or biological (sexual) divisions or practices, each of which is supposed to embody something genuine and cultural. Thus the "cultures," when it comes down to it, are white males, women, gays, and "peoples of color" (African American, Asians, Amerindians, and "browns"). Latinos sometimes slip in, notwithstanding that they are not a racial group. For the most part, they are presumed brown.

But these categories eliminate some of the real elements of "cultural" diversity, even in the ordinary understanding. Racialism and biologism, for example, deny religion as a source of culture. Hegel once wrote, "Religion is the sphere wherein a people gives itself the definition of what it regards as true."[14] By this criterion, one of the most important cultural divisions in modern American society might well be between secularists and Christian fundamentalists. Yet the latter have by and large been excluded from multicultural discourse. In a recent debate of a major college faculty, a suggestion that "diversity" in the faculty should reflect this religious dimension of culture was taken by multiculturalists to be a joke. Perhaps it was intended to be. But on whom?

Meanwhile, multiculturalism ascribes status to "cultures" that have scarcely existed as such but that have been called into being by multiculturalists and bureaucrats in order to derive and confer certain benefits (such as "minority" congressional districts, proportional representation on boards, and positions on university faculties). For example, one may question in what way Asian Americans form a distinct "culture." There are, of course, Japanese Americans, Korean Americans, Chinese Americans, Cambodian Americans, and so forth. But did these groups ever constitute a single "culture," except in the mind of a few intellectuals and governmental bureaucrats? Much the same can be said of "Hispanics" or "Latinos." While (once) sharing a common language, Latinos may have little more in common with each other than the members of the various cultural groups who speak English. The Hispanic "category," as anyone who has studied this issue recognizes, is in no meaningful sense a "culture." Yet multiculturalists have invested these entities (invented circa 1970) with all the reality and dignity of those who can trace their roots to a genuine cultural tradition.

Why should one demand precision in defining culture from multicultural theory, when no one else has succeeded in giving it a satisfactory definition? This is a fair question. But much more rides on multiculturalism's conception (or lack thereof) of culture, for multiculturalism has transformed "culture" into the major category of social reality. Many important benefits are now regularly distributed according to some understanding of the term. "Culture," or "minority status," is already ensconced in a myriad of laws and public policies and is used now as a matter of course in defining legislative constituencies, in allocating jobs, and in determining how to fulfill expectations for "diversity."

What Is Liberal Democracy?

Liberal democracy is a system that (a) provides the mass of citizens with the authority to select most public officials and determine the basic direction of government policy; and (b) guarantees the protection of basic rights for all individuals, and thereby as well in some degree for different groups or corporate entities.

What are the possible relations of liberal democracy to "cultures"? Scholars have recently sketched out three basic models or possibilities: (1) the public sphere designates one culture to be privileged and makes its maintenance an official project, but still provides adequate protection for individual rights and the rights (within reason) of minority cultures; (2) the public sphere is neutral among cultures, regarding individuals (not cultures) as the primary entities in the public space; (3) the public would seek to recognize, accommodate, and publicly promote the diversity of cultures as a primary object of society, while maintaining basic protection as well for the individual and individual rights.

The actual status of the American experience, however, fits none of these models exactly. Both opponents and proponents of multiculturalism—each for their own reasons—have found it expedient to identify traditional American liberal democracy (or at any rate its ideals) with the second model of "neutrality." While there is something to this characterization (especially when compared to the other two alternatives), this model remains something of a caricature. For one thing, the idea that American liberalism is— or would wish to be—wholly "neutral" is fanciful. Anyone who thinks realistically about society knows that a notion of neutrality as between all things now claimed as "cultural" is impossible. The Constitution does not say, for example, that English is the national language of the United States (though the Constitution was written in English); but the nation is not really "neutral" about this fact.

Nor can American liberalism be said to have ever been wholly individualistic. The character of American society has always involved extensive action and interaction of groups or (sub)cultures. For example, if one reads any account of how deals for representation were decided in cities like Chicago, one quickly sees that group (or cultural, or community) considerations were always extremely important. Any notion that American life has ignored such cultural factors—or even that most have pretended to ignore them—is chimerical. It was recognized, especially at lower levels of government and within various institutions (such as political parties), that group or "cultural" considerations would in fact play an enormous role, and their influence would be enmeshed, formally and informally, in all manner of ways. The most insidious of these ways were the laws and practices involving racial discrimination against Asians, Amerindians, women, and above all African Americans.

Whatever the role of these groups, however, the national ideal, or "best statement" of American liberal democracy—not always recognized in fact, to be sure—has been one that involved formally recognizing individuals, not cultural groups, as the core of the compact of society. The highest principle was that of all persons being created equal, with the rights and privileges attaching in the first instance to individuals. Cultural groups, in this view, are seen mostly as the associations of individuals, having a secondary status. This idea is now the one that multiculturalism implicitly calls into question.

The history of constitutional law of the past half century has consisted of two basic stages. First, in order to fight against the discrimination in the lower levels of government and in all the other major institutions, there was a massive extension of the "formal" principle of color-blind individualism into local spheres and into the practices of various institutions. The extension of this principle thus came to be thought of more and more (by many) as the ideal of American liberalism, because this extension was undertaken in the name of eliminating racial injustices. It went so far, as both a legal principle and a norm, as to call into question or discredit the idea of group institutions or associations. Integration was pushed as a norm or legal requirement into ever more areas of society, in many cases beyond the preferences of majorities of nearly all cultural groups.

The various groups under this regime did not always achieve what they wanted under this principle. Color-blind (or sex-blind) legal status for individuals did not bring the progress that many hoped for. The policies based on this idea could not root out all current discrimination. Many came to believe that it was necessary to go deeper than the problem of current discrimination and deal directly with historical legacies. Justice was to be attained more by correcting matters for groups than for individuals. Again, in a slightly different vein, African Americans now began to occupy major positions of power in local governments; as they did so, they found that many of the old mechanisms once used for "recognizing" groups were not easily available to them because of the constraints of all the new formal color-blind principles. (For example, black big-city mayors did not control delegates at the party conventions or have as much say over local jobs and contracts.)

The frustration at the lack of progress under the color-blind system brought another stage of constitutional development, which began about a quarter century ago and which has dramatically modified the previous individualist model. It has done so not by relaxing the degree of legal restrictions and allowing local and informal mechanisms to reassert themselves, but instead by a model that increasingly asks the government formally to recognize certain groups or "cultures" and then to require benefits to be distributed on the basis of this cultural identity. We have thus increasingly formalized and "constitutionalized" the cultural unit. American law and practice are now pervaded by "culture"-based principles, applied and sanctioned at the very highest levels of federal and constitutional law. This last legal transformation preceded in many respects the intellectual movement of multiculturalism. But it is fair to say that more and more, multiculturalism provides the contemporary grounding for this legal regime, incorporating the entire history of civil rights into the discourse of the Hegemon and Other.

Does Multiculturalism Help American Liberal Democracy?

Will multiculturalism strengthen or weaken American liberal democracy? It is quite possible, even likely, that the multicultural movement has contributed to achieving some goals sought by previous reformers. But at what cost? That cost, I would hazard, is to undermine some of the important props of liberal democracy, without offering any coherent idea of what alternative might replace it. Consider the following liberal doctrines that are threatened by multiculturalism.

1. Multiculturalism has shifted the relationship—both legally and in our general way of thinking—between the individual and the "culture" in a way that gives far more weight to the "culture" and far less to the individual. As a sociological matter, the "cultural" element has always played a significant role, but the legal standard of individualism provided support to individuals who sought to break from a currently constituted cultural group. Today, cultural identity has been recognized in the law and enshrined in the ideological notion that we are all "cultural" animals, with "cultural" referring mostly to biologically defined criteria. Individuals in many ways—witness our college campuses—are pushed into greater "cultural" solidarity.

2. Multiculturalism has "socialized" the notion of culture itself, making it into a matter of government determination. Whatever the idea of "culture" has meant inside of American liberal democracy, it has been left in large measure for private arrangement and adjustment to define—or at any rate within local communities. Culture was something too important—or too vague—to be defined directly by the government. Shifts that took place in cultural identity thus were not officially established and did not need to be disestablished at the national level. Being "German American" might once have been considered important for everything, from artistic projects to political representation. Now, however, "cultures" are locked in by formal rules and laws, with the determinations made by various public bodies, including the Congress and the Supreme Court. This is a system that we may find difficult, if not impossible, to adjust or dismantle.

3. Multiculturalism degenerates into culturalism based largely on race and biology. The problem of integrating a diverse populace into a people possessing sufficient unity has been ignored in favor of playing up our "needs" as cultural beings. The failure to concern ourselves with creating a primary national identity—to have people feel, as Lincoln once put it, that they are "blood of the blood, and flesh of the flesh, of the men who wrote [the] Declaration"—may be an omission we shall shortly begin to rue.

4. Multiculturalism perpetuates a perverse psychology. Proof of victimization, established generally today by the possession of some biological characteristic, is the basis of any claim to honor or position. People of different groups thus vie in an unseemly process to claim that they have been oppressed—even in cases when they manifestly have not been. The real differences among various groups are thus overlooked.

5. Multiculturalism blinds us to the (or a) meaning of our own history. In multicultural history, the heart of the American experience has been one of racism and biologism. The dominant strain of the American founders' thought rejected the notion of "culture" rooted in tribal and biological principles. This thought either has been ignored or else has been twisted into a principle that somehow is said to perpetuate racism and oppression. There is something more than merely ironic in a reading of American history that embraces a new yoke of biologism while dismissing a principle that has given hope that biologism might one day be overcome.

Can multiculturalism be eradicated in a way that will avoid the extremism of a "cultural" reaction? One would like to think it could be, but this is far from certain. The time, regrettably, may soon be approaching when each person may face the choice of attempting to save his or her own "culture" first. Any victory on these terms cannot be a victory for American liberal democracy.

Notes

1. *Multiculturalism and "The Politics of Recognition": An Essay by Charles Taylor, with Commentary by Amy Gutmann, Steven C. Rockefeller, Michael Walzer, and Susan Wolf,* ed. Amy Gutmann (Princeton: Princeton University Press, 1992).

2. Amy Gutmann, "Introduction," *Multiculturalism and "The Politics of Recognition,"* 3.

3. Incidentally, the same "art" dealer who supplied the King tape to the Whitney also offered Timothy Goldman's film, from the 1992 riots in Los Angeles, which features a

(white) truck driver being pulled from a truck and beaten by three (black) men. The Whitney curators decided against using this piece of art, judging that it lacked a comparable artistic "dynamic." See Suzanne Muchnic, "King Beating Footage Comes to the Art World," *Los Angeles Times*, 10 March 1993, F8.

4. Taylor, *Multiculturalism and "The Politics of Recognition*," 25, 26.

5. Iris Marion Young, *Justice and the Politics of Difference* (Princeton: Princeton University Press, 1990), 59.

6. Cornel West, *The American Evasion of Philosophy: A Genealogy of Pragmatism* (Madison: University of Wisconsin Press, 1989), 208.

7. Young, 98, 99, 111.

8. Richard Sennett, "The Identity Myth," *New York Times*, 30 January 1994, sec. 4, p. 17.

9. Joyce Appleby, "Recovering America's Historic Diversity: Beyond Exceptionalism," *Journal of American History* 79, no. 2 (September 1992), 430, 420, 429.

10. This connection has been noted by two leading political theorists, Charles Taylor, *Multiculturalism and "The Politics of Recognition*," 65, and Thomas Pangle, *The Ennobling of Democracy* (Baltimore: Johns Hopkins University Press, 1992), 79.

11. This is the thesis of Charles Taylor, which is seemingly endorsed by other political theorists writing in the same volume, including Amy Gutmann and Michael Walzer.

12. Thomas Hobbes's famous remark about commonwealths might nearly as easily apply to "cultures": "There is scarcely a Commonwealth in the world, whose beginning can in conscience be justified" (*Leviathan*, "Review and Conclusion").

13. Franz Boas, *The Mind of Primitive Man* (New York: Macmillan, 1938), 195.

14. Georg F. Hegel, *Reason in History*, trans. Robert Hartman (New York: Macmillan, 1988), 64.

Chapter 10

Liberal Democracy, Universalism, and Multiculturalism

Marc F. Plattner

I come to this subject as someone who has had no involvement in America's internal wars over multiculturalism but who has been engaged on a daily basis in a very different struggle—the effort to expand and strengthen democracy around the world. What has struck me, however, as news from the multicultural battlefront has filtered into my consciousness, is the extent to which these two intellectual and political struggles appear to be tending in opposite directions.

On the global front, at least insofar as one is speaking of the realm of ideas, the trend clearly seems to be toward universalism, while on the domestic front there seems to be an increasing swing toward particularism. Taking a closer look at this paradoxical situation may help to illuminate the question of multiculturalism and democracy.

The most important *international* political development of the past two decades has been the global resurgence of democracy. The courageous efforts of democratic movements have brought down a host of dictatorial governments around the world—a range of brutal and squalid tyrannies including the right-wing military regimes of Latin America, the one-party states of Africa, and of course communist totalitarianism in Eastern Europe and the former Soviet Union. The success of these democratic movements has both reflected and helped further to promote the growing worldwide acceptance of certain basic principles of liberal democracy—notably, the protection of individual rights and civil liberties and the right of people to choose their governments through free and fair elections.

Now it is true that recent events have demonstrated that building workable and durable democracies is much more complex and in some ways much harder than toppling dictatorships. It is also true that with the fall of authoritarian regimes there has been a marked upsurge in ethnic strife, most

157

dramatically illustrated by the former Yugoslavia. Yet it nonetheless remains clear that the principles (if not the practice) of liberal democracy today enjoy an unparalleled global ascendancy.

Prior to their revival during the past decade, these very same principles had gone into eclipse in much of the world. In part, this was owing to the impact of a Marxist critique that disparaged liberal democratic regimes and institutions as embodying merely "formal" or "bourgeois" democracy that served as a cover for class oppression. But perhaps even more damaging was the view that the principles of liberal democracy were distinctively "Western," not simply in their origins, but in their very essence. Hence there were no valid grounds for seeking to apply them in non-Western parts of the world, especially in countries that had recently thrown off the yoke of colonialism.

The global democratic resurgence of our time would not have been possible unless men and women throughout much of the non-Western world had emphatically rejected this view. Time and again I have heard from the lips and read from the pens of people from Asia and Africa (not to mention Latin America and Eastern Europe) that they had as much right as any North American or West European to appeal to universal principles of liberal democracy. Not only that, but that they regarded it as demeaning and even racist for Westerners to imply that any lesser standards should be applied to their countries.

Let me present some examples drawn solely from articles for the publication that I edit, the *Journal of Democracy*. Here are the words of Burmese democratic leader and Nobel Peace Prize recipient Aung San Suu Kyi:

> Opponents of the movement for democracy in Burma have sought to undermine it by . . . condemning the basic tenets of democracy as un-Burmese. There is nothing new in Third World governments seeking to justify and perpetuate authoritarian rule by denouncing liberal democratic principles as alien. . . . It was predictable that as soon as the issue of human rights became an integral part of the movement for democracy, the official media would start ridiculing and condemning the whole concept of human rights, dubbing it a Western artifact alien to traditional values. . . . [But it] is a puzzlement to the Burmese how concepts which recognize the inherent dignity and the equal and inalienable rights of human beings . . . can be inimical to indigenous values. . . . The proposition that the Burmese are not fit to enjoy as many rights and privileges as the citizens of democratic countries is insulting.[1]

Next, I quote from a talk by Wuer Kaixi, one of the two principal leaders of the Chinese student demonstrations in Tiananmen Square:

In the course of the prodemocracy movement, many of my fellow students, friends and comrades, along with doctors, nurses, and men and women from all walks of life, were killed in Tiananmen Square and on Changan Avenue in Beijing.... What were they demanding? It was very simple: freedom, democracy, human rights, and the rule of law. And a *true* republic. In name, China is called a "People's Republic," but even after the revolution initiated by Sun Yatsen we have continued to be governed by a series of dynasties. These feudal, imperial rulers have denied the Chinese people their natural and fundamental human rights and freedoms.[2]

Africans seem particularly incensed at the notion that they might somehow be exempted from adherence to liberal democratic principles. Peter Anyang' Nyong'o, a Kenyan who is secretary-general of the African Political Science Association, states:

Many Westerners ... think that Africans are basically backward and cannot be judged on the basis of any universal standard. From our point of view, however, human rights are universal; the right to be ruled democratically is enshrined in the UN Charter and the Universal Declaration of Human Rights. All human beings are born equal and are endowed by their Creator with basic rights that belong to them as human beings, and not as people of this or that color, continent, sex, nationality, or religion.[3]

Here is a quote from an article by journalist Bona Malwal, a southern Sudanese now in exile from the Islamic fundamentalist dictatorship that rules his country:

Among the obstacles that Sudanese democrats must overcome, one is particularly disheartening. This is the attitude of condescension that some politicians, public officials, and other elites in the West take towards democracy in the developing world.... Just as the people of the Sudan reject the notion that democracy is suitable only for the developed, as opposed to the developing world, so should the people of the developed world help them by standing firm for democratic principles [and] refusing to deal in double standards.[4]

Finally, let me cite an article by Cameroonian political scientist Paul Ntungwe Ndue, who rails against the notion that

human rights are chimerical abstractions; culture, race, or nationality is what really counts. In the case of Africa, such rights can be trumped easily by tribal customs and the cult of the chief.... These quite simply racist doctrines, coined in order to justify dictatorships, long misled even honest people.... In reality, this dangerous illusion merely makes possible the colonization of Africa by other means. The generation of Africans that is now calling for democratic pluralism has realized this. There is no such thing as white, black, yellow, Eastern, or Western human rights; there are universal human rights, applicable to human beings as such by virtue of their universal characteristics. It is because of the universality of these rights that one part of the world feels involved when they are violated elsewhere. Their recognition and safeguarding is a matter of urgency for Africa.[5]

There has been enormous sympathy in the United States for the cause of international human rights and for the recent triumphs of democracy abroad. Yet so far as I can discern, the universalistic outlook of these Third World democrats has had virtually no resonance in our domestic debate over multiculturalism. Indeed, my guess is that many of the same people who regard themselves as supporters of a vigorous human rights policy abroad—and are horrified by ethnic conflict in the postcommunist countries—also favor the trend toward multiculturalism at home.

Whether there is a real contradiction here depends, of course, on what one means by multiculturalism. If it amounts to no more than a recognition or even celebration of cultural pluralism, then it obviously poses no fundamental challenge to liberal democracy. My children get a steady diet of this brand of multiculturalism in their schools—ethnic festivals, lessons in the contributions made by various groups, and the like. Even this benign approach can be susceptible to abuses, ranging from distortions of the historical record to the "crowding out" from the curriculum of serious instruction about America's democratic political institutions. But in principle there is certainly no incompatibility and arguably even some mutual reinforcement between democracy and this sort of cultural pluralism.

There also seems to be another, more radical strain of multiculturalism, however, which holds that any principles that lay a claim to universality are merely instruments that some cultural groups use to exert dominance over others. According to this view, the injustices that have been visited upon various minorities during the course of American history are evidence not of America's failure to live up to its democratic principles in practice, but of the spurious or defective character of those principles themselves. Although this perspective typically presents itself as a defender of the marginalized and oppressed, it has always seemed to me that its attempt to "unmask" all allegedly universal moral and political principles as nothing more than rationales for domination ultimately points toward a politics of raw power. It is a view that would be much more congenial to the perpetrators of "ethnic cleansing" in Bosnia than to the brave and beleaguered Serbian democrats in Belgrade who criticize Milosevic and his supporters for their violation of universal democratic norms.

What strikes me most forcefully about the U.S. debate over radical multiculturalism is, to use a barbarous term, how "Americocentric" it is. My sense is that most supporters of radical multiculturalism take for granted (even as they threaten to undermine) the solidity of America's liberal democratic order and the relatively nonethnic character of the American national identity. They do not really contemplate the dangers or even envisage the possibility of setting America's various ethnic groups at one another's throats, of giving rise to a serious politics of ethnic struggle, or of turning America into a truly divided society. Even in severely divided societies democracy is not necessarily impossible, and there is a growing literature in comparative political science that explores how various electoral systems and federal arrangements can help to make it work.[6] But the sad experience of democratic breakdown in such cases as Lebanon, Sri Lanka, and Nigeria's First Republic indicates the scope of the difficulty.

The relationship of ethnicity and nationalism to democracy is one of the central questions of our age, at the level of both theory and practice. I am not among those who view ethnicity and nationalism as simply atavistic expressions of particularism wholly at odds with the universalist demands of liberal democracy. To take but one example, the democratic movements in the non-Russian republics of the former Soviet Union were inevitably nationalist movements as well. Liberal democracy simply could not have worked if the former Soviet empire had remained a single political unit, any more than it could have worked in Asia and Africa if the old West European colonial empires had maintained their territorial integrity. Nationalism can take a variety of political forms, however, just as ethnicity can find political expression in many different ways. The key desideratum for democrats must be to shape nationalism and ethnicity in such a fashion that they remain compatible with liberal democracy.[7]

On the whole, I would say that the United States has been generally successful in fashioning an American nationalism tied not to "blood and soil" but to the liberal democratic principles on which this country was founded. Despite certain "nativist" strands in our history and even in our current politics, this evolving national identity has remained largely accessible to people arriving on our shores from all over the globe. Expatriates from non-Western countries who have lived in both the United States and Western Europe almost invariably remark on how much easier it is for foreigners—and especially their children—to become Americans than to become Frenchmen, Englishmen, or Germans. One can be a hyphenated American without being any the less American.

In my view the pull of Americanism is strong enough, and the ethnic identities that might be arrayed against it are attenuated enough, that multiculturalism does not in itself pose a serious threat to American society. The power and prestige of radical multiculturalism in our universities, however, is a worrisome sign that Americans may be experiencing an accelerating loss of faith in the soundness of our own liberal democratic principles—at the very moment when they are being embraced by nations around the world.

It is striking that the democratic voices from the developing world I cited earlier frequently invoke not merely contemporary United Nations documents proclaiming universal human rights but also the language of the classic eighteenth-century American formulations of these ideas. In fact, today one is far more likely to find such terms as "natural" or "inalienable" rights used by democratic thinkers or activists from Africa, Asia, or the former Soviet Union than by those from the West. Today, as people from a multitude of cultures throughout the world are expressing their support for America's liberal democratic principles, it is not only ironic but also deeply troubling that the intellectual foundations of those principles are being eroded here at home.

Notes

1. Aung San Suu Kyi, "In Quest of Democracy," *Journal of Democracy* 3 (January 1992): 5, 10–11.

2. Wuer Kaixi, "After the Massacre," *Journal of Democracy* 1 (Winter 1990): 7.

3. Peter Anyang' Nyong'o, "Africa: The Failure of One-Party Rule," *Journal of Democracy* 3 (January 1992): 94.

4. Bona Malwal, "The Agony of the Sudan," *Journal of Democracy* 1 (Spring 1990): 77, 86.

5. Paul Ntungwe Ndue, "Africa's Turn Toward Pluralism," *Journal of Democracy* 5 (January 1994): 52–53.

6. See, for example, Larry Diamond and Marc F. Plattner, eds., *Nationalism, Ethnic Conflict, and Democracy* (Baltimore: Johns Hopkins University Press, 1994).

7. See Diamond and Plattner.

Part III

Multiculturalism and Civic Education

Chapter 11

Civic Education in a Changing Society

Linda Chavez

The face of America is changing. It's becoming more diverse and complex than at any time in our history. We're no longer a white-and-black society struggling to integrate two major groups of people who have been in this country for nearly four hundred years, but a multiracial and multiethnic society in which newcomers arrive in record numbers every day. The 1980s will be remembered as a period of one of the highest levels of immigration in our nation's history. Some ten million persons immigrated to the United States in that decade, a number as great as that of the previous peak decade, 1900 to 1910.[1] The 1990s will probably see even more arrivals.

Unlike the immigrants of the early part of this century, who were primarily from Europe, the great bulk of today's immigrants—about 80 percent—come from Asia and Latin America.[2] Much has been made of this phenomenon, and many who favor restricting immigration suggest that these new Asian and Latin immigrants will be less successfully absorbed into the fabric of American society. "I know that earlier large waves of immigrants didn't 'overturn' America," says former Colorado governor Richard Lamm, "but there are . . . reasons to believe that today's migration is different from earlier flows."[3]

But, in fact, when we look at one of these groups, we find that most Hispanics are assimilating into the social, educational, economic, and language norms of this society despite the image of Hispanics portrayed in the media and perpetuated by Hispanic leaders. A few facts:

- Mexican-origin men have a higher labor-force participation rate than non-Hispanic males.[4]
- U.S.-born Hispanics have rapidly moved into the middle class. The earnings of Mexican American men are now roughly 80 percent of those of non-Hispanic white men.[5]
- Mexican American men earn about 93 percent of the earnings of non-Hispanic white males with comparable education.[6]

- Most differences in earnings between Hispanics and non-Hispanics can be explained by educational differences between the two groups; but at the secondary school level, young Mexican Americans are closing the gap with their non-Hispanic peers. Seventy-eight percent of second-generation Mexican American men aged twenty-five to thirty-four have completed twelve years of school or more, compared with approximately 90 percent of comparable non-Hispanic whites.[7]
- English proficiency is also key to earnings among Hispanics, but here, too, conventional wisdom about Hispanics is mostly invalid. The overwhelming majority of U.S.-born Hispanics are English-dominant, and one-half of all third-generation Mexican Americans—like most other American ethnics—speak only one language: English.
- What's more, Hispanics, with the exception of Puerto Ricans, have marriage rates comparable to those of non-Hispanic whites. Mexican-origin and Cuban Hispanics are more likely to live in married-couple households than the general population, and almost half own their own homes.[8]

If these facts come as a surprise, it's largely because most of the analysis of Hispanics fails to note that nearly half of the adult Hispanic population is foreign-born.[9] And like new immigrants of the past, Hispanic immigrants will take at least one generation to move up the economic ladder and into the cultural mainstream.

Perhaps a little history is in order here. The current period is not the only time we have viewed new immigrants with distrust and suspicion. We tend to forget that Italians, Greeks, Jews, Poles, and others—whom some people lump together as "Europeans"—were considered alien to the white Americans of the early twentieth century, most of whom were of British, German, or Scandinavian descent. Anyone who believes that immigrants of an earlier day lived in halcyon times of tolerance and acceptance should read through the reports of the 1921 Dillingham Commission, which in 1924 ultimately recommended a quota system to keep out southern and eastern European immigrants and Asians.[10]

Despite these problems, most of those who came here found the struggle worth the effort. And these groups did, by and large, succeed in America. Today, the many different European immigrant groups are virtually indistinguishable from each other on measures of earnings, status, and education. Even Chinese and Japanese Americans, who endured much greater discrimination than southern and eastern Europeans, have done exceedingly well and outperformed most other groups on all indicators of social and economic success. But it took three generations for most of these groups to achieve this status. Italian Americans, for example, arrived at the same average educational attainment as other Americans only in 1970—some sixty years after the peak of their immigration to the United States.[11]

Is it possible simply to mimic what we did in the past in treating this generation of newcomers? No. Let me concede that we did a great deal of wrong in the past, and immigrants succeeded in spite of, not because of, our mistakes. It would be neither compassionate nor legal to return to a system in which we put non-English-speaking children into the public school classrooms in which the instruction was entirely in English and expect those children to "sink or swim." The United States Supreme Court in 1974 declared this approach in violation of our civil rights laws.[12] Nor should we hark back to the "good old days" when Anglo conformity was the sole acceptable cultural model. But in trying to right these wrongs, we should take care not to reverse ourselves 180 degrees by attempting to educate each group of immigrant children in their own native language and inculcate them in their own native culture. There is something wrong when two-thirds of children from Spanish-speaking homes are taught to read in Spanish when they enter first grade in American public schools and three-fourths are given Spanish oral language development. If we insist on separate language instruction for all immigrant children—who speak more than 120 different languages in New York City alone[13]—we will close the door on integration, divide ourselves along cultural and linguistic lines, and thereby perpetuate inequalities rather than eradicate them. The proponents of multicultural education are often so obsessed with the excesses of Anglo conformity that they fail to see the benefits of a shared, common culture—not entirely white, Anglo-Saxon, or Protestant—but common nonetheless. And they fail to see the dangers in substituting one orthodoxy with another, no less rigid.

The more diverse we become racially and ethnically, the more important it is that we learn to tolerate differences—and also to celebrate what we all have in common. Whether we came to the United States voluntarily or involuntarily, we all choose to live here now. And more people want to live here than anywhere else in the world. No other country accepts as many immigrants as we do. Surely, even those who criticize our so-called Eurocentric society must admit that it has something to offer or there would not be such long lines of those waiting to get in—very few of them European, by the way. What do we have that these Mexicans, Cambodians, Ethiopians, Filipinos, and others want? Two things primarily: economic opportunity and political freedom. The two, by the way, go hand in hand, and it is our legal and political institutions that protect both. Now it so happens that those political institutions did not, in fact, develop in Asia or Latin America or Africa or even throughout most of Europe. It happens that the framework for our political institutions comes from England. The basis for American jurisprudence comes from English common law—not Spanish adaptations of Roman law that governed most of Latin America, or from the legendary rulers of China or from the Hsia Dynasty or from Confucianism, or from the Ghanian Empire, the Kush state in Nubia, or from Mali. That is not to say that these others are not important civilizations deserving recognition in their own right, but it is to acknowledge the special importance to our particular political and legal system of the Magna Carta, habeas corpus, and trial by jury, all of which were handed down directly from England. Of course, not all of these concepts were totally indigenous to England; King Henry II adapted from the Franks the system of trial by jury to replace the oath, the ordeal, and the duel, which were used in both criminal and civil cases until the twelfth century.

In our zeal to tell the stories of other civilizations, to include the history of those whose ancestors came from places other than England, we should not attempt to rewrite the history of our own founding and our political antecedents. Nor should we blush at the thought that this history now belongs to children who come from Mexico, Vietnam, and Ghana, or whose parents came from these countries. These children are now American children, and this is their political inheritance as much as it is the inheritance of the child of Italian or Greek or Russian roots. As we hasten to promote diversity, we often forget that what makes this country unique in the world is that we have forged an identity as a people even though most of us share very little in common in terms of our personal histories. There is nothing wrong with holding onto personal history, but—given the incredible diversity of the country as a whole—it becomes increasingly difficult to expect the state to try to pass on that sense of personal history to each and every group. The most that can be expected, I think, is that we make sure that we recognize the contributions each group—once here—has made to the common history of this nation.

Is it possible to study the individual culture of the ancestors of each group represented in America? That depends on how superficial we're willing to be. We could develop a dictionary of cultural literacy of every major group and teach children to memorize a few facts and dates about each. Given our current success with children's learning to locate Arkansas on a map of the United States and China on a map of the world, or to tell in what half a century the Civil War was fought, or to name more than four past presidents of the United States, it seems doubtful that such a project would carry a lasting benefit. But there are other problems as well. Who decides what represents the "history" of each group? Take Hispanic children, for example. What do we teach them about the Maya, Aztecs, and Incas? They are all important civilizations, but relatively few Hispanics in the United States actually descend from them. And what about the history of Spain? Will Hispanic youngsters read Cervantes and Lope de Vega, or something else?

The problem is no less complicated when it comes to African Americans. In the name of multicultural education, many school systems have adopted an Afrocentric curriculum that mostly focuses on the contributions of ancient Egypt. There is no question about the fact that Egypt is on the continent of Africa, but that is about all traditional Egyptologists and Afrocentrists can agree upon. Is Egypt better understood as a part of the broader thalassic culture of the Mediterranean, which also includes the Middle East and southern Europe? The Sahara, which separates Egypt from the central and southern portions of the African continent, today remains a powerful cultural barrier. Are we to assume it was less so in the past? These issues are rarely addressed by Afrocentric curricula.

So if we cannot—and perhaps should not—try to teach each group its own individual history through multiple ethnocentric curricula, how do we try to deal with this increasingly diverse student population?

1. Black, Hispanic, Asian, and American Indian children need the same basic skills that we take for granted that white children need. This is an obvious point, but one that seems occasionally forgotten when we discuss multicultural education. All children in American public schools need to be taught to read, write, and speak standard English well. Their ability to master these skills will affect their life chances more than virtually anything else they learn—or fail to learn—in school.

2. They need to be taught the basic math and science that will enable them to function in an increasingly complex technological society.

3. They need a broad understanding of our form of government and its institutions. We live in a country in which we enjoy great freedom, but we also live in a country in which people are highly apathetic. If we hope to preserve democracy, our young people must develop a better appreciation for our heritage and be committed to preserving it. Somewhere along the way we have become reticent about instilling in our young an appreciation for democracy. If we expect to preserve our democratic way of life, we had better begin to develop that appreciation once again. And that means emphasizing the duties and responsibilities that go along with good citizenship.

4. We need to teach our children the history of this nation. Here, we sometimes failed in the past to include the contributions made by all the groups that compose this nation. While we should not shy away from teaching the essentially English antecedents of our political and legal institutions, neither should we forget that many who built this nation were not English, white, or male. There are many excellent histories to consult about the contribution of African Americans: W. E. B. DuBois, John Hope Franklin, Carter Woodson, to name only three. There are fewer familiar texts to consult on the contributions of Mexican Americans, Puerto Ricans, Chinese Americans, and other Asians, but two good books on the Latinos are *Hispanics in the United States* by Harry Pachon and Joan Moore[14] and *Puerto Rican Americans* by Father Joseph Fitzpatrick.[15] Both are short but comprehensive.

5. All American children need a better understanding of the world in which we live, an understanding that includes something of the history of other nations. They need a grounding in geography, which, if taught well, will also teach them why nations developed as they did. Rivers, seas, terrain, and climate are all important to the development of culture. Of course, learning the language of another country is the best way to develop a real depth of understanding in that culture, and I hope we do not ignore developing second-language proficiency in all of our students. In this respect, immigrant children have a real advantage.

These recommendations are not exhaustive. Nor are they geared only to the child who comes from a nonwhite, non-European background. These recommendations are suited for all of our children.

The American public school system was created on the premise that it would be a common school, one for all children. It has not always lived up to that ideal—certainly not before 1954—but that does not mean we should abandon the ideal. The face of America is changing, but we should not give up on the idea that we are one people and one nation.

Even under this regime there remains a place for the preservation of language and culture for new immigrants or others who wish to retain aspects of their former traditions. Some would have us believe that assimilation means every group must lose what makes it unique as it swirls about in an indifferent melting pot's colorless alloy. But, of course, this is not what has happened. As a trip into the heart of any American city will reveal, ethnic communities are alive and well, even as their inhabitants enjoy the fruits of social, political, and economic integration. The question is not whether any group has a right to maintain its language, culture, and traditions, but rather whose responsibility it is to do so: the individual's or the government's? This is the center of the multiculturalism debate.

If Hispanics, Koreans, Jews, Greeks, or the members of any other group wish to maintain their individual and unique cultures, languages, or traditions, it must be up to them to do so. Indeed, many groups have been quite successful in preserving their native cultures in the United States. Chinese parents often send their children to Saturday school to learn Cantonese or Mandarin and the history of their ancestors. Jewish children frequently attend Hebrew classes and receive religious instruction that teaches them the tenets of their faith and the history of their people. Greek Americans are among the most successful of any group in preserving their language in the United States; according to the 1980 census, a majority of Greek Americans say they still speak Greek in their homes at least occasionally.

Hispanics who wish to maintain their native language and culture should follow the examples of their fellow ethnic Americans. Frankly, given the tremendous diversity within the Hispanic community, the only successful way for each group to ensure that its members know its history and traditions is to undertake that education itself. If government assumes the responsibility, it is likely to amalgamate and homogenize in ways that make the original culture virtually indecipherable. The government, after all, is capable of lumping all 22 million Hispanics in this country into a single category that manages to include Cakchikel Indians from Guatemala, mestizos from Mexico, the descendants of Italian immigrants from Argentina, Japanese immigrants from Peru, Spaniards from Europe, and the descendants of colonists who settled the Southwest nearly four hundred years ago. Wouldn't it be better to entrust each of these very different groups with the responsibility of maintaining its own traditions without the interference—or assistance—of the government? The overwhelming majority of immigrants think so. They believe that it is the family's duty, not the government's, to help their children maintain their native language.[16]

Some critics warn that the United States is in danger of fragmenting into competing racial and ethnic groups. Nonetheless, I remain optimistic that we can—if we commit ourselves—successfully integrate the more than 70 million blacks, Hispanics, Asians, and American Indians into our society. That we can create a new *unum* out of the many here and the many more who will come. But to do so will require the cooperation of us all—those who have been here for generations as well as those who are arriving each day. It will require that each of us recognize the covenant that exists between the old and the new; that we respect the rights of individuals to maintain what is unique in their ancestral heritages; but that we understand that our future lies in forging a common identity of shared values and beliefs essential to the democratic ideal.

Notes

1. John J. Miller and Stephen Moore, *The Index of Leading Immigration Indicators* (Washington, D.C.: The Center for Equal Opportunity, 1995), 2.

2. Miller and Moore, 7.

3. Richard D. Lamm and Gary Imhoff, *The Immigration Time Bomb: The Fragmenting of America* (New York: Truman Talley Books, 1985), 77.

4. U.S. Census, *The Hispanic Population in the United States* (1990).

5. Linda Chavez, *Out of the Barrio: Toward a New Politics of Hispanic Assimilation* (New York: Basic Books, 1991), 112.

6. Chavez, 112.

7. Chavez, 113.

8. U.S. Census, *The Hispanic Population in the United States* (1992).

9. U.S. Census Bureau, 1990 Census, CP-3-3, "Persons of Hispanic Origin" (1990).

10. John Higham, *Strangers in the Land: Patterns of American Nativism 1860–1925* (New York: Atheneum, 1973), 310.

11. Commission on Civil Rights, *The Economic Status of Americans of Southern and Eastern Ancestry* (Washington, D.C.: GPO, 1986).

12. *Lau v. Nichols,* 414 U.S. 563 (1974).

13. John J. Miller, "The Rest of the 'Rainbow' Curriculum," *Wall Street Journal,* February 10, 1993.

14. Joan W. Moore and Harry Pachon, *Hispanics in the United States* (Englewood Cliffs, N.J.: Prentice-Hall, 1985).

15. Joseph P. Fitzpatrick, *Puerto Rican Americans: The Meaning of Migration to the Mainland* (Englewood Cliffs, N.J.: Prentice-Hall, 1987).

16. Linda Chavez, "One Nation, One Common Language," *Reader's Digest,* August 1995.

Chapter 12

Multiculturalism and Civic Education

Lorraine Pangle

Multicultural education is a new attempt to solve one of humanity's oldest social problems, the problem of ethnic division and conflict. The idea of multiculturalism was first popularized in Canada in the 1960s, as a result of rising tensions between Quebec nationalists and the English-speaking majority. In response to French discontent, the Canadian federal government began considering measures to strengthen the official status of the French language and culture, so as to put the two "founding races" on a more equal footing. This proposal, in turn, sparked a concern among Ukrainian Canadians and other ethnic groups that their own languages and cultures were being relegated to third-class status. Prime Minister Pierre Trudeau thereupon worked out the compromise of "multiculturalism within a bilingual framework," a policy which recognizes and encourages cultural diversity as a desirable feature of Canadian society. Official multiculturalism in Canada has included the promotion of bilingualism throughout the country, government support for the cultural activities of ethnic minorities, direct efforts to combat racism, and most importantly, programs of multicultural education that attempt to give all students a positive regard for the various ethnic groups that make up Canadian society.

The United States, having no such deep-seated language divisions as Canada, has not been pushed into an official policy of multiculturalism. Many American educators, however, have embraced multicultural education for the same reasons that recommend it to their northern neighbors. Both countries have large and diverse minority populations; both have found their ethnic diversity to be a source of conflict, and yet in both there is increasing doubt as to the viability or justice of old expectations that minorities should simply assimilate to the language and customs of the majority. Proponents of a new "cultural pluralism" argue that ethnicity is important to everyone's identity and that a fair and humane society must respect and even actively foster ethnic loyalties. Influential multicultural curricula, such as that of New

173

York State, emphasize the positive value of having a variety of cultures within the United States, call for a new "cultural democracy," and even assert a "right" to cultural diversity.[1]

The New Civics and Its Dangers

American advocates of multicultural education want to transform the entire school curriculum to make it more inclusive and less biased, but their central interest is naturally the social studies program, and especially the teaching of history. They point out a number of flaws in history programs as they have traditionally been taught in the United States. American schools have always neglected the study of other parts of the world, and until recently, they have tended to teach American history in a somewhat self-congratulatory spirit. Noah Webster set the tone for American schoolbooks with the stream of influential spellers and readers he began producing in the 1780s. He filled his books with American content and worked to instill in students a pride in their virtuous republic, contrasting it with the decadence of monarchic Europe. As he argued in his first speller, "Europe is grown old in folly, corruption, and tyranny—in that country laws are perverted, manners are licentious, literature is declining and human nature debased. For America in her infancy to adopt the present maxims of the old world, would be to stamp the wrinkles of decrepit age upon the bloom of youth and to plant the seeds of decay in a vigorous constitution."[2] In the early nineteenth century, Parson Weems began weaving about our national heroes such pious fictions as the story of George Washington and the cherry tree, which were soon taken up and immortalized by the *McGuffy Readers*. With the best of intentions, such stories rob history of life by presenting great leaders as less human, less complex, and hence less interesting than they really were. Traditional American textbooks have been criticized, with some justice, for presenting our history as chiefly a series of triumphs, for downplaying both darker incidents and controversial interpretations, and for telling the story from the point of view of white settlers and white slaveholders or liberators, neglecting the viewpoints of American Indians, slaves, and immigrants.

These criticisms, if taken seriously, suggest that American students need a history and civics program that is more objective, more probing, and above all less provincial than the courses their parents received. The criticisms would seem to call for a curriculum that would offer students not only a richer perspective on American history, but also an encounter with radically different outlooks and ways of life and a confrontation with controversial arguments about many issues. This could be accomplished through a sequence of in-depth studies of cultures or civilizations or regimes from many parts of the world and historical epochs. It could lead to a questioning and a reexamination of the assumptions and beliefs students have picked up from contemporary American society. To that extent, it might prove dangerous, and have more of a corrosive than a constructive effect on their political and moral beliefs. But if teachers took account of this danger and worked to make as strong a case as possible for the American principles and way of life that would be coming under scrutiny, the result could be an excellent civic education that would be politically responsible and liberating at the same time.

When one looks at the specific proposals and guidelines for multicultural education that have been produced in both the United States and Canada, however, one is struck by the extent to which they perpetuate precisely the aspects of the old civics education that critics find objectionable. In particular, it is surprising how provincial they still are, and how few issues they explore. Ontario's recent guideline, *The Common Curriculum,* is quite typical of programs on both sides of the border. The focus is entirely on the students' own country and the ethnic groups within it. Students are to study the contributions of each group to Canadian society, learn that cultural diversity is good, learn about the evils of racism, and study the ways in which everyone is formed willy-nilly by birth, class, culture, geography, race, and discrimination. Little attention is given either to the beliefs and principles that all Canadians hold in common or to the truly deep differences between Canada and many of the societies from which its immigrants have come. The guidelines for New York State's multicultural geography and history program are similarly narrow in focus. Although students are required to take a smattering of world history, no area except the United States is studied in any depth, and the central concepts around which American history is to be organized are virtually all related to ethnicity, race, and equity. The guidelines for American history pay no attention to, for example, the structure of the federal government, religion, the significance of the frontier, or international relations. The goal of these and similar guidelines in other states is not to provide a broad-based civic education or to expand students' minds through an encounter with a rich variety of cultures, historical figures, and interesting historical controversies. Rather, the goal is to solve specific social problems associated with ethnicity, and sometimes also with gender and disability:

to end inequities by promoting toleration in the majority and enhanced self-esteem for "marginalized" groups.[3]

Such social studies as social therapy is, I believe, a dangerous distraction from the real business of teaching and learning. If we conceive of multicultural education as a device for eradicating discrimination and inequities by instilling specific, officially approved feelings and beliefs, it can do significant harm. If, on the other hand, we accept it as a needed reminder that we must broaden and deepen students' study of the world and of genuinely different points of view, a multicultural approach can do much to revitalize American education and can promote social harmony at the same time.

Unfortunately, advocates of multicultural education have for the most part produced programs at least as dogmatic and manipulative as the old ones they criticize. Their guidelines place too much emphasis on molding the feelings, and give too little attention to provoking serious thought. One state, Pennsylvania, states explicitly in its curriculum guidelines that achieving the specified graduation outcomes "does not require students to hold or express particular attitudes, values, or beliefs," but such disclaimers are rare in multicultural programs. More typical are Iowa's instructional objectives, which stipulate that students shall "demonstrate understanding that cultural differences do not imply cultural deficiencies," shall "analyze U.S. diversity as a source of vitality, richness, and strength," shall "understand that no individual or group is inherently superior or inferior," and shall "demonstrate respect for physical and cultural differences by modeling nonsexist, culturally sensitive language and interaction patterns."[4]

Most interesting is the goal that appears in virtually all guidelines for multicultural education, that of persuading students that cultural diversity is good. This assertion is less than self-evident, as the New York Social Studies Review and Development Committee concedes at the very outset of *One Nation, Many Peoples:* "Certainly, contemporary trends toward separation and dissolution in such disparate countries as the Soviet Union, South Africa, Canada, Yugoslavia, Spain, and the United Kingdom remind us that different ethnic and racial groups have often had extraordinary difficulty remaining together in nation-states." Laying these grim object lessons before us, the authors then simply assert without evidence that diversity is the source of our national strength. There is no doubt that the colorful appeal of cities like New York and San Francisco depends largely upon their ethnic diversity, and American cuisine was indisputably dull before the proliferation of ethnic restaurants, but such things can hardly be put in the scales against the threat of national dissolution. Multicultural advocate assert that ethnic diversity provides us with a multiplicity of approaches to solving problems, but since they do not give examples of problems that have proved insoluble without the aid of some special ethnic point of view, this claim is hard to assess. *Individuals* from every corner of the earth certainly have made great contributions to American society, but that is not what is at issue here. Americans from many cultures have also derived strength and comfort from their separate traditions, but it is not clear that they are happier or contribute more to the country than their assimilated descendants who view themselves simply as Americans. The most serious reason for the argument that cultural diversity as such is a source of national strength appears in the next sentence of the New York committee's report: "If the United States is to continue to prosper in the 21st century, then all of its citizens, whatever their race or ethnicity, must believe that they and their ancestors have shared in the building of the country and have a stake in its success."[5] Cultural diversity must be celebrated as a positive good, it seems, because without such a celebration, not all citizens will feel a sense of belonging and dedication to America.

Ethnic Pride and Self-Esteem

In place of the old efforts to mold students' feelings by encouraging a patriotic devotion to national unity, we now have attempts to encourage feelings of ethnic solidarity and an attachment to diversity. Is it appropriate for schools to engage in *either* national or ethnic boosterism, in order to cultivate feelings of pride and belonging? The dangers of nationalism have been as evident in this century as the dangers of ethnic strife, and of course the two are closely related. It would nevertheless be unwise to try to root out or transcend national loyalties altogether: patriotic feeling has been an integral part of every healthy society, and the current American doctrine that our country is no better than others (or indeed a bit worse) is more likely to produce an apathetic disaffection from politics than a genuine love and concern for all of humanity. Patriotism can unify a country and draw citizens out of their private affairs into constructive efforts on the public behalf and noble acts of sacrifice. In the best case, patriotism gives citizens a sense that they belong to something important that is greater than themselves, a sense of what they must live up to, and a hope that indeed they can live up to standards set by others of their own kind who have gone before. Moreover,

American patriotism is less divisive than, say, the patriotism of the Serbs, because it does not depend upon the accidents of birth. What we take pride in, above all, is a set of principles that can potentially be accepted and implemented anywhere. To be an American means to be an immigrant or the descendant of immigrants. Hence our ability to admire Benjamin Franklin or Frederick Douglass and to count them as our own does not depend upon our being related to them by blood, or having ancestors who lived in the same country with them, or even knowing where our ancestors were when these men were alive.

Advocates of multiculturalism, however, tend to assume that the accidents of birth are all-important for everyone's sense of identity. They seek to give every child, or at least every nonwhite child, the same pride in his or her ethnic group that traditional American texts have endeavored to give American students in their nation. Arguing that self-esteem is an essential condition for success and that a positive attitude toward the group one was born into is an essential condition for self-esteem, these advocates seek to present minority groups as favorably as possible. This is why, although painstaking efforts have been made to remove the biases from American history texts, the controversy over these books rages hotter than ever. Representatives of various minorities, joined by representatives of women, homosexuals, and the handicapped, charge that their own groups are inadequately represented or not depicted in a sufficiently positive light.[6]

The project of rewriting history has been carried furthest by Molefi Kete Asante, Leonard Jeffries, and other proponents of an "Afrocentric" curriculum for black youth. These activists argue that American culture is, root and branch, Anglo-Saxon or Eurocentric culture, forgetting the American founders' deliberate efforts to take a critical distance from Europe and forge a new country with new principles. They teach that blacks must find their own, Afrocentric culture, suited to African modes of thinking and feeling, and that blacks can never be educated effectively by white teachers. An influential series of "African American Baseline Essays," edited by Asa Hilliard, has been used in Portland and other cities to teach black children that Africa is the true source of civilization and of Western science, medicine, mathematics, and democracy. They maintain that the Greeks "stole" philosophy from the ancient Egyptians, and that the Europeans have taken credit for it in a massive conspiracy. In a similar vein, Jeffries teaches that in contrast to the warm, humanistic Africans, Europeans are "cold, individualistic, materialistic, and aggressive 'ice people.' "[7] Quite apart from the unsubstantiated claims of the Afrocentrists, which have been critiqued by black and white scholars alike, such teachings add fuel to the very fire that multiculturalism was originally intended to quench. One does not put an end to bigotry by turning it on its head, or heal race relations by focusing children's minds on the question of which race is responsible for more good or more evil in the world.

Even when ethnic cheerleading is not taken to such lengths as it is in the African American Baseline Essays, direct efforts to change students' feelings about themselves are a central feature of most multicultural education proposals. In the blunt words of a 1989 New York State task force, the social studies curriculum should be revised in ways that will provide "children from Native American, Puerto Rican/Latino, Asian American, and African cultures" with "higher self-esteem and self-respect, while children from European cultures will have a less arrogant perspective." Other plans are rather more generous in attempting to nurture the self-esteem of everyone. As one of Iowa's policy statements puts it, "It is important that all students see themselves positively reflected in their curriculum, regardless of their sex, race, cultural background or disability. Students who do not, often feel alienated from the educational process and may soon question their own worth." Iowa's guidelines therefore mandate, among other things, that *all units* of Iowa and American history must include "the contributions and perspectives of both women and men, diverse cultural/racial groups, and the disabled." One wonders how a unit on, say, the Constitutional Convention could ever be taught. Making the curriculum as objective and unbiased as possible is important for many reasons, but when specific material is included or excluded chiefly on the basis of its presumed effect upon students' self-esteem, we must question the pedagogical soundness of the selection. When students spend extensive amounts of time examining ads for bias and writing letters of protest to advertisers, sampling one another's cuisines, recounting occasions when they experienced discrimination, and clarifying their feelings about their ancestors, we must wonder what more substantive lessons are being displaced.[8]

Educators routinely assume that self-esteem is an essential prerequisite for learning, and a tremendous amount of what they do is premised upon this belief, but in fact it is not well supported by empirical research. Studies have generally but by no means consistently found some *correlation* between self-esteem and academic achievement, but there is substantial evidence that achievement is more of a cause than an effect. Brent Bridgeman and Virginia Shipman have reported that the self-esteem of preschool children tends to be uniformly high, and unrelated to intelligence, whereas by grade three, children's self-esteem shows much more variation and is more strongly correlated with academic achievement. They conclude that the self-esteem of low-achieving students has fallen as a result of their difficulties in school. A study by Edward Kifer shows likewise that the self-esteem of children diverges over time, and reveals an especially strong correlation with academic achievement in children who have established a prolonged pattern of high or low achievement. Apparently it is the repeated experience of success or failure that tends to create a highly positive or negative self-image. Rubin, Dorle, and Sandridge conclude that "nowhere has it been convincingly demonstrated that raising self-esteem will lead to greater academic achievement," although scattered researchers propose this on the basis of the observed correlations.[9]

Even if self-esteem is more the result than the cause of achievement for students in general, however, the case may be different with minorities, for advocates of multicultural education argue that minority students' experience of exclusion and stigmatization has affected their self-esteem in particularly insidious ways. Yet it is here that research results are most surprising. Among black students, at any rate, studies have shown that there is no significant relationship between overall self-esteem and academic achievement. Despite the fact that they do more poorly in school on average than white students, blacks turn out to have equal or higher levels of self-esteem. Finally, researchers have found that high individual self-esteem among them is not related to levels of black pride. All of this casts serious doubt on the assumption of multicultural education proponents in general and Afrocentrists in particular that minority children's academic difficulties stem from low self-esteem and can best be overcome through programs that help them to identify more strongly and more positively with their ethnic heritage.[10]

It is even possible that a high self-esteem that is not grounded in an accurate appraisal of one's academic competence may in some ways impede learning. American students as a whole fare poorly on international mathematics assessments, yet the vast majority consider themselves to be good in math. To motivate students to work hard, every teacher must persuade them that it is important for them to know certain things that they do not know. This is always a humbling experience for a student. Humility, however, is inseparable from a recognition of what one needs, and a degree of humility can itself be quite constructive. It would of course be best if the simple desire to learn could provide sufficient motivation for a whole education, but it rarely if ever does. Everyone seems to need the reward of pride in one's accomplishments and an uneasiness at the prospect of doing poorly to keep oneself moving forward at moments when learning is not intrinsically fascinating. Hence having a self-esteem that is somewhat dependent on doing well at school is extremely helpful.

On the other hand, unless a student has real hope of being *able to* succeed at studies, it is simply too painful to acknowledge that this is important; one will do whatever one can to keep one's self-esteem from becoming dependent on academic success. Therefore, the goal of a good teacher is to create both humility and confidence, by showing students that they have work to do and that the teacher has faith in their ability to accomplish it. Studies of the teachers and teaching styles that have had the best results with disadvantaged students confirm what common sense suggests. These teachers do not try to build self-esteem unrelated to the work at hand by dwelling on the glories of their students' ancestors or telling the students that they are perfectly wonderful just as they are. Instead, they show through everything they do that academic achievement is important, that they take their students seriously and care deeply about their progress, and that they have complete faith in the students' ability to live up to high standards.[11]

Whatever disadvantaged minority students may feel about themselves in general, this sense of hope, this confidence that they can succeed at whatever they put their minds to, seems often to be fragile in them. Here is where the multicultural approach of telling stories of people of all races and both sexes who have overcome obstacles to lead remarkable lives can be so helpful. One need not be handicapped to be inspired by Franklin D. Roosevelt's accomplishments in the face of polio, or Indian to take inspiration, as Martin Luther King, Jr., did, from Mahatma Gandhi's ideals. However, the tendency of multicultural programs to dwell on the importance of race, sex, ethnicity, and physical handicaps can undermine children's confidence in their power to shape their own lives. Although these accidental qualities are normally not subject to change, their importance to us is. Efforts to sensitize all students to these issues and to show how deeply they affect us can create a self-fulfilling analysis. It is not inevitable that black children growing up will think of themselves as black first and Americans or, say, aspiring physicians second. It is not inevitable that they will see their race and the racism of whites as a central feature of their existence and carry the kind of bitterness within them that such a perception tends to spawn. The real and ugly history of racism in the United States must of course not be papered over. It nevertheless makes a difference whether teachers encourage students to define themselves by accidents of birth and the problems they create or by students' own accomplishments, virtues, and aspirations. The hope of Martin Luther King, Jr., that someday all Americans might be measured not by the color of their skin, but by the content of their characters, gives eloquent expression to what has always been one of America's noblest aims. Persuading students to judge themselves this way is the first step toward fully realizing this goal.

Over the past several years, American colleges have been paying increasing attention to accidents of birth, attempting to raise the self-esteem of some students and to heighten the sensitivity of others, in hopes of ending the inequities and tensions that turn upon ethnic and sexual differences. Millions of dollars have been spent, countless workshops and mandatory orientations have been held, and whole buildings have gone up to house new cadres of campus life administrators. Yet racial and ethnic tensions have not improved and may even have gotten worse, and charges of sexual harassment proliferate by the day. Is it possible that we are encouraging people to see an affront to the essence of their beings in what was only a display of bad manners and to become more the victims of their sex or skin color rather than less so? Is it possible that, with special treatment for all sorts of groups and with such pressures upon everyone to be sensitive, we are creating a backlash?[12] It would not be surprising if programs that encourage students to delve into and express their feelings of racial animosity or to elaborate their experiences of discrimination are failing to reduce racial tensions. Bad feelings usually do not go away when we dwell upon them.

Problems between the sexes are more complex and deeply rooted, but ethnic and racial tensions may well be amenable to the same solution that the early Americans found for religious enmities. As Thomas Jefferson said, observing the various states' responses to the quarrels that arose from the country's religious diversity, "Pennsylvania and New York . . . have made the happy discovery, that the way to silence religious disputes, is to take no notice of them."[13] If United States governments at all levels were consistently to refuse to take any notice of race (a policy that has never been tried), racial conflict might eventually become as insignificant as religious conflict in this country. If all schools were to treat their students' racial and ethnic origins as a matter of absolutely no relevance to the business of teaching and learning, they might achieve a similar result. Students would remain free to place a high personal value on their race or ethnic origins, just as many now place on their religions, but the schools would be officially neutral on both issues.

Such a policy, carried out in conjunction with humanities programs in which the only history studied was that of the United States and the only literature read was that of white Americans and Englishmen, surely would convey a message that the ethnic heritage of minority students was of little value. But if students were to study the history and literature of the whole world, minorities would be pressured neither to assimilate completely nor to maintain a strong sense of loyalty to their own ethnic group. All students would be encouraged to consider the world as their heritage, and to believe that they can reasonably aspire to be like anyone they choose, from either sex and from any nationality and historical epoch.

All in all, the central failing of multicultural education programs is their attempt to provide therapy for individuals' and society's perceived ills rather than to promote true education. Our society has always been tempted to try to solve its social problems by imposing new mandates on the schools. A century ago, one teacher commented, "You can't open your schoolroom door for a breath of fresh air without letting someone with a mission fall in."[14] Activists hold out the alluring hope that we can make a better society simply by giving children the right attitude to every issue: to drugs, to alcohol, to the environment, to nuclear weapons, to homosexuality, to race relations. The difficulty is that new issues and problems arise every year, and the solutions are rarely as straightforward and unambiguous as reformers would wish. Before long, the slow and serious business of training minds and building character gets lost in a panoply of noisy causes. Yet our social problems remain as troubling as ever. The great irony is that many of the same reformers who are busily shaping attitudes toward the issues of the day also cheerfully assert that our children will live in a world vastly and unpredictably different from the one we know. No doubt they exaggerate, but they have a point. What is needed is not to produce "right-thinking" people, but to nurture the virtues that every individual needs and every society values, and to cultivate minds that can assess unforeseen problems with sound judgment.

From Shallow Relativism to Serious Questioning

For such an education of the hearts and minds of citizens, multicultural studies that explore other cultures as deeply and as sympathetically as possible are admirably suited. Individuals become more thoughtful, and most able to contribute to the public life of their country, when they have an outside perspective on their own society. To gain such a perspective, it is essential to study other cultures on their own terms, on their own ground, and in their totality. This means going beyond a study of the remnants of other cultures retained by immigrants to North America, to a historical investigation of the countries they come from. Students need to move beneath the superficial differences of dress and cuisine and artistic styles to grapple with the issues that truly define and divide cultures: different conceptions of justice or of political legitimacy or of the best way to order citizens' common life together, and different religions. Students will profit very little from multicultural studies if they attend only to the colorful elements of other cultures and are not open to the possibility that these cultures have things to teach them about the very most important questions in life. Glib talk about giving students "cross-cultural competency," or the ability to function in a variety of cultures, willfully disregards these deep and often vexing differences that make culture something more than a matter of style.[15] Thomas Jefferson exemplified a more serious multicultural approach when he tried to reform the College of William and Mary in 1779. Among other changes, he proposed dropping the missionary who was sent to teach English, arithmetic, and Christianity to the Indians, and instead sending a scholar who would study and record their languages and laws. Jefferson was persuaded that Americans could learn a great deal from the Indians both about speculative questions such as the nature of languages and the history of human migrations and about the wise ordering of society.[16]

Without a willingness to learn lessons from other societies about the strengths and weaknesses of our own, multicultural studies in the schools will never be more than window dressing. There will always be a few people who care about such things as the genealogy of human languages, but most of us learn so that in one way or another we may make our lives better. A good multicultural program aims at educating not philosophers but moral human beings and citizens; hence it must focus on the questions of what is just and how we ought to live. If it is responsible, it must support decency; but if it is serious, it cannot escape being controversial: true education is inherently controversial. Now a valuable part of the multicultural education movement has been the desire to move history courses away from the presentation of a single, officially sanctioned story to an encounter with multiple perspectives and conflicting interpretations. Proponents rightly argue that this approach is both more honest and more likely to stimulate interest among students. But they often assume that the multiple perspectives that matter most are not those of, say, Marxists and Augustinians and liberals, but those of women and homosexuals and minorities, and that unlike the former perspectives, which can be adopted and modified through reasoned discourse, the latter cannot be understood by anyone outside the group in question.[17] This is an issue of the gravest moment. Is history only a tangle of different narratives, different points of view, each of which is bound by its own horizon, determined inescapably by circumstances, and ultimately self-serving? Or do we at least potentially have access to a common and comprehensive truth, of which the different interpretations and narrative accounts are all more or less distorted, more or less illuminating fragments? If the former is the case, there is little hope for a peaceful and rational resolution of our differences, and little reason for students to be interested in listening to other perspectives. What intrigues them in a controversy is, after all, the prospect of a puzzle to be solved. But even to state the two possibilities is to show the incoherence of the former argument, in asserting the objective truth that there is no objective truth.

Despite this illogic, the denial of objective truth about history in general and moral judgments in particular is extremely common. Instilling in students a belief in cultural relativism is one of the central goals of multicultural education advocates. Tolerance and mutual respect will follow, they believe, once students see that each culture is as good as every other, and that there is no objective basis for judging any of them as deficient. The assertion of the equality of cultures and the assertion of the incommensurability of cultures are, of course, contradictory. If there is really no basis for measuring cultures or their component beliefs and customs against one another, then there are no grounds for asserting that they are equal. Each of these assertions, however, is unsustainable when taken by itself; hence multiculturalists slide continually between the two. If one maintains openly that cultures really can be weighed and measured against one another, it is a little too absurd to assert that, on some objective scale of measurement, taking all the strengths and weaknesses of each into consideration, all of the thousands of cultures the world has seen come out precisely the same. On the other hand, if one tries to argue consistently that no such measures are possible, one gives up one's moral compass. One can make no rational objection to slavery, widow burning, clitoridectomies, infanticide, or many of the other practices that have formed an integral part of various cultures. Nor can one assert anything more than an idiosyncratic preference for liberal democracy. As Mussolini saw clearly, cultural relativism does not support democracy and tolerance any more than it supports any other political system:

> If relativism signifies contempt for fixed categories and men who claim to be the bearers of an objective, immortal truth ... then there is nothing more relativistic than Fascist attitudes and activity. . . . From the fact that all ideologies are of equal value, that all ideologies are mere fictions, the modern relativist infers that everybody has the right to create for himself his own ideology and to attempt to enforce it with all the energy of which he is capable.[18]

Indeed, it should not surprise us that those who begin with relativism should end with a fierce and intolerant assertion of their ideologies, because relativism is psychologically impossible to sustain. Everyone makes judgments about good and bad, right and wrong, all the time. People may say that these are just "value judgments," that they are entirely subjective and hold no universal validity, but no one can consistently live or even talk as if this were true. The principles that people believe in, that they want to pass on to their children and students, hold an entirely different meaning for them than what they recognize as their private, idiosyncratic preferences. Everyone holds his deepest principles to be universally valid, whether he believes above all in the virtue of faith or the virtue of humane tolerance or the virtue of authentic commitment.

The fact that the relativistic position is both dangerous and psychologically unsustainable does not, of course, prove that it is false, or that there is an absolute truth about right and wrong and the just ordering of society, or that such a truth is accessible to us through reason. It only means that we would do well to look for such a truth, rather than dogmatically insist that it is not to be found. Lessing once defined dogmatism as the confusion of the goal of one's thought with the point at which one becomes tired of thinking, and dogmatic relativists seem to grow tired of thinking before they even begin.[19] Dogmatic relativism is as inimical to the spirit of fair-minded inquiry as is dogmatic moralism or chauvinism. Although they appear to be opposites, these positions resemble each other in striking ways. Adherents of both views are self-satisfied, and hence unwilling to listen to other points of view and grapple with them seriously. As dogmatic moralists are certain that they possess the truth and have nothing to learn from anybody, dogmatic relativists are equally certain that no one possesses the truth and that those who disagree with them are no wiser than they are, but only different. The dogmatic moralists refuse to examine themselves because they are certain they are good, the relativists because they feel no need to justify their views since they can defend the views simply by saying, "These are my values." Both have an incomplete self-understanding. Traditional dogmatists tend to deceive themselves by denying whatever doubts they have; dogmatic relativists do the same thing by deny-ing their critical judgments. Both positions, in short, are shallow.

Students who are taught relativism year after year, although deeply af-fected by it, are never wholly convinced. As a result, they become an inco-herent mixture of these two extremes, with unfortunate consequences for education. Having heard time and again that no society is any better than any other, they have little motive for wanting to know about other societies; indifference is a much more common result of relativism than is true respect for other ways of life. But while relativism can sap their interest in history, geography, and literature, it does not dissolve the judgments that lurk deep within. These judgments tend to remain unacknowledged, however, and hence they cannot be educated and refined through reasoned discourse. The education that students need, and that multicultural studies can provide, is one that will bring them to a deeper thoughtfulness by helping them to inte-grate and develop their questions, their conscience, their common sense, and their capacity for reasoned judgment. They need to balance commitment and judgment with open-mindedness, and that requires a willingness to engage in serious discourse about what is good and bad, admirable and not admirable. How can teachers push beneath students' superficial relativism to create such genuine openness?

It is easy enough to show students that they do indeed believe in right and wrong and good and bad social institutions. One need only take extreme examples such as Nazis shooting babies, or slavery, or apartheid. The reason students keep slipping back into a relativistic position, despite their knowl-edge of these clear cases, is that they believe that they can be good and kind people only if they are tolerant and that they can be tolerant only if they are relativists. What they need is to see toleration in perspective, as one part but by no means the whole of the virtue of humanity. There are things that should be tolerated and things that it is inhumane to tolerate, and only with clarity about basic principles can one tell the difference. Students need to be shown, by the same token, that judgment is not inherently bad. The deroga-tory word "judgmental" that we now hear so often is one of those careless terms that blurs important distinctions. It conflates valid judgments with those that are hasty and groundless and judgments that are voiced with a constructive purpose with those that are spoken only in order to hurt. Judg-ments can indeed lead to hurt feelings, although hurt feelings are often the necessary prelude to growth or reformation. Such judgments should be voiced with great caution, then, but not banished altogether.

Students also need to be reminded that the mere fact of disagreement does not mean that there is no truth. It only means that some or all people are ignorant of it, and probably that the truth is difficult to find. Nor is it necessary to persuade everyone of one's view in order to in fact be right. There may always be diehard partisans of apartheid, yet one may rightly conclude from the evidence that the policy of apartheid is neither just nor well suited to promoting the happiness of nations. What is more important than convincing all opponents is being able to satisfy oneself that one has considered their arguments and has sufficient answers for them.

Inevitably, students will ask, "*Who's to say* which moral beliefs are right, or which culture's system of laws is best?" Teachers can reply that it is the responsibility of *everyone* to try to judge these things, in open and fair-minded discussion with one another. Students who are studying another society should make every effort to give the benefit of the doubt, and should also give greater weight to the testimony of those who know it firsthand than to their own judgments. There are societies that need barbed wire to keep people out and others that need it to keep people in, and it would be arrogant in the extreme to say that those who seek to escape oppression are wrong because all societies are equally good. The fact that people can assert the equality of all societies or cultures, despite their recognition of the evils of tyranny, suggests a naive ignorance of the power of the political regime to shape all aspects of culture. Reading the works of communist dissidents such as Vaclav Havel and Alexander Solzhenitsyn, who have written eloquently about the social and moral ills caused by communism, can help correct this misunderstanding, at the same time that it gives students an inside perspective on totalitarian society and an outside perspective on our own.

Reaching a thoughtful middle ground between relativism and dogmatism means knowing what one's principles are and what the arguments are for these principles, but also recognizing that at the root of cultural differences lie difficult questions, with cases to be made on both sides. Students should see, for instance, that there are good arguments for a close-knit, communitarian, tribal kind of life, as well as for extensive individual liberty. Even while they believe that democracy is the best form of government, they should recognize that it may not have all the advantages on its side, and that very thoughtful men and women have favored other forms of government. They should see that there is a case to be made for such systems as theocracy and aristocracy, and that we have things to learn by engaging in these arguments. Exploring alternatives and looking for answers to the challenges they present can lead students to a deeper grasp of their own country's principles. It can make them better democrats, not in the sense of being more partisan democrats, but in the sense of being more thoughtful and moderate, and hence better able to compensate for democracy's characteristic weaknesses or blind spots. For this purpose, reading a sympathetic critique of democracy from an aristocratic perspective, such as Tocqueville's *Democracy in America,* is extremely helpful. At the same time, a recognition of the depth of the issues that divide truly different cultures will help students to see that the United States, for all its vaunted cultural diversity, enjoys virtual unanimity regarding the most important aspects of culture: the political system and the relation of religious authorities to political ones.

Program Organization and Teaching Strategies

How would a serious multicultural education be structured, then, so as to foster the kind of thoughtful judgment that is needed? The program would balance the study of America with a study of the Western tradition of which it is a part and with explorations of wholly different traditions. It would include some knowledge of many societies throughout the world and throughout history, and a deeper knowledge of a few. By studying a variety of other societies, students can get a sense of what the range of human possibilities is and of what is constant in human nature. Ohio's guidelines for multicultural education express the usual aim of teaching students to value diversity in American society and, in Justice William O. Douglas's words, to appreciate "the flowering of man and his idiosyncrasies."[20] A more basic and valuable lesson to be gleaned from multicultural studies, however, is the knowledge of what is universal and what is only the growth of our own particular time and place. A recognition of the virtues that are respected everywhere can help correct the thoughtless assumption that morals are completely variable or relative. A study of many different political systems and political experiments gives citizens the foundation for prudence and good judgment in political affairs: an understanding of the natural limits of politics, or of what can reasonably be hoped for from political action and what is a utopian and dangerous dream.

A good program would be structured so as to give students extensive information with which to make judgments about social and political issues. Substantive knowledge of a number of different societies allows one to recall historical precedents and parallels for current developments and to assess them intelligently for oneself. There is no substitute for knowing a great deal of history, understanding it in context, and being able to make informed judgments about how events are likely to unfold. This is where some of the newer approaches to multicultural studies threaten to leave students seriously deprived. The New York Social Studies Review and Development Committee, wisely recognizing the impossibility of covering all parts of the world and all periods of history comprehensively and in meaningful depth (and at the same time wanting desperately to be evenhanded), advises schools to shift their emphasis away from information and toward the tools, concepts, and intellectual processes that allow one to be an "autonomous learner." Hence they recommend that schools abandon the traditional organization of history and geography courses in favor of courses organized around key concepts. Teachers would then draw relevant examples from a variety of cultures to illustrate each concept.[21] Taking events out of context in this way, however, will leave students dependent on their teachers' interpretations of the events, their causes, and the unfamiliar cultures in which they have taken place. Events viewed in isolation as examples of some general point are harder to retain in one's memory than events that make sense as part of a continuous narrative. Students educated in this way will come away without solid knowledge of any other society and without practice in marshaling their own knowledge to form independent assessments of events. In education circles it has become quite fashionable to de-emphasize facts at the expense of concepts or skills, on the questionable assumption that information is easy to obtain whenever one needs it—and on the strange assumption that one must choose between information and concepts or thinking skills. This approach neglects the consideration that students who are never required to move systematically and carefully from facts to general ideas may never feel the need for the knowledge that they lack. Rather than reaching independent conclusions, they will simply adopt the popular ideas of their times. There is much talk these days about critical thinking and much too little attention paid to the habits of patience and thoroughness and respect for knowledge that are its necessary foundation.

In addition to providing students with broad knowledge of the world and a habit of using it well, a good multicultural studies program would also focus in depth on a few societies that stand as challenging alternatives to our own. In the later grades especially, breadth of coverage would be foregone for the sake of depth, and teachers would have freedom to focus on the specific countries and periods that they know well and find most fruitful to teach. An intimate knowledge of one society that differs deeply from ours can provoke more thoughtfulness and more of a disposition to regard others with respectful openness than giving students a whirlwind tour of many cultures. One need not even go far afield to give students such a perspective. Ancient Greece, though the source of much that we cherish and much that we take for granted, can also provide some of the deepest challenges to us, with its paganism, its public supervision of religion and the arts, its variety of political regimes, brilliantly justified, and its dedication to smallness and military valor.

Allowing teachers to focus on the countries and periods of history that they themselves find most admirable can also help promote respect for other cultures as a whole. This is one of the great limitations of multicultural studies that look only at immigrant groups within North America. It is not reasonable to expect that a society's finest achievements will be particularly visible among immigrants to another country, since the immigrants' energies will be consumed in establishing a new life for themselves and fitting into a new society. American history courses should of course include the study of minorities as an integral part of our history, and the study of immigrant groups can be an excellent prelude to the study of the countries that they came from, especially for younger students. But if the goal is to provoke thought and respect for another group, the best multicultural literature for students to read will not be stories of immigrants' sufferings or of others who have been hurt by their contact with the West, but classics from within those cultures themselves.

Respect for other cultures also comes through learning about impressive individuals within those societies. Young people have a great need for models that they can admire and pattern their lives after, as George Washington did with Cato and as our students continue to do with rock stars and whoever else seizes their imagination. For all their talk about the importance of role models, many educators do not understand students' need for inspiration; and they single out figures for special attention not on the basis of their virtues or the captivating drama of their lives, but on the basis of skin color, gender, and physical disability. The Organization of American Historians recommends that "the history curriculum of public schools should be constructed around the principle that *all* people have been significant actors in human events."[22] The most thoroughly egalitarian form of history instruction would no doubt be to study lives chosen at random, but this would do nothing to nourish the mind or the heart. Stories and especially biographies of remarkable people are valuable in the same way that the best novels are: they give us models that we can keep in our minds as reference points all our lives and that we can use to help sort out our own aspirations. If we look impartially for inspiring models in all continents, they will naturally come in all colors. One who admires Anwar Sadat will care little about the color of his skin; and the more eclectic one's stock of heroes is, the harder it will be to be prejudiced.

Once students have a preliminary acquaintance with a society that they are studying, the teachers need to listen carefully to their judgments. If instructors do not elicit and address students' honest responses to the material, the students will remain detached, and the course will seem dry and "academic." Only by engaging students fully can teachers educate their judgments. Honest judgments can of course be explosive, especially if the subject is American ethnic groups. This is one advantage to studying the history and literature of other periods: if the class is investigating ancient Rome or Egypt, no one in the room need feel offended by criticisms leveled against that society. Once students have learned habits of judging carefully and giving the benefit of the doubt in their study of other cultures, they will be able to apply these same habits to their analysis of events near at hand.

The next step after clarifying one's initial judgments, however, is to suspend these judgments and try to understand the case for the other side. Despite their initial prejudices, students are often surprisingly willing to consider the arguments for other regimes and ways of life if they are given the task of defending these in essays or debates. Teachers can help them make serious arguments by pointing them to relevant texts and documents from the society under study. If they are assigned to explain the position of the elders of the Massachusetts Bay Colony who banished Anne Hutchinson, for instance, they would be encouraged to resist the initial temptation to judge them in terms of modern conceptions of religious liberty and first to give a sympathetic reading to the early Puritan speeches that show their very different conception of society's purpose and the spiritual duties of magistrates.

Meaningful courses can be structured so as to allow generous scope for the issues that provoke a strong reaction in students and hence engage their interest most fully. These initial reactions or judgments can be used to formulate guiding questions for research. In a unit on India, for example, students are likely to respond more intensely to the caste system or to arranged marriages than to issues of industrialization and sanitation. They might ask how the caste system got started, why it persisted so long, and why it is still powerful even now that it is illegal. Students would confront the injustice of the early Aryans, who set themselves up as the highest caste; but they would also learn about the Hindu teachings of reincarnation and the soul's gradual progress to Nirvana, in stages corresponding to the castes. They would consider the strong sense of community and belonging and order that such a system gives to life, and perhaps contrast an Indian community with utopian American attempts to forge close-knit communities.

Rather than criticize the caste system from the perspective of our principles, they would notice that there have been Indian critics of it from the outset and that their perspective is different from ours. Many of the protest movements that sprang up in the Middle Ages, such as the Virasaiva movement of the tenth to twelfth centuries, were egalitarian in a sense, not because they believed in democracy as such, but because they were trying to create a community of saints. They believed that enlightenment could come in one lifetime to members of any caste. If students compare their own tendency to value individual freedom for the sake of getting ahead in life with the Indian focus on spiritual things, their respect for India will grow. This comparison could lead them to a reexamination of their own understanding of human rights. Perhaps what is really best and most important about individual liberty is not its contribution to economic self-advancement, but the fact that it allows for freedom of thought and of conscience—a freedom to live a spiritual life, but also to follow the religion or philosophy that one finds most persuasive. A study of this nature would help students to see that the caste system is neither simply cynical nor simply destructive. Examining its power to persist and the nature of the protests against it can help Americans to see their lives in better perspective. In the end, such a process will give students wiser and more moderate judgments, judgments that reflect more understanding, a sense of the complexity of the issues, and a greater willingness to consider other views in the future.

This sketch of a multicultural civic education is undeniably ambitious. By the end of high school, students cannot be expected to attain a complete understanding of American principles or a full appreciation of what even one other culture has to offer. It is extraordinarily hard to get outside of one's own terms of reference and the prejudices of one's own culture to understand another on its own terms. Teachers who are to help students to make a successful start at this ought to have a thorough grounding in history themselves, which unfortunately most jurisdictions do not require social studies teachers to have. They need some understanding of world religions and of the arguments for and against different regimes, different family structures, and different ways of balancing the claims of the individual against the claims of society. They need, in the best case, some acquaintance with political philosophy. Yet any teacher who is thorough, openminded, and willing to learn can make progress together with her students; and in twelve years of serious and unhurried history and geography courses, students can make an excellent beginning. Even if the best civic education is rarely attained, having a clear vision of the goal is invaluable. A frank investigation of other societies that welcomes judgments about good and bad can be safely engaged in without fear of promoting more bigotry, because the issues that divide societies *are* hard issues. If questions about how human beings should live together and govern themselves were easy, everyone would adopt the same laws and customs, just as we all sleep lying down at night, and not sitting or standing in stalls. Because the questions are hard, there is almost always something to be said on both sides and almost always something to be learned from the other side. And the experience of learning from each other is in the end the best way to generate mutual respect and goodwill. At the same time, if teachers help students to understand the strongest case for liberal democracy, and if they investigate other countries not with a view to denigrating ours, but with a view to finding constructive lessons for it, such openness will promote not only tolerance but civic health more broadly. We close, then, with a paradox. Just as racism may best be overcome through a broad civic education that looks beyond race to deeper issues, so the best civic education for America may be a liberal education, which looks beyond the civic concerns of our society to contemplate humanity itself.

Notes

1. James Banks, *Multiethnic Education: Theory and Practice* (Boston: Allyn and Bacon, 1981), ch. 5; New York State Social Studies Review and Development Committee, *One Nation, Many Peoples: A Declaration of Cultural Interdependence* (June 1991), xii.

2. Noah Webster, *A Grammatical Institute, of the English Language, Comprising, an Easy, Concise, and Systematic Method of Education, Designed for the Use of English Schools in America. In Three Parts,* pt. 1 (Hartford, Conn.: Hudson and Goodwin, 1783; facsimile reprint, Menston, England: Scolar Press, 1968), 14.

3. Ontario Ministry of Education, *The Common Curriculum* (1993), 25–29; also New York State Social Studies Review and Development committee. In this context, see especially the dissenting opinions of Arthur M. Schlesinger, Jr., and Kenneth Jackson.

4. *Pennsylvania Bulletin* 23, no. 30 (July 24, 1993): 3553; State of Iowa Department of

Public Instruction, *A Guide to Developing Multicultural, Nonsexist Education Across the Curriculum* (May 1989), 14–17.

5. New York State Social Studies Review and Development committee, 1.

6. See Diane Ravitch, "Multiculturalism: E Pluribus Plures," *American Scholar* 59, no. 3 (Summer 1990): 337–54.

7. Molefi Kete Asante, "The Afrocentric Idea in Education," *Journal of Negro History* 60, no. 2 (Spring 1991): 170–80; Leonard Jeffries, quoted by Joseph Berger, "Professors' Theories on Race Stir Turmoil at City College," *New York Times,* 20 April 1990; Arthur M. Schlesinger, Jr., *The Disuniting of America* (n.p.: Whittle Direct Books, 1991), 35–43.

8. New York State Department of Education, *A Curriculum of Inclusion: Report of the Commissioner's Task Force on Minorities: Equity and Excellence* (July 1989), 35; State of Iowa Department of Public Instruction, *Multicultural Nonsexist Education: Social Studies* (1979, reprinted 1991), 3, 8: like *A Curriculum of Inclusion,* this document speaks of the need to root out "patronizing attitudes" toward females and minorities. See also Leroy G. Baruth and M. Lee Manning, *Multicultural Education of Children and Adolescents* (Boston: Allyn and Bacon, 1992), 148–52.

9. Brent Bridgeman and Virginia Shipman, "Preschool Measures of Self-Esteem and Achievement Motivation as Predictors of Third Grade Achievement," *Journal of Educational Psychology* 70, no. 1 (February 1978): 17–28; Edward Kifer, "Relation Between Academic Achievement and Personality Characteristics: A Quasi-Longitudinal Study," *American Educational Resources Journal* 12, no. 2 (Spring 1975): 191–210; Rosalyn A. Rubin, Jeanne Dorle, and Suzanne Sandridge, "Self-Esteem and School Performance," *Psychology in the Schools* 14, no. 4 (October 1977): 503–7; see also Barbara Byrne, "The General/ Academic Self-Concept Nomological Network: a Review of Construct Validation Research," *Review of Education Research* 54, no. 3 (Fall 1984): 427–56.

10. Craig Frisby and Carolyn Tucker, "Black Children's Perception of Self: Implications for Educators," *Educational Forum* 57, no. 2 (Winter 1993): 146–54.

11. Ronald Edmonds, "Effective Schools for the Urban Poor," *Educational Leadership* 37, no. 1 (October 1979): 15–24; Thomas Sowell, "Pattern of Black Excellence," ch. 2 in *Education: Assumptions vs. History* (Stanford, Calif.: Hoover Institution Press, 1986).

12. See especially Dinesh D'Sousa, *Illiberal Education: The Politics of Race and Sex on Campus* (New York: Vintage Books, 1992), ch. 5.

13. Thomas Jefferson, *Notes on the State of Virginia,* ed. William Peden (New York: W. W. Norton, 1954), Query XVII, 160–61.

14. Agnes Cameron, quoted in Andrew Nikiforuk, *School's Out* (Toronto: Macfarlane Walter & Ross, 1993), 26.

15. Banks, 26.

16. Thomas Jefferson, "A Bill for Amending the Constitution of the College of William and Mary, and Substituting More Certain Revenues for Its Support," in *The Papers of Thomas Jefferson,* ed. Julian P. Boyd et al. (Princeton, N.J.: Princeton University Press, 1950–   ), 539–40; *Notes on the State of Virginia,* Query XV, 150–51.

17. This position is often incoherent. There is great pressure to study literature and scholarship written by women and homosexuals and minorities, on the grounds that only in this way can one get a true diversity of views. It is thought, for example, that whites cannot study or write knowledgeably about blacks. But if we truly cannot understand one another's perspectives, why should a student study with or read the works of anyone of another race or gender?

18. Benito Mussolini, cited in Jerry Martin, "The Postmodern Argument Reconsidered," *Partisan Review* 60, no. 4 (Fall 1993): 653.

19. Gotthold Lessing, Letter to Mendelssohn, 9 January 1771, quoted in Leo Strauss, *Natural Right and History* (Chicago: University of Chicago Press, 1953), 22. The first two chapters of this book give an extremely helpful account of the philosophic roots of relativism.

20. Ohio Department of Education, *Citizenship, Multiculturalism, and Human Relations Education* (1985), 5.

21. New York State Social Studies Review and Development Committee, 16–17, 20–21.

22. New York State Social Studies Review and Development Committee, 20.

Part IV

Multiculturalism and the Arts

Chapter 13

What Is a Classic?

J. M. Coetzee

In October of 1944, as Allied forces were battling on the European mainland and German rockets were falling on London, Thomas Stearns Eliot, aged 56, gave his presidential address to the Virgil Society in London. In his lecture Eliot does not mention wartime circumstances, save for a single reference—oblique, understated, in his best British manner—to "accidents of the present time" that have made it difficult to get access to the books he needs to prepare the lecture. It is a way of reminding his auditors that there is a perspective in which the war is only a hiccup, however massive, in the life of Europe.

The title of the lecture was "What Is a Classic?" and its aim was to consolidate and reargue a case Eliot had long been advancing: that the civilization of Western Europe is a single civilization, that its descent is from Rome via the Church of Rome and the Holy Roman Empire, and that its originary classic must therefore be the epic of Rome, Virgil's *Aeneid*.[1] Each time this case was reargued, it was reargued by a man of greater public authority, a man who by 1944, as poet, dramatist, critic, publisher, and cultural commentator, could be said to dominate English letters. This man had targeted London as the metropolis of the English-speaking world, and with a diffidence concealing ruthless singleness of purpose had made himself into the deliberately *magisterial* voice of that metropolis. Now he was arguing for Virgil as the dominant voice of metropolitan, imperial Rome, and Rome, furthermore, imperial in transcendent ways that Virgil could not have been expected to understand.

"What Is a Classic?" is not one of Eliot's best pieces of criticism. The address *de haut en bas,* which in the 1920s he had used to such great effect to impose his personal predilections on the London world of letters, has become mannered. There is a tiredness to the prose, too. Nevertheless, the piece is never less than intelligent, and—once one begins to explore its background—more coherent than at first reading one might think. Furthermore, behind it is a clear awareness that the ending of World War II must bring

199

with it a new cultural order, with new opportunities and new threats. What struck me when I reread Eliot's lecture, however, was the fact that nowhere does Eliot reflect on the fact of his own Americanness, or at least his American origins, and therefore on the somewhat odd angle at which he comes, honoring a European poet to a European audience.

I say "European," but of course even the Europeanness of Eliot's British audience is an issue, as is the line of descent of English literature from the literature of Rome. For one of the writers Eliot claims not to have been able to reread in preparation for his lecture is Sainte-Beuve, who in *his* lectures on Virgil claimed Virgil as "the poet of all Latinity," of France and Spain and Italy but *not* of all Europe.[2] So Eliot's project of claiming a line of descent from Virgil has to start with claiming a fully European identity for Virgil and also with asserting for England a European identity it has not always been eager to embrace.[3]

Rather than trace in detail the moves Eliot makes to link Virgil's Rome to the England of the 1940s, let me ask how and why Eliot himself became English enough for the issue to matter to him.[4]

Why did Eliot "become" English? My sense is that at first the motives were complex: partly from Anglophilia, partly in solidarity with the English middle-class intelligentsia, partly as a protective disguise in which a certain shame about American barbarousness may have figured, partly as a parody from a man who enjoyed acting (passing as English is surely one of the most difficult acts to bring off). I would suspect that the inner logic was, first, residence in London (rather than England), then the assumption of a London social identity, then the specific chain of reflections on cultural identity that would eventually lead him to claim a European and *Roman* identity in which London identity, English identity, and Anglo-American identity were subsumed and transcended.[5]

By 1944 the investment in this identity was total. Eliot *was* an Englishman—though, in his own mind at least, a Roman Englishman. He had just completed a cycle of poems in which he named his roots and reclaimed as his own East Coker in Somersetshire, home of the Elyots. "Home is where one starts from," he writes. "In my beginning is my end." "What you own is what you do not own"—or, to put it another way, what you do not own is what you own.[6] Not only would he now claim for himself that sense of roots that is so important to his understanding of culture, but he had equipped himself with a theory of history that defined England and America as provinces of an eternal metropolis, Rome.

So one can understand how it is that in 1944 Eliot feels no need to present himself to the Virgil Society as an American talking to Englishmen. But how does he present himself?

For a poet who had such success, in his heyday, in importing the yardstick of *impersonality* into criticism, Eliot's poetry is astonishingly personal, not to say autobiographical.[7] So it is not surprising to discover, as we read the Virgil lecture, that it has a subtext concerning Eliot himself. But the figure of Eliot in the lecture is not in the first place Virgil, but Aeneas, the hero of Virgil's epic poem—Aeneas understood or even transformed in a particularly Eliotic way into a rather weary middle-aged man who "would have preferred to stop in Troy, but becomes an exile, . . . exiled for a purpose greater than he can know, but which he recognises." "Not, in a human sense, a happy or successful man," whose "reward [is] hardly more than a narrow beachhead and a political marriage in a weary middle age: his youth interred."[8]

From the major romantic episode of Aeneas's life, the affair with Queen Dido that ends with Dido's suicide, Eliot singles out for mention neither the high passion of the lovers nor Dido's *Liebestod,* but what he calls the "civilised manners" of the couple when they meet later in the underworld, and the fact that "Aeneas does not forgive himself . . . in spite of the fact that all that he has done has been in compliance with destiny."[9] It is hard not to see here a covert reference to Eliot's own unhappy first marriage.[10]

The element of what I would call compulsiveness—just the opposite of impersonality—that makes Eliot articulate the story of Aeneas, in this lecture and before this audience, as an allegory of his own life is not my concern here. What I want to point to is that in reading the *Aeneid* in this way, Eliot is not only using its fable of exile followed by home founding—"In my end is my beginning"—as the pattern of his own intercontinental migration—which I do not call an odyssey precisely because Eliot is concerned to validate the destiny-inspired trajectory of Aeneas over the idle and ultimately circular wanderings of Odysseus—but is also appropriating the cultural weight of the epic to back himself.

Thus in the palimpsest Eliot sets before us, he, Eliot, is not only Virgil's dutiful *(pius)* Aeneas, who leaves the continent of his birth to set up a beachhead in Europe (*beachhead* is a word one could not have used in October of 1944 without evoking the landings in Normandy just a few months earlier, as well as the 1943 landings in Italy), but Aeneas's Virgil. If Aeneas is recharacterized as an Eliotic hero, Virgil is characterized as a rather Eliot-like "learned author," whose task, as seen by Eliot, was that of "re-writing Latin poetry" (the phrase Eliot preferred for himself was "purifying the dialect of the tribe").[11]

Of course I would be traducing Eliot if I created the impression that in 1944 he was in any simple-minded way setting himself up as the reincarnation of Virgil. His theory of history and his conception of the classic are much too sophisticated for that. To Eliot, there can be only one Virgil because there is only one Christ, one Church, one Rome, one western Christian civilization, and one originary classic of that Roman-Christian civilization. Nevertheless, while he does not go so far as to identify himself with the so-called adventist position that Virgil prophesies a new Christian era, he does leave the door open to the suggestion that Virgil was being used by an agency greater than himself for a purpose of which he could not have been aware—that is, that in the greater pattern of European history he may have fulfilled a prophetic role.[12]

Read from the inside, Eliot's lecture is an attempt to reaffirm the *Aeneid* as a classic not just in Horatian terms—as a book that has lasted a long time[13]—but in allegorical terms: as a book that will bear the weight of having read into it a meaning for Eliot's own age. The meaning for Eliot's age includes not only the allegory of Aeneas the sad, long-suffering middle-aged widower hero, but the Virgil who appears in the *Four Quartets* as one element of the composite "dead master" who speaks to fire-warden Eliot in the ruins of London, the poet without whom, even more than Dante, Eliot would not have become himself. Read from the outside, and read unsympathetically, it is an attempt to give a certain historical backing to a radically conservative political program for Europe, a program opened up by the imminent end of hostilities and the prospect of reconstruction. Broadly stated, this would be a program for a Europe of nation-states in which every effort would be made to keep people on the land, in which national cultures would be encouraged and an overall Christian character maintained—a Europe, in fact, in which the Catholic Church would be the principal supranational organization.

Continuing this reading from the outside, at a personal but still unsympathetic level, the Virgil lecture can be fitted into a decades-long program on Eliot's part to redefine and resituate nationality in such a way that he, Eliot, cannot be sidelined as an eager American cultural arriviste lecturing the English and/or the Europeans about their heritage and trying to persuade them to live up to it—a stereotype into which Eliot's one-time collaborator Ezra Pound all too easily fell. At a more general level, the lecture is an attempt to claim a cultural-historical unity for Western European

Christendom, including its provinces—which Eliot considered to be the home of the world's major culture[14]—within which the cultures of its constituent nations would belong only as parts of a greater whole.

This is not quite the program that would be followed by the new North Atlantic order that was to emerge after the war—the urgency for its own program came from events Eliot could not have foreseen in 1944—but it is highly compatible with that program. If Eliot got it wrong, it was by not foreseeing that the new order would be directed from Washington, not London and certainly not Rome. Looking further into the future, Eliot would of course have been disappointed by the form toward which western Europe in fact evolved—toward economic community but even more toward cultural homogeneity.[15]

The process I have been describing, extrapolating from Eliot's 1944 lecture, is one of the more spectacular examples of a writer attempting to *make* a new identity, claiming that identity not on the basis of immigration, settlement, residence, domestication, acculturation, as other people do, or not only by such means—since Eliot with characteristic tenacity did all of the above—but by defining nationality to suit himself and then using all of his accumulated cultural power to impose that definition on educated opinion, and by resituating nationality within a specific—in this case Catholic—brand of internationalism or cosmopolitanism, in terms of which he would emerge not as a Johnny-come-lately but as a pioneer and indeed a kind of prophet; a claiming of identity, furthermore, in which a new and hitherto unsuspected paternity is asserted—a line of descent less from the Eliots of New England and/or Somerset than from Virgil and Dante, or at least a line in which the Eliots are an eccentric offshoot of the great Virgil-Dante line.

"Born in a half-savage country, out of date," Pound called his Hugh Selwyn Mauberley. The feeling of being out of date, of having been born into too late an epoch, or of surviving unnaturally beyond one's term, is all over Eliot's early poetry, from "Prufrock" to "Gerontion." The attempt to understand this feeling or this fate, and indeed to give it meaning, is part of the enterprise of his poetry and criticism. This is a not uncommon sense of the self among colonials—whom Eliot subsumes under what he calls provincials—particularly young colonials struggling to match their inherited culture to their daily experience. The high culture of the metropolis provides them with extraordinarily powerful experiences, which cannot, however, be embedded in their lives in any obvious way and which seem therefore to have their existence in some transcendent realm.

In extreme cases, such provincials blame their environment for not living up to art and take up residence, even live out their lives, in an art-realm. This is a provincial fate—Gustave Flaubert diagnosed it in Emma Bovary, subtitling his case study *Moeurs de province*—but particularly a colonial fate, for those colonials brought up in the culture of what is usually called the mother country but in this context deserves to be called the father country.

Eliot as a man and particularly as a young man was open to experience, both aesthetic and real-life, to the point of being suggestible and even vulnerable. His poetry is in many ways a meditation on, and a struggling with, such experiences; in the process of making them over into poetry, he makes himself over into a new person. The experiences are perhaps not of the order of religious experience, but they are of the same genre.

There are many ways of understanding a life's enterprise like Eliot's, among which I will isolate two. One, broadly sympathetic, is to treat these transcendental experiences as the subject's point of origin and read the entirety of the rest of the enterprise in their light. This is an approach that would take seriously the call from Virgil that seems to come to Eliot from across the centuries. It would trace the self-fashioning that takes place in the wake of that call as part of a lived poetic vocation. That is, it would read Eliot very much in his own framework, the framework he elected for himself when he defined tradition as an order you cannot escape, in which you may try to locate yourself, but in which your place gets to be defined, and continually redefined, by succeeding generations—an entirely transpersonal order, in fact.

The other (and broadly unsympathetic) way of understanding Eliot is the sociocultural one I outlined a moment ago: of treating his efforts as the essentially magical enterprise of a man trying to redefine the world around himself—redefining America, redefining Europe—rather than confronting the reality of his not-so-grand position, namely, that of a man whose highly academic and Eurocentric education had prepared him rather narrowly for life as a mandarin in one of the New England ivory towers.

I would like to interrogate these alternative readings—the transcendental-poetic and the sociocultural—further, and bring them closer to our own times, following an autobiographical path that may be methodologically risky but has the virtue of dramatizing the issue.

One Sunday afternoon in the summer of 1955, when I was fifteen years old, I was mooning around our back garden in the suburbs of Cape Town, wondering what to do, boredom being the main problem of existence for me in those days, when from the house next door I heard music. As long as the music lasted, I was frozen, I dared not breathe. I was being spoken to by the music as music had never spoken to me before.

What I was listening to was a recording of Bach's *Well-Tempered Clavier,* played on the harpsichord. I learned this name only some time later, when I had become more familiar with what, at the age of fifteen, I knew only— in a somewhat suspicious and even hostile teenage manner—as "classical music." The house next door had a transient student population; the student who was playing the Bach record must have moved out soon afterward, or lost his/her taste for Bach, for I heard no more, though I listened intently.

I don't come from a musical family. There was no musical instruction offered at the schools I went to, nor would I have taken it if it had been offered: in the colonies classical music was sissy. I could identify Khachaturian's "Sabre Dance," the overture to Rossini's *William Tell,* Rimsky-Korsakov's "Flight of the Bumble-Bee"—that was the level of my knowledge. At home we had no musical instrument, no record player. There was plenty of the blander American popular music on the radio (heavy emphasis on George Melachrino and his Silver Strings), but it made no great impact on me.

What I am describing is middle-class musical culture of the Age of Eisenhower, as it was to be found in the ex–British colonies, colonies that were rapidly becoming cultural provinces of the United States. The so-called classical component of that musical culture may have been European in origin, but it was Europe mediated and in a sense orchestrated by the Boston Pops.

And then the afternoon in the garden, and the music of Bach, after which everything changed. A moment of revelation that I will not call Eliotic—that would insult the moments of revelation celebrated in Eliot's poetry—but that was of the greatest significance in my life nevertheless: for the first time I was undergoing the impact of *the classic.*

What did Bach give me? He gave me, so to speak, the idea of form. In Bach nothing is obscure, no single step that he takes is beyond imitation. Yet when the chain of sounds is realized in time, the building process ceases at a certain moment to be the mere linking of units; the units cohere as a higher-order object in a way that I can only describe by analogy as incarnation. Bach's music is not just the incarnation of certain musical ideas, but the incarnation of higher-order ideas of exposition, complication, and resolution that are more general than music. Bach thinks in music. Music thinks itself in Bach.[16]

The revelation in the garden was a key event in my formation. Now I wish to interrogate that moment again, using as a framework both what I have been saying about Eliot—specifically, using Eliot the provincial as a pattern and figure of myself—and, in a more skeptical way, invoking the kinds of questions that contemporary cultural analysis asks about culture and cultural ideals.

The question I put to myself, somewhat crudely, is this: Is there some nonvacuous sense in which I can say that the spirit of Bach was speaking to me across the ages, across the seas, putting before me an ideal of form; or was what was really going on at that moment that I was symbolically electing high European culture, and command of the codes of that culture, as a route that would take me out of my class position in white South African society and ultimately out of what I must have felt, in whatever obscure and mystified terms, as the dead end of that society itself—a road that would culminate (again symbolically) with me writing an essay for a cosmopolitan audience on Bach, T. S. Eliot, and the question of the classic? In other words, was the experience what I understood it to be—a disinterested and in a sense impersonal aesthetic experience—or was it really the masked expression of a material interest?

This is a question of a kind that one would be deluded to think one could answer about oneself. Any autobiographical answer must be open to endless suspicion. But that does not mean it should not be asked; and asking it means asking it properly, in terms that are as clear and as full as possible. As part of the enterprise of asking the question clearly, let me therefore ask what I might mean when I talk of being spoken to by the classic across the ages.[17]

In two out of the three senses, Bach is a classic of music. Sense one: the classic is that which is not time-bound, which retains meaning for succeeding ages, which "lives." Sense two: a proportion of Bach's music belongs to what are loosely called "the classics," that part of European musical canon that is still widely played, if not particularly often or before particularly large audiences. The third sense, the sense that Bach does not satisfy, is that he does not belong to the revival of so-called classical values in European art starting in the second quarter of the eighteenth century.

Bach was not only too old, too old-fashioned, for the neoclassical movement: his intellectual affiliations and his whole musical orientation were toward a world that was in the process of passing from sight. In the popular and somewhat romanticized account, Bach, obscure enough in his own day and particularly in his later years, dropped entirely out of public consciousness after his death, and was resurrected only some eighty years later, mainly through the enthusiasm of Felix Mendelssohn. For several generations, in this popular account, Bach was hardly a classic at all: not only was he not neoclassical, but he spoke to no one across those generations. His music was not published; it was rarely played. He was part of music history, he was a name in a footnote in a book, that was all.[18]

It is this unclassical history of misunderstanding, obscurity, and silence, which if not exactly history as truth is history as one of the overlays of the historical record, that I wish to emphasize, since it calls into doubt facile notions of the classic as the timeless, as that which unproblematically speaks across all boundaries. Bach the classic was historically constituted, as I will remind you, constituted by identifiable historical forces and within a specific historical context. Only once we have acknowledged this point are we in a position to ask the more difficult questions: What, if any, are the limits to that historical relativization of the classic? What, if anything, is left of the classic after the classic has been historicized, that may still claim to speak across the ages?

In 1737, in the middle of the third and last phase of his professional life, Bach was the subject of an article in a leading musical journal. The article was by a one-time student of Bach's named Johann Adolf Scheibe. In it, Scheibe attacked Bach's music as "turgid and sophisticated" rather than "simple and natural," as merely "sombre" when it meant to be "lofty," and generally as marred by signs of "labour and . . . effort."[19]

As much as it was an attack by youth upon age, Scheibe's article was a manifesto for a new kind of music based on Enlightenment values of feeling and reason, dismissive of the intellectual heritage (scholastic) and the musical heritage (polyphonic) behind Bach's music. In valuing melody above counterpoint, unity, simplicity, clarity, and decorum against architectonic complexity, and feeling above intellect, Scheibe speaks for the blossoming modern age and in effect makes Bach, and with Bach the whole polyphonic tradition, into the last gasp of the dead Middle Ages.

Scheibe's stance may be polemical, but when we remember that Haydn was only a child of five in 1737 and Mozart not yet born, we must recognize that his sense of where history was going was accurate.[20] Scheibe's verdict was the verdict of the age. By his last years Bach was a man of yesterday. What reputation he had was based on what he had written before he was forty.

All in all, then, it is not so much the case that Bach's music was forgotten after his death as that it did not find a place in public awareness during his lifetime. So if Bach before the Bach revival was a classic, he was not only an invisible classic but a dumb classic. He was marks on paper; he had no presence in society. He was not only not canonical, he was not public.

How, then, did Bach come into his own? Not, it must be said, via the quality of the music pure and simple, or at least not via the quality of that music until it was appropriately packaged and presented. The name and the music of Bach had first to become part of a cause, the cause of German nationalism rising in reaction to Napoleon and of the concomitant Protestant revival. The figure of Bach became one of the instruments through which German nationalism and Protestantism were promoted; reciprocally, in the name of Germany and Protestantism Bach was promoted as a classic; the whole enterprise being aided by the Romantic swing against rationalism and by enthusiasm for music as the one art privileged to speak directly from soul to soul.

The first book on Bach, published in 1802, tells much of the story. It was entitled *The Life, Art and Works of J. S. Bach: For patriotic admirers of genuine musical art*. In his introduction the author writes: "This great man . . . was a German. Be proud of him, German fatherland. . . . His works are an invaluable national patrimony with which no other nation has anything to be compared."[21] We find the same emphasis on the Germanness and even the Nordicness of Bach in later tributes. The figure and the music of Bach became part of the construction of Germany and even of the so-called Germanic race.

The turning point from obscurity to fame came with the oft-described performances of the *St. Matthew Passion* in Berlin in 1829, directed by Mendelssohn. But it would be naive to say that in these performances Bach returned to history on his own terms. Mendelssohn arranged Bach's score not only in the light of the larger orchestral and choral forces at his command but also in the light of what had been going down well recently with Berlin audiences, audiences that had responded rapturously to the Romantic nationalism of Weber's *Der Freischütz*. It was Berlin that called for repeat performances of the *Matthew Passion*. In Königsberg, Kant's city and still a center of rationalism, by contrast, the *Matthew Passion* flopped, and the music was criticized as "out-of-date rubbish."[22]

I am not criticizing Mendelssohn's performances for not being "the real Bach"—that will just land us in a metaphysical forest. The point I make is a simple and limited one: the Berlin performances, and indeed the whole Bach revival, were powerfully historical in ways that were largely invisible to the moving spirits behind them. Furthermore, one thing we can be certain of about our own understanding and performance of Bach, even—and perhaps even particularly—when our intentions are of the purest, the most puristic, is that it is historically conditioned in ways invisible to us. And the same holds for the opinions about history and historical conditioning that I am expressing at this moment.

By saying this I do not mean to fall back into a helpless kind of relativism. The Romantic Bach was partly the product of men and women responding to unfamiliar music with a stunned overwhelmedness analogous to what I myself experienced in South Africa in 1955 and partly the product of a tide of communal feeling that found in Bach a vehicle for its own expression. Many strands of that feeling—its aesthetic emotionalism, its nationalistic fervor—are gone with the wind, and we no longer weave them into our performances of Bach. Scholarship since Mendelssohn's day has given us a different Bach, enabling us to see features of Bach invisible to the revivalist generation—for instance, the sophisticated Lutheran scholasticism within whose context he worked.[23]

Such recognitions constitute a real advance in historical understanding. Historical understanding is understanding of the past as a shaping force upon the present. Insofar as that shaping force is tangibly felt upon our lives, historical understanding is part of the present. Our historical being is part of our present. It is that part of our present—namely, the part that belongs to history—that we cannot fully understand, since it requires us to understand ourselves not only as objects of historical forces but as subjects of our own historical self-understanding.

It is in the context of paradox and impossibility I have been outlining that I ask myself the question: Am I far away enough from 1955, in time and in identity, to begin to understand my first relation to the classic—which is a relation to Bach—in a historical way? And what does it mean to say that I was being spoken to by a classic in 1955 when the self that is asking the questions acknowledges that the classic—to say nothing of the self—is historically constituted? As Bach for Mendelssohn's 1829 Berlin audience was an occasion to embody and, in memory and reperformance, to express aspirations, feelings, self-validations that we can identify, diagnose, give names to, place, even foresee the consequences of, what was Bach in South Africa in 1955, and in particular what was the nomination of Bach as the classic, the occasion for? If the notion of the classic as the timeless is undermined by a fully historical account of Bach-reception, then is the moment in the garden—the kind of moment that Eliot experienced, no doubt more mystically and more intensely, and turned into some of his greatest poetry—undermined as well?

Is being spoken to across the ages a notion that we can entertain today only in bad faith?

To answer this question, to which I aspire to give the answer no, and therefore to see what can be rescued of the idea of the classic, let me return to the story of Bach, to the half of the story that I have not yet told.

A simple question. If Bach was so obscure a composer, how did Mendelssohn know his music?

If we follow closely the fortunes of Bach's music after his death, attending not to the reputation of the composer but to actual performance, it begins to emerge that, though obscure, Bach was not quite as forgotten as the revivalist history would lead us to believe. Twenty years after his death, there was a circle of musicians in Berlin regularly performing his instrumental music in private, as a kind of esoteric recreation. The Austrian ambassador to Prussia was for years a member of this circle and on his departure took copies of Bach back to Vienna, where he held performances of Bach in his home. Mozart was part of his circle; Mozart made his own copies and studied the *Art of Fugue* closely. Haydn was also in the circle.

Thus a certain limited Bach tradition, which was not a Bach revival simply because continuity with Bach's own time was never broken, existed in Berlin and branched to Vienna, among professional musicians and serious amateurs, though it did not express itself in public performance.

As for the choral music, a fair amount of it was known to professionals like C. F. Zelter, director of the Berlin Singakademie. Zelter was a friend of Mendelssohn's father. It was at the Singakademie that the young Felix Mendelssohn first came across the choral music, and, against the general uncooperativeness of Zelter, who regarded the *Passions* as unperformable and of specialist interest only, had his own copy of the *Matthew Passion* made and plunged into the business of adapting it for performance.

I say *of specialist (or professional) interest only.* This is the point where parallels between literature and music, the literary classics and the musical classics, begin to break down, and where the institutions and practice of music emerge as perhaps healthier than the institutions and practice of literature. The musical profession has ways of keeping what it values alive that strike me as qualitatively different from the ways in which the institutions of literature keep submerged but valued writers alive.

Because becoming a musician, executant or composer, not only in the Western tradition but in other major traditions of the world, entails long training and personal apprenticeship to a succession of teachers; because the nature of the training entails repeated performance for the ears of others and minute listening and practical criticism, together with memorization; because a range of kinds of performance, from playing for one's teacher to playing for one's class to varieties of public performance, has become institutionalized—for all of these reasons, it is possible to keep music alive and indeed vital within professional circles while it is not part of public awareness, even among educated people.

If there is anything that gives one confidence in the classic status of Bach, it is the *testing* process that he has been through within the profession. Not only did this provincial religious mystic outlast the Enlightenment turn toward rationality and the metropolis, but also he survived what, for many others, would have been the kiss of death, namely, being promoted during the nineteenth-century revival as a great son of the German soil. And today, every time a beginner stumbles through the first prelude of the "48," Bach is being tested again, within the profession. Dare I suggest that the classic in music is what emerges intact from this process of day-by-day testing?

The criterion of testing and survival is not just a minimal, pragmatic, Horatian standard (Horace says, in effect, that if a work is still around a hundred years after it was written, it must be a classic). It is a criterion that expresses a certain confidence in the tradition of testing and a confidence that professionals will not devote labor and attention, generation after generation, to sustaining pieces of music whose life functions have terminated.

It is this confidence that enables me to return to the autobiographical moment at the center of this essay, and to the alternative analyses I proposed of it, with a little more optimism. About my response to Bach in 1955, I asked whether it was truly a response to some inherent quality in the music and not in fact a symbolic election on my part of European high culture as a way out of a social and historical dead end. It is of the essence of this skeptical questioning that the term *Bach* should stand simply as a counter for European high culture, that Bach or *Bach* should have no value in himself or itself—that the notion of "value in itself" should in fact be the object of skeptical interrogation.

By not invoking any idealist justification of "value in itself" or trying to isolate some quality, some essence of the classic, held in common by works that survive the process of testing, I hope I have allowed the terms *Bach* and *the classic* to emerge with a value of their own, even if that value is only in the first place professional and in the second place social. Whether at the age of fifteen I understood what I was getting into is beside the point: Bach is some kind of touchstone because he has passed the scrutiny of hundreds of thousands of intelligences before me, by hundreds of thousands of fellow human beings.

What does it mean in living terms to say that the classic is what survives? How does such a conception of the classic manifest itself in people's lives?

For the most serious answer to this question, we cannot do better than turn to the great poet of the classic in our own day, the Pole Zbigniew Herbert. To Herbert the opposite of the classic is not the Romantic but the barbarian; furthermore, classic versus barbarian is not so much an opposition as a confrontation. Herbert writes from the historical perspective of Poland, a country with an embattled Western culture caught between intermittently barbarous neighbors. It is not the possession of some essentialist quality that, in Herbert's eyes, makes it possible for the classic to withstand the assault of barbarism. Rather, what survives the worst of barbarism, surviving because generations of people cannot afford to let go of it, and therefore hold on to it at all costs—that is the classic.

So we arrive at a certain paradox. The classic defines itself by surviving. Therefore the interrogation of the classic, no matter how hostile, is part of the history of the classic, inevitable and even to be welcomed. For as long as the classic needs to be protected from attack, it can never prove itself classic.

One might even venture further along this road, to say that the function of criticism is defined by the classic: criticism is that which is duty bound to interrogate the classic. Thus the fear that the classic will not survive the decentering acts of criticism may be turned on its head: rather than being the foe of the classic, criticism, and indeed criticism of the most skeptical kind, may be what the classic uses to define itself and ensure its survival. Criticism may in that sense be one of the instruments of the cunning of history.

Notes

1. T. S. Eliot, *What Is a Classic?* (London: Faber, 1945). Hereafter cited as WIC.

2. "Le poète de la latinité tout entière," quoted in Frank Kermode, *The Classic* (London: Faber 1975), 16. Sainte-Beuve's lectures were published as *Etude sur Virgile* in 1857.

3. In a *Criterion* article of 1926, Eliot claims that Britain is part of "a common culture of Western Europe." The question is, "Are there enough persons in Britain believing in that European culture, the Roman inheritance, believing in the place of Britain in that culture?" Two years later he assigns Britain a mediating role between Europe and the rest

of the world: "She is the only member of the European community that has established a genuine empire—that is to say, a world-wide empire as was the Roman empire—not only European but the connection between Europe and the rest of the world." Quoted in Gareth Reeves, *T. S. Eliot: A Virgilian Poet* (London: Macmillan, 1989), 111, 85. Reeves is rightly puzzled by the passing over of the French and other empires.

4. Eliot left Harvard to study in Germany, then moved to Oxford when the war broke out, then married an Englishwoman, then tried to return to Harvard to defend his doctoral dissertation (but the ship on which he had a berth did not sail), then tried to get a job in the U.S. Navy but failed, then—it seems—simply gave up trying, stayed in England, and eventually became a British subject. If the dice had fallen another way, it is not impossible to see him getting his Ph.D., taking up the professorship that awaited him at Harvard, and resuming his American life.

For facts and chronology here, I depend on Roger Kojecky, *T. S. Eliot's Social Criticism* (London: Faber, 1971), 43–47.

5. Eliot made no major public statement on his decision to leave the United States. However, in a 1928 letter to Herbert Read he did, somewhat plaintively, articulate his sense of rootlessness within the country of his birth: "Some day I want to write an essay about the point of view of an American who wasn't an American, because he was born in the South and went to school in New England as a small boy with a nigger drawl, but who wasn't a southerner in the South because his people were northerners in a border state and looked down on all southerners and Virginians, and who so was never anything anywhere and who therefore felt himself to be more a Frenchman than an American and more an Englishman than a Frenchman and yet felt that the U.S.A. up to a hundred years ago was a family extension." Quoted in Russell Kirk, *Eliot and his Age* (New York: Random House, 1971), 56.

Three years later, in the *Criterion*, he saw the plight of the American intellectual as follows: "The American intellectual of today has almost no chance of continuous development upon his own soil and in the environment which his ancestors, however humble, helped to form. He must be an expatriate: either to languish in a provincial university, or abroad, or, the most complete expatriation of all, in New York." Quoted in William M. Chace, *The Political Identities of Ezra Pound and T. S. Eliot* (Stanford: Stanford University Press, 1973), 155. Eliot stresses, however, that this enforced deracination is more a feature of modern life than of specifically American circumstances.

6. T. S. Eliot, "East Coker," in *Four Quartets* (London: Faber, 1944), 22, 15, 20.

7. "Poetry is not a turning loose of emotion, but an escape from emotion; it is not the expression of personality, but an escape from personality." T. S. Eliot, "Tradition and the Individual Talent" (1919), in *Selected Prose,* ed. John Hayward (Harmondsworth: Penguin, 1953), 30.

8. WIC, 28, 32.

9. WIC, 21.

10. Reeves quotes the address of the Cumaean Sibyl to Aeneas (*Aeneid* VI. 93–94): "The

cause of all this Trojan woe is again an alien bride *[coniunx hospita],* again a foreign marriage." The alien brides who cause "Trojan woe" are Helen of Troy, Phoenician Dido, and
Latin Lavinia. Reeves writes, "Is not at least a portion of Eliot's woe his marriage to Vivien,
an Englishwoman, a *coniunx hospita*?" Reeves, 47.

I might add that Eliot's reading of the meeting of Dido and Aeneas in the Underworld
is hard to understand. After Aeneas has addressed her, Dido

> fixed her eyes on the ground.
> Her features were not more stirred by his speech
> Than if they were made of hard flint or Marpesian marble.
> Then she flung herself off *[sese corripuit]* and fled back to the
> shadowy grove,
> Still hostile *[inimica].*

Aeneid VI. 469–73, trans. L. R. Lind (Bloomington: Indiana University Press, 1963), 117.

11. WIC, 21. The degree of Eliot's conscious identification with Virgil and with Aeneas
is further discussed in Reeves, 158–59.

12. In "Virgil and the Christian World" (1951), Eliot distinguishes Virgil's "conscious
mind" from an aspect of his mind that remains discreetly unnamed but may be responding to higher direction. T. S. Eliot, *On Poetry and Poets* (London: Faber, 1957), 129. See
also Reeves, 102.

13. Horace, *Ep.,* II. i, 39: *est vetus atque probus, centum qui perfecit annos.* Quoted in
Frank Kermode, *The Classic* (London: Faber, 1975), 117.

14. Western culture is "the highest culture that the world has ever known," wrote Eliot
in 1948 (quoted in Chace, 203).

15. *Notes toward a Definition of Culture,* completed in 1948, is in effect a response to
Karl Mannheim, who in *Man and Society in an Age of Reconstruction* argued that the
problems of the industrial Europe of the future could be solved only by a shift to conscious social planning, and more generally by the encouragement of new modes of
thought. Direction would have to be given by an elite that had transcended class constraints.

Eliot opposed social engineering, future planning, and *dirigisme* in general. He foresaw that the cultivation of elites would foster class mobility and thereby transform society. It was better, he said, "that the great majority of human beings should go on living
in the place where they were born." The self-consciousness Mannheim envisaged should
remain a faculty of some form of aristocracy or presiding class. See Chace, 197.

Eliot's response to the moves toward European unity represented by the Hague conference of 1948 (which mooted the idea of a European Parliament) and the founding of
the Council of Europe in 1949 is contained in a public letter of 1951, in which, distinguishing cultural questions from political decisions, he advocates a long-term effort to
convince the people of Western Europe of their common culture and to conserve and
cultivate regions, races, languages, each having a "vocation" in relation to the others. See

Kojecky, 214; see also T. S. Eliot, "The Man of Letters and the Future of Europe" (1944), reprinted in *Sewanee Review* (1945): 336–40, and quoted in Kojecky, 202. For fuller discussion of Eliot's debate with Mannheim, see Chace, 196–207.

16. Goethe: "It is as if the eternal harmony were conversing with itself as it may have done in the bosom of God just before the creation of the world." Quoted in Friedrich Blume, *Two Centuries of Bach,* trans. Stanley Godman (London: Oxford University Press, 1950), 47.

17. I do not address the hypothetical question of whether I could have been "spoken to" by Bach if I had been not only a musical illiterate but a musical illiterate brought up in a non-Western cultural tradition. The answer is very likely no: the modalities and sonorities might have been too foreign, the rhythms too unarresting. On the other hand, one should not underestimate the seductive power of the exotic, particularly in so eclectic an age as ours.

18. Certain pieces did keep their place in specialized repertories—some of the motets, for instance, remained in the repertory of the Thomaskirche in Leipzig, where Mozart heard "Singet dem Herrn" in 1789.

19. Blume, p. 12. I have amended Godman's translation slightly.

20. The historical sense of Bach's musician sons Wilhelm Friedemann, Carl Philipp Emmanuel, and Johann Christian was accurate too: not only did they do nothing after their father's death to promote his music or keep it alive, but they swiftly established themselves as leading exponents of the new music of reason and feeling.

During his later years in Leipzig Bach was regarded as what Blume calls "an intractable oddity, a sarcastic old fogey." The authorities of the St. Thomas Church in Leipzig, where he was cantor, were all too visibly relieved when he died and they could hire a younger man more in tune with the times. Of his two most famous contemporaries, one (Telemann) expressed the verdict that Bach's sons, particularly Carl Philipp Emmanuel, were his greatest gift to the world, while the other (Handel) took not the slightest notice of him. See Blume, 15–16, 23, 25–26.

21. The author was J. N. Forkel, director of music at Göttingen University. Quoted in Blume, 38.

22. Blume, 52–53, 56.

23. As Blume points out, we have got beyond the ahistorical liberal idea of Bach as a creature of lonely genius fighting against the restrictions that church, dogma, family, and craft imposed on him—what he calls "Bach the restless titan." We now recognize the tradition of mysticism he inherited; we can also recognize the uncomfortable and paradoxical coexistence in him of a certain resignation of the will (identified by Nietzsche) with a certain violence of temperament (identified by Dilthey). See Blume, 69, 72–73.

Chapter 14

Fiction: The Power of Lies

Mario Vargas Llosa

Ever since I wrote my first short story, people have asked if what I wrote "was true." Though my replies sometimes satisfy their curiosity, I am left each time, no matter how sincere my answer, with a nagging sense of having said something that is not quite on target.

Whether novels are accurate or false is as important to certain people as whether they are good or bad, and many readers, consciously or unconsciously, link the two together. The Spanish Inquisitors, for example, prohibited novels from being published or imported in the Hispano-American colonies, claiming that those nonsensical, absurd books—untruthful, that is—could be harmful to the spiritual health of the Indians. Thus, for three hundred years, Hispano-Americans read only contraband works of fiction, and the first novel published as such in Spanish America did not appear until after Independence (1816, in Mexico). The Holy Office, in banning not only specific works but a literary genre in general, established what in its eyes was a law without exception: novels always lie, they all present a false view of life. Some years ago, I wrote a piece ridiculing those arbitrary fanatics. I now believe that the Spanish Inquisitors were the first to understand—before critics and even novelists—the nature of fiction and its subversive tendencies.

In fact, novels do lie—they cannot help doing so—but that is only a part of the story. The other is that, through the lying, they express a curious truth, which can be expressed only in a veiled and concealed fashion, masquerading as what it is not. This statement has the ring of gibberish. But actually it is quite simple. Men are not content with their lot, and nearly all—rich or poor, brilliant or mediocre, famous or obscure—would like to have a life different from the one they lead. To (cunningly) appease this appetite, fiction was born. It is written and read to provide human beings with the lives they are unresigned to not having. The germ of every novel contains an element of nonresignation and desire.

216

Does this mean that a novel is synonymous with unreality? That Conrad's introspective pirates, Proust's languid aristocrats, Kafka's anonymous, beleaguered little men, and the erudite metaphysical characters in Borges's stories arouse or move us because they have nothing to do with us and because it is impossible to identify their experiences with ours? Not at all. One must proceed cautiously, for this road—of truth and falsehood in the realm of fiction—is riddled with traps, and any enticing oasis is usually a mirage.

What does it mean to say that a novel always lies? Not what the officers and cadets believed at the Leoncio Prado Military Academy where—seemingly, at least—my first novel, *The Time of the Hero,* takes place, and where it was burned, accused of slandering the institution. Not what my first wife thought after having read another of my novels, *Aunt Julia and the Scriptwriter,* which she incorrectly construed as a portrait of herself, and which led her to publish a book purporting to restore the truth that had been altered by fiction. Both stories, of course, contain more inventions, deviations, and exaggerations than memories, and at no point in writing them did I seek to be literally faithful to certain persons and events prior to and extraneous to the novel. In both instances, as in everything I have written, I began with experiences still vivid in my memory and stimulating to my imagination and then fantasized something that is an extremely unfaithful reflection of that material.

Novels are not written to recount life but to transform it by adding something to it. In the novellas of the French writer Restif de la Bretonne, reality is as photographic as can be, a cataloguing of the eighteenth-century French customs. And yet, within that utterly painstaking enumeration of customs, where everything resembles real life, there is something else, different, minimal, and revolutionary—the fact that in this world men do not fall in love with women for the purity of their features, the grace of their body, their spiritual endowments, and so on, but *exclusively* for the beauty of their feet.

All novelists, less crudely, less explicitly, and also less consciously, remake reality—embellishing it or diminishing it—as did the prodigious Restif with delightful ingenuousness. These subtle, or crude, additions to life—wherein the novelist materializes his obsessions—constitute the originality of a work of fiction. Its profundity depends on how fully it expresses a general need and on the number of readers, through time and space, who can identify their own obscure, haunting demons with those contraband infiltrations of life. Could I, in those novels of mine, have attempted an exact correlation with actual memories? Of course. But even if I had accomplished that tedious feat of simply narrating actual events and describing people whose biographies fit their models like a glove, my novels would not thereby have been any less truthful or untruthful than they are.

Anecdote is not what essentially determines the truth or falsehood of a work of fiction, but rather the idea that it be not lived but written, that it be made up of words and not live experiences. Events translated into words undergo a profound modification. The actuality—the glory battle I participated in, the Gothic profile of the girl I loved—that is one thing, whereas the signs that describe it are countless. By selecting some and discarding others, the novelist favors one and kills off infinite other possibilities or versions of what he is describing. The novelist therefore changes nature; *what describes* becomes *what is described.*

I am referring here only to the case of the realistic writer, that sect, school, or tradition to which I belong, whose novels relate events that readers can recognize as plausible from their own experience of reality. It might, in fact, appear that the connection between reality and fiction is not even an issue for the novelist of a fantastic vein, who describes irreconcilable and clearly nonexistent worlds. Actually, it is an issue, but in another way. The "unreality" of fantastic literature becomes, for the readers, a symbol or allegory, in other words, a representation of realities, of experiences they can identify as being possible in life. What is important is this—the "realistic" or "fantastic" nature of an anecdote is not what marks the boundary line between truth and falsehood in fiction.

Along with this first modification—the imprint of words or events—there is another, no less fundamental: that of time. Real life flows without pause, lacks order, is chaotic, each story merging with all stories and hence never having a beginning or ending. Life in a work of fiction is a simulation in which that dizzying disorder achieves order, organization, cause and effect, beginning and end. The scope of a novel is not determined merely by the language in which it is written, but also by its temporal scheme, the manner in which existence transpires within it—its pauses and accelerations and the chronological perspective employed by the narrator to describe that narrated time.

Though there is a distance between words and events, there is always an abyss between real time and fictional time. Novelistic time is a device created to attain certain psychological effects. In it, the past can be subsequent to the present—effect preceding cause—as in the Alejo Carpentier story, *Journey to the Seed,* which begins with the death of an old man and continues until his conception within the maternal womb. Or it can merely be a remote past that never actually dissolves into the recent past, the point from which the narrator is narrating, as in most classical novels. Or it can be an eternal present without either past or future, as in Samuel Beckett's fictional works. Or a labyrinth in which past, present, and future coexist, annihilating each other, as in Faulkner's *The Sound and the Fury.*

Novels have a beginning and an end; and, even in the loosest and most disjointed ones, life takes on a discerning meaning, for we are presented with a perspective never provided by the real life in which we are immersed. This order is an invention, an addition of the novelist, that dissembler who appears to re-create life when, in fact, he is rectifying it. Fiction betrays life, sometimes subtly, sometimes brutally, encapsulating it in a weft of words that reduce it in scale and place it within the readers' reach. Thus the readers can judge it, understand it, and, above all, live it with an impunity not granted them in real life.

What difference is there, between a work of fiction and a journalistic report or a history book? Are they not, too, composed of words? And do they not, within the artificial time of the account, encapsulate that shoreless torrent, real time? It is a question of opposing systems in the approach to what is real: the novel rebels against life and transgresses it, other genres are unceasingly its slave. The notion of truthfulness or deception functions differently in both instances. In journalism or history, it hinges on the correlation between what is written and the corresponding reality: the closer it is the truer, and the farther away the falser. To say that Michelet's *History of the French Revolution,* or Prescott's *Conquest of Peru,* is "novelistic" is a criticism, an insinuation that they lack seriousness. Documenting the historical error of *War and Peace* with respect to the Napoleonic Wars would be a waste of time—the truth of the novel does not depend on facts.

On what, then, does it depend? On its own persuasive powers, on the sheer communicative strength of its fantasy, on the skill of its magic. Every good novel tells the truth and every bad novel lies. For a novel "to tell the truth" means to be unable to accomplish that trickery. The novel, thus, is an amoral genre; or rather, its ethic is sui generis, one in which truth and falsehood are exclusively esthetic concepts.

My foregoing remarks might suggest that fiction is a gratuitous fabrication, a juggling devoid of transcendence. On the contrary, wild as it may be, fiction's roots are submerged in human experience, from which it derives sustenance and which it in turn nourishes. A recurrent theme in the history of fiction is the risk incurred in taking what novels say literally, in believing that life is the way novelists describe it to be. Books on chivalry addle Don Quixote's brain and set him on the road to spearing windmills, and Emma Bovary's tragedy would not have occurred if Flaubert's character had not attempted to be like the heroines of the romantic novels she read.

By believing that reality is like fiction, Alonso Quijano and Emma Bovary undergo terrible upheavals. Do we condemn them for that? No, their stories move and awe us; that impossible determination to live fiction seems to personify for us an idealistic attitude that honors the species. To want to be different from the way one is, is the human aspiration par excellence. It has engendered the best and worst in recorded history. Including works of fiction.

When we read novels, we are not only who we are, but, in addition, we are the bewitched beings into whose midst the novelist transfers us. The transfer is a metamorphosis—the asphyxiating constriction of our lives opens up and we sally forth to be others, to have vicarious experiences that fiction converts into our own. A wondrous dream, a fantasy incarnate, fiction completes us, mutilated beings burdened with the awful dichotomy of having only one life and the ability to desire a thousand. This gap between real life and the desires and fantasies demanding that it be richer and more varied is the realm of fiction.

At the heart of all fictional work there burns a protest. Their authors created these lives because they were unable to live them, and their readers (and believers) encounter in these phantom creatures the faces and adventures needed to enhance their own lives. That is the truth expressed by the lies in fiction—the lies that we ourselves are, the lies that console us and make up for our longings and frustrations. How trustworthy then is the testimony of a novel on the very society that produced it? Were those people really that way? They were, in the sense that that was how they wanted to be, how they envisioned themselves loving, suffering, and rejoicing. Those lies document not their lives, but rather their driving demons—the dreams that intoxicated them and made the lives they led more tolerable. An era is populated not merely by flesh and blood creatures, but also by the phantom creatures into which they are transformed in order to break the barriers that confine them.

The lies in novels are not gratuitous—they fill in the insufficiencies of life. Thus, when life seems full and absolute, and people, out of an all-consuming faith, are resigned to their destinies, novels perform no service at all. Religious cultures produce poetry and theater, not novels. Fiction is an art of societies in which faith is undergoing some sort of crisis, in which it is necessary to believe in something, in which the unitarian, trusting, and absolute vision has been supplanted by a shattered one and an uncertainty about the world we inhabit and the afterworld.

Every novel, aside from being amoral, harbors at its core a certain skepticism. When religious culture enters into crisis, life seems divested of any binding schemes, dogma, and precepts and turns into chaos. That is the optimum moment for fiction. Its artificial orders offer refuge, security, and the free release of those appetites and fears that real life incites and cannot gratify or exorcise. Fiction is a temporary substitute for life. The return to reality is almost a brutal impoverishment, corroboration that we are less than we dreamed. Which means that fiction, by spurring the imagination, both temporarily assuages human dissatisfaction and simultaneously incites it.

The Spanish Inquisition understood the danger. Leading lives through fiction that one does not live in reality is a source of anxiety, a maladjustment to existence that can turn into rebelliousness, an unsubmissive attitude toward the establishment. One can well understand why regimes that seek to exercise total control over life mistrust works of fiction and subject them to censorship. Emerging from one's own self, being another, even in illusion, is a way of being less a slave and of experiencing the risks of freedom.

"Things are not as we see them but as we remember them," wrote Valle Inclan. He was undoubtedly referring to the way things are in literature, that spurious world that acquires a precarious sense of reality through the persuasive powers of the good writer and a certain readiness to accept on the part of the good reader.

For almost every writer, memory is the starting point of the imagination; it is the springboard that precipitates it on its indeterminate journey toward fiction. In creative literature, that which emanates from the memory and that which is invented are so inextricably interwoven that it is often quite impossible even for the author to distinguish one from the other; and although he may claim otherwise, he knows that any attempt to recuperate lost time through a work of literature can never be more than mere pretense, a work of fiction in which memories merge into fantasies and vice versa.

That is why literature is the domain par excellence of ambiguity. It is always subjective; it deals in half truths, relative truths, literary truths that frequently constitute flagrant historical inaccuracies or even lies. Although the almost cinematographic description of the battle of Waterloo that features in *Les Misérables* may exalt us, we are aware that this was a contest fought and won by Victor Hugo, and not the one lost by Napoleon. Or—to cite a Valencian medieval classic, Joanot Martorell—the conquest of England by the Moors described in *Tirant lo Blanc* is totally convincing, and no one would think of questioning its credibility with the petty argument that historically no Moorish army ever crossed the English Channel.

The reconstruction of the past through literature is almost always misleading in terms of historical objectivity. Literary truth is one thing, historical truth another. But, although it may be full of fabrication—or for that very reason—literature presents us with a side of history that cannot be found in history books. For literature does not lie gratuitously. All its deceits, devices, and hyperbole only serve to express those deep-seated and disturbing truths that come to light only in this oblique way.

When Johannot Martorell relates in *Tirant lo Blanc* that the Princess of France had such a white skin that one could see the wine going down her throat, he is telling us something technically impossible; and yet, captivated by the author's magic, we accept it as an incontrovertible truth because, in the simulated world of the novel (unlike what happens in real life), excess is never the exception, always the rule. Nothing appears excessive if everything is.

In *Tirant*, for instance, there are apocalyptic battles fought with a punctilious sense of ritual and exploits of a hero who, single-handed, routs the mob and literally ravages half of Christendom and the whole of Islam. There are comic rituals too, as demonstrated by that pious and lustful character who kisses women three times on the mouth in homage to the Holy Trinity. Everywhere we find excess—as with war, love too has generally cataclysmic consequences. Tirant, when he sees Carmesina's swelling breasts for the first time in the half-light of the funeral chamber, becomes nothing less than cataleptic, collapsing on a bed, where he remains without sleeping or eating or uttering a single word for several days. When he finally recovers, it is as if he were learning to speak again. The first words he stammers out are "Yo amo": "I am in love."

These fictitious events tell us not what the Valencians were really like at the end of the fifteenth century, but how they would have liked to have been and what they would have liked to have done; they depict not the characters of flesh and blood who actually lived in those terrible times, but merely ghosts that haunted them. It is their insatiable appetites, their fears and cravings, their grudges, that are brought to life. In a successful work of fiction it is the individual's experience of an age that comes to life; and that is why novels, although, when compared with history, they may be full of fabrication, nonetheless communicate to us certain transitory, evanescent truths that always defy purely scientific descriptions of reality. Only literature has the powers and techniques at its disposal to distil the delicate elixir of life: the truth that lies hidden at the heart of the human imagination.

Now there is nothing deceptive about the deceits of literature; at least, there should not be. Only simpletons who believe that literature must be objectively faithful to life and as dependent on reality as history is might think so. There is no deception, because when we open a work of fiction, we adjust our minds to participate in a performance where we know very well that the extent to which we are moved or bored will depend exclusively on the narrator's talent to captivate us and draw us into the world of his imagination—making us accept and experience his lies as if they were the truth—and not on his ability to reproduce faithfully what actually happened.

These well-defined boundaries between literature and history—between literary truth and historical truth—are a prerogative of open societies. There they exist side by side, independently and in their own right, although complementing each other in a Utopian attempt to encompass the whole of life. And perhaps the most effective proof of an open society, in the sense Karl Popper used the term, is when the following occurs: when literature and history coexist autonomously without either encroaching on the territory or usurping the role of the other.

In closed societies the exact opposite occurs. And perhaps the best way of defining a closed society would be to say that in such a society, history and fiction have ceased to be two separate entities; they have become muddled up, each taking the other's place and swapping identities as at a masked ball.

In a closed society the authorities not only assume the right to control people's actions, what they do and what they say, but also aim to control their imaginations, their dreams and aspirations—and, of course, their memories. In a closed society, sooner or later the past becomes subject to a sort of manipulation specially designed to justify the present. The official version of history, the only one tolerated, is the setting for the extraordinary *volte-faces* made famous by the Soviet *Encyclopedia*. Protagonists appear and disappear without trace according to whether they have been redeemed or purged by the authorities; and the exploits of past heroes and villains alter, with every new edition, in sign, valency, and substance in accordance with the requirements of the dictatorial elite of the moment. This is a practice that modern totalitarianism has perfected but not invented; it dates back as far as the dawn of civilization, which, let us not forget, until relatively recently was always despotic and dictatorial.

To organize the collective memory, to turn history into an instrument of the government whose role is to legitimize whoever is in power and to find alibis for their crimes, is a temptation inherent in all authority. Totalitarian states can make it a reality. In the past, countless civilizations put it into practice.

Take my ancient compatriots, the Inkas, for example. They effected it in a brutal and theatrical manner. When the *emperador* died, not only did his wife and concubines die with him, but also the court intellectuals who were known as *amautas,* or wise men. Their talents were applied essentially to performing the following little conjuring trick: creating history out of fiction. The new Inka would come to power with a brand new court of *amautas* responsible for renewing the official records, revising the past, by bringing it up-to-date so to speak, so that all the accomplishments, conquests, feats of engineering or architecture, and the like that were previously attributed to his predecessor would be from now on transferred to the new emperor's personal record of achievements. Gradually his predecessors would be forgotten—lost in oblivion.

The Inkas knew how to put the past to good use, turning it into literature, so that it could contribute toward the stabilization of the present—the ultimate ideal of any dictatorship. They prohibited personal accounts of what happened because those must always be at odds with an official account, which is of necessity coherent and unappealable. The result is that the Inka Empire is a society without a history, at least without any anecdotal history; for no one has been able to reconstruct with any degree of reliability a past that has been so systematically dressed up and undressed like a professional striptease artist.

In a closed society history becomes steeped in fiction, and so it actually becomes a work of fiction, because it is constantly being written and rewritten to serve religious orthodoxy or contemporary political theory or, even more crudely, to accord with the whims of the ruling power.

At the same time, a strict system of censorship is usually introduced, so that imaginative literature is kept within narrow limits, so that its subjective truths do not contradict or cast aspersions on the official version of history, but rather popularize and illustrate it. The difference between historical truth and literary truth disappears; and the two become fused into a sort of hybrid that imbues history with a sense of unreality and empties fiction of any mystery, originality, or spirit of nonconformity it may have toward the establishment.

To condemn history to tell lies and literature to propagate facts specially concocted by the authorities is no obstacle to the scientific or technological development of a country or the establishment of a certain social justice. It seems to have been proved that the Inka period—an extraordinary achievement for its time and for ours—put an end to hunger: everyone in the kingdom had enough to eat. And modern totalitarian societies have given a great impetus to education, medicine, sport, and employment, making them accessible to the majority of the people, something that open societies, despite their widespread prosperity, have not yet succeeded in doing, for the price of the freedom they enjoy is paid sometimes by enormous inequalities of wealth and—even worse—inequalities of opportunity among their members.

But when a state, in its zeal to control and decide everything, deprives human beings of the right to create freely and believe whatever lies they choose to believe, when it appropriates that right and exercises it like a monopoly through its historians or censors—as the Inkas did through their *amautas*—one of the great nerve centers of life is destroyed. And men and women suffer a sort of mutilation that impoverishes their existence even when their basic needs are taken care of.

Because the real world, the material world, has never been adequate, and never will be, to fulfill human desires. And without that essential dissatisfaction with life that is both exacerbated and at the same time assuaged by the lies of literature, there can never be any genuine progress.

The gift of the imagination with which we are all endowed is a diabolical one. It constantly opens up the abyss between what we are and what we would like to be, between what we have and what we covet.

But it has also produced an ingenious and gentle palliative to relieve the pain of the inevitable breach between our boundless desires and our practical limitations: fiction. Thanks to fiction we can grow and diversify without losing our basic identities. We can immerse ourselves in it, proliferate, living out many more lives than the ones we have, and many more than we would be able to were we to remain confined to reality without ever venturing out of the prison of history.

Men cannot live by truth alone; they also need lies—those they invent of their accord, not those foisted on them by others; those that emerge undisguised, not those that insinuate themselves through the trapping of history. Fiction enriches life, complements it, and offers fleeting compensation for man's tragic condition: that of always wanting and dreaming of more than he can realistically attain.

When literature is allowed to supply this alternative life, unimpeded, without any constraints except the limitations of the creator, then it extends

the range of human experience by adding to it that dimension which nourishes our inner life—that intangible, elusive, yet invaluable one we experience only vicariously.

It is a right we must defend without shame. Because to play a game of
lies, as the authors of works of fiction do with their readers—lies writers
invent according to their own personal demons—is a way of asserting individual sovereignty and defending it when it is threatened. It is a way of preserving one's own sphere of freedom, a bastion beyond the control of the
authorities, protected from the interference of others, inside which we are
truly the masters of our own destinies.

And from that freedom other freedoms are born. Those private havens,
the subjective truths of literature, give historical truth, their counterpart, a
viable existence and a function of its own: that of recovering an important
part—but only a part—of our past . . . those moments of glory and wretchedness we share with others in our capacity as ordinary human beings. And
there is no substitute for historical truth—it is indispensable if we are to know
what we were and what we may become in terms of human society. But what
we are as individuals, what we wanted to be and could not really be and therefore had to be in our dreams and imaginations—that secret side of our history—only literature can relate. That is why Balzac remarked that fiction was
"the private history of nations."

By its very existence, it is a terrible indictment of life under any regime
or ideology: a flagrant testimony of the inadequacies, the inability of such
systems to fulfil us . . . and therefore a permanent antidote to all authority
that attempts to keep men content and compliant. The lies of literature, if
they are allowed to flourish freely, are proof to us that this never was the case.
And they are a permanent source of intrigue that ensures that it never will
be in the future.

CONTRIBUTORS

K. ANTHONY APPIAH is professor of Afro-American studies and philosophy at Harvard University. His most recent books are *In My Father's House: Africa in the Philosophy of Culture* (1992), *Identities* (1995), and (with Amy Guttmann) *Color Conscious: The Political Morality of Race* (1996). He is the editor (with Henry Louis Gates, Jr.) of *The Dictionary of Global Culture* (1997).

WALTER BERNS is professor emeritus of government at Georgetown University. His books include *For Capital Punishment: Crime and the Morality of the Death Penalty* (1979), *In Defense of Liberal Democracy* (1984), and *Taking the Constitution Seriously* (1987). He is resident scholar at the American Enterprise Institute.

BERNARD BOXILL is professor of philosophy at the University of North Carolina, Chapel Hill. He is the author of *Blacks and Social Justice* (1992).

JAMES CEASER is professor of government at the University of Virginia. His books include *Reforming the Reforms* (1982), *Liberal Democracy and Political Science* (1990), (with Andrew Busch) *Upside Down and Inside Out: The 1992 Elections and American Politics* (1992), and *Reconstructing America: The Symbol of America in Modern Thought* (1997).

LINDA CHAVEZ is president of the Center for Equal Opportunity. She is the author of *Out of the Barrio: Toward a New Politics of Hispanic Assimilation* (1991). She has served as White House director of public liaison, executive director of the U.S. Commission on Civil Rights, and president of U.S. English.

J. M. COETZEE'S most recent novels are *Foe* (1986), *Age of Iron* (1990), and *Master of Petersburg* (1994). His other works include *White Writing: On the Culture of Letters in South Africa* (1988), *Doubling the Point: Essays and Interviews* (1992), and *Giving Offense: Essays on Censorship* (1996). He is professor of general literature at the University of Cape Town.

STANLEY FISH is Arts and Sciences Professor of English and professor of law at Duke University. His books include *Doing What Comes Naturally: Change, Rhetoric, and the Practice of Theory in Literary and Legal Studies* (1989), *There's No Such Thing as Free Speech and It's a Good Thing Too* (1994), and *Professional Correctness: Literary Studies and Political Change* (1995). He serves as executive director of Duke University Press.

NATHAN GLAZER is professor of education and sociology emeritus at Harvard University. His most recent books are *Ethnic Dilemmas* (1983), *The Limits of Social Policy* (1988), and *We Are All Multiculturalists Now* (1997). He serves as coeditor of *Public Interest.*

WILSON CAREY MCWILLIAMS is professor of political science at Rutgers University, New Brunswick. His books include *The Idea of Fraternity in America* (1973) and *The Politics of Disappointment: American Elections, 1976–1994* (1995).

ARTHUR M. MELZER is professor of political science at Michigan State University. He is the author of *The Natural Goodness of Man: On the System of Rousseau's Thought* (1990). He is a director of the Symposium on Science, Reason, and Modern Democracy and an editor of its first two volumes of essays, *Technology in the Western Political Tradition* (1993) and *History and the Idea of Progress* (1995).

ANNE NORTON is professor of political science at the University of Pennsylvania. She is the author of *Alternative Americas: A Reading of Antebellum Political Culture* (1986), *Reflections on Political Identity* (1988), and *Republic of Signs: Liberal Theory and American Popular Culture* (1993).

LORRAINE PANGLE has taught at Groton School and the Community Hebrew Academy of Toronto. She is the author (with Thomas L. Pangle) of *The Learning of Liberty: The Educational Ideas of the American Founders* (1993).

MARC F. PLATTNER is coeditor of the *Journal of Democracy,* codirector of the International Forum for Democratic Studies, and counselor at the National Endowment for Democracy. He is the author of *Rousseau's State of Nature* (1979) and editor (with Larry Diamond) of *The Global Resurgence of Democracy* (1993), *Nationalism, Ethnic Conflict, and Democracy* (1994), and *Civil-Military Relations and Democracy* (1996).

MARIO VARGAS LLOSA'S most recent novels are *The Storyteller* (1989), *In Praise of the Stepmother* (1990), and *Death in the Andes* (1996). His other works include *A Writer's Reality* (1991) and *A Fish in the Water: A Memoir* (1994).

JERRY WEINBERGER is professor of political science at Michigan State University. His books include *Science, Faith, and Politics: Francis Bacon and the Utopian Roots of the Modern Age* (1985) and *The History of the Reign of King Henry the Seventh: A New Edition and Interpretation* (1996). He is a director of the Symposium on Science, Reason, and Modern Democracy and an editor of its first two volumes of essays, *Technology in the Western Political Tradition* (1993) and *History and the Idea of Progress* (1995).

C. VANN WOODWARD is Sterling Professor of History emeritus at Yale University. His most recent books are *Mary Chestnut's Civil War* (1981), *Thinking Back: The Perils of Writing History* (1986), *The Future of the Past* (1989), and *The Old World's New World* (1991).

M. RICHARD ZINMAN is professor of political theory in James Madison College at Michigan State University. He is executive director of the Symposium on Science, Reason, and Modern Democracy and an editor of its first two volumes of essays, *Technology in the Western Political Tradition* (1993) and *History and the Idea of Progress* (1995).

INDEX

Abrams v. United States, 81
Achebe, Chinua, 37, 41, 42
Accommodation, 30, 107–8, 122, 139–40
Acculturation. *See* Assimilation
Addams, Jane, 22
Adorno, Theodore, 144
Aeneid, the, 201–2
Africa
 and colonial rule, 38, 57–58
 creative arts in, 57
 cultural and racial identity in, 38–46,
  49, 55–56, 58–59
 and democracy, 159–60
 ethnicity, 56, 58–59
 and multiculturalism, 38, 46, 49, 57, 59
 religion in, 43–44, 56–57
African American Baseline Essays, 178–79
African Americans
 assimilation and exclusion of, 5, 16, 18,
  19, 20, 22, 25–26, 27, 28, 29–32, 34,
  62–64
 and cultural identity, 55–56
 and discrimination, 28, 29, 31–32,
  63–66, 103–4, 152
 and education, 63, 66–68, 169, 178–82
 integration of, 34, 63, 153
African Development Bank, 42
Afrocentrism, 6, 32, 41, 49–50, 51, 66–67,
  69, 169, 178–79, 180
Alexander, Larry, 87n25
Algeria, 58

Amalgamation, 20–21, 33
American Civil Liberties Union, 66
American Dilemma, An (Myrdal), 31
American identity, 16–18
Americanization Day, 21, 28
Americanization movement, 5, 19–25, 29,
  62. *See also* Assimilation
Americans by Choice (Gavit), 22
Angola, 58
Appleby, Joyce, 145
Arendt, Hannah, 132
Areopagitica (Milton), 70
Arieli, Yehoshua, 18
Arnold, Matthew, 92
Asante, Molefi Kete, 178
Asian Americans, 19, 22, 27, 28, 29, 34,
  73, 115, 151–52, 166–67, 169
Assimilation
 of African Americans, 5, 18, 20, 22,
  25–26, 28, 29–32, 34, 62–64
 of Asian Americans, 27, 29–34
 in Canada, 106–7
 criticism of, 25–27, 171
 definition of, 16, 17
 disreputation of, 5, 15, 25, 33
 and education, 23–24
 as it exists today, 5, 15, 16, 33, 171–72
 of Hispanic Americans, 27, 29, 34
 of immigrants, 23–24, 25–28, 29, 30,
  32–33, 62, 94, 107
 of Jews, 31

Assimilation *(continued)*
  liberals on, 30, 32
  responsibility for, 171
  prior to the twentieth century, 16,
    18–19, 62–63, 94
  during the World Wars, 27–29
Azikiwe, Nnamdi, 43

Bach, Johann Sebastian, 11, 205–12
Balzac, Honoré de, 226
Beckett, Samuel, 219
Belgium, 61
Berlant, 87n30
Biafra, 43
Biologism, 9, 150, 155
"Black English," 63, 64
Black No More (Schuyler), 54n18
Black Reconstruction (Du Bois), 45, 54n18
Bloom, Allan, 92
Boaz, Franz, 150
Borglum, Gutzon, 22
Bosnia-Herzegovina, 59
Bouchard, Lucien, 107
Bourassa, Robert, 106
Bourne, Randolph, 26, 123
Brandeis, Louis, 21
Bretonne, Restif de la, 217
Bridgeman, Brent, 179
British North American Act of 1867, 106
Brown v. Board of Education, 63
Bryce, James, 62
Burke, Edmund, 130
Burma, 158

Canada, 62, 92–93, 106–7, 140, 173, 175
Carlin, David, 126
Carlyle, Thomas, 91–92
Carnegie Corporation Americanization
    Studies series, 22, 23, 29
Carpentier, Alejo, 218
Catholicism, 121–22

Censorship, 221, 224
Charlottetown Accord, 107
Chesterton, G. K., 126
Chicago Cultural Studies Group, 85n15
Childhood and Society (Erikson), 17
China, 158–59
Chinese Americans, 166–67
Closed societies, 223, 224
Cohen, Avern, 66
Coleridge, Samuel, 92
Communist party, 97, 98
Conference on Security and Cöoperation
    in Europe, 61
Constitution, U.S.
  and discrimination, 153
  and minority rights, 104–5, 112, 113
  and multiculturalism, 6–7, 8, 91,
    93–95, 120–21, 122–24, 127, 133, 153
Coolidge, Calvin, 96
Crèvecoeur, J. Hector St. John de, 16,
    62–63
Croatia, 59
Crummell, Alexander, 41
Cultural conflicts, 43–44, 58–62
Cultural pluralism, 15, 26, 27, 28, 91,
    94–95, 101, 112, 160, 173
Cultural separatism, 63, 65–66, 67
Culture
  and the arts, 57, 108, 141, 142
  definition of, 46–47, 51–52, 55, 91–92,
    118, 140, 147–48, 149–51
  and diversity, 51–52, 72, 125, 151, 152
  and education, 48–51, 183–84
  and equality, 8, 125–26, 188
  maintaining a, 171
  and the media, 47–48
  and religion, 56–57, 94–95, 105, 150,
    220–21
*Culture and Democracy in the United
    States* (Kallen), 27
Czechoslovakia, 59

Dannhauser, Werner J., 109
Declaration of Independence, 17, 120, 124
Democracy
  definition of, 130
  liberal, 7, 8, 105, 151–52, 154, 158, 161–62, 185
  and majority rule, 7, 112–13, 115–16, 118–19, 124
  and religion, 121, 122
  resurgence of, 157–62
Democratic institutions, 123–24
Democratic movements, 59, 157–62
Derrida, Jacques, 144
Dewey, John, 26
Disuniting of America, The (Schlesinger), 64
Dogmatism, 187, 188
Dorle, Jeanne, 180
Douglas, Stephen, 98, 102
Douglas, William O., 189
Douglass, Frederick, 65, 178
Du Bois, W. E. B., 41, 45, 54n18, 63, 65, 131, 170

Economic Community of West African States (ECOWAS), 42
Education
  and culture, 32, 47–51, 65, 66–67, 91, 108
  and curriculum, 169–70, 173–77, 178–79, 189–94
  of immigrants, 23–24
  in Iowa, 176, 179
  and multiculturalism, 9–10, 32, 34, 48–51, 65, 66, 67, 77, 91, 108, 123, 141, 160, 168–70, 173–94
  in New York, 173–74, 175, 176–77, 179, 190
  in Ohio, 189
  in Pennsylvania, 176

and segregation, 63, 66–68
and self esteem, 178–82
Supreme Court rulings on, 63, 100, 167
See also African Americans, and education
Eliot, T. S., 11, 199–204, 206
Emerson, Ralph Waldo, 18
Equality, 8, 23, 91, 102, 124, 125–26, 188
Equal opportunity, 113, 116, 125
Equal rights, 71–72, 96, 104–5, 106, 122, 145, 149, 151, 152, 157, 158–60, 162
Erikson, Erik H., 17
Ethnic conflicts, 42–45, 58–59, 60, 105, 157–58
Ethnicity, 17–18, 19, 33, 37, 42–44, 161, 171, 173, 175, 182
European Community, 61

Fabian, Johannes, 43
Fanon, Franz, 146
Faulkner, William, 219
Federalist, The, 93, 95–96, 97, 105, 120, 135
Fiction, 11–12, 216–26
Fitzpatrick, Father Joseph, 170
Flaubert, Gustave, 204
France, 61
Franklin, Benjamin, 178
Franklin, John Hope, 65, 170
Frazier, E. Franklin, 31
Frost, Robert, 130

Garveyism, 31
Gates, Henry Louis Jr., 66
Gavit, James A., 22
German Americans, 28
Ghana, 37, 43, 49
Gandhi, Mahatma, 181
Ghetto, The (Wirth), 31
Gleason, Philip, 16, 17–18
Gobineau, Arthur de, 143

Goldberg, David Theo, 85n15
Great Britain, 61, 98–100, 104
Gutmann, Amy, 78–82, 86n23,
    87nn25,28,29,30, 92, 103, 104–5, 140

Habermas, Jürgen, 80–81, 82, 87n25
Hare, Thomas, 7, 119
Hate speech, 72, 79–81, 82–84, 87
Havel, Vaclav, 188
Hegel, Georg, 146, 150
Hegemon and the Other, 142–44, 147
Heidegger, Martin, 144
Herbert, Zbigniew, 212
Herzfeld, Michael, 125
Higham, John, 19
Hilliard, Asa, 178
Hirsch, E. D., 48
Hispanic Americans, 27, 29, 34, 49, 63,
    147, 151, 165–66, 169, 170, 171
Historical truth and understanding, 41,
    130, 132, 168, 170, 174, 209, 222,
    223, 224, 225–26
Hitler, Adolf, 27, 28, 29
Holmes, Oliver Wendell, 81
Houghton, James, 76
Huntington, Samuel P., 105

"I am an American Day," 28
Idea of the University, The (Pelikan), 67
Immigrants
    assimilation of, 17, 19–22, 23–24,
        25–28, 29, 30, 32–33, 62, 94, 107
    and education, 23–24, 167
    restriction of, 26, 97
    in the twentieth century, 165, 166
Inclan, Valle, 221
Integration, 31, 153, 155, 172
Intermarriage, 5, 21, 34
Inter-Racial Council, 21–22
Italian Americans, 28, 167

Japanese Americans, 28, 115, 166–67
Jefferson, Thomas, 94, 100, 101, 102, 108,
    123, 182, 184
Jeffries, Leonard, 178
Jews, 19, 31, 33, 50, 64, 104, 115
Journey to the Seed (Carpentier), 218
Jurisprudence, 168
Jury trials, 103–4, 105

Kahane, Rabbi Meir, 103
Kaixi, Wuer, 158–59
Kallen, Horace, 26, 27, 30, 94
Keats, John, 92
Kellor, Frances, 20–21
Khomeini, Ayatollah Ruholla, 73, 103
Kifer, Edward, 180
King, Martin Luther Jr., 63, 181, 182
Kohn, Hans, 18
Ku Klux Klan, 19, 26
Kunstler, William, 103
Kyi, Aung San Suu, 158
Kymlicka, Will, 86n21, 87n30

Laitin, David, 43
Lamm, Richard, 165
Language
    and bilingualism, 49, 63, 106, 173
    and cultural diversity, 56
    and multilingualism, 47
Lenin, 146
Lessing, Gotthold, 186
Letter on Toleration (Locke), 101
Letters from an American Farmer (Crève-
    coeur), 16
Levesque, Rene, 106
Lewis, Arthur, 119n5
Lewis, Bernard, 99
Lewis, Read, 33
Liberalism, 2, 6, 9, 30, 32, 81–82, 83–84, 86n21,
    87n28, 142–43, 145, 149, 152, 153

Liberia, 58, 63
Liberty, 108–9, 145, 157, 193
Lincoln, Abraham, 96–97, 98, 102, 155
Lindsay, Vachel, 132, 138n7
Lipset, S. M., 18
Literature, 199–206, 210, 216–26
Locke, John, 92, 101, 102, 132, 136
Los Angeles riots, 37, 44, 53n2

McLaren, Peter, 85n15
Madison, James, 94, 95–96, 97, 100, 131, 135, 136
Majorities, 112–19, 123, 135, 142–44
Malwal, Bona, 159
Mansfield, Harvey, 124
Marcuse, Herbert, 3
Martorell, Johannot, 222
Marx, Karl, 3, 4
Marxism, 1, 3–4, 31, 45, 67–68, 146, 158
Meech Lake Accord, 106
Melville, Herman, 133
Mendus, Susan, 86n23, 87n30
Merchant of Venice, The (Shakespeare), 91
Mill, John Stuart, 7, 71, 92, 113, 117, 118, 119
Milton, John, 70, 75
Minorities, 7, 112–19, 142–44
Moore, Joan, 170
Mormons, 97–98
Mulroney, Brian, 106
Multiculturalism
   in Africa, 38, 46
   and the arts, 108
   boutique, 69–73, 74, 75
   in Canada, 62, 92–93, 106–7, 173, 175
   categorization of, 142–44, 146–47
   definition of, 1–4, 5, 6, 46, 48, 69– 70, 75, 76, 77, 78, 92, 123, 139–42, 147, 148, 160

and democracy, 123–26, 127, 133, 135, 160
   democratic, 123–26
   and demographics, 75–76
   effects of, 7, 8, 51, 52, 131–35, 154–55
   and equality, 71–72, 91
   in Europe, 59–61, 99, 104
   and exclusion, 80, 81–82, 87n28, 103
   in Great Britain, 99–100, 104
   limitations of, 8–9, 10, 146–48, 150
   moderate, 10–11
   origin of, 144, 146
   radical, 10, 161–62
   and self-esteem, 178–82
   strong, 69, 73–75
   in the work place, 76–77
   See also Constitution, U.S., and multiculturalism; Cultural pluralism; Education, and multiculturalism
Multiculturalism and the Politics of Recognition, 140
Multicultural separatist movements, 64, 65–66
Music, 205–12
Muslims, 98, 99, 100
Mussolini, Benito, 185–86
Myrdal, Gunnar, 31, 62

National identity, 16, 17–18
Nationalism, 43, 62, 93, 161, 208
Native Americans, 18, 62, 73, 152, 169
Naturalization, 22, 25, 94
Ndue, Paul Ntungwe, 159
New Left, 3, 4
New York Social Studies Review and Development Committee, 176–77, 190
Nietzsche, Friedrich, 3, 4, 136
Nigeria, 43–44, 56, 58
Northern Ireland, 104

Northern Peoples' Congress, 43
Norton, Anne, 120
Nosair, El Sayyid A., 103
Nyong'o, Peter Anyang', 159

On Liberty (Mill), 71, 117
Organization of African Unity (OAU),
    40, 42, 45

Pachon, Harry, 170
Pan-Africanism, 45–56
Park, Robert E., 29–31
Particularism, 157
Patriotism, 177–78
Pelikan, Jaroslav, 67
Pinckney, Charles Cotesworth, 124
Plunkitt, George Washington, 122
Pluralism, 2, 5, 10, 38, 50, 52, 108, 109n7,
    123. *See also* Cultural pluralism
Politics of difference, 72–73
Politics of Difference (Young), 142
Popper, Karl, 223
Pound, Ezra, 202
Pupin, M. I., 22

Race
    in Africa, 38–46
    alliances based on, 40
    definition of, 22, 28, 39–40, 41
    and minorities, 29
    misconceptions of, 39–41
Racialism, 9, 150
Racism, 28, 39, 40, 44, 45, 72–73, 83–84,
    86n23, 145, 155, 181–82
Rationalism, 3, 144, 145
Rawls, John, 85n9, 86n23, 87n30
Relativism, 185–87, 188
Religion, 47, 71, 220–21
    in Africa, 43–44, 56–57
    and the Constitution, 97, 98, 101–3,
        122

and culture, 56–57, 94–95, 150,
    220–21
and ethnic conflict, 43–44, 105
in Great Britain, 98–100
Supreme Court rulings on, 100
and tolerance, 97–98, 121, 122
Religious fundamentalism, 69, 73, 74,
    80–81
Representation, 7, 113–16, 119, 124, 157
Representative Government (Mill), 113
Robinson, Cedric, 54n18
Rockefeller, Steven C., 70, 71, 82, 87n30
Roosevelt, Franklin D., 28, 181
Roosevelt, Theodore, 28
Rorty, Richard, 87n29
Ross, David, 108
Rousseau, Jean-Jacques, 131, 146
Rubin, Rosalyn A., 180
Rushdie, Salman, 6, 7, 69, 73, 74, 99, 103
Russia, 60

Sandridge, Suzanne, 180
Scheibe, Johann Adolf, 207
Schiff, Jacob, 22
Schlesinger, Arthur Jr., 37, 64
Schooling of the Immigrant, The (Thompson), 23
Schuyler, George, 54n18
Sedgwick, Theodore, 94
Segregation, 34, 63, 66–68, 116, 119
Sennett, Richard, 145
Shakespeare, William, 91, 95
Shelley, Percy, 92
Shipman, Virginia, 179
Sixties radicalism, 2–3, 4
Slaughter, M. M., 74
Slavery, 57, 96, 102, 120–21, 124, 145
Smith, Adam, 92
Solzhenitsyn, Alexander, 188
Sound and the Fury, The (Faulkner), 219
South Africa, 56

Southern African Development Coordination Conference (SADCC), 42
Soviet Union, 60, 161
Soyinka, Wole, 41
Spain, 61
Speech codes, 72, 82–84
Stella, Antonio, 22
Strauss, Leo, 108
Sudan, the, 159
Supreme Court, U.S., 63, 97–98, 100, 104, 167
Sutherland, George, 98
Swartz, Marc, 125

Taylor, Charles, 71–72, 76, 92, 140, 142, 146
Theroux, Paul, 74, 82
Thomas, Clarence, 144
Thompson, Frank V., 23–24
Tirant lo Blanc (Martorell), 222
Tocqueville, Alexis de, 8, 62, 91, 92, 99, 120, 121–22, 135, 189
Tolerance, 23, 29, 73–74, 97–98, 117, 120, 121, 122, 142, 143, 147, 148, 167, 176, 185, 187
Tradition, 204
Tribalism, 42–44, 45, 59
Trudeau, Pierre Elliott, 92, 106, 173

Uganda, 56
United Nations, 42, 61
Universalism, 9, 83, 136, 157, 160–61

Virgil, 200–202, 204
(Virginia) Bill for Religious Freedom, 101, 102

Wald, Lillian, 22
Walker, David, 63
Warner, Michael, 87n30
Warren, Earl, 63
Washington, George, 110n24
Waters, Mary, 33
Webster, Noah, 174
West, Cornel, 144–45
Whitman, Walt, 18, 131, 136
Whitney Museum Biennial Exhibition of American Art, 108, 141, 142
Wilson, Woodrow, 21, 28
Wiredu, Kwasi, 41
Wirth, Louis, 31
Wolfe, Tom, 69
Woodsen, Carter, 170
Wordsworth, William, 92
World Bank, 42

Yeltsin, Boris, 60
Young, Iris Marion, 142, 145
Yugoslavia, 59–60, 61, 158

Zaire, 43–44, 56, 58

NIGGER

ALSO BY **RANDALL KENNEDY**

Race, Crime, and the Law

NIGGER

The Strange Career of
a Troublesome Word

RANDALL KENNEDY

Pantheon Books, New York

All rights reserved under International and Pan-American
Copyright Conventions. Published in the United States by
Pantheon Books, a division of Random House, Inc., New York,
and simultaneously in Canada by Random House of Canada
Limited, Toronto.

Pantheon Books and colophon are registered trademarks of
Random House, Inc.

Library of Congress Cataloging-in-Publication Data

Kennedy, Randall, 1954–
 Nigger / Randall Kennedy.
  p. cm.
 Includes bibliographical references and index.
 ISBN 0-375-42172-6
 1. United States—Race relations—Psychological aspects.
2. African Americans—Social conditions. 3. African
Americans—Race identity. 4. Racism in language.
5. Racism—United States—Psychological aspects.
6. English language—United States—Slang—Social aspects.
7. English language—United States—Slang—Psychological
aspects. 8. Invective—United States—Psychological aspects.
9. Invective—United States—History—Anecdotes.
I. Title.
E185.625 .K46 2002 305.896'073—dc21 2001036442

www.pantheonbooks.com

Book design by Johanna S. Roebas

Printed in the United States of America
First Edition

2 4 6 8 9 7 5 3 1

CONTENTS

One   The Protean N-Word   3

Two   *Nigger* in Court   56

Three   Pitfalls in Fighting *Nigger:*
Perils of Deception, Censoriousness,
and Excessive Anger   113

Four   How Are We Doing with *Nigger?*   172

Endnotes   177
Acknowledgments   211
Index   213

NIGGER

CHAPTER ONE

The Protean N-Word

How should *nigger* be defined? Is it a part of the American cultural inheritance that warrants preservation? Why does *nigger* generate such powerful reactions? Is it a more hurtful racial epithet than insults such as *kike, wop, wetback, mick, chink,* and *gook*? Am I wrongfully offending the sensibilities of readers right now by spelling out *nigger* instead of using a euphemism such as *N-word*? Should blacks be able to use *nigger* in ways forbidden to others? Should the law view *nigger* as a provocation that reduces the culpability of a person who responds to it violently? Under what circumstances, if any, should a person be ousted from his or her job for saying "nigger"? What methods are useful for depriving *nigger* of destructiveness? In the pages that follow, I will pursue these and related questions. I will put a tracer on *nigger,* report on its use, and assess the controversies to which it gives rise. I have invested energy in this endeavor because *nigger* is a key word in the lexicon of race relations and thus an important term in American politics. To be ignorant of its meanings and effects is to make oneself vulnerable to all manner of perils, including the loss of a job, a reputation, a friend, even one's life.[1]

Let's turn first to etymology. *Nigger* is derived from the Latin word for the color black, *niger.*[2] According to the *Random House Historical Dictionary of American Slang,* it did not originate as a slur but took on a derogatory connotation over time. *Nigger* and other words related to it have been spelled in a variety of ways, including niggah, nigguh, niggur, and niggar. When John Rolfe recorded in his journal the first shipment of Africans to Virginia in 1619, he listed them as "negars." A 1689 inventory of an estate in Brooklyn, New York, made mention of an enslaved "niggor" boy. The seminal lexicographer Noah Webster referred to Negroes as "neg-

4

ers." (Currently some people insist upon distinguishing nigger—which they see as exclusively an insult—from nigga, which they view as a term capable of signaling friendly salutation.)[3] In the 1700s *niger* appeared in what the dictionary describes as "dignified argumentation" such as Samuel Sewall's denunciation of slavery, *The Selling of Joseph*. No one knows precisely when or how *niger* turned derisively into *nigger* and attained a pejorative meaning.[4] We do know, however, that by the end of the first third of the nineteenth century, *nigger* had already become a familiar and influential insult.

In *A Treatise on the Intellectual Character and Civil and Political Condition of the Colored People of the United States: and the Prejudice Exercised Towards Them* (1837), Hosea Easton wrote that *nigger* "is an opprobrious term, employed to impose contempt upon [blacks] as an inferior race. . . . The term in itself would be perfectly harmless were it used only to distinguish one class of society from another; but it is not used with that intent. . . . [I]t flows from the fountain of purpose to injure." Easton averred that often the earliest instruction white adults gave to white children prominently featured the word *nigger*. Adults reprimanded them for being "worse than niggers," for being "ignorant as niggers," for having "no more credit than niggers"; they disciplined them by telling them that unless they behaved they would be carried off by "the old nigger" or made to sit with "niggers" or consigned to the "nigger seat," which was, of course, a place of shame.[5]

Nigger has seeped into practically every aspect of American culture, from literature to political debates, from cartoons to song. Throughout the 1800s and for much of the 1900s as well, writers of popular music generated countless lyrics that lampooned blacks, in songs such as "Philadelphia Riots; or, I Guess It Wasn't de Niggas Dis Time," "De Nigga Gal's Dream," "Who's Dat Nigga Dar A-Peepin?," "Run, Nigger, Run," "A Nigger's Reasons," "Nigger Will Be Nigger," "I Am Fighting for the Nigger," "Ten Little Niggers," "Niggas Git on de Boat," "Nigger in a Pit," "Nigger War Bride Blues," "Nigger, Nigger, Never Die," "Li'l Black Nigger," and "He's Just a Nigger." The chorus of this last begins, "He's just a nigger, when you've said dat you've said it all."[6]

Throughout American history, *nigger* has cropped up in children's rhymes, perhaps the best known of which is

Eeny-meeny-miney-mo!
Catch a nigger by the toe!
If he hollers, let him go!
Eeny-meeny-miney-mo!

But there are scores of others as well, including

Nigger, nigger, never die,
Black face and shiny eye.[7]

And then there is:

Teacher, teacher, don't whip me!
Whip that nigger behind that tree!
He stole honey and I stole money.
Teacher, teacher, wasn't that funny?[8]

Today, on the Internet, whole sites are devoted to nigger jokes. At KKKomedy Central–Micetrap's Nigger Joke Center, for instance, the "Nigger Ghetto Gazette" contains numerous jokes such as the following:

Q. What do you call a nigger boy riding a bike?
A. Thief!

Q. Why do niggers wear high-heeled shoes?
A. So their knuckles won't scrape the ground!

Q. What did God say when he made the first nigger?
A. "Oh, shit!"

Q. What do niggers and sperm have in common?

A. Only one in two million works!

Q. Why do decent white folk shop at nigger yard sales?

A. To get all their stuff back, of course!

Q. What's the difference between a pothole and a nigger?

A. You'd swerve to avoid a pothole, wouldn't you?

Q. How do you make a nigger nervous?

A. Take him to an auction.

Q. How do you get a nigger to commit suicide?

A. Toss a bucket of KFC into traffic.

Q. How do you keep niggers out of your backyard?

A. Hang one in the front yard.

Q. How do you stop five niggers from raping a white woman?

A. Throw them a basketball.[9]

Nigger has been a familiar part of the vocabularies of whites high and low. It has often been the calling card of so-called white trash—poor, disreputable, uneducated Euro-Americans. Partly to distance themselves from this ilk, some whites of higher standing have aggressively forsworn the use of *nigger*. Such was the case, for example, with senators Strom Thurmond and Richard Russell, both white supremacists who never used the N-word. For many whites in positions of authority, however, referring to blacks as niggers was once a safe indulgence. Reacting to news that Booker T. Washington had dined at the White House, Senator Benjamin Tillman of South Carolina predicted, "The action of President Roosevelt in entertaining that nigger will necessitate our killing a thousand niggers in the South before they will learn their place again."[10] During his (ultimately successful) reelection campaign of 1912, the governor of South Carolina, Coleman Livingston Blease, declared with reference to his opponent, Ira Jones, the chief justice of the state supreme court, "You people who want social equality [with the Negro] vote for Jones. You men who have nigger children vote for Jones. You who have a nigger wife in your back yard vote for Jones."[11]

During an early debate in the United States House of Representatives over a proposed federal antilynching bill, black people sitting in the galleries cheered when a representative from Wisconsin rebuked a colleague from

Mississippi for blaming lynching on Negro criminality. In response, according to James Weldon Johnson of the National Association for the Advancement of Colored People (NAACP), white southern politicians shouted from the floor of the House, "Sit down, niggers."[12] In 1938, when the majority leader of the United States Senate, Allen Barkley, placed antilynching legislation on the agenda, Senator James Byrnes of South Carolina (who would later become vice president and secretary of state) faulted the black NAACP official Walter White. Barkley, Byrnes declared, "can't do anything without talking to that nigger first."[13]

Nigger was also a standard element in Senator Huey P. Long's vocabulary, though many blacks appreciated the Louisiana Democrat's notable reluctance to indulge in race baiting. Interviewing "The Kingfish" in 1935, Roy Wilkins (working as a journalist in the days before he became a leader of the NAACP) noted that Long used the terms "nigra," "colored," and "nigger" with no apparent awareness that that last word would or should be viewed as offensive.[14] By contrast, for Georgia governor Eugene Talmadge, *nigger* was not simply a designation he had been taught; it was also a tool of demagoguery that he self-consciously deployed. Asked by a white constituent about "Negroes attending our schools," Talmadge happily replied, "Before God, friend, the niggers will never go to a school which is white while I am governor."[15]

As in Georgia, so in Mississippi, where white judges routinely asked Negro defendants, "Whose nigger are you?"[16] Reporting a homicide, the Hattiesburg *Progress* noted: "Only another dead nigger—that's all."[17] Three decades later, the master of ceremonies at a White Citizens Council banquet would conclude the festivities by remarking, "Throughout the pages of history there is only one third-rate race which has been treated like a second-class race and complained about it—and that race is the American nigger."[18]

Nor was nigger confined to the language of local figures of limited influence. Supreme Court Justice James Clark McReynolds referred to Howard University as the "nigger university."[19] President Harry S Truman called Congressman Adam Clayton Powell "that damned nigger preacher."[20] *Nigger* was also in the vocabulary of Senator, Vice President, and President Lyndon Baines Johnson. "I talk everything over with [my wife]," he proclaimed on one occasion early in his political career. Continuing, he quipped, "Of course . . . I have a nigger maid, and I talk my problems over with her, too."[21]

A complete list of prominent whites who have re-ferred at some point or other to blacks demeaningly as niggers would be lengthy indeed. It would include such otherwise disparate figures as Richard Nixon and Flan-nery O'Connor.[22]

Given whites' use of *nigger,* it should come as no sur-prise that for many blacks the N-word has constituted a major and menacing presence that has sometimes shifted the course of their lives. Former slaves featured it in their memoirs about bondage. Recalling her lecherous master's refusal to permit her to marry a free man of color, Harriet Jacobs related the following colloquy:

> "So you want to be married do you?" he said, "and to a free nigger."
>
> "Yes, sir."
>
> "Well, I'll soon convince you whether I am your master, or the nigger fellow you honor so highly. If you *must* have a husband, you may take up with one of my slaves."[23]

Nigger figures noticeably, too, in Frederick Douglass's autobiography. Re-creating the scene in which his master objected to his being taught to read and write, the great abolitionist imagined that the man might have said, "If you give a nigger an inch he will take an ell. A nigger should know nothing but to obey his master. . . . Learning would *spoil* the best nigger in the world."[24]

In the years since the Civil War, no one has more searingly dramatized *nigger*-as-insult than Richard Wright. Anyone who wants to learn in a brief compass what lies behind African American anger and anguish when *nigger* is deployed as a slur by whites should read Wright's *The Ethics of Living Jim Crow*. In this memoir about his life in the South during the teens and twenties of the twentieth century, Wright attacked the Jim Crow regime by showing its ugly manifestations in day-to-day racial interactions. Wright's first job took him to a small optical company in Jackson, Mississippi, where things went smoothly in the beginning. Then Wright made the mistake of asking the seventeen-year-old white youth with whom he worked to tell him more about the business. The youth viewed this sign of curiosity and ambition as an unpardonable affront. Wright narrated the confrontation that followed:

"What yuh tryin' t' do, nigger, git smart?" he asked.

"Naw; I ain' tryin' t' git smart," I said.

"Well, don't, if yuh know what's good for yuh! . . . Nigger, you think you're *white,* don't you?"

"No sir!"

"This is *white* man's work around here, and you better watch yourself."[25]

From then on, the white youth so terrorized Wright that he ended up quitting.

At his next job, as a menial worker in a clothing store, Wright saw his boss and his son drag and kick a Negro woman into the store:

Later the woman stumbled out, bleeding, crying, and holding her stomach. . . . When I went to the rear of the store, the boss and his son were washing their hands in the sink. They were chuckling. The floor was bloody and strewn with wisps of hair and clothing. No doubt I must have appeared pretty shocked, for the boss slapped me reassuringly on the back.

"Boy, that's what we do to niggers when they don't want to pay their bills," he said, laughing.[26]

Along with intimidation, sex figured in Wright's tales of Negro life under segregationist tyranny. Describing his job as a "hall-boy" in a hotel frequented by prostitutes, the writer remembered

a huge, snowy-skinned blonde [who] took a room on my floor. I was sent to wait upon her. She was in bed with a thick-set man; both were nude and uncovered. She said she wanted some liquor and slid out of bed and waddled across the floor to get her money from a dresser drawer. I watched her.

"Nigger, what in hell you looking at?" the white man asked me, raising himself up on his elbows.

"Nothing," I answered, looking miles deep into the black wall of the room.

"Keep your eyes where they belong if you want to be healthy!" he said.

"Yes, sir."

On a different evening at this same hotel, Wright was leaving to walk one of the Negro maids home. As they passed by him, the white night watchman wordlessly slapped the maid on her buttock. Astonished, Wright instinctively turned around. His doing so, however, triggered yet another confrontation:

> Suddenly [the night watchman] pulled his gun and asked: "Nigger, don't you like it?"
>
> I hesitated.
>
> "I asked yuh don't yuh like it?" he asked again, stepping forward.
>
> "Yes, sir," I mumbled.
>
> "Talk like it then!"
>
> "Oh, yes, sir!" I said with as much heartiness as I could muster.
>
> Outside, I walked ahead of the girl, ashamed to face her. She caught up with me and said: "Don't be a fool! Yuh couldn't help it!"
>
> This watchman boasted of having killed two Negroes in self-defense.[27]

Among the ubiquitous stories featuring *nigger* that appear in literature by and about black Americans, several others also stand out.

In the summer of 1918, Lieutenant George S. Schuyler, proudly dressed in the uniform of the United States Army, stopped to get his boots shined at the Philadelphia railroad station. The bootblack, a recent immigrant from

Greece, refused in a loud voice to serve "a nigger." This affront helped push Schuyler into going absent without leave, an infraction for which he was briefly imprisoned.[28] Although Schuyler became a writer and mined his own life for much of his material, this encounter with *nigger*-as-insult was so upsetting that he never publicly mentioned it.

In 1932 a young black Communist named Angelo Herndon found himself on trial for his life in Atlanta, Georgia, for allegedly organizing an insurrection. Testifying against him was a hostile witness who referred to him as a nigger. Herndon's black attorney, Benjamin Jefferson Davis, requested that the white judge intervene, prompting an ambiguous ruling:

> *Davis*: I object, Your Honor. The term "nigger" is objectionable, prejudicial, and insulting.
> *Judge Wyatt*: I don't know whether it is or not. . . . However, I'll instruct the witness to call [Herndon] "darky," which is a term of endearment.[29]

Radicalized by this experience, Davis himself soon thereafter joined the Communist party.

The civil rights activist Daisy Bates recalled an episode from her childhood in which a butcher refused to take her order until he had served all of the white customers in the shop, regardless of whether she had preceded them. "Niggers have to wait," the butcher stated.[30]

When a clerk at a drugstore soda fountain called him "nigger," nine-year-old Ely Green asked his foster mother what it meant. "Why should I be called a nigger?" he inquired. "It must be very bad to be a nigger." Bothered by her refusal or inability to explain, the boy spent a sleepless night trying to decipher the meaning of this mysterious word. "What could a nigger be," he wondered, and "why should God make me a nigger?"[31]

Paul Robeson earned a degree from Columbia Law School but turned his back on a career as an attorney after, among other incidents, a stenographer refused to work for him, declaring, "I never take dictation from a nigger."[32]

Malcolm X remembered that during his childhood, after his family fell apart following the murder of his father, the whites who served as his guardians openly referred to blacks as niggers. And then there was his encounter with a white teacher who, in recommending a career in carpentry rather than the law, urged young Malcolm to be "realistic about being a nigger."[33]

When Jackie Robinson reported to the Brooklyn

Dodgers' top minor-league team, the manager earnestly asked the team's owner whether he really thought that niggers were human beings.[34] Robinson, of course, would have to contend with *nigger* throughout his fabled career. During a game played on April 22, 1947, he recalled hearing hatred pour forth from the dugout of the Philadelphia Phillies "as if it had been synchronized by some master conductor":

"Hey, nigger, why don't you go back to the cotton field where you belong?"

"They're waiting for you in the jungles, black boy!"

"We don't want you here, nigger."[35]

On a tour of the South in 1951, the journalist Carl Rowan tried to buy a newspaper in the white waiting room of a train depot since there were no papers in the colored waiting room. As he was about to pay, a white station agent hurriedly intervened to stop the transaction. Rowan complained that under the separate-but-equal theory of segregation he should be able to purchase any item in the colored waiting room that was available in the white waiting room. But the station agent was insistent:

"Well, you'll have to go back and let the redcap come and get the paper," he explained.

"The redcap? He's darker than I am and I've got the nickel—what's the logic there?" I argued.

"He's in uniform."

"Suppose I were in uniform—[the uniform] of the United States Navy?"

"You'd still have to go where niggers belong."[36]

In the early 1960s, at the height of his celebrity as a comedian, Dick Gregory ventured south to join other activists in protesting blacks' exclusion from the voting booth. In his autobiography, he recounted an altercation he had with a policeman in Greenwood, Mississippi, who, without just provocation, shoved him and ordered,

"Move on, nigger."

"Thanks a million."

"Thanks for what?"

"Up north police don't escort me across the street against the red light."

"I said, move on, nigger."

"I don't know my way, I'm new in this town."

The cop yanked on my arm and turned his head.

"Send someone over to show this nigger where to go," he hollered. . . .

I pulled one of my arms free and pointed at the crowd.

"Ask that white woman over there to come here and show me where to go."

The cop's face got red, and there was spittle at the corner of his mouth. All he could say was: "Nigger, dirty nigger. . . ."

I looked at him. "Your momma's a nigger. Probably got more Negro blood in her than I could ever hope to have in me."

He dropped my other arm then, and backed away, and his hand was on his gun. I thought he was going to explode. But nothing happened. I was sopping wet and too excited to be scared.[37]

Either Gregory was lucky or his celebrity gave him more protection than others enjoyed. When Charles McLaurin, an organizer with the Student Nonviolent Coordinating Committee (SNCC), was jailed in Columbia, Mississippi, a patrolman asked him, "Are you a Negro or a nigger?" When McLaurin responded, "Negro," another patrolman hit him in the face. When he gave the same reply to the same question, McLaurin was again beaten. Finally, asked the question a third time, he answered, "I am a nigger." At that point the first patrolman told him to leave town and warned, "If I ever catch you here again I'll kill you."[38]

As a child, the playwright August Wilson stopped going to school for a while after a series of notes were left in his desk by white classmates. The notes read: "Go home nigger."[39]

The olympic sprinter Tommie Smith remembers an incident from his boyhood in which a white child snatched an ice cream cone out of his hand and snarled, "Niggers don't eat ice cream."[40]

Michael Jordan was suspended from school for hitting a white girl who called him "nigger" during a fight over a seat on a school bus in Wilmington, North Carolina.[41]

Tiger Woods was tied up in kindergarten by older schoolmates who called him "nigger."[42]

Recalling the difficulties she faced in raising her black son in a household with her white female lover, the poet Audre Lorde noted that "for years in the name-calling at school, boys shouted at [her son] not—'your mother's a lesbian'—but rather—'your mother's a nigger.'"[43]

The musician Branford Marsalis has said he cannot

remember a time when he was *not* being called "nigger." "If you grew up in the South," he observed, whites "called you nigger from the time you were born."[44]

Reminiscing about the first time someone called her "nigger," the journalist Lonnae O'Neal Parker described a trip she took to Centralia, Illinois, with her parents when she was five years old. She was playing in a park when

> two white girls walked up to me. . . . They were big. Impossibly big. Eleven at least. They smiled at me.
>
> "Are you a nigger?" one of the girls asked. . . .
>
> I stood very still. And my stomach grew icy. . . . "I, I don't know," I told her, shrugging my shoulders high to my ears. . . .
>
> Then the other repeated, more forcefully this time, "Are you a nigger? You know, a black person?" she asked.
>
> I wanted to answer her. To say something. But fear made me confused. I had no words. I just stood there. And tried not to wet my panties.
>
> Then I ran.[45]

Responding to Parker's published recollection, a reader shared two stories of her own. Brenda Woodford wrote that in the predominantly white middle-class community where she grew up, little white boys on bicycles would constantly encircle her, chanting, "Nigger, nigger, nigger." Later Woodford continued to be shadowed by *nigger*. On one occasion, the word flew out of the mouth of a white man during an argument; at the time, she thought he loved her.[46]

In 1973, at the very moment he stood poised to break Babe Ruth's record for career home runs, the baseball superstar Hank Aaron encountered *nigger*-as-insult on a massive scale, largely in the form of hateful letters:

Dear Nigger,

Everybody loved Babe Ruth. You will be the most hated man in this country if you break his career home run record.

Dear Black Boy,

Listen Black Boy, we don't want no nigger Babe Ruth.

Dear Mr. Nigger,

I hope you don't break the Babe's record. How can I tell my kids that a nigger did it?

Dear Nigger,

   You can hit all dem home runs over dem short fences, but you can't take dat black off yo face.

Dear Nigger,

   You black animal, I hope you never live long enough to hit more home runs than the great Babe Ruth. . . .

Dear Nigger Henry,

   You are [not] going to break this record established by the great Babe Ruth if you can help it. . . . Whites are far more superior than jungle bunnies. . . . My gun is watching your every black move.[47]

An offshoot of *nigger* is *nigger lover,* a label affixed to nonblacks who become friendly with African Americans or openly side with them in racial controversies. In the Civil War era, Republicans' antislavery politics won them the appellation "black Republicans" or "nigger lovers." To discredit Abraham Lincoln, his racist Democratic party opponents wrote a "Black Republican Prayer" that ended with the "benediction"

May the blessings of Emancipation extend through-out our unhappy land, and the illustrious, sweet-scented Sambo nestle in the bosom of every Abolition woman . . . and the distinction of color be forever consigned to oblivion [so] that we may live in bands of fraternal love, union and equality with the Almighty Nigger, henceforth, now and forever. Amen.[48]

One of Senator Charles Sumner's white constituents in Massachusetts suggested sneeringly that his exertions in favor of abolition amounted only to "riding the 'nigger' hobby."[49] Another dissatisfied constituent main-tained that the senator suffered from "a deep-seated nigger cancer," that he could "speak of nothing but the 'sublime nigger,' " and that his speeches offered nothing but "the nigger at the beginning, nigger in the middle, and nigger at the end."[50]

A century later, during the civil rights revolution, whites who joined black civil rights protesters were frequently referred to as nigger lovers. When white and black "freedom riders" rode together on a bus in vio-lation of (unlawful) local Jim Crow custom, a bigoted white driver took delight in delivering them to a furious crowd of racists in Anniston, Alabama. Cheerfully anticipating the beatings to come, the driver yelled to the mob, "Well, boys, here they are. I brought you some niggers and nigger lovers."[51] Speaking to a rally in Baltimore, Maryland, a spokesman for the National States Rights Party declared confidently that most "nigger lovers are sick in the mind" and "should be bound, hung, and killed."[52]

The term *nigger lover* continues to be heard amid the background noise that accompanies racial conflict. Whites who refrain from discriminating against blacks, whites who become intimate with blacks, whites who confront antiblack practices, whites who work on the electoral campaigns of black candidates, whites who nominate blacks for membership in clubs, whites who protect blacks in the course of their official duties, and whites who merely socialize with blacks are all subject to being derided as "nigger lovers."[53]

Over the years, *nigger* has become the best known of the American language's many racial insults, evolving into the paradigmatic slur. It is the epithet that generates epithets. That is why Arabs are called sand niggers, Irish the niggers of Europe, and Palestinians the niggers of the Middle East; why black bowling balls have been called nigger eggs, games of craps nigger golf, watermelons nigger hams, rolls of one-dollar bills nigger rolls, bad luck nigger luck, gossip nigger news, and heavy boots nigger stompers.[54]

Observers have made strong claims on behalf of the special status of *nigger* as a racial insult. The journalist Farai Chideya describes it as "the all-American trump card, the nuclear bomb of racial epithets."[55] The writer Andrew Hacker has asserted that among slurs of any sort, *nigger* "stands alone [in] its power to tear at one's insides."[56] Judge Stephen Reinhardt deems *nigger* "the most noxious racial epithet in the contemporary American lexicon."[57] And prosecutor Christopher Darden famously branded *nigger* the "filthiest, dirtiest, nastiest word in the English language."[58]

The claim that *nigger* is the superlative racial epithet—the *most* hurtful, the *most* fearsome, the *most* dangerous, the *most* noxious—necessarily involves comparing oppressions and prioritizing victim status. Some scoff at this enterprise. Objecting to a columnist's assertion that being called a honky was not in the same league as being called a nigger, one reader responded, "We should be in the business of ending racism, not measuring on a politically correct thermometer the degree to which one is more victimized than another."[59] Declining to enter into a discussion comparing the Holocaust with American slavery, a distinguished historian quipped that he refused to become an accountant of atrocity. His demurral is understandable: sometimes the process of comparison degenerates into divisive competitions among minority groups that insist upon jealously defending their victim status.[60] Because the Jewish Holocaust is the best known and most widely vilified atrocity in modern times, many use it as an analogical yardstick for the purpose of highlighting their own tragedies. Hence Iris Chang dubbed the Japanese army's Rape of Nanking during World War II "the forgotten holocaust,"[61] Larry Kramer titled his reportage on the early days of the AIDS crisis *Reports from the Holocaust*,[62] and Toni Morrison dedicated her novel *Beloved* to the "sixty million and more"—a figure undoubtedly calculated to play off the familiar six million, the number of Jews generally thought to have perished at the hands of the Nazis.[63] At the same time, some who are intent upon propounding the uniqueness of the Holocaust aggressively reject analogies to it, as if comparing it to other atrocities could only belittle the Nazis' heinous crime.[64]

We could, of course, avoid making comparisons. Instead of saying that the Holocaust was the *worst* atrocity of the twentieth century, we could say simply that the Holocaust was terrible. Instead of saying that *nigger* has been the *most* socially destructive racial epithet in the American language, we could say merely that, when used derogatorily, *nigger* is a socially destructive epithet. Although such a strategy may have certain diplomatic merits, it deprives audiences of assistance in making qualitative judgments. After all, there is a difference between the massacre that kills fifty and the one that kills five hundred—or five thousand or fifty thousand. By the same token, the stigmatizing power of different racial insults can vary.

A comedy sketch dramatized by Richard Pryor and Chevy Chase on the television show *Saturday Night Live* makes this point vividly. Chase is interviewing Pryor for a job as a janitor and administers a word-association test that goes like this:

" 'White,' " says Chase.

" 'Black,' " Pryor replies.

" 'Bean.' "

" 'Pod.' "

" 'Negro.' "

" 'Whitey,' " Pryor replies lightly.

" 'Tarbaby.' "

"What did you say?" Pryor asks, puzzled.

" 'Tarbaby,' " Chase repeats, monotone.

" 'Ofay,' " Pryor says sharply.

" 'Colored.' "

" 'Redneck!' "

" 'Jungle bunny!' "

" 'Peckerwood,' " Pryor yells.

" 'Burrhead!' "

" 'Cracker.' "

" 'Spearchucker!' "

" 'White trash!' "

" 'Jungle bunny!' "

" 'Honky!' "

" 'Spade!' "

" 'Honky, honky!' "

" 'Nigger,' " says Chase smugly [aware that, when pushed, he can always use that trump card].

" 'Dead honky!' " Pryor growls [resorting to the threat of violence now that he has been outgunned in the verbal game of racial insult].[65]

It is impossible to declare with confidence that when hurled as an insult, *nigger* necessarily inflicts more distress than other racial epithets. Individuals beset by thugs may well feel equally terrified whether those thugs are screaming "Kill the honky" or "Kill the nigger." In the aggregate, though, *nigger* is and has long been the most socially consequential racial insult. Consider, for example, the striking disparity of incidence that distinguishes *nigger* from other racial epithets appearing in reported court opinions. In reported federal and state cases in the LEXIS-NEXIS data base (as of July 2001), *kike* appears in eighty-four cases, *wetback* in fifty, *gook* in ninety, and *honky* in 286.[66] These cases reveal cruelty, terror, brutality, and heartache. Still, the frequency of these slurs is overwhelmed by that of *nigger,* which appeared in 4,219 reported decisions.[67]

Reported court opinions are hardly a perfect mirror of social life in America; they are merely an opaque reflection that poses real difficulties of interpretation. The social meaning of litigation is ambiguous. It may represent an attempt to remedy real injury, or it may mark cynical exploitation of increased intolerance for racism. The very act of bringing a lawsuit may express a sense of empowerment, but declining to bring one may do so as well, signaling that a person or group has means other than cumbersome litigation by which to settle scores or vindicate rights. That there is more litigation in which *nigger* appears could mean that usage of the term is more prevalent than usage of analogous epithets; that its usage is associated with more dramatic injuries; that targets of *nigger* are more aggrieved or more willing and able to sue; or that authorities—police, prosecutors, judges, or juries—are more receptive to this species of complaint. I do not know which of these hypotheses best explains the salience of *nigger* in the jurisprudence of racial epithets. What cannot plausibly be doubted, however, is the fact of *nigger*'s baleful preeminence.

Nigger first appears in the reports of the United States Supreme Court in a decision announced in 1871. The case, *Blyew v. United States*,[68] dealt with the prosecution for murder of two white men who, for racial reasons, had hacked to death several members of a black family. According to a witness, one of the codefendants had declared that "there would soon be another war about the niggers" and that when it came, he "intended to go to killing niggers."[69]

In the years since, federal and state courts have heard hundreds of cases in which the word *nigger* figured in episodes of racially motivated violence, threats, and arson. Particularly memorable among these was the successful prosecution of Robert Montgomery for violation of federal criminal statutes.[70] In 1988, in Indianapolis, state authorities established a residential treatment center for convicted child molesters in an all-white neighborhood. From the center's opening until mid-1991—a period during which all of the residents of the center were white—neighbors voiced no objections. In June 1991, however, authorities converted the center into a shelter for approximately forty homeless veterans, twenty-five of whom were black. Soon thereafter trouble erupted as a group of whites, including Montgomery, loudly proclaimed their opposition to the encroachment of "niggers" and burned a cross and vandalized a car to express their feelings. An all-white cadre of child molesters was evidently acceptable, but the presence of blacks made a racially integrated group of homeless *veterans* intolerable!

If *nigger* represented only an insulting slur and was associated only with racial animus, this book would not exist, for the term would be insufficiently interesting to warrant extended study. *Nigger* is fascinating precisely because it has been put to a variety of uses and can radiate a wide array of meanings. Unsurprisingly, blacks have often used *nigger* for different purposes than racist whites. To lampoon slavery, blacks created the story of the slave caught eating one of his master's pigs. "Yes, suh, Massa," the slave quipped, "you got less pig now, but you sho' got more nigger."[71] To poke fun at the grisly phenomenon of lynching, African Americans told of the black man who, upon seeing a white woman pass by, said, "Lawd, will I ever?" A white man responded, "No, nigger, never." The black man replied, "Where there's life, there's hope." And the white man declared, "Where there's a nigger, there's a rope."[72] To dramatize the tragic reality of Jim Crow subjugation, African Americans recounted the tale of the Negro who got off a bus down south. Seeing a white policeman, he politely asked for the time. The policeman hit him twice with a club and said, "Two o'clock, nigger. Why?" "No reason, Cap'n," the black man answered. "I's just glad it ain't twelve."[73] And to satirize "legal" disenfranchisement, African Americans told the joke about the black man who attempted to register to vote. After the man answered a battery of questions that were far more difficult than any posed to whites, an official confronted him with a headline in a Chinese paper and demanded a translation. "Yeah, I know what it means," the black man said. "It means that niggers don't vote in Mississippi again this year."[74]

In the 1960s and 1970s, protest became more direct and more assertive. Drafted to fight a "white man's war" in Vietnam, Muhammad Ali refused to be inducted into the U.S. Army, explaining, "No Vietcong ever called me 'nigger.' "[75] Emphasizing the depth of white racism all across the United States, activists joked, "What is a Negro with a Ph.D.?" Their response? "Dr. Nigger."

In his famous "Letter from a Birmingham Jail," Martin Luther King Jr. continued to agitate, listing in wrenching detail the indignities that prompted his impatience with tardy reform. He cited having to sleep in automobiles because of racial exclusion from motels, having to explain to his children why they could not go to amusement parks open to the white public, and being "harried by day and haunted by night by the fact that you are a Negro, living constantly at tip-toe stance never quite knowing what to expect next." Among King's litany of abuses was the humiliating way in which whites routinely addressed blacks: "Your wife and mother," he observed, "are never given the respected title 'Mrs.,' " and under the etiquette of Jim Crow, "your first name becomes 'nigger' and your middle name becomes 'boy' (however old you are) and your last name becomes 'John.' "[76]

For some observers, the only legitimate use of *nigger* is as a rhetorical boomerang against racists. There are others, however, who approvingly note a wide range of additional usages. According to Professor Clarence Major, when *nigger* is "used by black people among themselves, [it] is a racial term with undertones of warmth and good will—reflecting . . . a tragicomic sensibility that is aware of black history."[77] The writer Claude Brown once admiringly described *nigger* as "perhaps the most soulful word in the world,"[78] and journalist Jarvis DeBerry calls it "beautiful in its multiplicity of functions." "I am not aware," DeBerry writes, "of any other word capable of expressing so many contradictory emotions."[79] Traditionally an insult, *nigger* can also be a compliment, as in "He played like a nigger." Historically a signal of hostility, it can also be a salutation announcing affection, as in "This is my main nigger." A term of belittlement, *nigger* can also be a term of respect, as in "James Brown is a straight-up nigger." A word that can bring forth bitter tears in certain circumstances, *nigger* can prompt joyful laughter in others.[80]

A candid portrayal of the N-word's use among African Americans may be found in Helen Jackson Lee's autobiography, *Nigger in the Window*. It was Lee's cousin who first introduced her to *nigger*'s possibilities. As Lee remembered it, "Cousin Bea had a hundred different ways of saying *nigger*; listening to her, I learned the variety of meanings the word could assume. How it could be opened like an umbrella to cover a dozen different moods, or stretched like a rubber band to wrap up our family with other colored families. . . . *Nigger* was a piece-of-clay word that you could shape . . . to express your feelings."[81]

Nigger has long been featured in black folk humor. There is the story, for example, of the young boy inspired by a minister's sermon on loving all of God's creatures. Finding a frozen rattlesnake, he nicely put the animal under his shirt to warm it up. "Nigger, I'm gonna bite the hell out of you!" the snake announced upon its revival. "Mr. Snake," the boy asked, "you mean to say you gonna bite me after I followed the preacher's teaching and took you to my bosom?" "Hell yeah, nigger," the snake replied. "You knew I was a snake, didn't you?"[82]

Before the 1970s, however, *nigger* seldom figured in the routines of professional comedians. It was especially rare in the acts of those who performed for racially mixed audiences. Asserting that unmentionable slurs derived much of their seductive power from their taboo status, the iconoclastic white comedian Lenny Bruce recommended a strategy of subversion through overuse. In a 1963 routine, Bruce suggested with characteristic verve that "if President Kennedy got on television and said, 'Tonight I'd like to introduce the niggers in my cabinet,' and he yelled 'Niggerniggerniggerniggernigger-niggernigger' at every nigger he saw . . . till *nigger* didn't mean anything anymore, till *nigger* lost its meaning . . .

you'd never hear any four-year-old nigger cry when he came home from school."[83]

But Bruce was unusual, and in terms of the N-word, he failed to inspire emulation. While the hip comedians of the 1950s and 1960s—Dick Gregory, Nipsey Russell, Mort Sahl, Godfrey Cambridge, Moms Mabley, Redd Foxx—told sexually risqué or politically barbed jokes, *nigger* for the most part remained off-limits.

All that changed with the emergence of Richard Pryor.[84] Through live performances and a string of albums, he brought *nigger* to center stage in stand-up comedy, displaying with consummate artistry its multiple meanings.

Pryor's single best performance may be heard on the aptly titled *That Nigger's Crazy,* winner of the 1974 Grammy Award for best comedy recording. The album explores Pryor's professional fears ("Hope I'm funny . . . because I know niggers ready to kick ass"), blacks' alleged ability to avoid certain sorts of danger ("Niggers never get burned up in buildings. . . . White folks just panic, run to the door, fall all over each other. . . . Niggers get outside, *then* argue"), black parenting styles ("My father was one of them eleven-o'clock niggers"), comparative sociology ("White folks fuck quiet; niggers make noise"), racial anthropology

("White folks . . . don't know how to play the dozens"), and social commentary ("Nothin' can scare a nigger after four hundred years of this shit").

The bit that often provokes the most applause from black listeners is Pryor's "Niggers vs. Police":

> Cops put a hurtin' on your ass, man, y'know? They really degrade you.
>
> White folks don't believe that shit, don't believe cops degrade you. [They say,] "Oh, c'mon, those people were resisting arrest. I'm tired of this harassment of police officers." Police live in [a white] neighborhood, and [all his white neighbors] be knowin' the man as Officer Timson. "Hello, Officer Timson, going bowling tonight? Yes, nice Pinto you have. Ha, ha."
>
> Niggers don't know 'em like that. See, white folks get a ticket, they pull over [and say], "Hey Officer, yes, glad to be of help." Nigger got to be talkin' about "I am reaching into my pocket for my license! 'Cause I don't wanta be no muthafuckin' accident!"

Mel Watkins has rightly maintained that what made Richard Pryor a pathbreaking figure was that he "intro-

duce[d] and popularize[d] that unique, previously concealed or rejected part of African-American humor that
thrived in the lowest, most unassimilated portion of the
black community."[85] He broke free, at least for a while,
of all those—whites and blacks alike—who, sometimes
for different reasons, shared an aversion to too much
realism. He seemed radically unconcerned with deferring to any social conventions, particularly those that
accepted black comedians as clowns but rejected them
as satirists. Nothing more vividly symbolized his defiant,
risk-taking spirit than his unprecedented playfulness
regarding the explosive N-word in performances before
racially mixed audiences.[86]

In the years since the release of *That Nigger's Crazy,*
the N-word has become a staple in the routine of many
black comedians. Among these, the one who most jar-
ringly deploys it is Chris Rock, whose signature skit
begins with the declaration "I love black people, but I
hate niggers." He goes on:

> It's like our own personal civil war.
> On the one side, there's black people.
> On the other, you've got niggers.
> The niggers have got to go. Every time black
> people want to have a good time, niggers mess it

up. You can't do anything without some ignorant-ass niggers fucking it up.

Can't go to a movie the first week it opens. Why? Because niggers are shooting at the screen. . . .

You can't have anything in your house. Why? Because the niggers who live next door will break in, take it all, and then come over the next day and go, "We heard you got robbed."

According to Rock, "niggers always want credit for some shit they're *supposed* to do. They'll say something like 'I took care of my kids.'" Exploding with impatience, Rock interjects:

You're *supposed* to, you dumb motherfucker.
"I ain't never been to jail."
Whaddya want? A cookie? You're not *supposed* to go to jail, you low-expectation-having motherfucker.

Rock asserts that "the worst thing about niggers is that they love to *not know*." That's because, he says, "niggers don't read. Books are like Kryptonite to a nigger."

Aware that some may condemn his routine as latter-day minstrelsy, racial betrayal, or a false pandering to antiblack prejudice, Rock exclaims near the end of his performance,

> I know what all you black [listeners] think.
>
> "Man, why you got to say that? . . . It isn't us, it's the *media*. The media has distorted our image to make us look bad. Why must you come down on us like that, brother? It's not us, it's the media."
>
> Please cut the shit. When I go to the money machine at night, I'm not looking over my shoulder for the media.
>
> I'm looking for niggers.
>
> Ted Koppel never took anything from me. Niggers have. Do you think I've got three guns in my house because the media's outside my door trying to bust in?[87]

Rap is another genre of entertainment suffused with instances of *nigger*. A cursory survey just of titles yields Dr. Dre's "The Day the Niggas Took Over," A Tribe Called Quest's "Sucka Nigga," Jaz-Z's "Real Nigger," the Geto Boys' "Trigga Happy Nigga," DMX's "My Niggas," and Cypress Hill's "Killa Hill Nigga." In "Gangsta's Paradise," meanwhile, Coolio declares,

I'm the kind of nigga
little homies want to be like
on their knees in the night
saying prayers in the streetlights.[88]

Ice-T says in one of his songs, "I'm a nigger not a colored man or a black or a Negro or an Afro-American."[89] Ice Cube, for his part, dubs himself "the Nigga ya love to hate,"[90] And Beanie Sigel promises

I'ma ride with my niggas
die with my niggas
get high with my niggas
split pies with my niggas
till my body gets hard
soul touch the sky
till my numbers get called
and God shuts my eyes.[91]

One of the seminal influences in gangsta rap called itself NWA, short for "Niggaz Wit Attitude." One of this group's most popular albums was *Efil4zaggin,* which, read backward, is "Niggaz 4 Life." Tupac Shakur proclaimed that for him, *nigga* stood for "Never Ignorant, Gets Goals Accomplished."[92]

Some people—I call them eradicationists—seek to drive *nigger* out of rap, comedy, and all other categories of entertainment even when (perhaps *especially* when) blacks themselves are the ones using the N-word. They see this usage as bestowing legitimacy on *nigger* and misleading those whites who have little direct interaction with African Americans. Eradicationists also maintain that blacks' use of *nigger* is symptomatic of racial self-hatred or the internalization of white racism, thus the rhetorical equivalent of black-on-black crime.

There is something to both of these points. The use of *nigger* by black rappers and comedians has given the term a new currency and enhanced cachet such that many young whites yearn to use the term like the blacks whom they see as heroes or trendsetters. It is undoubtedly true, moreover, that in some cases, blacks' use of *nigger* is indicative of an antiblack, self-hating prejudice. I myself first became aware of the term as a child in an all-black setting—my family household in Columbia, South Carolina—in which older relatives routinely attributed to negritude traits they disparaged, including tardiness, dishonesty, rudeness, impoverishment, cowardice, and stupidity. Such racial disparagement *of* blacks *by* blacks was by no means idiosyncratic. It is a widespread feature of African American culture that has given rise to a distinctive corpus of racial abasement typified by admonishments, epigraphs, and doggerel such as:

Stop acting like a nigger.

I don't want nothing black but a Cadillac.[93]

Niggers and flies. Niggers and flies. The more I see niggers, the more I like flies.[94]

If you're white, you're right,
If you're yellow, you're mellow,
If you're brown, stick around,
If you're black, step back.[95]

This tendency toward racial self-abnegation has been much diminished since the civil rights revolution. But it still retains a grip on the psyches of many black Americans and is searingly evident in a phrase well known in black circles: "Niggers ain't shit."[96]

Self-hatred, however, is an implausible explanation for why many assertive, politically progressive African Americans continue to say "nigger" openly and frequently in conversations with one another. These are African

Americans who, in their own minds at least, use *nigger* not in subjection to racial subordination but in defiance of it. Some deploy a long tradition, especially evident in black nationalist rhetoric, of using abusive criticism to spur action that is intended to erase any factual predicate for the condemnation voiced. An example is writing by the Last Poets, a group established in 1968 that merged poetry, music, and politics in forms that anticipated certain types of rap. A famous item in the Last Poets' repertoire was "Niggers Are Scared of Revolution," in which they charged that:

> Niggers are scared of revolution but niggers shouldn't be scared of revolution because revolution is nothing but change, and all niggers do is change. Niggers come in from work and change into pimping clothes to hit the streets to make some quick change. Niggers change their hair from black to red to blond and hope like hell their looks will change. Niggers kill other niggers just because one didn't receive the correct change. . . .
>
> Niggers shoot dope into their arms. Niggers shoot guns and rifles on New Year's Eve a new year that is coming in where white police will do more shooting at them. Where are niggers when the rev-

olution needs some shot? Yeah . . . you know, niggers are somewhere shooting the shit. Niggers are
scared of revolution.[97]

Describing their intentions, Umar Bin Hassan writes
that the poem constituted a "call to arms" because "niggers are human beings lost in somebody else's system of
values and morals."[98]

Many blacks also do with *nigger* what other members
of marginalized groups have done with slurs aimed at
shaming them. They have thrown the slur right back
in their oppressors' faces. They have added a positive
meaning to *nigger*, just as women, gays, lesbians, poor
whites, and children born out of wedlock have defiantly
appropriated and revalued such words as *bitch, cunt,
queer*, *dyke*, *redneck*, *cracker*, and *bastard*.[99]

Yet another source of allegiance to *nigger* is a pes-
simistic view of the African American predicament. Many
blacks who use *nigger* in public before racially mixed audiences disdain dressing up their colloquial language. They
do not even attempt to put their best foot forward for the
purpose of impressing whites or eroding stereotypes
because they see such missions as lost causes. They like
to use *nigger* because it is a shorthand way of reminding themselves and everyone else precisely where they

perceive themselves as standing in American society—the message being, "Always remember you's a nigger." As Bruce A. Jacobs observes, "To proclaim oneself a nigger is to declare to the disapproving mainstream, 'You can't fire me. I quit.' Hence the perennial popularity of the word. Among poor black youth who . . . carry a burning resentment of white society. To growl that one is a nigga is a seductive gesture . . . that can feel bitterly empowering."[100]

Two additional considerations also warrant notice here, both of them having to do with the power of words to simultaneously create and divide communities. Some blacks use *nigger* to set themselves off from Negroes who refuse to use it. To proclaim oneself a nigger is to identify oneself as real, authentic, uncut, unassimilated, and unassimilable—the opposite, in short, of a Negro, someone whose rejection of *nigger* is seen as part of an effort to blend into the white mainstream. Sprinkling one's language with *nigger*s is thus a way to "keep it real."[101]

Roping off cultural turf is another aim of some blacks who continue to use *nigger* in spite of its stigmatized status. Certain forms of black cultural expression have become commercially valuable, and black cultural entrepreneurs fear that these forms will be exploited by

49

white performers who will adopt them and, tapping white-skin privilege, obtain compensation far outstripping that paid to black performers. This is, of course, a realistic fear in light of the long history of white entertainers' becoming rich and famous by marketing in whiteface cultural innovations authored by their underappreciated black counterparts. A counterstrategy is to seed black cultural expression with gestures that are widely viewed as being off-limits to whites. Saying "nigger" is one such gesture. Even whites who immerse themselves in black hip-hop culture typically refrain from openly and unabashedly saying "nigger" like their black heroes or colleagues, for fear that it might be perceived as a sign of disrespect rather than one of solidarity.

Some non-white entertainers have used *nigger* in their acts. John Lennon and Yoko Ono, for example, entitled a song "Woman Is the Nigger of the World,"[102] and Patti Smith wrote "Rock 'n' Roll Nigger."[103] But Lennon, Ono, and Smith performed in overwhelmingly white milieus. Rap, by contrast, is dominated by blacks. A few white rappers have achieved commercial success and won the respect of black artists and audiences. I am thinking here especially of the white rapper Eminem, a superstar in the hip-hop culture. Eminem has assumed many of the distinctive mannerisms of his black rap col-

leagues, making himself into a "brother" in many ways—
in his music, his diction, his gait, his clothes, his associations. He refuses to say, however, any version of a word
that his black hip-hop colleagues employ constantly as a
matter of course; the nonchalance with which he tosses
around epithets such as *bitch* and *faggot* does not extend
to *nigger*. "That word," he insists, "is not even in my
vocabulary."[104]

Eminem is certainly following a prudent course, for
many people, white and black alike, disapprove of a
white person saying nigger under virtually any circumstance. "When we call each other 'nigger' it means no
harm," Ice Cube remarks. "But if a white person uses it,
it's something different, it's a racist word."[105] Professor
Michael Eric Dyson likewise asserts that whites must
know and stay in their racial place when it comes to saying "nigger." He writes that "most white folk attracted to
black culture know better than to cross a line drawn in
the sand of racial history. *Nigger* has never been cool
when spit from white lips."[106]

The race line that Dyson applauds, however, is a spe-
cious divide. There is nothing necessarily wrong with
a white person saying "nigger," just as there is nothing
necessarily wrong with a black person saying it. What
should matter is the context in which the word is spo-

ken—the speaker's aims, effects, alternatives. To condemn whites who use the N-word without regard to context is simply to make a fetish of *nigger*. Harriet Beecher Stowe (*Uncle Tom's Cabin*), Mark Twain (*Huckleberry Finn*), William Dean Howells (*An Imperative Duty*), Edward Sheldon (*The Nigger*), Eugene O'Neill (*All God's Chillun*), Lillian Smith (*Strange Fruit*), Sinclair Lewis (*Kingsblood Royal*), Joyce Carol Oates (*Them*), E. L. Doctorow (*Ragtime*), John Grisham (*A Time to Kill*), and numerous other white writers have unveiled *nigger*-as-insult in order to dramatize and condemn racism's baleful presence.

In 1967, President Lyndon Baines Johnson decided to appoint an African American to the Supreme Court for the first time in American history. First on Johnson's list of candidates was Thurgood Marshall—"Mr. Civil Rights," the hero of *Brown v. Board of Education* and, of course, the man he ended up putting on the Court. But before he announced his selection, Johnson asked an assistant to identify some other possible candidates. The aide mentioned A. Leon Higginbotham, whom Johnson had appointed to the federal trial bench. Reportedly, the president dismissed the suggestion with the comment "The only two people who have ever heard of Judge Higginbotham are you and his momma. When I appoint a nigger to the [Supreme Court], I want everyone to know he's a nigger."[107] Was the use of *nigger* in this context a venting of racial prejudice? Maybe. Johnson had been raised in a thoroughly racist environment, had supported racist policies for a long period, and, as we have seen, casually used *nigger* as part of his private vocabulary before he became president. On this particular occasion, however, it seems likely that he was merely seeking to highlight the racial exclusion against which he was acting, parodying the old regime even as he sought to reform it. If this is an accurate assessment of the situation, I see nothing wrong with what Johnson said, and I applaud what he did.

Can a relationship between a black person and a white one be such that the white person should properly feel authorized, at least within the confines of that relationship, to use the N-word? For me the answer is yes. Carl Van Vechten, for instance, wrote of "niggers" in correspondence with his friend Langston Hughes,[108] and Hughes did not object (though he did once write that *nigger* was a red flag for all Negroes).[109] *Should* Hughes have objected? No. Van Vechten, a key supporter of the Harlem Renaissance, had shown time and again that he abhorred racial prejudice, would do what he could to improve the fortunes of African Americans, and treasured his black friends. It was against this backdrop of achieved trust that Hughes (and other black writers) rightly permitted Van Vechten to use *nigger* as so many African Americans have used it—as an ironic, shorthand spoof on the absurdity of American race relations.[110]

As we have seen, *nigger* can mean many different things, depending upon, among other variables, intonation, the location of the interaction, and the relationship between the speaker and those to whom he is speaking. Generally a reference to people of color, particularly blacks, *nigger* can refer to people of any hue. Senator Robert C. Byrd (D. West Virginia) got into trouble for saying publicly that he "had seen a lot of white niggers in [his] time."[111] But more and more the word is being applied ecumenically. Sociologist John Hartigan reports that poor whites in Detroit often refer to their white neighbors as *niggers*.[112] Typically they mean the word as an insult. But they do not necessarily mean for it to be a *racial* insult. Responding to an inquiry about a white-on-white deployment of *nigger*, one of the participants in Hartigan's study remarked: "He's a nigger, man, and you know what I mean by that. He's an asshole, and it doesn't matter whether a person's black or white, orange or plaid, he can still be a nigger if he runs his mouth like that asshole."[113] Another white Detroiter observed by Hartigan echoed this sentiment. "You don't have to be black to be a nigger," he declared. "Niggers come in all colors." (Interestingly, he added: "We are all colored. . . . There's about a hundred shades of white.")[114]

The linguist Arthur K. Spears has also discerned an appreciable revision of *nigger*'s racial usage. He writes that "White public school teachers hear themselves referred to as 'that White nigga' or simply 'nigga,' and [that] Asian Americans in San Francisco can be heard, as they navigate high school hallways, to call one another niggas."[115]

More vividly than most words, then, *nigger* illustrates Justice Oliver Wendell Holmes's observation that "a word is not a crystal, transparent and unchanged." A word is instead "the skin of a living thought [that] may vary greatly in color and content according to the circumstances and the time in which it is used."[116]

CHAPTER TWO

Nigger in Court

I n September 1957, Congressman Charles C. Diggs Jr. of Michigan traveled to Sumner, Mississippi, to see firsthand the trial of two white men charged with the murder of a black fourteen-year-old from Chicago. Emmett Till had been killed for violating Jim Crow etiquette by, among other things, whistling at the wife of one of the defendants. In Sumner, Diggs encountered segregation in full bloom. Greeting a bevy of black reporters from across the country, the local sheriff cheerfully shouted, "Hello, niggers," without a hint of self-consciousness. One of these reporters, James Hicks of the *Amsterdam News,* sought to secure a seat in the segregated courtroom for Representative Diggs. Professor Stephen J. Whitfield tells what happened:

Diggs had wired Judge Curtis L. Swango of the Seventeenth Judicial District to ask whether he might attend the trial. The judge, a tall, informal forty-seven-year-old, a graduate of Millsaps College in Jackson and of the law school at "Ole Miss," invited him down. But by the time the representative got inside the courtroom, the whites and then the blacks had already taken all the seats. Diggs gave his card to Hicks, who started to walk up to the judge's bench but was accosted by a deputy who inquired: "Where you going, nigger?" When Hicks explained his mission and showed the deputy the card, another deputy was called over and told: "This nigger said there's a nigger outside who says he's a Congressman. . . ."

"A nigger Congressman?"

"That's what this nigger said," and then the first deputy laughed at so blatant a contradiction in terms. But the sheriff was summoned and then told Hicks: "I'll bring him in here, but I'm going to sit him at you niggers' table." And that is where the representative sat.[1]

Although *nigger* was in the air throughout the Emmett Till case—from the promising indictment to the appalling acquittal—debate over the word did not play a central role in the litigation. In many other cases, though, such debate has occupied a salient place in the legal wrangling, generating a distinctive jurisprudence that can be divided into at least four categories. The first of these comprises cases in which a party seeks relief after it is revealed that officials within the criminal justice system—jurors, lawyers, or judges—have referred to blacks as niggers. The second encompasses cases in which an individual who kills another seeks to have his culpability diminished on the grounds that he was provoked when the other party called him a nigger. The third type of case involves controversies surrounding targets of racial invective who sue for damages under tort law or antidiscrimination statutes. And the fourth category consists of situations in which a judge must decide whether or not to permit jurors to be told about the linguistic habits of witnesses or litigants.

———

In 1978 in Columbus, Georgia, a jury handed down a death sentence for one William Henry Hance, who had committed multiple murders. After the trial two jurors revealed that they had heard fellow jurors make racially derogatory remarks about the defendant. More specifically, one juror maintained that during their deliberation, other jurors had referred to Hance as a "typical nigger" and "just one more sorry nigger that no one would miss." No court investigated the accuracy of these allegations prior to Hance's execution.[2]

Any defendant who seeks to challenge a conviction or sentence on the basis of prejudiced jury deliberations is very unlikely to prevail. First, federal and state rules of evidence stringently exclude juror testimony that impeaches a jury's verdict. And second, many jurisdictions require defendants to show actual prejudice resulting from juror misconduct.[3]

It is understandable that the legal system should want to promote finality, protect jurors from harassment, and shield the privacy and independence of jury deliberations. Still, it is chilling to think that a person could be sentenced to death pursuant to deliberations tainted by *nigger*.[4] The use of the word raises concerns not only about the attitudes of the jurors who said it but also about the attitudes of the jurors who *heard* it. In 1985 social psychologists Jeff Greenberg and Tom Pyszczynki performed an experiment aimed at determining how listeners were affected by overhearing racial slurs directed at specific targets. They asked groups of white college students to judge debates between white and black contestants. Immediately after the debates, persons working in concert with the experimenters either derogatorily referred to the black contestants as niggers, criticized them in a nonracist manner, or made no comment at all. Greenberg and Pyszczynki found that observers who overheard the insult exhibited a marked tendency to lower their evaluation of the slurred black debaters. This suggested, the researchers argued, that racial slurs "can indeed cue prejudiced behavior in those who are exposed to [such slurs]," a phenomenon that could well have practical significance in such settings as "parole board meetings, promotion committee meetings, and jury deliberations, in which [racial] slurs may be expressed by one member of a group, be overheard, and then affect the evaluations of the target by other members of the group." *Nigger,* Greenberg and Pyszczynki concluded, was not merely a symptom of prejudice but a carrier of the disease.[5] The risk in *Hance* was thus not simply that the manifest racial prejudice of two jurors might have eroded *their* ability to determine facts and set an appropriate punishment, but also that the use of *nigger* might have transmitted the pair's prejudice to other jurors, awakening latent biases or creating racial animus where none had previously existed.

Judges, too, use the N-word. In the late 1960s, H. Rap Brown, the former head of the Student Nonviolent Coordinating Committee (SNCC), was convicted of a firearms violation. After the conviction, a lawyer stepped forward with information suggesting that the judge who had presided over the trial harbored a prejudice against Brown. According to this lawyer, the judge had said that he was "going to get that nigger."[6] At a postconviction hearing, a new judge found the lawyer's statement to be credible but decided nonetheless to affirm the conviction and sentence. He ruled that notwithstanding the initial judge's unfortunate comment, the defendant had had a fair trial. The court of appeals subsequently reversed his decision and vacated Brown's conviction. In doing so, it relied on a federal statute that requires the mandatory disqualification of a judge " 'in any proceeding in which his impartiality might reasonably be questioned' or 'where he has a personal bias or prejudice concerning a party.' "[7] The court of appeals emphasized that the trial judge's remark had undercut the appearance of impartiality. It also concluded that it could not suitably determine from the trial record alone whether or not the defendant had received a fair trial.

The reversal of Brown's conviction is an inspiration compared to *Hance*. Still, there remains the disquiet of knowing that the judge remained in office, in a position to adjudicate disputes involving others whom he may well have called niggers in private. How must it have felt to be a black litigant in Judge Lansing L. Mitchell's courtroom the day *after* the reversal of H. Rap Brown's conviction?

This raises the question of what should be done about officials such as Judge Lansing. The federal constitution offers great—in my view *excessive*—security to federal judges inasmuch as they cannot be removed from office except by the famously cumbersome process of impeachment by the United States House of Representatives and conviction by the United States Senate. Other jurisdictions are able to handle matters of judicial bias more expediently. In 1994, for example, the California Supreme Court suspended Judge Stanley Z. Goodfarb for making repeated derogatory references to "niggers" off the record in his chambers, where he believed himself to be immune from the disapproval of observers.[8] In

1998 the Supreme Court of Michigan removed a judge who, in tapes surreptitiously made by her husband, was revealed as a person who constantly referred to blacks demeaningly as niggers.[9]

In 1999 a state court in New York removed J. Kevin Mulroy from a judgeship based on several incidents. In one case, Judge Mulroy had attempted to persuade a prosecutor to accept a plea bargain from four men indicted for murdering and robbing a sixty-seven-year-old African American woman. The judge told the prosecutor that he should not worry about the case since the victim had been just "some old nigger bitch."[10] In castigating Mulroy for this remark, the court observed that he had "devalued the life of the victim in a most nonprofessional, disturbing, and inappropriate way. . . . A judge's use of such language indicates an unacceptable bias and insensitivity that [have] no place on the bench and [warrant] the severest possible sanction."[11]

Case law documents instances in which prosecutors in open court have referred to African American defendants as niggers.[12] In 1911 a Mississippi prosecutor told a jury, "This bad nigger killed a good nigger. The dead nigger was a white man's nigger and these bad niggers like to kill that kind. The only way you can break up this pistol toting among these niggers is to have a necktie party."[13] (Decades later, the good nigger/bad nigger distinction would remain in force: explaining why he had killed a black man and his wife shortly after World War II, one white bigot recalled, "Up until George went into the Army, he was a good Nigger. But when he came out, [he and his wife] thought they were as good as any white people.")[14] In 1907 a prosecutor in Texas stated that he was well enough acquainted with a certain "class of niggers to know that they have got it in for the [white] race."[15] A prosecutor in Alabama in 1922 demanded of a presumably all-white jury, "Are you gentlemen going to believe that nigger [defendant] sitting over there . . . in preference to the testimony of [white] deputies?"[16] A prosecutor in Texas in 1970 asked a witness if he would have gotten out of his car "for three nigger men at night if they hadn't had guns."[17] Although there has long been a consensus that such slurs are prohibited, courts have generally declined to reverse convictions stemming from proceedings in which the N-word was used if the trial judge admonished the prosecutor and instructed the jury to disregard the offending language. Such was the outcome, for example, in the 1922 and 1970 cases described above. Appellate judges are understandably loath to award a windfall to a vicious criminal who happens to have been prosecuted by an undisciplined bigot.

That is why they tend to uphold convictions provided they have some indication that the original trials were not irredeemably polluted by racist language. There is no good excuse, though, for the general failure of judges and local bar associations to discipline lawyers who demean courtroom proceedings with blatantly racist language. I have never heard of a case in which a prosecutor faced discipline for using an insulting version of *nigger* in the courtroom.

In one remarkable case, however, a prosecutor was disciplined for using the N-word outside of court.[18] In the early-morning hours of June 30, 1995, Jerry L. Spivey, the elected district attorney of the Fifth Prosecutorial District of North Carolina, got inebriated in a bar in Wrightsville Beach and was heard to say regarding another patron, "Look at that nigger hitting on my wife." The patron to whom he was referring was Ray Jacobs, a professional football player with the Denver Broncos who had previously been a college star in North Carolina. A little later, when Spivey's wife sought to introduce the two men and began by asking her husband whether he recognized Jacobs, the district attorney responded by saying, "He looks like a nigger to me." That comment was followed by others in which District Attorney Spivey, with an increasing degree of drunken agitation, repeatedly referred to

Jacobs as a nigger. Eventually the bartender ejected the district attorney from the establishment.[19]

Soon thereafter, several attorneys petitioned a judge to remove Spivey from his post pursuant to a state law authorizing such an action in the event of misconduct prejudicial to the administration of justice and bringing an office into disrepute. During a hearing, expert testimony was elicited from the distinguished historian John Hope Franklin on the history and meaning of the word *nigger*. The judge also heard testimony from other members of the community who told the court about experiences they had had with the N-word and described their perception of the district attorney in light of his racial language. One man recounted the following painful memory from his days in the air force in the 1950s: "I was coming in from an overseas assignment and I stopped in Arkansas to get some gas and a sandwich. Three kids with me. We walked up, put the gas in the car. Stopped at the side window to get a sandwich and from the inside we were told, 'We don't serve niggers here.' I said, 'We simply want to get a sandwich.' He took my money for the gas and we turned and walked [away]. My little kid asked me, 'Daddy, what's a nigger?' "[20] Questioned about the effect that incident had had on him, the man responded tearfully that he had never stopped hurt-

ing. When asked to react to the district attorney's use of
the N-word, he remarked, "To me it says that it doesn't
matter what you have accomplished in life . . . if you have
a black face . . . you are less than a person."[21]

The judge removed Spivey from office. The former
district attorney appealed, arguing, among other things,
that his federal First Amendment rights had been violated. There was some irony in his claiming that the state
had wrongfully punished him for giving voice to protected expression, since he simultaneously insisted that
what he had said did not at all express his true sentiments or beliefs. "I am sorry," he testified, that "I used
the word *nigger*. . . . That word occupies no place in my
day-to-day vocabulary, and that word in no way reflects
my beliefs about, or feelings and attitude toward, people
of African American heritage."[22] While in one breath
Spivey complained of being a victim of censorship based
on the substance of disfavored remarks, in the next he
asserted that his outburst had been little more than a
verbal belch—rude, yes, but substantively meaningless.

The North Carolina Supreme Court affirmed Spivey's
removal and in the course of doing so rebuffed his First
Amendment challenge, ruling that his language was
covered by that amendment's fighting-words exception.
In *Chaplinsky v. New Hampshire,* the 1942 case that es-

tablished the fighting-words doctrine, the United States Supreme Court observed, "There are certain well-defined and narrowly limited classes of speech, the prevention and punishment of which have never been thought to raise any constitutional problem. These include the lewd and obscene, the profane, the libelous, and the insulting or 'fighting' words—those which by their very utterance inflict injury or tend to incite an immediate breach of the peace."[23] Applying *Chaplinsky,* the North Carolina court ruled that Spivey's outburst had constituted a "classic" case of unprotected fighting words.[24] Elaborate hearings, the court maintained, were not needed to determine the effects of *nigger* on black targets. "No fact is more generally known," it declared, "than that a white man who calls a black man a 'nigger' within his hearing will hurt and anger the black man and often provoke him to confront the white man and retaliate."[25]

While the court ruled rightly in *Spivey,* there is good reason to reject the fighting-words doctrine on which its decision largely rested. Although *Chaplinsky* offers two bases on which language may be deemed fighting words, subsequent case law makes it clear that the primary and perhaps the exclusive grounds for declining to give First Amendment protection to so-called fighting words is that under certain circumstances, such language will either incite or be likely to incite an immediate breach of the peace by a target who responds impulsively and with violence. Thus, in a hypothetical dispute between an offensive speaker and a violent target, the fighting-words doctrine favors the target. Rather than insisting that the target of the speech control himself, the doctrine tells the offensive speaker to shut up. This is odd and objectionable. It allows "speech to be [regulated] . . . when directed at someone who would react violently to a verbal assault, but not [regulated] . . . when directed at someone with a more pacific bent."[26] It thus gives more leeway to insult a nun than a prizefighter since the nun is presumably less likely to retaliate.[27] The fighting-words doctrine is in tension, moreover, with the dominant (and good) rule in criminal law that prevents "mere words standing alone . . . no matter how insulting, offensive, or abusive," from constituting the predicate for a provocation excuse.[28] In those jurisdictions that abide by the so-called mere-words doctrine (which we will examine further below), legal authority instructs everyone to exercise self-discipline even in the face of inflammatory taunts. The fighting-words doctrine weakens that salutary message.

In *Spivey,* the North Carolina Supreme Court wrote that the district attorney's "use of the word *nigger* . . . did not in any way involve an expression of his viewpoint on any local or national policy."[29] But clearly those who petitioned for his removal did believe that his utterance of the N-word revealed something—and something very disturbing—about his view of blacks. They would not have moved for his ouster had he merely called Jacobs, say, an asshole. That, too, would have been rude and abusive and indicative of a lack of self-discipline and decorum that would have reflected badly on the office of the district attorney. But *asshole* does not carry the ideological baggage that burdens the term *nigger*. During the United States presidential campaign of 2000, George W. Bush was overheard describing a reporter for the *New York Times* as "an asshole."[30] The incident raised a few eyebrows, to be sure, but it did not seem to cost him much, if anything, in public esteem. Had he been overheard describing a reporter (or anyone else) as a "nigger," however, his candidacy would have been doomed. That is because when whites use the word *nigger*, they are widely perceived to be showing their true colors as bigots. It is precisely because *nigger* is thought to indicate the presence of racist beliefs or sentiments that many people take such strong objection to it—as did the people who demanded Spivey's ouster.

The real reason and the better justification for Spivey's removal were that the statements he made rendered him unfit to fulfill his public responsibility. Such a responsibility entails a commitment to the idea that all people, regardless of race, should be treated equally and with respect before the bar of justice. By calling Ray Jacobs a nigger, Jerry Spivey cast a pall over public confidence in his commitment to accord all people due respect regardless of race.

In condemning officials or other leaders who use *nigger* or related terminology, we would do well to remember how complex people can be. Many unreconstructed white bigots have refrained from using the N-word even as they have continued to do everything in their power to hold blacks back.[31] At the same time, whites who use the N-word have made important contributions to the advancement of African Americans. Two politicians who come to mind here are Harry S Truman and Lyndon B. Johnson. Both used *nigger* in private conversation, and yet both surprised observers by taking unprecedented steps to elevate the fortunes of Negro Americans. Jerry Spivey's use of the N-word does not necessarily mean that he harbored racist views or would have failed to apply the law evenhandedly. Perhaps his remarks that night were an aberration. The problem is that his words raised justifiable doubts in the minds of North Carolinians, especially black North Carolinians, about whether he would or could treat all individuals equally, regardless of race. Spivey's misstep might have been reasonably overlooked or forgiven if he had occupied a position of lesser responsibility. But as the district attorney, he wielded massive and discretionary authority (it was up to him, for instance, to decide whether or not to seek capital punishment in a given case) that was effectively outside the scope of judicial review. In light of that power, and of the doubts raised regarding Spivey's ability to wield it effectively and fairly in the aftermath of his N-word incident, the North Carolina judiciary did just the right thing in removing him from office.[32]

The law of murder is a second area shadowed by *nigger*. Murder is the unjustified and intentional or reckless killing of a person. One way that society could signal that it abhors *nigger*-as-insult would be to deem justifiable the killing of anyone who insultingly deployed the epithet. No sensible person would seriously propose such a policy, of course, but what about excusing to some extent those who respond violently when provoked by the N-word?

That question has hovered in the background of several noteworthy cases. Consider the following episode, the basis for Richard Wright's short story "The Man

Who Killed a Shadow."[33] On March 1, 1944, Julius Fisher, a black janitor at the National Cathedral in Washington, D.C., complained to a white librarian named Catherine Cooper Reardon about statements she had made to his boss regarding his poor performance on the job. She responded, he said, by calling him a "black nigger." He later testified that no white person had ever before spoken to him in this way. Angered, he slapped Reardon, who screamed. To stop her from screaming, he beat, choked, and stabbed her to death.[34]

At Fisher's trial for murder, his counsel, the redoubtable Charles Hamilton Houston—the great teacher of Thurgood Marshall—offered a defense of partial responsibility. While conceding that his client had killed the victim, Houston argued that he should be found guilty of second- as opposed to first-degree murder because he suffered from a mental deficiency. The difference in culpability amounted literally to a difference between life and death, since first-degree murder carried a mandatory death sentence, whereas second-degree murder carried a prison sentence of twenty years to life.

The trial judge allowed Houston to present evidence intended to show that Fisher suffered from a diminished capacity to control himself and that Reardon had disastrously triggered this weakness by calling him a "black nigger." The judge refused, however, to instruct the jury that in reaching a decision it should consider evidence of the defendant's alleged mental deficiency. The jury convicted Fisher of first-degree murder. A court of appeals subsequently affirmed the trial judge's decision, as did, in its turn, the Supreme Court of the United States. Three justices dissented, maintaining that the trial judge had erred in refusing to instruct the jury specifically that it could consider Houston's theory of diminished capacity.

One of the dissenting justices was Felix Frankfurter, who, in an early draft of his dissent, suggested that "Miss Reardon's [reference to the defendant as a] 'black nigger' pulled the trigger that made the gun go off."[35] In the published version of the dissent, however, Frankfurter turned his attention from the specificity of the N-word as an incitement and instead focused on the defendant's deficiencies, observing that Fisher's "whole behavior seems that of a man of primitive emotions reacting to the stimulus of insult and proceeding from that point without purpose or design."[36]

Nearly a quarter of a century later, the N-word emerged as an important feature of another interracial killing in Washington. On June 4, 1968—two months after the assassination of Martin Luther King Jr. sparked major riots in the District of Columbia and throughout the country—Benjamin Murdock killed two white marines in a Little Tavern hamburger shop.[37] In the middle of a verbal altercation, one of the marines called Murdock a nigger, whereupon he drew a revolver and shot his antagonists. At trial, Murdock's attorney attempted to present a defense similar to the one Houston had mounted on Fisher's behalf. He argued that his client's "rotten social background" had contributed to a diminished capacity to control the rage that exploded when the marine referred to him and his buddies as niggers. The trial judge, however, instructed the jury to disregard the "rotten social background" defense, whereupon the jury convicted Murdock of second-degree murder.[38]

In neither Fisher's nor Murdock's case did the defense lawyer argue that the jury ought to be instructed that the word *nigger* alone could be such a powerful incitement to violence that it should be deemed a provocation sufficient to reduce the defendant's crime from murder to manslaughter. Every jurisdiction in the United States allows a murder defendant to claim, under certain conditions, that his killing of another was sufficiently provoked that his crime should be demoted from murder—the acme of all crimes against persons—to manslaughter, a lesser (albeit still serious) offense. The question that could have been posed in both *Fisher* and *Murdock* was whether being called a nigger constituted a circumstance that might allow a defendant to claim that the provocation had been such that he had lost control of himself, killed in the heat of passion, and therefore committed a crime that, though terrible, was nonetheless less morally condemnable than a killing done in cold blood. The likely reason that the two men's lawyers refrained from pressing the question is that in Washington in those years—and the same is true today[39]—the mere-words doctrine was well-established law.

That doctrine would be squarely confronted in *State of North Carolina v. Rufus Coley Watson, Jr.,* a 1975 case in which a black inmate in a corrections facility killed a white inmate over his use of the word *nigger.*[40] At trial, Watson's attorney argued that in view of the verbal provocation the defendant had faced, the jury should at least be given instructions that would permit it to consider whether he had committed manslaughter rather than murder. The trial judge, however, thwarted that strategy by instructing the jury that "Words and gestures alone[,] . . . regardless of how insulting or inflammatory those words or gestures may be, do not constitute adequate provocation for the taking of human life."[41] The jury convicted Watson of second-degree murder.

On appeal, the defense counsel sought to oust the mere-words doctrine as the governing law. In asserting his position, he cited as precedent an early-nineteenth-century case in which a white man named Tackett had been charged with murdering a black slave named Daniel.[42] There was enmity between the two men because Tackett had made sexual overtures toward Daniel's wife, a free woman of color. Tackett wanted to offer evidence that Daniel had been a turbulent man, impudent and insolent to white people. He argued that this fact in itself should allow a jury to reduce his crime from murder to manslaughter. The judge excluded the proposed testimony, ruling that the defendant's argument could be predicated only upon evidence that the deceased slave had been impudent and insolent to Tackett himself. A jury convicted Tackett and sentenced him to death.

The North Carolina Supreme Court, ruling on Tackett's appeal, held that the trial judge should have allowed the defendant to present evidence regarding Daniel's general comportment around whites. The trial judge's fundamental mistake, according to Chief Justice Taylor, had consisted in his erroneous belief that "the case was to be determined by the same rules and principles of law as if the deceased had been a white man.[43] The law of provocation in antebellum North Carolina had thus served to cheapen the lives of black slaves who failed to be properly deferential to whites. One hundred fifty-five years later, in *Watson*, the defense counsel tried to turn the same ruling around to mitigate his (black) client's actions. But the North Carolina Supreme Court would have none of it. Instead, it indicated that its earlier, racially discriminatory conception of provocation was long dead and had been superseded by a clear, clean rule that applied to all: no mere words could provide any degree of excuse warranting a lessening of punishment for the taking of another's life.

That rule is law throughout much, though by no means all, of the United States. Several states, including California, permit juries to consider the provocation excuse whenever the evidence points to any circumstances, including mere words or gestures, that might cause a reasonable person to lose to control over himself or herself. But a majority of the states still embrace the rule that words alone cannot constitute provocation sufficient to diminish murder to manslaughter.

Is the mere-words doctrine a good rule in light of everything we know about the turmoil, distress, and rage that *nigger*-as-insult can generate within its targets?[44] An argument for reform might begin with the proposition that *nigger* and similar slurs are not mere words. Professor Charles Lawrence has described them as "assaultive" and classified them as "a form of violence by speech" that causes a target to feel as though he or she had been slapped in the face.[45] Professor Richard Delgado similarly refers to such speech as "words that wound."[46] The likening of racist speech to violence is significant in this context because violence is universally recognized as creating a predicate for a provocation excuse. If calling someone a nigger is indeed a "form of violence by speech," then it seems reasonable that at least in some circumstances, the N-word should be deemed a provocation in the eyes of the law.

An argument against this reform is that black people can and do routinely show discipline, intelligence, and productiveness even in the face of *nigger,* and that the law should undergird such conduct by offering no excuse to those who react with violence. People who hold this view may fear what Professor Ann Coughlin has termed "the perils of leniency,"[47] believing that a modification of the mere-words doctrine out of concern over the *nigger* insult will result in an entrenchment of the notion that blacks are less capable of self-control than others and ought, on that account, to be forgiven for their putatively unavoidable impulsiveness.

Adherents to this view can take inspiration from

Ralph Ellison. There is an American Negro tradition, he wrote, "which teaches one to deflect racial provocation and to master and contain pain. It is a tradition which abhors as obscene any trading on one's own anguish for gain or sympathy; which springs not from a desire to deny the harshness of existence but from a will to deal with it as men at their best have always done."[48]

The issue is agonizingly close, with strong arguments on both sides. One's conclusion turns largely on one's belief regarding the primary purpose of criminal law. If the primary purpose is utilitarian crime control, the mere-words doctrine should be retained. If the primary purpose of the criminal law is retribution—dishing out just desserts—reform of the mere-word doctrine is preferable. An ambivalent retributivist, I choose the latter alternative. I am persuaded that there should be no bright-line limits to the array of provocations that a jury is permitted to consider for the purposes of mitigation. It should be up to a jury to determine whether, in fact, a defendant lost control of himself or herself in the face of *nigger* or any other alleged provocation and whether society should soften its punishment in the event of such a loss of control.[49]

———

The third category of *nigger* litigation is composed of cases in which targets of the slur have invoked tort law or antidiscrimination law to sue their tormentors.

Many jurisdictions offer individuals the possibility of obtaining relief for what tort law terms "the intentional infliction of emotional distress."[50] This legal weapon emerged from the notion that under certain circumstances, even in the absence of offensive touching or threats of force, some conduct may be so outrageous that a formal means of redress should be available to offended parties. Successful applications of this idea in its early years involved malevolent practical jokes, as in the case of a plaintiff who was told that her husband had been severely injured, while the defendant knew that he was in fact safe.[51] Other scenarios that have given rise to successful lawsuits include instances of a defendant's spreading false rumors that a plaintiff's son had hanged himself,[52] a defendant's bringing a mob to a plaintiff's door at night and voicing a threat to lynch him unless he left town,[53] and a defendant's telephoning the plaintiff around the clock seeking repayment of a debt.[54] The jurisprudence of emotional distress also contains a body of precedent related to *nigger*. Consider the following cases: *Wiggs v. Courshon*[55] and *Nims v. Harrison*.[56]

Wiggs involved black customers at a motel restaurant

in Miami, Florida, who became embroiled in an argument with a waitress over a food order. Among these customers were several adults and one seven-year-old boy. At one point in the dispute, the waitress exclaimed to one of the adults, "You can't talk to me like that, you black son of a bitch. I will kill you."[57] Later, outside of the immediate presence of the plaintiffs but within earshot of them, the waitress shouted, "They are nothing but a bunch of niggers."[58] The plaintiffs immediately checked out of the motel. The next day, when they returned to tell a manager what had happened, they were advised, "You shouldn't feel so bad. . . . [That waitress] is prejudiced against Catholics, Jews, and all other kinds of minorities."[59] Upset, the plaintiffs cut short their vacation, went home, and eventually sued, persevering through trial to win a jury verdict.

The plaintiff in *Harrison* was a black high school teacher, Rosalind Nims, who sued several graduating students because of the nature of comments about and threats toward her that they published in a newsletter distributed at the school. The newsletter described Nims as the "most fucked-up teacher," assailed her as "a stupid bitch . . . who has black skin and is a fucking gigaboo [*sic*]," and contained the declarations "I will kill you

you fucking whore" and "I will rape you and all of your children and cousins you stupid motherfucking bitch." For good measure, the writer added, "Die nigger."[60]

Nims charged the students responsible with intentional infliction of emotional distress and sued for damages. A trial court judge dismissed the complaint, ruling that even if the facts alleged by the plaintiff were true, they failed as a matter of law to reach the level of outrageousness required for a recovery of damages. An appellate court reversed, concluding that "justice, reason and common sense compel a remedy for the revilement inflicted upon the teacher . . . provided that the facts alleged are proven." The Florida Court of Appeal found that the conduct alleged "is so outrageous in character, and so extreme in degree, as to go beyond all possible bounds of decency; it is utterly intolerable in a civilized community."[61]

While these cases demonstrate that it is possible to recover in tort for racial insults, imposing difficulties lie in wait for those who attempt to do so. First, seeking redress through litigation is typically expensive, nerve-racking, fatiguing, and time-consuming. Second, the formal requirements of the tort of intentional infliction of emotional distress are daunting. Plaintiffs must show that the offending conduct was extreme and outrageous; that it was intentional or reckless; that it caused emotional distress; and that the emotional distress caused was severe. According to the American Law Institute:

> It has not been enough that the defendant has acted with an intent which is tortious or even criminal, or that he has intended to inflict emotional distress, or even that his conduct has been characterized by "malice," or a degree of aggravation which would entitle the plaintiff to punitive damages for another tort. Liability has been found only where the conduct has been so outrageous in character, and so extreme in degree, as to go beyond all possible bounds of decency, and to be regarded as atrocious, and utterly intolerable in a civilized community. Generally, the case is one in which the recitation of the facts to an average member of the community would arouse his resentment against the actor and lead him to exclaim, "Outrageous!"[62]

Third, many judges have been reluctant to permit damage awards based on claims of emotional distress caused solely or even primarily by verbal abuse. They fear trumped-up charges and injuries. They fear infringements upon liberty in general and, more particularly, upon that guaranteed by the First Amendment to the United States Constitution. They also fear encouraging a debilitating oversensitivity and an overdependence on courts. Scores of judges embrace the proposition that "against a large part of the frictions and irritations and clashing of temperaments incident to participation in a community life, a certain toughening of the mental hide is a better protection than the law could ever be."[63] This attitude is mirrored in many judicial decisions. In *Wiggs*, for example—the case of the foulmouthed waitress—the plaintiffs prevailed, but that did not prevent the judge from intervening to lower the damage award. After the jury awarded $25,000 in damages, the trial judge stated that he would order a new trial unless the plaintiffs accepted a lesser sum. According to the judge, the jury had "plainly embarked on a giveaway program far out of line with common sense and experience."[64] While he condemned "the uncivil outburst and rude remarks made by [the restaurant] waitress," he concluded that "a line would quickly form by members of any ethnic group to receive $25,000 as balm for an ethnic or racial epithet."[65] To prevent the plaintiffs from reaping what he perceived as a windfall, he reduced the money damages to one tenth of the amount awarded by the jury, or $2,500.

In other instances, judges have not even allowed juries to decide the matter. Consider the following episodes:

A lawyer twice called a young black man a nigger while trying to collect on a debt. When the target of the insult sued, the trial judge granted summary judgment in favor of the defendant. He was upheld by the Kansas Court of Appeals, which ruled, "It appears to us that the trial judge was fully justified in regarding the epithets as 'mere insults' of the kind which must be tolerated in our rough-edged society."[66]

A black man went to a store to return merchandise that he believed to be subpar. As a precondition for giving him a refund, a sales clerk insisted that the man sign a sales slip on which was written the notation "Arrogant nigger refused exchange—says he doesn't like products." Courts in Illinois ruled that the notation, albeit rude, was insufficiently extreme and outrageous to serve as a predicate for the plaintiff's lawsuit.[67]

An employee in a Zayre's department store called a customer a nigger during a dispute over goods. When the customer subsequently sued, a judge ruled that even if the defendant had in fact said what the plaintiff alleged she had said, that conduct, though offensive, did not reach the level of outrageousness required for a recovery. Insulting and abusive though *nigger* might be, the court observed, "taken in this context it does not amount to the type of extreme and outrageous conduct which gives rise to a cause of action. Clearly the law cannot serve to redress all indignities."[68]

A black man alleged that a white bartender had referred to him angrily as a nigger when he saw him speaking to some white women seated at the bar. When the man sued for damages, a judge granted summary judgment to the defendant. While referring to a person as a nigger was indeed outrageous, the court declared, the defendant should nonetheless prevail because the plaintiff had failed to show to the satisfaction of the court that his distress was severe.[69]

An employee responsible for looking after parking spaces called a person "nigger" in the course of an argument over a space. When the insulted party sued, the court ruled in favor of the defendant, essentially reasoning that the conduct complained of, albeit regrettable, had not been so bad and injurious as to warrant legal interference.[70]

An employee sued a supervisor who had referred

to him as a "sleazy nigger." A judge disallowed the claim for intentional infliction of emotional distress on the grounds that the remark did not rise to the level of intolerable conduct. Affirming the trial judge, an appellate panel commented that "as part of living in our society, we must tolerate a certain amount of offensive expression."[71]

A plaintiff alleged that his employer had called him a "stupid nigger" and a "token nigger" and proclaimed that the firm "would never pay a nigger $75,000 a year." Noting that "rarely will conduct in the employment context rise to the level of outrageousness necessary to establish a basis of recovery for intentional infliction of emotional distress," the trial judge dismissed this aspect of the plaintiff's suit. The alleged statements were "inconsiderate," the judge conceded, but they did not, he said, rise to the level of outrageousness the law required.[72]

Statutes prohibiting racial discrimination in employment provide yet another means by which the law offers recourse to targets of *nigger*. The most widely used of these statutes is Title VII of the Civil Rights Act of 1964. Two questions typically confront Title VII plaintiffs in suits involving *nigger*. The first arises in situations in which a plaintiff complains that his or her race has prompted an adverse decision regarding hire, promotion, or term of employment. In such cases, the question is whether a decision maker's use of the word *nigger* provides direct evidence of racial discrimination. The second question arises in situations in which a plaintiff charges that use of the N-word in the workplace has created a hostile work environment. Here the key issue is often whether such usage has been sufficiently burdensome that the legal system ought to make relief available. Consider the following cases, which illustrate these two scenarios.

In 1967 Henry Brown, a black man, got a job as a janitor with the East Mississippi Electric Power Association (EMEPA). Over the years he won promotions within the company, eventually attaining the position of serviceman, a post in which he performed such tasks as installing meters, pulling meters, troubleshooting in instances of malfunction, and, occasionally, collecting on overdue accounts. Servicemen work alone and enjoy a degree of independence that other EMEPA employees do not have. Brown was the company's first African American serviceman.

In 1989, EMEPA higher-ups informed Brown that he would have to either accept reassignment or else leave the company. His supervisors maintained that their action was prompted by complaints from customers, several of whom had asserted that Brown was rude and had cursed at them. One had charged that he engaged in reckless driving. The complaints had continued even after Brown had received an earlier warning to avoid consumer dissatisfaction. Faced with a choice between reassignment (and therefore the loss of his post as a serviceman) and termination, Brown ceased working for EMEPA and thereafter sued, charging that the company had subjected him to racial discrimination. According to Brown, EMEPA treated him differently, more harshly, than it did its white servicemen. Under similar circumstances, he averred, a white serviceman would not even have been reprimanded, much less demoted.[73]

As a key piece of evidence in his case, Brown cited a supervisor's use of *nigger*. In 1985, prior to becoming a serviceman, Brown had overheard an EMEPA supervisor on the radio discussing a traffic accident. At some point in the conversation, he testified, the supervisor said something to the effect of, he felt like getting a gun and shooting the offending "nigger." A couple of months later, after he became a serviceman, Brown heard this same supervisor say to another serviceman, "You should have hooked that power up for that nigger [presumably a customer]. You know how they are." According to Brown, he complained about this use of the N-word to a company official, who told him he would take care of the problem. A while later, however, the supervisor called him into his office and demanded that he stop calling him by his first name over the company radio. "If you call me [by my first name] one more time on that radio," the supervisor threatened, "I'll call you 'nigger.' " Brown said he subsequently overheard the same supervisor referring to him as a nigger on two occasions. In one instance the supervisor said, "Look at my little nigger going down the hall. We brung him to his knees." At another time he declared, "We finally got what we wanted. We got rid of that little nigger."

That the supervisor occasionally used the N-word was uncontested; other EMEPA employees, including several whites, confirmed this. And the supervisor himself admitted that *nigger* was part of his vocabulary. He insisted, though, that he did not use the word in front of blacks and that he had largely stopped saying "nigger" after company officials instructed him to do so.

After a trial, United States District Court Judge Tom S. Lee ruled in favor of EMEPA. He gave several reasons for his decision. Contrary to what Brown alleged, he said,

white servicemen *had* been reprimanded following customer complaints; one had even been fired. Then, too,
Brown had offered no evidence to show that the company
condoned the use of racial slurs. After the serviceman
complained to company officials about the supervisor's
use of the N-word, they responded by telling the supervisor to stop doing it or risk being fired. The judge dis-
believed Brown's testimony regarding the supervisor's
alleged continued use of the N-word after that warning
and expressly credited the supervisor's denial that he had
referred to Brown as a "little nigger." The judge noted
that it was this very supervisor who had been instrumental in getting Brown promoted to the position of serviceman in the first place. Judge Lee stressed, moreover, that
in the final confrontation between Brown and company
officials, it was the supervisor who had sought to intervene on Brown's behalf and implored him to cool off
before quitting and thus throwing away the benefits
he had accrued over twenty years of employment at
EMEPA.

The Fifth Circuit Court of Appeals reversed Judge
Lee. It ruled that the supervisor's "routine use of racial
slurs constitutes direct evidence that racial animus was
a motivating factor in the contested disciplinary deci-

sions."[74] According to the appellate judges, the supervisor's repeated use of *nigger* could not be dismissed as an innocent habit: "Unlike certain age-related comments [e.g., 'young tigers'] which we have found too vague to constitute evidence of discrimination, the term *nigger* is a universally recognized opprobrium, stigmatizing African-Americans because of their race. That [the supervisor] usually was circumspect in using the term in the presence of African-Americans underscores that he knew it was insulting. Nonetheless, he persisted in demeaning African-Americans by using it among whites. This is racism."[75] Concluding that this individual's racism had infected the decision to reassign and demote Brown, the court of appeals asserted that the supervisor's " 'I had to dust my little nigger' comment . . . demonstrates that his racism distorted Brown's employment record and extended to decisions of the type at bar."[76] Furthermore, the appeals court took the unusual step of deciding key factual issues of the sort that are typically remanded to the trial judge for determination. When a plaintiff shows that racial bias played a role in a challenged decision, for example, the defendant is offered the opportunity to show that he would have made the same decision even absent the racial bias. Usually trial

courts make such findings. In this case, however, the
court of appeals decided the issue on its own, circum-
venting the trial judge—purportedly out of "a pruden-
tial concern for scarce judicial resources."[77]

Mr. Brown was very lucky; other appellate courts
might well have decided the case differently. For one
thing, appellate courts generally defer to the factual
findings of trial judges. But in this case—though without
expressly saying so—the appeals court declined to accept Judge Lee's findings of fact. Whereas Judge Lee had
explicitly discredited Brown's testimony about hearing
the supervisor refer to him as a "little nigger," the appellate court cited this very testimony as the predicate
for its conclusions that the supervisor was racially biased
and had contaminated EMEPA's decision making with
his prejudice.

The probable mainsprings of the decision in *Brown*
were an appreciation of the likelihood that extraordinary scrutiny had been focused upon EMEPA's first
black serviceman; a realistic sense that he was bound to
receive more than his fair share of white customer complaints regardless of his actual conduct; distrust of the
trial judge's perception of the situation; and, outweigh-
ing any other single consideration, a deep reluctance to
rule in favor of a white employer whose place of busi-

ness echoed with *nigger* references. "At the heart of this appeal," the appellate court declared, "is the significance of [the supervisor's] routine use of the term *nigger*."[78] Contradicting the defendant's dismissal of such language as "isolated remarks," the plaintiff had succeeded in persuading the appellate court that the supervisor's use of *nigger* constituted "direct evidence" of illegal racial discrimination. Direct evidence is evidence that, if believed, proves a fact without inference or presumption. It precludes the necessity of inferring whether a challenged action constitutes (in this context) racial discrimination, because it *compels* that conclusion.

Given the protean character of *nigger,* which may signal several different (even contradictory) meanings, it is probably erroneous to conclude that the word itself *necessarily* furnishes proof of racial discrimination, even when the speaker is white and the target black. Automatic labeling of *nigger* may be an efficient shorthand method for judicially assessing the N-word—a method whose inevitable mistakes may be tolerable given the savings it affords in labor and time. Perhaps in the context of antidiscrimination law at the workplace, moreover, it is better to err on the side of overenforcement rather than underenforcement. Still, even if that is so, it is important to remember that the N-word is not self-defining. Its actual meaning in any given instance always depends on surrounding circumstances. Deriving an understanding of *nigger* thus always requires interpretation.

The second category of Title VII cases featuring *nigger* comprises lawsuits alleging that an employer has either knowingly or negligently condoned a racially hostile workplace environment. One such suit was filed by James H. Spriggs, an African American who worked at the Diamond Auto Glass Company in Forestville, Maryland, as a customer service representative in the 1990s.[79] Spriggs left Diamond because of what he viewed as the company's inadequate response to misconduct on the part of his supervisor, a white man named Ernest Stickell. According to Spriggs, Stickell, in his presence, constantly referred to African American customers and employees as monkeys and niggers. Stickell himself was married to a black woman, but according to Spriggs, she, too, was subjected to her husband's racial vilification. Stickell referred to her as a black bitch and directed racial slurs at her in agitated phone conversations that Spriggs said he could not help but overhear. Angered, Spriggs quit Diamond but returned after the company's management assured him it would force Stickell to clean up his language. Spriggs maintained, however, that Diamond failed to make good on its promise and that Stickell's verbal conduct did not improve; indeed, in Spriggs's view, his supervisor's behavior worsened. Stickell continued to describe his wife in racially derogatory terms and repeatedly called Spriggs a monkey and a nigger to his face. Spriggs claimed that Stickell also inserted between pages of a manual that he (Spriggs) regularly consulted a picture of a monkey, with a notation that read, "So you'll never forget who you are."[80]

Spriggs eventually resigned and sued, charging that he had been victimized by harassment that created a racially hostile workplace in violation of Title VII. In order to prevail, he would have to satisfy both a subjective and an objective requirement: he needed to show that he himself had actually perceived the work environment to be abusive and that a reasonable person would also view it thus.[81] According to the Supreme Court, "Conduct that is not severe or pervasive enough to create an objectively hostile or abusive work environment . . . is beyond Title VII's purview."[82] The "mere utterance of an . . . epithet which engenders offensive feelings in an employee" is insufficient grounds;[83] the conduct objected to must be sufficiently bad that "a reasonable person" would find it to be intolerably hostile. Many judges demand that "reasonable people" be thick-skinned and have a high threshold for tolerating irksome, even deplorable, conduct. Spriggs drew such a judge. United States District Court Judge Frederic N. Smalkin granted summary judgment to Diamond, holding that, even assuming that his factual allegations were accurate, Spriggs's suit failed as a matter of law. But the Fourth Circuit Court of Appeals reversed, remanding the case for trial. The appellate court concluded that the language Spriggs had found objectionable was sufficiently injurious to be deemed a violation of Title VII if, upon trial, his allegations were determined to be true. Central to the court's ruling was the special place of *nigger* in the lexicon of verbal abuse. "Perhaps no single act," the court remarked, "can more quickly alter the conditions of employment and create an abusive working environment than the use of . . . 'nigger' by a supervisor in the presence of his subordinates."[84] Elaborating, the court averred that "far more than a 'mere offensive utterance,' the word 'nigger' is pure anathema to African-Americans."[85]

Hostile-workplace litigation—like every other kind—is frustrating, expensive, and risky. Corporate employers are liable for abuse committed by their employees, but only if they are put on notice that such abuse is occurring.

This poses a dilemma for victims. If they repeatedly report abusive behavior by coworkers, they may improve their chances of obtaining legal relief in the event of litigation, but they also run the risk of poisoning relations with colleagues and alienating supervisors. Compounding this conundrum is the difficulty of predicting whether or not a court will see the reported misconduct as unlawful. No bright line authoritatively distinguishes mere rudeness from illegal abuse; drawing the line is a matter of judgment, and judgments vary.

Consider the plight of James L. Bolden Jr., an African American who worked as an electrician for eight years for PRC, Inc. Long tormented by his coworkers, Bolden finally quit and sued his employer. He alleged that his coworkers had constantly called him "faggot," "fool," "dickhead," and "dumbshit"; that one coworker had walked over to his work area and farted directly at him; that several others had said "nigger" in his presence; and that on one occasion a colleague had warned, "You better be careful because we know people in [the] Ku Klux Klan."[86]

A federal district judge, affirmed by a court of appeals, ruled that even if Bolden's allegations were accurate, they failed as a matter of law to constitute the predicate for a hostile-work-environment claim. While the judges acknowledged that the racial abuse alleged was deplorable, they found that it was insufficiently deplorable to trigger the remedies contained in Title VII. Echoing established doctrine, the judges declared that a plaintiff must prove more than the occurrence of "a few isolated incidents of racial enmity" or the utterance of "sporadic racial slurs."[87] What a plaintiff needed to show, they suggested, was "a steady barrage of opprobrious racial comments."[88] In the judges' view, Bolden's complaints fell far short of this threshold. "The blatant racial harassment," they pointed out, "came from only two of his co-workers on a couple of occasions," and the "racial jokes and slurs were infrequent."[89]

The appellate judges who affirmed dismissal erred in ruling that, as a matter of law, no reasonable juror could find for Bolden based on the evidence he presented. They saw a wholly one-sided case when they should have seen a more complicated controversy. The evidence was such that reasonable jurors could have disagreed— meaning that the judges should have permitted a jury to resolve the dispute.

In light of the outcome in Bolden's case, can a plaintiff successfully sue if he or she is referred to "only" once with hostility as a nigger? How about twice? Or three times? At what point does race-baiting on the job become illegal? The only way to answer such questions sensibly is in terms of probabilities, taking into account such considerations as where a lawsuit is filed and before which judge the suit will be heard.[90] While certain judges stress that episodic misconduct is usually insufficient to support a hostile-work-environment claim, others make rulings and generate rhetoric friendlier to plaintiffs, including the observation that "even a single episode of harassment, if severe enough, can establish a hostile work environment."[91]

Linda Jackson's fate, like Bolden's, exemplifies the variability of different listeners' assessments of *nigger* even in the context of federal statutory law. Jackson sued the Quanex Corporation of Detroit, Michigan, alleging that it fostered a racially hostile work environment.[92] To make her case, she introduced evidence that racial slurring insulting to blacks was rife in the workplace. She testified, for example, that at a staff meeting a superior stated, "We are up to our asses in nigger sludge."[93] Jackson also introduced evidence that racist graffiti was prevalent and that white workers constantly attempted to sabotage or otherwise injure their black colleagues. In one incident, a fellow worker had called Jackson a nigger bitch and physically assaulted her. In the aftermath, *both* workers had been suspended for three days, and Jackson had been denied the opportunity to work overtime.

United States District Court Judge Avern Cohn disposed of Jackson's case by granting judgment to the defendant. He found that in some instances the company had not been notified of objectionable conditions and that in others management had responded adequately. Judge Cohn also stressed that several of the racist acts that Jackson had entered into evidence either had not occurred in her presence or had not been directed at her, and that several of the actions she was objecting to were so commonplace at Quanex as to have become "conventional conditions on the factory floor."[94]

A federal court of appeals reversed Judge Cohn in an unusually harsh ruling that branded his view of the relevant law and facts as "myopic." According to the appellate court, Judge Cohn had erroneously chopped the evidence into unconnected bits that robbed the plaintiff of a fair chance to show that, in their accumulated totality, the individual episodes and incidents constituted an ugly portrait of intolerable racial hostility. Unlike the trial judge, the appellate judges deemed the defendants' reactions to racism on the factory floor to be both tardy and deficient, insofar as management had made no effort whatsoever to discover the identity of those behind the graffiti. And unlike the trial judge, the appellate judges focused not on what had been reported to management by victims but instead on what management actually knew or should have known about racial abuse among its workers. Finally, the appellate court took strong exception to what it saw as "potentially the most disturbing" aspect of Judge Cohn's ruling: the "decision to minimize proof of persistent racial slurs and graffiti at Quanex" on the grounds that their very prevalence made them less rather than more problematic as a legal matter. Averring that Judge Cohn's reasoning reflected an unseemly class bias that would impose lower demands on blue-collar than on white-collar worksites, the appellate judges "squarely denounce[d] the notion that increasing regularity of racial slurs and graffiti renders such conduct acceptable, normal, or part of 'conventional conditions on the factory floor.' "[95]

Were the appellate judges correct with respect to this last point? Yes, they were. It would have been a mistake to have offered safe harbor to racially abusive language because such language was pervasive and customary at a given worksite. To have done so would have encouraged inertia when clearly the express aim of Title VII and similar statutes is to uproot racist custom.[96] This was not a case in which a defendant was contesting whether a particular usage of *nigger* should be deemed insulting; here that was conceded. Rather, the defendant in Jackson's case was arguing that, given the facts she alleged, and given the law of Title VII, no juror could reasonably conclude the plaintiff had been subjected to racial harassment that was sufficiently bad to warrant legal relief. That is an argument that the defendant rightly lost.

A fourth setting in which *nigger* arises as a focal point in litigation involves cases in which the judge must decide whether certain evidence that one party wants to offer to the jury should be admitted. The party seeking to exclude the evidence from the trial argues that it is more prejudicial than probative—or in layman's terms, more likely to impede than to advance the search for truth, in that its inclusion is inessential to a sound adjudication of the facts in dispute and will poison the minds of the jurors, making them unable to attend fairly to their task. Examples abound of *nigger* in this context.

Michael Brad Magleby, for instance, was charged with committing crimes in connection with burning a cross on the property of an interracial family. During the trial, over defense counsel's objections, prosecutors read lyrics of a song that Magleby was said to have listened to on the evening of the cross burning. The lyrics featured numerous references to nigger, as in "Nigger, nigger, get out of here."[97] A court of appeals upheld Magleby's conviction, holding that the trial judge had not abused his discretion by admitting the song lyrics into evidence.

In another case, Jack William Tocco was prosecuted for racketeering. During his trial, prosecutors played taped conversations for the jury in which the defendant and a close associate could be heard saying, among other things, that they "might win up here [in Detroit] with a nigger trial, nigger jury."[98] While agreeing with the defendant that "those particular denigrating comments were unfairly prejudicial," an appellate court affirmed his conviction because the prejudicial comments constituted only a small portion of the captured discussion, and other evidence also pointed to his guilt.[99]

The issue surfaces in civil as well as criminal cases. Aleia Robinson sued the United States Postal Service for violating Title VII of the Civil Rights Act by discriminating against her on racial grounds. At trial she sought to introduce into evidence a document entitled "Nigger

Employment Application," which in her view supported her contention that racism was pervasive at the Cincinnati, Ohio, facility where she worked. A parody of a standard employment application, this document listed as possible choices for birthplace the zoo, a cotton field, a back alley, and an animal hospital. Robinson stated that she was prepared to present witnesses who would testify that the parody had been widely circulated at her workplace, that no one had ever been disciplined in connection with it, and that it had prompted nothing more than laughter on the part of several supervisors. A magistrate judge excluded the application from evidence, declaring that it was irrelevant to the legal issues in question and would be more prejudicial than probative in resolving the dispute. A court of appeals disagreed, finding that the magistrate judge's evidentiary ruling had been overly restrictive. Robinson was awarded a new trial.[100]

In a suit charging police officers with using excessive force in making a lawful arrest, a judge excluded from evidence a portion of a tape recorded during the incident in question. The excluded portion would have revealed that an arresting officer shouted at one point, "Did you get that nigger?"[101] A court of appeals reversed and granted the plaintiff a new trial. Exasperated, the appellate tribunal declared, "It is difficult to understand why [the trial judge] believed that all of the words uttered at the time of the arrest and beating were probative and helpful to the task the jury faced, except the phrase containing the word 'nigger.' . . . Because the district court did not state for the record any reason for excluding this evidence, and neither the parties nor this court can discern any reason for its exclusion, we hold that the district court abused its discretion."[102]

Of course, the most famous evidentiary ruling involving the N-word came in response to efforts to bring a witness's use of the term to the attention of the jury in the murder trial of O. J. Simpson.[103] In that case, Simpson was charged with murdering his former wife Nicole Brown Simpson and an acquaintance of hers named Ronald Goldman. The police had allegedly found incriminating evidence at the murder site and at Simpson's residence, including a bloody glove presumably worn by the murderer. Simpson's attorneys maintained that the bloody glove had been planted by police officer Mark Fuhrman.

The prosecutors requested that the presiding judge, Lance Ito, prevent defense counsel from questioning Fuhrman with regard to his racial attitudes, including his alleged penchant for derogatorily referring to blacks as niggers. The title of the prosecution's motion—"People's Motion . . . to Exclude from Trial Remote, Inflammatory, and Irrelevant Character Evidence regarding L.A.P.D. Detective Mark Fuhrman"—revealed its essential argument. Pleading for the judge to exclude any inquiry into Fuhrman's linguistic habits, prosecutor Christopher Darden declared that because the N-word "is the filthiest, dirtiest, nastiest word in the English language," references to it "will blind the jury. It will blind them to the truth. . . . It will affect their judgment. It will impair their ability to be fair and impartial. . . . If you allow [the defense] to use their word and play this race card, not only [do] the direction and the focus of the case change, but the entire complexion of the case changes. It is a race case then. It is white versus black, African American versus Caucasian, us versus them, us versus the system."[104]

The defense responded with a dual argument. First, it maintained that evidence relating to Fuhrman's racial views was relevant to its theory that for reasons of racial animus, the officer had planted evidence. Second, it derided the notion that testimony regarding Fuhrman's use of the word *nigger* would prevent jurors from sensibly evaluating the evidence at hand. It was "demeaning," defense counsel Johnny Cochran argued, to suggest that black jurors—"African Americans [whose forebears] have lived under oppression for two hundred-plus years in this country," and who themselves had lived with "offensive words, offensive looks, [and] offensive treatment every day of their lives"—would be unable to deliberate fairly if they were made aware of a witness's racial views, as evidenced in part by his usage of the N-word.[105]

Judge Ito rightly decided to permit Simpson's attorneys to ask Fuhrman whether, over the preceding ten years, he had ever used the N-word. Fuhrman denied that he had—a statement that, instead of ending the matter, set the stage for a second controversy. Several months after Fuhrman's denial, audiotapes were discovered on which he was heard using the N-word repeatedly and with relish. The defense attorneys, not surprisingly, sought to introduce this new evidence in its entirety. The prosecution, for its part, sought to prevent or at least to minimize the jury's exposure to the tapes. Judge Ito compromised: he permitted the jury to hear Fuhrman say "nigger" twice and also allowed the defense to elicit an acknowledgment that in the taped conversations he used the N-word some forty-one times. The jury subsequently acquitted Simpson, in perhaps the most hotly debated jury verdict in American legal history.

———

Like every other significant feature of American life—including cigarettes, guns, pornography, drugs, stock trading, sex, religion, and money—*nigger* is thoroughly enmeshed in litigation. The disorderly diversity of the conflicts in which it figures is remarkable. The following three cases illustrate that variety.

Otis Ross successfully sued the Douglas County, Nebraska, correctional facility for violating federal antidiscrimination law. Ross, a black prison guard, complained of being subjected to a constant barrage of abuse by a supervisor who addressed him as "nigger" and "black boy" and referred to Ross's white wife as "whitey." The abusive supervisor was also black. The county posited that as a matter of law, blacks could not subject other blacks to a racially hostile workplace. The judges, however, wisely rejected that argument, quoting Thurgood Marshall's observation that given the mysteries of human motivation, "it would be unwise to presume as a matter of law that human beings of one definable group will not discriminate against other members of their group."[106]

In a second case, a white woman sued for and won a divorce after forty years of marriage and three children. She alleged that her husband had subjected her to cruel and inhuman treatment due to his rage at their daughter's decision to marry someone whom the court described as "a gentleman of Puerto Rican descent." The husband had refused to attend the wedding and would not speak to his daughter or acknowledge his son-in-law. Infuriated by his wife's acceptance of the marriage, he told her that her presence made him feel like puking. For good measure, he repeatedly called her a nigger lover.[107]

A third memorable case arose from one man's efforts to effectuate Lenny Bruce's strategy to defang *nigger* through continuous use. Russell Lawrence Lee petitioned a court to change his name to "Mister Nigger."[108] His intention in doing this, he wrote, was to "steal the stinging degradation—the thunder, the wrath, the shame and racial slur—from the word *nigger*."[109] A trial court, affirmed by the California Court of Appeals, rejected his petition. The appellate court maintained that while the petitioner had a common-law right to use whatever name he chose, the judiciary did not have to assist him in his experiment and could, in this instance, properly refrain from doing so, since the "proposed surname is commonly considered to be a racial epithet and has the potential to be a 'fighting word.' "[110]

These three cases, unusual though they all are, nonetheless represent a type of conflict that judges will continue to face. For *nigger* and its variants will keep

111

showing up in court so long as they remain key words that tap into and reflect powerful emotions. For the forseeable future, at least, *nigger* will constitute a peculiar, resilient, ever-changing fixture in the American jurisprudence of epithets.

CHAPTER THREE

Pitfalls in Fighting *Nigger:* Perils of Deception, Censoriousness, and Excessive Anger

fter the Civil War, a former master approached a former slave while she was tending livestock. "What you doin', nigger?" he asked, as he had probably done on many previous occasions. But this time her response was different: she replied, "I ain't no nigger. I's a Negro and I'm Miss Liza Mixon." Stung, the former master chased his former slave with a whip.[1]

Until the civil rights revolution of the 1960s, whites in the South typically refrained from addressing blacks as "Mr." or "Mrs." but instead called them by their first names or by titles signifying a senior with servile status—titles such as "Uncle" or "Auntie." Addressing all black men as "boys," regardless of their age, was another way for whites to observe Jim Crow etiquette.

Positive modifications to such practices have been effected only through struggle. To avoid or at least minimize belittlement, some blacks made a habit of identifying themselves only by their last names. Blacks furiously objected to *Negro* being spelled with a lower- as opposed to an uppercase *N,* and on March 7, 1930, the editors of the *New York Times* announced that the paper would henceforth capitalize the *N* in *Negro.* The U.S. Government Printing Office followed suit three years later. Within a decade, capitalization would become the rule at the Supreme Court as well.[2]

Referring to blacks derogatorily as niggers, however, was the custom to which blacks objected most strongly. In 1939, when David O. Selznick was in the throes of producing *Gone With the Wind,* he received hundreds of letters from blacks warning him to remove all "nigger" references from his upcoming film. The letter writers were concerned because the novel on which the film was based was full of such references. So, too, were early drafts of the film script. Initially Selznick sought to solve the problem by promising that the N-word would not be spoken by any white characters, but once he had been made aware of the intensity of blacks' feelings, he resolved to prohibit its use entirely and took pains to publicize his decision. A form letter declared that his studio had been "in frequent communication with Mr. [Walter] White of the Society for the Advancement of Colored People, and has accepted his suggestions concerning the elimination of the word 'nigger' from our picture."[3]

In the years that followed, blacks began to win other, similar battles. By the 1940s, "sensitivities were sufficiently aroused for Joseph Conrad's *The Nigger of the Narcissus* (1897) to be removed from open shelves in school libraries; for Marjorie Kinnan Rawlings's *The Yearling* (1938) to be released in a 'school edition' that omitted two passages containing the word [*nigger*]; and for Agatha Christie's play *Ten Little Niggers* (1939) to be retitled for American consumption as *Ten Little Indians* (and then retitled again as *And Then There Were None)*."[4]

In the 1960s and the decades thereafter, campaigns against racial indecency gained unprecedented support in mounting countless challenges to racist cultural artifacts. Scores of landmarks on official maps, for example, once bore such names as Nigger Lake, Niggerhead Hill, and Old Nigger Creek. *Nigger,* as we have seen, can have many meanings. But in the context of naming landmarks—an endeavor monopolized until recently by white men—it is clear that the *nigger* memorialized on maps was not the *nigger* of irony or affection but the *nigger* of insult and contempt. Widespread anger at cartographic slurs prompted Secretary of the Interior Stewart Udall to insist in 1963 that the Board on Geographic Names replace all references to *Nigger* with *Negro*.[5]

That same year, during court proceedings in Etowah County, Alabama, a prosecutor insisted upon addressing white witnesses by their last names and black witnesses by their first. At issue in the proceedings was the legality of arrests of civil rights protesters. The prosecutor began his cross-examination of one of the protestors by asking her name. She replied, "Miss Mary Hamilton." Addressing her as "Mary," he asked who had arrested her. She repeated her full name and added, "Please address me correctly." The prosecutor nevertheless continued to call her simply Mary, and the judge directed her to answer the question. She refused, whereupon the judge held her in contempt of court and immediately imposed a jail sentence and a fine. His ruling, however, would not stand; the Supreme Court of the United States would later reverse it.[6]

In Mississippi in 1964, during a *successful* gubernatorial campaign, Paul Johnson repeatedly joked that the acronym NAACP stood for "Niggers, Apes, Alligators, Coons, and Possums."[7] Such an electoral outcome would be inconceivable today in any state. No serious politician, not even a David Duke, could casually and unapologetically refer to "niggers" and hope to win an election. *Nigger* has been belatedly but effectively stigmatized—an important, positive development in American culture.

Progress, however, begets new problems, and our subject is no exception. The very conditions that have helped to stigmatize *nigger* have also been conducive to the emergence of certain troubling tendencies. Among these latter are unjustified deception, overeagerness to detect insult, the repression of *good* uses of *nigger*, and the overly harsh punishment of those who use the N-word imprudently or even wrongly.

The stigmatization of *nigger* has unavoidably created an atmosphere in which people may be tempted to make false charges in order to exploit feelings of sympathy, guilt, and anger. The most notorious instance of such deception involved an allegation made by a black teenager named Tawana Brawley, who claimed that several white men had abducted her, raped her, and scrawled *nigger* on her body with feces. Her charges have now been fully discredited, though some still profess to believe her story.[8] Brawley, however, was not alone in seeking to exploit goodwill through a hoax. In 1995 Tisha Anderson, a black woman, and William Lee, her white boyfriend, insisted that they had received hateful messages ("Niggers don't belong here") and been victimized by vandals who had scrawled racist slurs on the walls and steps of their apartment building ("Niggers live here"). It was all a lie: *they* were the ones who had defaced the building, in an attempt to escape their lease.[9] In another case, Persey Harris III filed charges against the owner of a restaurant, asserting that the man had come after him with a stick while shouting racial epithets. Harris later confessed that he had lied and explained that he had been trying to create the predicate for a civil lawsuit.[10] A Maryland woman, Sonia James, charged that thugs had flooded her home, slashed her furniture, and spray-painted racial slurs on her walls. Insurance companies covered her claims, the police set up a station near her house, and many people, after hearing of the alleged hate crime, sent gifts of money, food, and clothes. In actuality, the vandal was James herself.[11]

In yet another case, Sabrina Collins, a black freshman at Emory University, claimed that someone had targeted her with death threats and racist graffiti. Her alleged ordeal became national news. At one point it was reported that she had been so traumatized by racist mis-treatment that she had curled up into a fetal position and ceased speaking. Subsequently, however, it became clear that Collins herself had committed the acts in question. That a college student would perpetrate such a hoax was bad enough, but worse still was the reaction voiced by Otis Smith, the president of the Atlanta branch of the NAACP, who dismissed as largely irrelevant the find-ing that Collins had lied. Echoing Tawana Brawley's apologists, he maintained that to him, it did not matter "whether [Collins] did it or not."[12] Rather, what con-cerned Smith was "all the pressure these black students are under at these predominantly white schools."[13] If the hoax served to highlight that issue, he suggested, then he had no problem with Collins's means of publicity. It is difficult to imagine anything that could be more discred-iting to a civic leader than the remarks attributed to Smith. Not only do they exhibit an egregious indiffer-ence to truthfulness in public discussion; they also indi-cate an inability to distinguish between a coherent po-litical strategy and a pathetic escapade that was probably nothing more than a desperate plea for help.

Of all the things that have hurt the campaign against *nigger*-as-insult, unjustifiable lying and silly defenses have inflicted the most damage. But worrisome, too, are the badly mistaken attacks undertaken against people who never should have been seen as enemies.

One infamous round of wrongheaded protest was directed against David Howard, the white director of a municipal agency in Washington, D.C. Howard unwittingly entered the fray when he told members of his staff that in light of budgetary constraints, he would have to be "niggardly" with the money at his disposal. Apparently believing that *niggardly* (which means miserly or stingy) was related to *nigger,* a couple of Howard's black subordinates began a whispering campaign that blossomed into a public outcry. Howard resigned. The mayor of Washington, Anthony Williams, immediately accepted his resignation, declaring that Howard had shown poor judgment.

For several days afterward this incident became a focus of discussion in forums high and low. Some observers voiced indignation at Howard's language and refused to be mollified by explanations of the etymological difference between *nigger* and *niggardly*. "Do you really think," asked one Washingtonian, "[that Howard] didn't notice he had to pass 'nigger' before he could get to the 'dly'?"[14] In print, too, a few commentators maintained that Howard had shown poor judgment, a lapse for which he could justly be sanctioned. Julianne Malveaux, for example, wrote, "I have a bunch of dictionaries and I understand that 'niggardly' and 'niggling' are not the same as the N-word. But I am still annoyed, amazed, outdone [by Howard]. . . . He understands that perhaps there are other ways to indicate a tightness in a budget—that one might say 'parsimonious,' 'frugal,' or 'miserly.' No matter how many times teutonics attempts to trump ebonics, the fact is that the n-words—be it the N-word or 'niggardly'—rankle."[15] Others declined to attack Howard but suggested that *niggardly* and other, similar words prone to be misunderstood might be best avoided.[16] "Would the openly gay Howard not flinch, not even a little bit," columnist Debra Dickerson asked, "if a superior found a reason to mention tossing a 'faggot' on the fire or going outside to smoke a 'fag'? Two more perfectly harmless and obscure words—but why go there?"[17] Refusing to be bound by the dictionary definition of *niggardly,* Courtland Milloy of the *Washington Post* asserted that "when the subject of race is at hand . . . the only dictionary that counts is the one that gives meaning to human experience." Milloy placed a question mark over "any white person who says 'niggardly' . . . when [that person] could have said miserly."[18]

Many other commentators, however, took the opposite view, and sharply criticized the way Howard had been treated. Julian Bond, the chairman of the board of directors of the NAACP, remarked facetiously that "the Mayor has been niggardly in his judgment on this issue."[19] Writing in the Raleigh, North Carolina, *News and Observer,* Barry Saunders averred that the episode demonstrated the malevolent influence of "people whose antennae are always up, seeking out an affront where none exists so they can respond out of all proportion."[20] Similarly dismissive was the columnist Tony Snow, who pronounced Howard the victim of a "linguistic lynching." According to Snow, "David Howard got fired because some people in public employ were morons who a) didn't know the meaning of 'niggardly,' b) didn't know how to use a dictionary to discover the word's meaning and c) actually demanded that he apologize for their ignorance."[21]

Eventually Mayor Williams, who has been criticized as insufficiently "black" by many Washingtonians, offered Howard another position in the D.C. government and admitted that he had been wrong to accept his resignation without first educating himself fully about what had transpired. By then, though, the damage had been done. By fearfully deferring to excessive and uninformed outrage, the mayor had lowered his own standing in public opinion.

What happened in Washington will forever shadow the history of *niggardly* and serve as a benchmark of hypersensitivity. Around the same time, however, an even more alarming incident involving *niggardly* occurred at the University of Wisconsin at Madison, where a professor used the word during a lecture in a class he was teaching on Chaucer. A black student who was upset by the similarity between *niggardly* and *nigger* approached the professor after class to express her concerns. He apparently thanked her for sharing her perceptions with him and proceeded to explain the origin of *niggardly* and hence its distance from the N-word. In the next session the professor once again referred to *niggardly* and then defined it for the class. Notwithstanding the clarification, the same black student who had previously spoken with the professor stormed out of the classroom, crying. According to one news report, she referred to her experience in the Chaucer class as evidence of the need for a stringent speech code that would apply to all members of the faculty, regardless of the intent behind their "offensive" words. [22]

A misplaced protest notable for the distinguished

character of its antagonists erupted in the pages of *Boston Magazine* in May 1998, following the publication of a long, largely complimentary article by Cheryl Bentsen about Henry Louis Gates Jr., the chair of the Department of Afro-American Studies at Harvard University. Gates is a controversial figure about whom it is virtually impossible to write without getting involved in the disputes that surround his celebrity. In this instance, however, disputation arose not from Bentsen's profile itself but from the title given to it by the editors of the magazine. The cover of the April issue featured the phrase "Head Negro in Charge," a softened version of a term well known in black circles: "Head Nigger in Charge," or HNIC. Scores of readers objected, including one who declared in an agitated letter to the editor:

The title is EXTREMELY RACIST!!! As a black American, I am outraged and insulted. The term [HNIC] was used in the days of slavery when white foremen would designate a black person to oversee (that is to keep in check) other blacks. The title shows your ignorance and indifference to the black community. I vow NEVER to purchase or support your magazine in any way. I will also rally every single person I know to boycott your magazine.[23]

Another reader wrote:

> I am a subscriber . . . who is really offended by
> the headline of the Gates article. I can accept that
> you did not mean offense; but if members of the
> black community express dismay at the use of lan-
> guage, it is appropriate to say: I am sorry. . . . I will
> refrain from using such language in the future.[24]

Craig Unger, then the editor of *Boston Magazine*,
responded to the controversy by asserting:

> The term HNIC is part of the vernacular of
> black writers and intellectuals. It denotes the phe-
> nomenon of the white establishment selecting one
> African-American to speak for the race. It was in
> that context that we used HNIC, and there was
> clearly no intent to offend. On the contrary, we are
> proud of our story, and we want nothing to over-
> shadow it. Our use of the expression, however, has
> obviously upset some people, and I sincerely regret
> that.[25]

Many critics of the "HNIC" title proceeded as if their
offended sensibilities alone should settle the matter—as

if their sense of outrage necessarily made the act they objected to a bad act warranting an apology. Repeatedly, people voiced anger at *Boston Magazine* without troubling to state what justified their anger. Natalie Anderson's letter to the editor, for example, charged that the title of the article was "EXTREMELY RACIST," but it neglected to explain what was so racist about it. True, "HNIC" has historically denoted a black person who is in command of a given situation only thanks to the backing of whites.[26] But clearly the editors of *Boston Magazine* were aware of that meaning and simply wished to add a provocative and ironic twist to a largely admiring profile of a prominent black figure by suggesting that despite massive changes in race relations, whites still retain the power to select who among blacks will be accorded the mantle of leadership—a point that has been made by numerous black intellectuals, including Gates himself.

In truth, the anger directed at *Boston Magazine* had to do not so much with the content of the disparaged title as with its provenance—that is, the fact that the phrase had been co-opted by the magazine's white editors. For many people, *nigger* and its cognates take on completely different complexions depending on the speaker's race. Had the "HNIC" profile and title appeared in *Essence,*

Emerge, Ebony, or some other black-owned publication, there would have been no controversy. But *Boston Magazine* is white-owned and marketed mainly to whites, situating "HNIC" in a context that, for some observers, raised several difficulties: the embarrassment of discussing certain racial topics before a predominantly white audience; fear of, and anger about, a white entrepreneur intruding into black cultural territory; and the suspicion that whatever the setting, whites derive racist pleasure out of hearing, saying, or even alluding to "nigger." For these reasons, even blacks who use *nigger* themselves adamantly insist that it is wrong for whites to do so.[27] On the album containing his "I hate niggers" skit, for example, Chris Rock also presents a sketch in which a white man approaches him after a performance and appreciatively repeats some of what Rock has just said onstage. The next sound heard is that of the white man being punched.[28] Rock's message is clear: white people cannot rightly say about blacks some of the things that blacks themselves say about blacks. Just as a son is privileged to address his mother in ways that outsiders cannot (at least not in the son's presence), so, too, is a member of a race privileged to address his racial kin in ways prescribed to others.

Although many whites follow this convention, some rebel. Two noteworthy examples are Carl Van Vechten and Quentin Tarantino.

Van Vechten sparked controversy when, in 1926, he published *Nigger Heaven,* a novel about black life in Harlem. The title alone alienated many blacks, including some who knew the author personally. Van Vechten had, for example, selected some lines of poetry by his friend Countee Cullen to serve as the epigraph for his book, but when he told the poet about his proposed title, he turned, in Van Vechten's words, "white with rage."[29] And soon their friendship ended. At an antilynching rally in Harlem, a protester burned a copy of *Nigger Heaven*. And in Boston, the book was banned.

Van Vechten was well aware that the title would singe the sensibilities of many potential readers. Even his own father objected to it: "Your 'Nigger Heaven' is a title I don't like," Charles Duane Van Vechten informed his son in 1925. "I have myself never spoken of a colored man as a 'nigger.' If you are trying to help the race, as I am assured you are, I think every word you write should be a respectful one towards the blacks."[30] Yet the younger Van Vechten persisted, emblazoning upon his novel a title that still sparks resentment.

It should not be overlooked, however, that while

many blacks condemned *Nigger Heaven,* others—including some of the most admired black intellectuals of the day—applauded it. Charles Chesnutt, the first black professional man of letters, praised Van Vechten in a letter, telling him that he hoped that the novel would "have the success which its brilliancy and obvious honesty deserve." Walter White, himself a novelist as well as a leading official with the NAACP, expressed both admiration and regret that he had not thought of the title first. Paul Robeson sent Van Vechten a congratulatory telegram that stated, in part, "NIGGER HEAVEN AMAZING IN ITS ABSOLUTE UNDERSTANDING AND DEEP SYMPATHY THANKS FOR SUCH A BOOK." Charles S. Johnson, editor of *Opportunity*, one of the key journals of the Harlem Renaissance, commented that he "wish[ed] a Negro had written it." Along the same lines, novelist Nella Larsen mused, "Why, oh, why, couldn't we have done something as big as this for ourselves?"[31]

James Weldon Johnson, author of "Lift Evr'y Voice and Sing" (the "Negro National Anthem"), wrote an effusive review in which he declared that Van Vechten had paid colored people "the rare tribute of writing about them as people rather than as puppets."[32] Later, in his autobiography, Johnson would assert that "most of the Negroes who condemned *Nigger Heaven* did not read it; they were estopped by the title." Looking toward the future, he would conjecture that "as the race progresses it will become less and less susceptible to hurts from such causes."[33] On this point he was clearly wrong, for as we have seen, even in this new century *nigger* retains its capacity to anger, inflame, and distract.

The white film director Quentin Tarantino has recently updated the racial politics triggered by Van Vechten's novel by writing film scripts in which *nigger* figures prominently. Tarantino's leading man in *Jackie Brown,* a black gun runner, casually uses the word throughout the film; in one sequence he hugs a black underling and, with apparent affection, calls him "my nigger," only to murder him in cold blood a few minutes later. In *True Romance,* Tarantino orchestrates a confrontation between a white man and a Sicilian mobster. The man knows that the mobster is about to kill him, and in a final gesture of defiance, he laughingly tells him that since North African moors—"niggers"—conquered Sicily and had sex with Sicilian women, his ancestors must have been niggers. Further, the condemned man speculates that the Sicilian's grandmother "fucked a nigger" and that therefore the mobster himself is "part eggplant." And in Tarantino's *Pulp Fiction,* a scene featuring a black hit man, his white partner, and a white friend of the black hit man has the professional assassins showing up unexpectedly at the home of the friend to dispose of a bloody car with a corpse inside. Exasperated, the white friend complains to his black hitman buddy that "storing dead niggers ain't my fucking business." It isn't so much the fact that he will be breaking the law by helping to conceal a murder that worries him; rather, it's the fear that his wife will divorce him if she comes home while the hit men are still in the house. This white man who talks of "dead-nigger storage" loves his wife and is absolutely terrified by the prospect of losing her. It is important to note that she is black.

Spike Lee, among others, has taken exception to Tarantino's playfulness with *nigger*. When it was noted in response that some of his own films also make extensive use of *nigger,* the director replied that as an African American, he had "more of a right to use [the N-word]."[34] Lee himself has not articulated the basis for that asserted "right," but at least three theories are plausible. One is that the long and ugly history of white racist subordination of African Americans should in and of itself disqualify whites from using *nigger*. A second holds that equity earned through oppression grants cultural ownership rights: having been made to suffer by being called "nigger" all these years, this theory goes, blacks should now be able to monopolize the slur's peculiar cultural capi-

tal.[35] A third theory is that whites lack a sufficiently intimate knowledge of black culture to use the word *nigger*
properly.

All three of these theories are dramatized in Lee's
film *Bamboozled,* a farce about a black scriptwriter who,
in order to keep his job, creates a television-network
variety show featuring all of the stereotypical characteristics through which blacks have been comically de-
famed: blackface, bugging eyes, extravagant buffoonery,
the omnipresent grin. Lee takes care to make the worst
of *Bamboozled*'s many villains an obnoxious, presumptu-
ous, ignorant white man—Dunwitty—who deems himself sufficiently "black" to boast to his African American
subordinates that he knows more about "niggers" than
they do.[36]

The great failing of these theories is that, taken seriously, they would cast a protectionist pall over popular
culture that would likely benefit certain minority entrepreneurs only at the net expense of society overall.
Excellence in culture thrives, like excellence elsewhere,
in a setting open to competition—and that includes competition concerning how best to dramatize the N-word.
Thus, instead of cordoning off racially defined areas of the
culture and allowing them to be tilled only by persons of
the "right" race, we should work toward enlarging the

common ground of American culture, a field that is open to all comers regardless of their origin. Despite Spike Lee's protests to the contrary, Quentin Tarantino is talented and has the goods to prove it. That is not to say that he should be exempt from criticism, but Lee's racial critique of his fellow director is off the mark. It is almost wholly ad hominem. It focuses on the character of Tarantino's race rather than the character of his work—brilliant work that allows the word *nigger* to be heard in a rich panoply of contexts and intonations.

In 1997 in Ypsilanti, Michigan, a computer technician named Delphine Abraham decided to look up the definition of *nigger* in the tenth edition of *Merriam-Webster's Collegiate Dictionary*.[37] This is what she found:

> **1:** a black person—usu. taken to be offensive **2:** a member of any dark-skinned race—usu. taken to be offensive **3:** a member of a socially disadvantaged class of persons <it's time for somebody to lead all of America's ~s . . . all the people who feel left out of the political process—Ron Dellums>
>
> **usage** *Nigger* in senses 1 and 2 can be found in the works of such writers of the past as Joseph Conrad, Mark Twain, and Charles Dickens, but it

now ranks as perhaps the most offensive and inflammatory racial slur in English. Its use by and among blacks is not always intended or taken as offensive, but, except in sense 3, it is otherwise a word expressive of racial hatred and bigotry.

Abraham recorded what she subsequently felt and did:

I felt that the first two definitions labeled me and anyone else who happened to be Black or have dark skin a nigger. Outraged, I called Merriam-Webster in Springfield, Massachusetts. I reached the company's president and publisher, John Morse, who was polite but really didn't seem to understand my concerns. Not getting a response that satisfied me, I told him before hanging up, "Something should be done about this, and I think I'm going to start a petition drive to have the word removed or redefined."

Just by speaking locally, I gathered more than 2,000 signatures within the first month. I was interviewed by the Associated Press news service, on radio talk shows, and even on CNN. Newsgroups on the Internet joined the campaign. Syndicated newspaper columnists weighed in. The NAACP, through its president and CEO, Kweisi Mfume, suggested organizing a boycott if Merriam-Webster did not review the definition.

Most people believe, as I do, that the N-word needs a more accurate first definition reflecting that it is a derogatory term used to dehumanize or oppress a group or race of people.[38]

The question is, should Abrahams, Mfume, or anyone else have felt insulted by Merriam-Webster's definition?

No.

The definition notes that the term is usually taken to be offensive and then states, for good measure, that the N-word "now ranks as perhaps the most offensive and inflammatory racial slur in English." Abrahams claimed that the Merriam-Webster definition labeled as a nigger anyone who happened to be black. But that view is unreasonable given the totality of the definition offered by the dictionary. In defining *nigger,* moreover, *Webster's 10th* does not vary from its typical practice. For instance, in defining *honky,* the dictionary posits: "*usu. disparaging:* a white person."

In response to Abraham's petition drive, representatives of Merriam-Webster tried to depoliticize the matter by portraying the dictionary as a mechanical, autonomous linguistic mirror. To this end, the marketing director repeatedly averred that "a dictionary is a scholarly reference, not a political tool. As long as the word is in use, it is our responsibility as dictionary publishers to put the word into the dictionary."[39] Similarly, the company president, John R. Morse, portrayed his editors as mere technicians lacking independent powers of their own. Dictionary makers, Morse maintained, "do not invent the words that go into the dictionary, and they don't decide what meanings they will have."[40] Morse simultaneously undermined his own point, however, by noting that "offensive words . . . appear only in hardcover college-level dictionaries, which are edited expressly for adults. Slurs and other offensive words are not included in dictionaries intended for children. Nor are they published in any smaller, abridged dictionaries, such as paperbacks." With respect to these other dictionaries, the managers of Merriam-Webster had decided, for various reasons, to excise the N-word. Whether or not this decision was a sound one is, for the moment, irrelevant. The important thing to recognize is that dictionary makers do, in fact, exercise judgment, notwithstanding Morse's evasive denial.

Deciding whether to note or how to define a deeply controversial word is an inescapably "political" act, and claims to the contrary are either naive or disingenuous.

The issue, then, is not whether editors shape the substance of their dictionaries. Of course they do. The issue is the substance of the choices made. Some of Merriam-Webster's critics have condemned the editors' decision to include any reference at all to *nigger*. "If the word is not there [in the dictionary], you can't use it," one protester asserted in favor of deleting the N-word altogether.[41] That tack, however, is glaringly wrongheaded. Many terms that are absent from dictionaries are nonetheless pervasive in popular usage. Moreover, so long as racist sentiments exist, they will find linguistic means of expression, even if some avenues are blocked. There are, after all, numerous ways of insulting people.

In sum, the campaign against *Merriam-Webster's Collegiate Dictionary* was misguided. The dictionary defined the term adequately, and the dictionary's editors were correct in including the N-word despite the embarrassment and hurt feelings the term inflicts. *Nigger* should have a place in any serious dictionary. The word is simply too important to ignore.

A second, and achingly poignant, example of mistaken protest is the widespread repudiation of *Huckleberry Finn*, now one of the most beleaguered texts in American literature. Monthly, it seems, someone attacks Mark

Twain's most famous book on the grounds that it is racist. The novel's most energetic foe, John H. Wallace, calls it "the most grotesque example of racist trash ever written."[42] For many of *Huckleberry Finn*'s enemies, the most upsetting and best proof of the book's racism is the fact that *nigger* appears in the text some 215 times. At one point, for example, Huck's aunt Sally asks him why he is so late arriving at her house:

> "We blowed a cylinder head."
> "Good gracious! Anybody hurt?"
> "No'm. Killed a nigger."
> "Well, it's lucky; because sometimes people do get hurt."[43]

Wallace asserts that this exchange, within the context of the novel as a whole, strives to make the point that blacks are not human beings.[44] That interpretation, however, is ludicrous, a frightening exhibition of how thought becomes stunted in the absence of any sense of irony. Twain is not willfully buttressing racism here; he is seeking ruthlessly to unveil and ridicule it. By putting *nigger* in Aunt Sally's mouth, the author is not branding blacks, but rather branding Aunt Sally.

There was a time when Twain's own use of *nigger* signaled contempt. As a young man inculcated with white-supremacist beliefs and sentiments, he viewed blacks as inferior and spoke of them as such.[45] As he matured and traveled and became more cosmopolitan, however, Twain underwent a dramatic metamorphosis. He grew to hate slavery and the brutality of Jim Crow and began to express his antiracist perspective satirically through his writings. *Huckleberry Finn* is the best fictive example of Twain's triumph over his upbringing. In it he creates a loving relationship between Huck and Jim, the runaway slave, all the while sardonically impugning the pretensions of white racial superiority. Among Twain's nonfiction, a striking example of his revolt against bigotry is his piece "Only a Nigger," in which he speaks in the voice of an apologist for a lynching:

Ah, well! Too bad, to be sure! A little blunder in the administration of justice by southern mob-law: but nothing to speak of. Only "a nigger" killed by mistake—that is all. . . . But mistakes will happen, even in the conduct of the best regulated and most high-toned mobs, and surely there is no good reason why Southern gentlemen should worry themselves with useless regrets, so long as only an innocent "nigger" is hanged, or roasted or [ ] to death now and then. . . . What are the lives of a few "niggers" in comparison with the impetuous instincts of a proud and fiery race? Keep ready the halter, therefore, o chivalry of Memphis! Keep the lash knotted; keep the brand and the faggots in waiting, for prompt work with the next "nigger" who may be suspected of any damnable crime![46]

Wallace, I suppose, would read this as an endorsement of lynching. But obviously it is intended to be just the opposite. The same holds true for *Huckleberry Finn*, which Twain designed to subvert, not to reinforce, racism.

I am not ruling out criticism of the novel. Perceptive commentators have questioned its literary merits.[47] It is undoubtedly true, moreover, that regardless of Twain's intentions, *Huckleberry Finn* (like *any* work of art) can be handled in a way that is not only stupid but downright destructive of the educational and emotional well-being of students. To take a contemporary example, the producers of *Mississippi Burning* intended their film to carry an antiracist message, but that did not prevent it from contributing inspiration to a wayward youth who, in 1990, burned crosses outside the residence of a black family in St. Paul, Minnesota, in an effort to frighten them into moving.[48]

Such concerns, however, are different from the one I am addressing. I am addressing the contention that the presence of *nigger* alone is sufficient to taint *Huckleberry Finn* or any other text. I am addressing those who contend that *nigger* has *no* proper place in American culture and who thus desire to erase the N-word totally, without qualification, from the cultural landscape. I am addressing parents who, in numerous locales, have demanded the removal of *Huckleberry Finn* from syllabi *solely* on the basis of the presence of the N-word—without having read the novel themselves, without having investigated the way in which it is being explored in class, and without considering the possibilities opened up by the close study of a text that confronts so dramatically the ugliness of slavery and racism. I am addressing eradicationists who, on grounds of racial indecency, would presumably want to bowdlerize or censor poems such as Carl Sandburg's "Nigger Lover," stories such as Theodore Dreiser's "Nigger Jeff," Claude McKay's "Nigger Lover," or Henry Dumas' "Double Nigger," plays such as Ed Bullins' "The Electronic Nigger," and novels such as Gil Scott-Heron's *The Nigger Factory*.

A third category of misguided protest involves cases in which insulted parties demand excessive punishment.

Consider what happened in 1993 at Central Michigan University (CMU).

Keith Dambrot was in his third year as the school's varsity men's basketball coach.[49] CMU also designated him as an "assistant professor"; presumably his subject was basketball. At halftime during a game against Miami University of Ohio, Dambrot tried to focus and inspire his team, made up of eleven blacks and three whites. He asked his players for permission to use with them a term that they often used with one another: the N-word. They nodded their assent, at which point Coach Dambrot said, "We need to be tougher, harder-nosed, and play harder. . . . We need to have more niggers on the team."[50] He then admiringly referred to one white member of the team as a nigger and went around the locker room categorizing the other players, by name, as either niggers or half-niggers. The niggers were the players who were doing their jobs well. The half-niggers or non-niggers were the ones who needed to work harder. Coach Dambrot later explained that he had used the term *nigger* "for instructional purposes with the permission of my African American players, and I used the term in the sense in which it is used by my African American players . . . to connote a person who is fearless, mentally strong, and tough."[51]

Despite the halftime pep talk, Central Michigan lost the game. But that was merely the beginning of Coach Dambrot's problems.

Word soon spread on campus about Coach Dambrot's locker-room speech. He must have become aware of this, and realized that some observers might take offense, because he asked the university's athletic director to speak to the members of the team about the incident. None of them voiced any objection to what the coach had said. Nonetheless, the athletic director told Dambrot that regardless of his intentions, his use of *nigger* had been "extremely inappropriate."[52] The director then warned the coach that if he used the term again, he would be fired.

Soon thereafter, a student who had previously quit the basketball team complained about the coach's language to the university's affirmative-action officer. This administrator, a white woman, demanded that the coach be punished. She insisted that a formal reprimand be placed in his personnel file, that he be suspended without pay for five days, and that during his suspension he arrange for a sensitivity trainer to meet with the team to explain why the use of *nigger* was always inappropriate. She further specified that attendance at this sensitivity-training session should be made mandatory, that Coach

Dambrot should "help assure that the team is not hostile to the training," and that he should "convey his support of this training session to the players and the staff."[53]

The coach did not resist, hoping that the incident would blow over quietly. His hopes, however, were shortly to be dashed. Publicity triggered two demonstrations at which eighty to a hundred protestors expressed their disapproval of the coach's purported "racism." The president of the university responded by announcing that the coach had been disciplined, declaring that "the term [*nigger*] is inappropriate under any circumstances," and avowing that he was "deeply sorry about the hurt, anger, [and] embarrassment its use ha[d] caused individuals as well as the entire university community."[54] By that time, though, critics of the university, including state legislators, were calling for harsher punishment, which was soon forthcoming.

On April 12, 1993, the university administration fired Coach Dambrot on the grounds that "public reaction to the incident [had] created an environment that makes it impossible for the university to conduct a viable basketball program under [his] leadership."[55]

Dambrot then sued the university, claiming that his discharge constituted a violation of his First Amendment rights. In a gesture of solidarity, members of the basketball team also sued the university, claiming that its speech code violated *their* First Amendment rights. The students prevailed—judges invalidated CMU's speech code—but not so their coach: judges ruled that the First Amendment did not bar the university from firing him. As interpreted by the Supreme Court, the First Amendment protects (to some extent) speech that touches upon matters of public concern. Therefore, if the coach had been talking to his team at halftime about, say, the racist history of the term *nigger*, his comments probably would have been protected. But in the view of the judges, Dambrot's speech did not touch upon a matter of public concern and was therefore fully vulnerable to the university's censure.

Here, however, I am interested not so much in the courts' conclusion that the university had the authority to fire the coach—a legal conclusion that seems to me to have been correct—as in the judgment that the university officials exercised pursuant to that authority. That judgment—or, more accurately, that *mis*judgment—casts a revealing light on our society's continued grappling with *nigger* and the cultural dynamics that surround it. The initial response by the athletic director—ordering the coach to desist—was sufficient. It recognized the undue risk that the coach's words might be misunderstood by members of the wider university community, while acknowledging that Dambrot had meant no harm.

Subsequent actions taken by university officials were excessive. First, the sensitivity-training session ordered by the affirmative-action officer was just the sort of Orwellian overreaching that has, unfortunately, tarnished the reputation of multiculturalist reformism. Among her requirements in regard to the session, after all, were that it must brook no debate over the propriety of the coach's language; that it must involve the coach in pacifying his players' resistance; that player attendance must be mandatory; and that the coach must explicitly state his support for the process regardless of his own opinions. Second, prior to firing Coach Dambrot, CMU officials seem to have made little effort to clarify the controversy or to suggest to the university community that this was a situation in which underlying realities were considerably more ambiguous than surface appearances might indicate. The fact is that Dambrot, though imprudent, was obviously employing *nigger* in a sense embraced by his players—a sense in which the term was a compliment, not an insult.[56] Sometimes it may be necessary for an administration to sacrifice a deserving employee in order to mollify public anger that might otherwise pose a threat to the institution's future. In this case, however, the CMU authorities capitulated too quickly to the formulaic rage of affronted blacks, the ill-considered sentimentality of well-meaning whites, and their own crass, bureaucratic opportunism.

An even more deplorable incident took place in 1998 at Jefferson Community College in Louisville, Kentucky, where an adjunct professor named Ken Hardy taught a course on interpersonal communications.[57] In a class exploring taboo words, students cited a number of insulting terms such as *faggot* and *bitch*. A member of the class mentioned *nigger*, and in the course of the discussion, Hardy repeated it. One of the nine black students in the twenty-two-person class objected to the airing of *that* word. Classmates disagreed, giving rise to a debate in which most of those present participated. At one point Hardy lent his support to the student who had first objected, suggesting that the class should take seriously the proposition that certain words were simply too volatile to be spoken out loud.

During a break, the student who had objected approached Hardy and requested that he stop using the N-word. Hardy defended the class discussion that had transpired but offered the student the option of sitting out the remainder of the session. She rejected that alternative. Subsequently she noted her continued disapproval in a letter to Hardy and also relayed her complaint to the Reverend Louis Coleman, a prominent local civil rights activist. Coleman, in turn, called the president of the college and asked him to "look into the matter." Hardy soon found himself in a tense meeting with the acting dean of academic affairs, who indicated, among other things, that the school could ill afford to antagonize prominent citizens. Although Hardy did not know it at the time, his career at Jefferson was at an end. A few days later the dean left a message on his phone stating that he would have no job at the college come fall.

The dismissal at Jefferson was worse than the one at CMU because it arose from a teacher's effort to make a point that was directly relevant to the intellectual concerns of a college-level course. By contrast, Coach Dambrot had acted imprudently in gratuitously using the word *nigger* in a context readily available to misinterpretation. Common to both cases, however, was the overeagerness of academic administrators to fire a subordinate for a *single* perceived misstep, even in circumstances in which the alleged wrongdoer had quite obviously been innocent of any intention to insult or otherwise harm those whom he addressed.

A much more sensible and humane response was modeled by high school students in Gould, Arkansas, in

1988.[58] A white teacher got into trouble because of a remark she made to an all-black class of students who were, according to her, becoming rambunctious. Exasperated, she said something designed to get their attention: "I think you're trying to make me think you're a bunch of poor, dumb niggers, and I don't think that." Upon hearing about her comment, ninety-one parents signed a petition demanding her removal. The school board requested the teacher's resignation after she acknowledged that she had committed "a dumb, stupid mistake." She was reportedly about to leave the town for good when students circulated petitions asking the board to reconsider its decision. The petitions were signed by 124 out of the town's 147 high school students, only two of whom were white. In light of this development, the school board, chaired by a black man, reversed itself. Asked to explain the students' intervention, a student leader replied, "We were ready to forgive and go on. . . . Anybody ought to get a second chance."

The student's statement, generous as it is, needs a bit of qualification. The offer of a second chance ought not to be automatic but should instead hinge on such variables as the nature of the offender's position and the purpose behind his or her remark. In contrast to District Attorney Spivey, the teacher held a position that, while

149

important, did not entail her exercising powers like those wielded by a prosecutor. Moreover, again in contrast to District Attorney Spivey, the teacher was not attempting to humiliate anyone. She was simply trying to instruct her students for their own benefit, albeit in a regrettable manner. In such circumstances she, like Coach Dambrot, deserved a second chance.

Advocates of broader prohibitions against "hate speech" maintain that the current legal regime is all too tolerant of *nigger*-as-insult and other forms of racial abuse. Several of the most prominent of these advocates—notably Charles Lawrence, Mari Matsuda, and Richard Delgado—have, in their positions as professors in law schools, provided intellectual underpinnings for campaigns aimed at banishing hate speech.[59] They and their allies have succeeded in persuading authorities at some colleges and universities to enact new speech codes. They have succeeded, too, in shaking up and enlivening civil libertarians, a group that had become intellectually complacent in the absence of a strong challenge. They have been unable, however, to sway the judiciary and have thus been forced to witness the invalidation of speech codes tested in litigation.[60] They have also largely failed to capture opinion. In the American culture wars of the 1980s and 1990s, the left-liberal multiculturalists who sought increased regulation of hate speech were soundly trounced by a coalition of opponents who effectively derided them as censorious ideologues—otherwise known as the P.C. (Political Correctness) Police.

The point, however, is not simply that the champions of speech codes lost on a variety of important fronts; it is that they *rightly* lost. For one thing, proponents of enhanced hate-speech regulation have typically failed to establish persuasively the asserted predicate for their campaign—that is, that verbal abuse on college campuses and elsewhere is a "rising," "burgeoning," "growing," "resurgent" development demanding countermeasures.[61] Regulationists do cite racist incidents on campus—the African student at Smith College who found a message slipped under her door reading, "African Nigger do you want some bananas?";[62] the counselor at Purdue University who was greeted by the words "Death Nigger" etched onto her door;[63] the taunt written on a blackboard at the University of Michigan: "A mind is a terrible thing to waste—especially on a nigger"[64]—but too often the dramatic retelling of an anecdote is permitted to substitute for a more systematic, quantitative analysis. Indeed, some commentators do not even seriously attempt to document their assertions but instead simply note a number of apparently outrageous events and then charge, without substantiation, that these episodes are, for example, representative of "a rise in the incidence of verbal and symbolic assault and harassment to which black and other traditionally subjugated groups are subjected."[65] A list of twenty, fifty, one hundred, or even three hundred racist incidents may appear to offer a terrible indictment of race relations on American campuses—until one recalls that there are hundreds of institutions of higher education across the country. Bearing in mind the numbers of young collegians who are constantly interacting with one another, often in close quarters, is a useful aid for keeping in perspective the catalogue of racist episodes that regulationists point to as the predicate for what they see as urgently needed reform.

A persuasive assertion that racially assaultive speech is on the rise ought logically to entail positing that there was a greater incidence of such speech in year Y than in year X. Demonstrating such a trajectory, however, is a daunting enterprise. After all, even when one is able to say that the number of reported incidents in a certain year was greater than the number of reported incidents in another year, there remains the problem of determining whether the reporting itself was a mirror of reality or a result of efforts to elicit from subjects their dissatisfaction with conduct they perceived to be offensive. Acknowledging such complications opens the way to considering alternative interpretations to those put forth by the regulationists. One alternative is that the growing number of reported episodes involving hate speech is a function of both an increased willingness to report perceived insults and an increased willingness to record them, which would mean that the perception of a rising tide of racial vilification is an illusion that paradoxically signals progress rather than regress. Or it may be that the regulationists are correct—that increased reporting does in fact reflect a greater incidence of verbal abuse. Even if that is so, however, there remains a question of interpretation. Here again, it is possible that episodes of verbal abuse are actually indicative of racial progress. On some campuses, for example, racist verbal abuse may not previously have been a problem simply because there were too few blacks around to generate racial friction. More recently, with the advent of a critical mass of black students, the possibilities for racial conflict may have escalated. At institutions where this is the case, increasing numbers of racial insults could be merely a function of more frequent interracial interaction and all that comes with it—for good and for ill.

Proponents of enhanced speech codes portray blacks on predominantly white campuses as being socially isolated and politically weak. Yet the regulationists clearly believe that the authorities to whom they are appealing are likely to side with these students and not with their antagonists. This, as Henry Louis Gates Jr. observes, is the "hidden foundation for the [anti–] hate speech movement. . . . You don't go to the teacher to complain about the school bully unless you know the teacher is on your side."[66]

Resorting to school authorities, however, has had its own costs. In stressing the "terror" of verbal abuse, proponents of hate-speech regulation have, ironically, empowered abusers while simultaneously weakening black students by counseling that they should feel grievously wounded by remarks that their predecessors would have shaken off or ignored altogether.

An examination of the substance of the regulationists' proposals turns up suggested reforms that are puzzlingly narrow, frighteningly broad, or disturbingly susceptible to discriminatory manipulation. In 1990, after much debate, Stanford University prohibited "harassment by personal vilification," which it defined as speech or other expression that

a) is intended to insult or stigmatize an individual or a small number of individuals on the basis of their race, color, handicap, religion, sexual orientation, or national and ethnic origin; and

b) is addressed directly to the individual or individuals whom it insults or stigmatizes; and

c) makes use of insulting or "fighting" words or nonverbal symbols.[67]

Perhaps the most notable feature of this provision is how little it accomplished. One of the incidents at Stanford that had fueled the call for a speech code in the first place involved the defacement of a poster bearing a likeness of Beethoven. After an argument with a black student who claimed that the composer had been partly of African descent, white students darkened a portrait of him and exaggerated the curliness of his hair and the thickness of his lips. They then affixed their negrofied poster to the door of the black student's room. Regulationists were outraged by this conduct, which they perceived as being aggressively racist. But the Stanford code would not have covered this action or, for that matter, most of the other verbal or symbolic "assaults" about which regulationists complain. During the first five years of Stanford's code, in fact, no one was ever charged with a violation. Some might argue that this record suggests that the code effectively prevented bad conduct, thus obviating the need for disciplinary proceedings. But a more plausible explanation is that conduct of the sort prohibited by the code was virtually nonexistent before its enactment and virtually nonexistent afterward—a veritable straw man.[68]

The Stanford code covered a single, specific type of speech: vulgar racial insults directed from one person to another in a face-to-face encounter. Such exchanges do happen; at the University of Wisconsin, for instance, a group of white male students reportedly followed some black female students, all the while shouting, "I've never tried a nigger before."[69] But conduct of this sort is sanctionable via traditional legal machinery (or if not through reputation-besmirching publicity), without resort to newfangled modes of repression. It is likely, moreover, that especially on a college campus, antiblack polemics that are polite, skillful, and conventionally garbed—think of *The Bell Curve*—will be far more hurtful to African Americans than the odd *nigger, coon, jiga-*

boo, or other racial insult, which in any case will almost certainly be more discrediting to the speaker than to the target. Yet under the Stanford code, the damaging but polite polemic is protected, while the rude but impotent epithet is not. This problem of underinclusiveness is a major embarrassment for the regulationist camp because, as Gates notes, "the real power commanded by the racist is likely to vary inversely with the vulgarity with which it is expressed. Black professionals soon learn that it is the socially disenfranchised—the lower class, the homeless—who are more likely to hail them as 'niggers.' The circles of power have long since switched to a vocabulary of indirection." By focusing on vulgar words that wound, regulationists "invite us to spend more time worr[ying] about speech codes than [about] coded speech."[70]

Because speech codes of the Stanford variety fail to address what some regulationists see as intolerable forms of speech, broader prohibitions have been proposed. Professor Charles Lawrence, for example, has urged that the ban on racial epithets be extended beyond the context of face-to-face encounters, while Professor Mari Matsuda has advocated punishing "racist speech" in general. Such proposals, however, encroach upon legal doctrines that have helped to make American culture among the most open and vibrant in the world.[71] Under the overbreadth doctrine, regulation must be narrowly drawn so as to touch only that conduct which a governing authority may validly repress; where a regulation sweeps within its ambit a substantial amount of protected speech along with unprotected conduct, the overbreadth doctrine instructs courts to invalidate the regulation. Under the vagueness doctrine, regulation that may chill protected expression must be drawn with especially rigorous exactitude. And under the doctrine of content neutrality, a governmental authority cannot prohibit certain forms of speech merely because it objects to the ideas or sentiments the speaker seeks to communicate. To quote one of many Supreme Court pronouncements on this theme: "If there is one star fixed in our constitutional constellation, it is that no official, high or petty, can prescribe what shall be orthodox in politics, nationalism, religion or other matters of opinion."[72] The cumulative effect of these and related speech-protective doctrines is a conspicuous toleration of speech and other representations that many people— in some instances the vast majority of people—find deeply, perhaps even viscerally, obnoxious, including flag burning, pornography, Nazis' taunting of Holocaust survivors, a jacket emblazoned with the phrase "Fuck the Draft" worn in a courthouse, *The Satanic Verses*, *The Birth of a Nation*, *The Last Temptation of Christ*. And just as acute wariness of public or private censorship has long furthered struggles for freedom of expression in all its many guises, so has resistance against censorship always been an important and positive feature of the great struggles against racist tyranny in the United States, from the fight against slavery to the fight against Jim Crow.[73] For this reason, we may count ourselves fortunate that the anti–hate-speech campaign of the regulationists fizzled and has largely subsided. This particular effort to do away with *nigger*-as-insult and its kindred symbols was simply not worth the various costs that success would have exacted.

Finally, I turn to the eradicationists—those who maintain that *all* uses of *nigger* are wrongful and hurtful and ought to be condemned by dint of public opinion. Their absolutist position simply fails to acknowledge adequately either the malleability of language or the complexity of African American communities. Even the proponents of enhanced speech codes—the "regulationists" whom I have just criticized—make a distinction

159

between racist and nonracist, impermissible and permissible usages of the N-word. Professor Delgado has proposed, for example, that whites who insultingly call blacks niggers should be subject to suit for money damages. He goes on to explain, however, that the salutation " 'Hey, nigger,' spoken affectionately between black persons and used as a greeting, would not be actionable" under his scheme.[74] Similarly, though without expressly mentioning *nigger,* Professor Matsuda has indicated that her approach would allow words generally seen as racial insults, and thus otherwise prohibitable, to be protected in the context of a "particular subordinated community" that tolerated the use of such terms as a form of "wordplay."[75] She elaborates, "Where this is the case, community members tend to have a clear sense of what is racially degrading and what is not. The appropriate standard in determining whether language is persecutorial, hateful, and degrading is the recipient's community standard. We should avoid further victimization of subordinated groups by misunderstanding their linguistic and cultural norms."[76]

Matsuda, however, minimizes the reality of cultural conflict within groups. As we have seen, for example, blacks differ sharply over the use of *nigger*. Some condemn it absolutely, unequivocally, across the board, no matter who is voicing the hated N-word and no matter what the setting. This has long been so. Writing in 1940, Langston Hughes remarked:

> The word *nigger* to colored people of high and low degree is like a red rag to a bull. Used rightly or wrongly, ironically or seriously, of necessity for the sake of realism, or impishly for the sake of comedy[,] it doesn't matter. Negroes do not like it in any book or play whatsoever, be the book or play ever so sympathetic in its treatment of the basic problems of the race. The word *nigger*, you see, sums up for us who are colored all the bitter years of insult and struggle in America.[77]

Hughes overgeneralized. *All* Negroes do not react to *nigger* in the way he described. Hughes himself did not; he applauded his friend Carl Van Vechten's novel *Nigger Heaven*. He was also certainly aware that blacks used "nigger" freely when outside the presence of whites.[78] Hughes was correct, though, in suggesting that some blacks—then as now—detest *nigger* so thoroughly that they eschew efforts to distinguish between good and bad usages of the term and instead condemn it out of hand. "Everyone should refrain from [using the N-word] and provide negative sanctions on its use by others," black-studies professor Halford H. Fairchild has argued. What about blacks' using the term ironically, as a term of affection? "The persistent viability of the N-word in the black community," Fairchild writes, "is a scar from centuries of cultural racism."[79] Voicing the same message, Ron Nelson, an editor of the University of North Carolina newspaper, notes that while "most blacks . . . understand the implications and racist history of the word *nigger,* it has somehow dangerously and disturbingly found its way into everyday language." Castigating blacks' playful use of the N-word as "self-defeating," "hypocritical," and "absurd," Nelson asserts that its usage "creates an atmosphere of acceptance [in which whites wonder,] After all, if blacks themselves do it, why can't others[?]"[80] The Pulitzer Prize–winning journalist E. R. Shipp is of the same opinion. In an article revealingly entitled "N Word Just as Vile When Uttered by Blacks," Shipp declared that "there needs to be no confusion. . . . The N-word has no place in contemporary life or language."[81]

Bill Cosby is another who attacks blacks' use of *nigger*. Addressing African American comedians, Cosby has argued that when *nigger* pops out of their mouths as entertainment, all blacks are hurt. He fears that white onlookers will have negative impressions of African

Americans reinforced when blacks laughingly bandy about the N-word. He fears that many whites largely ignorant of black America will be all too literal-minded and will fail to understand the joke. Notwithstanding Cosby's criticisms and pleas, many black comedians have continued to give *nigger* a prominent place in their acts. Several of them were mainstays of *Def Comedy Jam,* a popular show that appeared on the Home Box Office cable-television network in the 1990s. Taking aim at *Def Comedy Jam,* Cosby likened it to an updated *Amos 'n' Andy*: "When you watch [*Def Comedy Jam*], you hear a statement or a joke and it says 'niggers.' And sometimes they say 'we niggers.' And we are laughing [at it], just as we laughed at *Amos 'n' Andy* in the fifties. But we don't realize that there are people watching who know nothing about us. This is the only picture they have of us other than our mothers going to work in their homes and pushing their children in the carriages and dusting their houses. . . . And they say, 'Yeah, that's them. Just like we thought.' "[82]

Cosby's reference to *Amos 'n' Andy* was intended to damn *Def Comedy Jam* by associating it with a program that some blacks regard as a terrible affront to African Americans.[83] *Amos 'n' Andy* began as a radio show in 1928. It was written and dramatized by two white men with roots in minstrelsy who animated the misadventures of a group of blacks living and working in Harlem. Episodes of the show focused on marital woes and infidelities, inept efforts to realize professional or entrepreneurial ambitions, and petty bickering within a semisecret fraternal order named the Mystic Knights of the Sea. Among the show's personalities were Andy (an amiable dunce), the Kingfish (a schemer who constantly bilked stupid Andy), Amos (an earnest taxicab driver), Algonquin J. Calhoun (an inept and unethical attorney), Sapphire (Andy's angry, contemptuous, shrewish wife), and Lightnin' (a slow, easily befuddled housepainter).

Amos 'n' Andy was one of the most successful programs in the history of radio. It inspired a comic strip, a candy bar, greeting cards, phonograph records, and a film. It coined phrases—for example, "holy mackerel"—that have become embedded in colloquial speech, and touched hundreds of thousands of Americans in all manner of surprising ways. Owners of restaurants, hotels, and movie theaters piped the show into their establishments for fear that if they didn't, customers would leave in droves to hear the latest installment. Eleanor Roosevelt was a fan, as was Huey P. Long, the flamboyant, demagogic governor of Louisiana, who nicknamed himself Kingfish under the show's influence.

In 1951, when *Amos 'n' Andy* moved to television, an all-black cast (the first on network TV) superseded the white men who had previously supplied the voices of the black characters. Although the show lasted only two seasons, syndicated reruns would be aired on local television stations until the mid 1960s.

Amos 'n' Andy's harshest critics denounced it as "the ultimate metaphor of whites' casual contempt for blacks."[84] W. J. Walls, a bishop in the African Methodist Episcopal Zion Church, contended in 1929 that the radio program degraded blacks by presenting African American characters with "crude, repetitional, moronic mannerisms" who spoke "gibbberish." Bishop Walls stated that there did exist "unlettered and mentally imbecilic" Negroes. But *Amos 'n' Andy,* in his view, focused unduly on that "rapidly decreasing" portion of the African American population, thereby allowing "the crude deeds of unfortunates to be paraded as the order and pattern of a whole people." Responding to defenders who pointed out that the word *nigger* was never heard on the show, the bishop suggested that blacks needed to cease being satisfied with merely the absence of the worst racial derogation.[85]

Robert L. Vann, the editor of the *Pittsburgh Courier,* also attacked *Amos 'n' Andy*. In 1931 he launched a drive to obtain one million signatures on a petition demanding that the Federal Radio Commission ban the program. The petition complained that "two white men . . . have been exploiting certain types of American Negro for purely commercial gain" and that their representations "are of such character as to prove detrimental to the self-respect and general advancement of the Negro." More specifically, "Negro womanhood has been broadcast to the world as indulging in bigamy, lawyers as schemers and crooks and Negro Secret Orders as organizations where money is filched from . . . members by dishonest methods, thereby placing all these activities among Negroes in a most harmful and degrading light."[86] According to the *Courier*, 740,000 people eventually signed the petition.

A third important critic of *Amos 'n' Andy* was the NAACP. When the program switched over to television in 1951, the country's foremost guardian of black advancement vigorously objected. Until that point the organization had refrained from criticism, but according to the NAACP leadership, "The visual impact [of the television show makes it] infinitely worse than the radio version." Anticipating Bill Cosby's annoyance with *Def Comedy Jam,* NAACP officials asserted that *Amos 'n' Andy* "say[s] to millions of white Americans who know nothing about Negroes . . . that this is the way Negroes are."[87]

A thorough assessment of such critiques requires an acknowledgment of the plurality of tastes, aspirations, interests, and perspectives within African American communities.[88] While an appreciable number of blacks repudiated *Amos 'n' Andy*, many others enjoyed it, a fact memorialized in letters, newspaper accounts, and the racial demographics of the show's audience. Black support, moreover, extended beyond the ranks of ordinary folk, finding a foothold in institutions and among cadres of intellectuals and activists. Thus, even as the *Pittsburgh Courier* was railing against the white authors of *Amos 'n' Andy,* the Chicago *Defender,* the nation's leading black weekly newspaper, was designating them honored guests at a parade and picnic on that city's South Side. In 1930, a young black journalist who would eventually head the NAACP defended *Amos 'n' Andy* and criticized its critics. According to Roy Wilkins, black opponents of the show should stop "sniffing about with [their] heads in the clouds," put aside "false pride," and start producing some humor of their own that would earn a share of the hundreds of thousands of dollars that the white producers of *Amos 'n' Andy* were making. Wilkins saw nothing wrong with the portraiture generated by *Amos 'n' Andy*. How would critics wish to have the show's characters presented? he asked. "In plug hats, with morning coat, striped trousers, glassined hair, spats, patent leather shoes, and an Oxford accent? Instead of having them struggling with the immediate and universal problem of how to get and keep a decent and usable spare tire for the taxicab, would [the critics] have them prating about mergers, mortgages, international loans and foreign trade balances?" Praising its "universal appeal," Wilkins concluded that *Amos 'n' Andy* was "clean fun from beginning to end," with "all the pathos, humor, vanity, glory, problems and solutions that beset ordinary mortals."[89]

Wilkins's perspective was by no means idiosyncratic. A prominent black attorney in Worcester, Massachusetts, declared that he could discern no good objection to *Amos 'n' Andy;* he found the show truly funny and dismissed the racial critique of the series as nothing more than the whining of blacks who were "thin-skinned" and "supersensitive."[90] Interpreting the show completely differently than its detractors, a black fan in Chicago maintained that *Amos 'n' Andy* showed that "the Negro race has and does . . . produce people who are worthwhile."[91] Theophilus Lewis, an acerbic black columnist for the *Amsterdam News,* suggested that the *Courier*'s petition campaign against the program would serve one good end: "When they complete their tally of signatures we will know precisely how many half wits there are in the race."[92]

In the 1950s, when debate shifted to the fate of *Amos 'n' Andy* on television, black opinion remained divided, though its opponents had gained considerable ground. As head of the NAACP, Roy Wilkins switched sides and called for the show to be taken off the air. In adopting that position he was supported by, among others, Thurgood Marshall (who would later, as we have seen, become the first black Supreme Court justice) and William Hastie (who would be the first black to sit on a federal court of appeals). Nevertheless, as Bill Cosby recognized, many blacks continued to support the show. In an ad hoc "man in the street" survey conducted by the black *Journal and Guide* newspaper in Norfolk, Virginia, a large majority of blacks voiced approval of *Amos 'n' Andy*. A poll taken by an opinion-research firm hired by an advertiser found the same result: among 365 black adults contacted in New York and New Jersey, 70 percent expressed a favorable view of the program.[93]

Today's conflicts over *nigger* replicate yesterday's conflicts over *Amos 'n' Andy*. Among the supporters of that show were black entertainers who stood to make money and gain visibility by participating in its production. Among the supporters of *Def Comedy Jam* and other, similar programs of our own day are black performers hungry for a break; to them, Bill Cosby's militant aversion to the N-word as entertainment is an indulgence that they themselves are hardly in a position to afford. Black critics of the campaign against *Amos 'n' Andy* charged that the show's detractors were excessively concerned about white people's perceptions. Today a similar charge is leveled. Some entertainers who openly use *nigger* reject Cosby's politics of respectability, which counsels African Americans to mind their manners and mouths in the presence of whites. This group of performers doubts the efficacy of seeking to burnish the image of African Americans in the eyes of white folk. Some think that the racial perceptions of most whites are beyond changing; others believe that whatever marginal benefits a politics of respectability may yield are not worth the psychic cost of giving up or diluting cultural rituals that blacks enjoy. This latter attitude is effectively expressed by the remark "I don't give a fuck." These entertainers don't care whether whites find *nigger* upsetting. They don't care whether whites are confused by blacks' use of the term. And they don't care whether whites who hear blacks using the N-word think that African Americans lack self-respect. The black comedians and rappers who use and enjoy *nigger* care principally, perhaps exclusively, about what they *themselves* think, desire, and enjoy—which is part of their allure. Many people (including me) are drawn to these performers despite their many faults because, among other things, they exhibit a bracing independence. They eschew boring conventions, including the one that maintains, despite massive evidence to the contrary, that *nigger* can mean only one thing.

CHAPTER FOUR

How Are We Doing with *Nigger?*

Although references to *nigger* continue to cause social eruptions, major institutions of American life are handling this combustible word about right. Where the most powerful and respected political and professional positions are at stake, public opinion has effectively stigmatized *nigger*-as-insult. Anyone with ambitions to occupy a high public post, for example, had better refrain from *ever* using *nigger* in any of its various senses, because the N-word rankles so many people so deeply. Political prudence counsels strict avoidance. We now know that a man can become president of the

United States even if he is overheard calling someone an asshole, but the same is no longer true of a person who refers to another as a nigger: too many voters view such conduct as utterly disqualifying. It is precisely because seasoned politicians know better than ever to utter the word *nigger* publicly that mouths dropped open when, during a television appearance in March 2001, Senator Robert C. Byrd of West Virginia talked about having seen "a lot of white niggers in [his] time"—a remark for which he quickly apologized.[1]

Reinforcing public opinion is the coercive power of government as manifested in tort law and antidiscrimination statutes. As we have seen, in certain situations victims of racial harassment can obtain money damages and other relief from their tormentors or from employers who fail to address harassment that is brought to their attention.

Various forces prevent the complete eradication of *nigger*-as-insult. Some of these are negative, such as vestigial racism and toleration of it; in many settings it is still the case that a habit of using *nigger*-as-insult does not much hurt one's reputation. It is also true, however, that positive forces militate in favor of the survival of *nigger*-as-insult. One such is libertarianism in matters of linguistic expression. Protecting foul, disgusting, hateful, unpopular speech against governmental censorship is a great achievement of American political culture.

As a linguistic landmark, *nigger* is being renovated. Blacks use the term with novel ease to refer to other blacks, even in the presence of those who are not African American. Whites are increasingly referring to other whites as niggers, and indeed, the term both as an insult and as a sign of affection is being affixed to people of all sorts. In some settings, its usage is so routine as to have become virtually standard. *Nigger* as a harbinger of hatred, fear, contempt, and violence remains current, to be sure. But more than ever before, *nigger* also signals other meanings and generates other reactions, depending on the circumstances. This complexity has its costs. Miscues are bound to proliferate as speakers and audiences misjudge one another. The latina singing star Jennifer Lopez said that she was surprised when some African Americans accused her of bigotry on account of lyrics in one of her songs that referred to *niggers*. Maybe she was merely posturing; controversy is often good for record sales. But maybe she was expressing genuine astonishment; after all, many African American female entertainers sing lyrics containing *nigger* without raising eyebrows. Perhaps a dual misunderstanding was at work, as Lopez mistook how she would be perceived and disappointed listeners mistook her sentiments.[2] The popular film *Rush Hour* spoofs this reality. In one of its scenes, a black character (played by Chris Tucker) is warmly received after saluting a black acquaintance as "my nigger," while a Chinese man (played by Jackie Chan) sparks fisticuffs when he innocently mimics Tucker's use of the N-word.[3]

A diminished ability to stigmatize the word is another cost. As *nigger* is more widely disseminated and its complexity is more widely appreciated, censuring its use—even its use as an insult—will become more difficult. The more aware judges and other officials become of the ambiguity surrounding *nigger,* the less likely they will be to automatically condemn the actions taken by whites who voice the N-word. This tendency will doubtless, in certain instances, lead to unfortunate results, as decision makers show undue solicitude toward racists who use the rhetoric of complexity to cover their misconduct.

Still, despite these costs, there is much to be gained by allowing people of all backgrounds to yank *nigger* away from white supremacists, to subvert its ugliest denotation, and to convert the N-word from a negative into a positive appellation. This process is already well under way, led in the main by African American innovators who are taming, civilizing, and transmuting "the

filthiest, dirtiest, nastiest word in the English language."
For bad and for good, *nigger* is thus destined to remain
with us for many years to come—a reminder of the
ironies and dilemmas, the tragedies and glories, of the
American experience.

1. The Protean N-Word

1. See, e.g., *Ohio v. Howard,* 1995 Ohio App. LEXIS 750 (Ohio Ct. App.) (man killed in altercation sparked by his calling the defendant a nigger); *State v. Higginbotham,* 212 N.W. 2d 881 (Minn. Sup. Ct. 1973) (man killed after calling a woman a nigger lover); "Black Judge Adds 35 Years to Robber's Sentence after Felon Made Racial Slur," *Jet,* October 10, 1994; "School Superintendent in Nevada under Fire for Using Word *Nigger,*" *Jet,* August 28, 2000; "White Bishop Steps Down from Charity amid Controversy over Racial Slur," *Jet,* April 21, 1997; "Jaguar Official Suspended after Using Racial Slur," *Jet,* June 13, 1994.

2. On the etymology of *nigger,* see the *Random House Historical Dictionary of American Slang*, ed. J. E. Lighter (1997), 2:657. See also the *Oxford English Dictionary,* eds. J. A. Simpson and E. S. C. Weiner, (2d ed., 1989), 10:402–4; Geneva Smitherman, *Black Talk: Words and Phrases from the 'Hood to the Amen Corner* (rev. ed., 2000), 210–13; H. L. Mencken, *The American Language: An Inquiry into the Development of English in the United States,* abridged with annotations and new material by Raven I. McDavid Jr., with the assistance of David W. Maurer (1979), 383–84; Hugh Rawson, *Wicked Words* (1989), 268–70.

3. See Rawson, *Wicked Words*, 268–70; Smitherman, *Black Talk*, 210–13.

4. The linguist Robin Tolmach Lakoff speculates that *nigger* became a slur when users of the term became aware that it was a mispronunciation of *Negro* and decided to continue using the mispronunciation to signal contempt—in much the same way that certain individuals choose to insult others by deliberately mispronouncing their names. Robin Tolmach Lakoff, "The N-Word: Still There, Still Ugly," *Newsday,* September 28, 1995. But see the *Random House Historical Dictionary of Slang,* 2:656, where this theory of mispronunciation is discounted.

5. Hosea Easton, *A Treatise on the Intellectual Character and Civil and Political Condition of the Colored People of the United States; and the Prejudice Exercised Towards Them* (1837), 40–41.

6. See Sam Dennison, *Scandalize My Name: Black Imagery in American Popular Music* (1982).

7. Rawson, *Wicked Words,* 268.

8. Kenneth Porter, "Racism in Children's Rhymes and Sayings, Central Kansas, 1910–1918," *Western Folklore* 24 (1965): 191.

9. The NAACP has registered Internet addresses that contain the word *nigger* in order to preempt their use by racists. Even so, there remains plenty of opportunity for mischief. An Internet search performed in July 2001 using *nigger* as the key word pulled up 241 Web sites. See Julie Salomon, "The Web as Home for Racism and Hate," *New York Times,* October 23, 2000; Michael Mechanic, "Prempting Cyberhate," *Mother Jones,* September 1999; Mark Leibovich, "A New Domain for Hate Speech: Civil Rights Groups Struggle to Buy Racist Web Addresses," *Washington Post*, December 15, 1999.

10. Quoted in Stephen Kantrowitz, *Ben Tillman and the Reconstruction of White Supremacy* (2000), 259.

11. Quoted ibid., 297.

12. Sandra Kathryn White, ed., *In Search of Democracy: The NAACP Writings of James Weldon Johnson, Walter White, and Roy Wilkins, 1920–1977* (1999), 43.

13. John Egerton, *Speak Now Against the Day: The Generation before the Civil Rights Movement in the South* (1994), 117.

14. T. Harry Williams, *Huey Long* (1978), 705–6.

15. William Anderson, *The Wild Man from Sugar Creek: The Political Career of Eugene Talmadge* (1975), 207. Talmadge is also reported to have said, "No niggah's good as a white man because the niggah's only a few shawt yea-ahs from cannibalism" (quoted in Rawson, *Wicked Words,* 269).

16. Neil R. McMillen, *Dark Journey: Black Mississippians in the Age of Jim Crow* (1989), 205.

17. Ibid, 204.

18. Quoted in Len Holt, *The Summer That Didn't End: The Story of the Mississippi Civil Rights Project of 1964* (1965; Da Capo Press ed., 1992), 311.

19. William O. Douglas, *The Court Years 1939–1975: The Autobiography of William O. Douglas* (1980), 15.

20. See David G. McCollough, *Truman* (1992), 576.

21. Robert A. Caro, *The Years of Lyndon Johnson: The Means of Ascent* (1990), 70.

22. See, e.g., Anthony Summers with Robbyn Swan, *The Arrogance of Power: The Secret World of Richard Nixon* (2000), 354; Seymour Hersh, *The Price of Power: Kissinger in the Nixon White House* (1983), 110–11; Hilton Als, "This Lonesome Place: Flannery O'Connor on Race and Religion in the Unreconstructed South," *The New Yorker,* Jan. 29, 2001; Ralph C. Wood, "Flannery O'Connor's Racial Morals and Manners," *The Christian Century,* Nov. 16, 1994.

23. Harriet Jacobs, *Incidents in the Life of a Slave Girl,* eds. Nellie Y. McKay and Frances Smith Foster, Norton critical Edition (2001), 34.

24. Frederick Douglass, *Narrative of the Life of Frederick Douglass, an American Slave, Written by Himself,* eds. William Andrews and William S. McFeeley (Norton critical ed. 1997), 29.

25. Richard Wright, *The Ethics of Living Jim Crow in Uncle Tom's Children* (1940; Harper Perennial ed., 1993), 4–5.

26. Ibid., 8.

27. Ibid., 12–13.

28. Kathryn Talalay, *Composition in Black and White: The Life of Philippa Schuyler* (1995), 67–68.

29. Quoted in Susan Spotts, "Benjamin Jefferson Davis" (unpublished paper on file at Harvard Law School), 15. Also see Charles H. Martin, *The Angelo Herndon Case and Southern Justice* (1976), 48; Benjamin J. Davis Jr., *In Defense of Negro Rights* (1950).

30. Lerone Bennett Jr., "Chronicles of Black Courage: The Little Rock Ten," *Ebony,* December 1997.

31. Ely Green, *Ely: An Autobiography* (1966), 13–17, 24. See also Leon Litwack, *Trouble in Mind: Black Southerners in the Age of Jim Crow* (1998), 20.

32. Martin B. Duberman, *Paul Robeson* (1988), 55.

33. *The Autobiography of Malcolm X* (1965), 30–37.

34. Arnold Rampersad, *Jackie Robinson: A Biography* (1997), 142.

35. Ibid., 172.

36. Carl T. Rowan, *South of Freedom* (1954), 125.

37. Dick Gregory with Robert Lipsyte, *nigger* (1964), 185–86. See also idem with James R. McGraw, *Up from Nigger* (1976).

38. Holt, 258.

39. William Plummer and Toby Kahn, "Street Talk," *People,* May 13, 1996.

40. Kenny Moore, "The 1968 Olympics: A Courageous Stand," *Sports Illustrated,* August 5, 1991.

41. Marc Appleman, "The Kid!," *Sports Illustrated for Kids,* July 1, 1995.

42. Gary Smith, "The Chosen," *Sports Illustrated,* December 23, 1996.

43. Audre Lorde, *Sister Outsider: Essays and Speeches* (1984), 72.

44. Branford Marsalis, interview, *Playboy,* December 1993.

45. Lonnae O'Neal Parker, "White Girl?," *Washington Post,* August 8, 1999.

46. "White Girl—The Dialogue Continues," *Seattle Times*, October 22, 1999.

47. Henry Aaron with Lonnie Wheeler, *I Had a Hammer: The Hank Aaron Story* (1991), 230–48.

48. Forrest G. Wood, *Black Scare: The Racist Response to Emancipation and Reconstruction* (1970), pl. 4, foll. p. 84.

49. Quoted in David Donald, *Charles Sumner,* pt. 2 (Da Capo Press ed., 1996), p. 49.

50. Ibid., 84.

51. David Halberstam, *The Children* (1998), 261.

52. *Lynch v. State*, 236 A.2d 45, 48 (Md. Ct. Spec. App. 1967).

53. See, e.g., *United States v. Pospisil,* 186 F.3d 1023 (8th Cir. 1999); *Clifton v. Mass. Bay Transp. Auth.,* 2000 Mass. Super. LEXIS 22; *Guillory v. Godfrey,* 134 Cal. App. 2d 628 (1955); *United States v. Smith,* 1998 U.S. App. LEXIS 16406 (4th Cir.); *United States v. Hartberger,* 148 F.3d 777 (7th Cir. 1998); *Ohio v. Faye,* 2000 Ohio App. LEXIS 1971; *Norris v. City of Anderson,* 1999 U.S. Dist. LEXIS 22612; *Black Voters v. McDonough,* 421 F.Supp. 165 (D. Mass. 1976); *Solomon v. Liberty County, Fla.,* 951 F.Supp. 1522 (E.D. Fla. 1997); *United States v. Lansdowne Swim Club,* 713 F.Supp. 785 (E.D. Pa. 1989); *People v. MacKenzie,* 34 Cal. App. 4th 1256 (1995); *State v. Palermo,* 765 So.2d 1139 (2000); *State v. Colella,* 690 A.2d 156 (N.J. Super. Ct. 1997); *Mancha v. Field Museum of Natural History,* 283 N.E.2d 899 (1972); *City of Minneapolis v. State of Minnesota,* 310 N.W.2d 485 (1981).

54. *Random House Historical Dictionary of American Slang,*

2:664–65; *DuFlambeau v. Stop Treaty Abuse,* 991 F.2d 1249 (7th Cir. 1993).

55. Farai Chideya, *The Color of Our Future* (1999), 9.

56. Andrew Hacker, *Two Nations: Black and White, Separate, Hostile, Unequal* (1992), 42.

57. *Monteiro v. Tempe Union High School District,* 158 F.3d 1022 (9th Cir. 1998). Also see *Random House Webster's College Dictionary* (2000), 894: "*Nigger* is now probably the most offensive word in English."

58. Margaret M. Russell, "Representing Race: Beyond 'Sell-outs' and 'Race Cards': Black Attorneys and the Straitjacket of Legal Practice," Michigan Law Review 95 (1997): 765.

59. Letter to the editor, "End Hatred and Its Code Words," *Des Moines Register,* December 28, 1999.

60. Ian Buruma, "Joys of Victimhood," *New York Review of Books,* April 8, 1999.

61. Iris Chang, *The Rape of Nanking: The Forgotten Holocaust of World War II* (1997).

62. Larry Kramer, *Reports from the Holocaust: The Making of an AIDS Activist* (1989).

63. Toni Morrison, *Beloved* (1987), v. Also see Stanley Crouch's review of *Beloved* in the *New Republic,* October 19, 1987.

64. For useful commentary on this point, see Peter Novick, *The Holocaust in American Life* (1999); Samantha Power, "To Suffer by Comparison? Genocide and the Jewish Holocaust," *Daedalus* 128 (1999): 31.

65. Quoted in Joseph Boskin, *Rebellious Laughter* (1997), 161–62.

66. See, e.g., *Goldberg v. City of Philadelphia,* 1994 U.S.

Dist. LEXIS 8969 (D.C.E.D. Pa. 1994) (kike); *Vigil v. City of Las Cruces*, 119 F.3d 871 (10th Cir. 1997) (wetback); *United States v. Piche*, 981 F.2d 706 (4th Cir. 1992) (gook); *Huckaby v. Moore*, 142 F.3d 233 (5th Cir. 1998) (honky).

67. See, e.g., *Gant v. Wallingford Bd. of Educ.*, 69 F.3d 669 (2d Cir. 1995); *United States v. Sowa,* 34 F.3d 447 (7th Cir. 1994); *United States v. Ramey,* 24 F.3d 602 (4th Cir. 1994); *United States v. Juvenile Male J.H.H.,* 22 F.3d 821 (8th Cir. 1994); *United States v. McInnis,* 976 F.2d 1226 (9th Cir. 1992). See also chapter two, ahead, *Nigger* in Court.

68. 80 U.S. 585 (1871). Also see Robert D. Goldstein, "*Blyew*: Variations on a Jurisdictional Theme," *Stanford Law Review* 41 (1988): 469.

69. 80 U.S. at 589.

70. *United States v. Montgomery,* 23 F.3d 1130 (7th Cir. 1994).

71. Lawrence W. Levine, *Black Culture and Black Consciousness: Afro-American Folk Thought from Slavery to Freedom* (1977), 309.

72. Ibid., 341.

73. Ibid., 344.

74. Ibid., 319.

75. Howard Bingham and Max Wallace, *Muhammed Ali's Greatest Fight: Cassius Clay vs. the United States of America* (2000), 119.

76. *A Testament of Hope: The Essential Writings and Speeches of Martin Luther King, Jr.,* ed. James M. Washington (1986), 293.

77. Clarence Major, *Dictionary of Afro-American Slang* (1970), 84.

78. Claude Brown, "The Language of Soul," *Esquire,* April 1968.

79. Jarvis DeBerry, "Keeping a Hateful Word Inside a Dictionary," *New Orleans Times-Picayune,* June 23, 1998.

80. For an excellent discussion about *nigger*, on which I have drawn, see Smitherman, *Black Talk,* 210–13.

81. Helen Jackson Lee, *Nigger in the Window* (1978), 27.

82. Levine, *Black Culture and Black Consciousness,* 328.

83. *The Essential Lenny Bruce,* ed. Joel Cohen (1967), 16.

84. On Richard Pryor, see Richard Pryor with Mike Gold, *Pryor Convictions and Other Life Sentences* (1995); John A. Williams and Dennis A. Williams, *If I Stop I'll Die: The Comedy and Tragedy of Richard Pryor* (1991); Jim Haskins, *Richard Pryor: A Man and His Madness* (1984); Jeff Rovin, *Richard Pryor: Black and Blue* (1983).

85. Mel Watkins, *On the Real Side* (1994), 550.

86. In the early 1980s Richard Pryor announced that he would no longer use the word *nigger*. Explaining that a three-week stay in Africa (mainly Kenya) had had a profound effect on him, Pryor later wrote (in prose that initially makes one wonder whether he is being facetious) that "the land had been timeless, the people majestic. I had seen and felt things impossible to experience any place else on Earth. I left enlightened. I also left regretting ever having uttered the word *nigger* onstage or off it. It was a wretched word. Its connotations weren't funny, even when people laughed. To this day I wish I'd never said that word. I felt its lameness. It was misunderstood by people. They [didn't] get what I was talking about. Neither did I." (Pryor with Gold, *Pryor Convictions,*

175. Luckily Pryor's racial enlightenment was delayed until *after* he had produced *Bicentennial Nigger* (1976) and other comedy albums reflecting his genius.

87. In print, see Chris Rock, *Rock This!,* 17–19 (1997). In audio, listen to Chris Rock, *Roll with the New* (1997). To view the performance, see the video, Chris Rock, *Bring the Pain* (1996).

88. Coolio, "Gangsta's Paradise," *Gangsta's Paradise* (Tommy Boy, 1995).

89. Ice-T, "Straight up Nigga," *OG: Original Gangster* (Sire Records, 1991).

90. Ice Cube, "The Nigga Ya Love to Hate," in *Amerikkka's Most Wanted* (Priority Records, 1990).

91. Beanie Sigel, "Ride 4 My," *The Truth* (Island Def Jam Music Group, 2000).

92. Listen to 2pac, *2pacalypse Now* (Interscope, 1991).

93. Eldridge Cleaver, *Soul on Ice* (1968), 9.

94. Harlon Dalton, *Racial Healing* (1995), 169.

95. Daryl Cumbers Dance, *Shuckin' and Jivin': Folklore from Contemporary Black Americans* (1978), 77.

96. Ibid.

97. Abiodun Oyewole and Umar Bin Hassan with Kim Greene, *The Last Poets—On a Mission: Selected Poems and a History of the Last Poets* (1996), 6–63.

98. Ibid., 60.

99. See Michael Thomas Ford, *That's Mr. Faggot to You: Further Trials from My Queer Life* (1999); Michael Warner: *The Trouble with Normal: Sex, Politics and the Ethics of Queer Life* (1999); Eve Ensler, *The Vagina Monologues* (1998); Inga Muscio, *Cunt: A Declaration of Independence* (1998); Elizabeth Wurtzel, *Bitch: In Praise of Difficult Women* (1998); Jim Goad, *The Redneck Mani-*

festo (1997); *Dyke Life: From Growing Up to Growing Old, a Celebration of the Lesbian Experience* (Karla Jay, ed. 1996); Jonathan Eig, "This Woman Wants You to Call Her Bastard," *Offsping*, June/July 2000 (describing Marley Greiner, founder of Bastard Nation); Kathleen Bishop, "Cracker Day Fun for All," Flagler—*Palm Coast Community Times*, March 29, 2000.

100. Bruce A. Jacobs, *Race Manners: Navigating the Minefield Between Black and White Americans* (1999), 102.

101. See Robin D. G. Kelly, *Race Rebels: Culture, Politics, and the Black Working Class* (1994), 209–14.

102. John Lennon and Yoko Ono, *Some Time in New York City* (Apple Records, 1972)

103. Patti Smith, *Easter* (Arista Records, 1978).

104. Anthony DeCurtis, interview with Eminem, *Rolling Stone,* July 15, 2000.

105. Quoted in Kelly, *Race Rebels,* 209–10.

106. Michael Eric Dyson, "Nigger Gotta Stop," *The Source,* June 1999.

107. Quoted in Robert Dallek, *Flawed Giant: Lyndon Johnson and His Times, 1961–1973* (1998), 44.

108. See Emily Bernard, ed., *Remember Me to Harlem: The Letters of Langston Hughes and Carl Van Vechten, 1925–1964* (2001).

109. See Langston Hughes, *The Big Sea* (1940), 268. See also p. 161.

110. Pertinent here is the following story, an anecdote saved from oblivion by the great sociologist Erving Goffman:

I was once admitted to a group of Negro boys of about my own age with whom I used to fish. When I first began to join them, they would carefully use the word *Negro* in my presence. Gradually, as we went fishing more and more often, they began to joke with each other in front of me and to call each other "nigger." . . . One day when we were swimming, a boy shoved me with mock violence and I said to him, "Don't give me that nigger talk."

He replied, "You bastard," with a big grin.

From that time on, we could all use the word *nigger* but the old categories had totally changed. Never, as long as I live, will I forget the way my stomach felt after I used the word *nigger* without any reservation.

Erving Goffman, *Stigma: Notes on the Management of Spoiled Identity* (1963), 29 (quoting Ray Birdwhistell).

111. Susan Schmidt, "Senator Byrd Apologizes for Racial Remarks," *Washington Post*, March 5, 2001.

112. See John Hartigan: *Racial Situations: Class Predicaments of Whiteness in Detroit* (1999). Related is the increasing use of "wigger," a reference to so-called white niggers—whites who immerse themselves in and express themselves through cultural styles, gestures, and tastes that are generally identified as "black."

113. Ibid., 116.

114. Ibid.

115. Arthur K. Spears, *African-American Language Use: Ideology and So-Called Obscenity* in *African-American English: Structure, History and Use* (eds. Salikoko S. Mufwene, Jahn S. Rickford, Guy Bailey, and John Baugh, 1998), 241.

116. *Towne v. Eisner*, 245 U.S. 418, 425 (1918).

2. *Nigger* in Court

1. Stephen J. Whitfield, *A Death in the Delta: The Story of Emmett Till* (1988), 37–38.

2. See *Hance v. Zant,* 696 F.2d 940 (11th Cir. 1983), *cert. denied,* 463 U.S. 1210 (1994); 114 S.Ct. 1392 (1994) (denying application for stay of execution). See also Bob Herbert, "Mr. Hance's 'Perfect Punishment,' " *New York Times,* March 27, 1994; idem, "Jury Room Injustice," *New York Times,* March 30, 1994.

3. See Randall Kennedy, *Race, Crime, and the Law* (1997), 277–84.

4. In the middle of William Andrews's trial for murder, for example, a juror handed the bailiff a napkin on which was drawn a man on a gallows above the inscription "Hang the Niggers." Whether a juror did the drawing and whether other jurors saw it are questions that remain unanswered, since courts declined even to order a hearing into the matter. Andrews was sentenced to death by firing squad; see *Andrews v. Shulsen,* 485 U.S. 919 (1988). See also *Callins v. Collins,* 998 F.2d 269, 277 (5th Cir. 1993) (issue involving a potential juror's reference to the defendant as a nigger).

5. Jeff Greenberg and Tom Pyszczynski, "The Effect of an Overheard Ethnic Slur on Evaluations of the Target: How to Spread a Social Disease," *Journal of Experimental Social Psychology* 61 (1985), 21.

6. *United States v. H. Rap Brown,* 539 F.2d 467, 468 (5th Cir. 1976).

7. Ibid., 469–70.

8. See In re *Stanley Z. Goodfarb,* 880 P. 2d 620 (1994).

9. See In re *Ferrara,* 582 N.W. 2d 817 (1998).

10. See "Disciplinary Proceeding in Relation to J. Kevin Mulroy," *New York Law Journal,* August 23, 1999, 8.

11. Ibid.

12. See Kennedy, *Race, Crime, and the Law,* 256–62.

13. *Collins v. State,* 100 Miss. 435, 440 (1911). The Mississippi Supreme Court reversed the conviction and ordered a new trial, declaring, "The appellant may be a bad Negro . . . yet he is entitled to go before the jury of the land untrammeled by voluntary epithets" (ibid.).

The term *white man's nigger* was once common among blacks. Now it is seldom heard. The defense counsel in *Collins* offered a useful elucidation of the phrase:

> It has two meanings, one which endears the possessor of the name to the average white man who looks upon this class as willing and obedient servants, ready to execute any commission a white man may set, whether lawful or not, and to the better white men, it often carries with it an idea that a white man's nigger is loyal, peaceful and faithful to the last degree to white ideals and white control. The average white jury would take it for granted that the killing of a white man's nigger is a more serious crime than the killing of a plain, every-day black man.

Ibid., at 435, 436–37.

14. John Egerton, *Speak Now Against the Day: The Generation Before the Civil Rights Movement in the South* (1994), 369.

15. *Taylor v. State,* 50 Texas Criminal Reports 560, 561 (1907).

16. *James v. State,* 92 So. 909, 910 (Ala. Ct. App. 1922).

17. *Thornton v. State,* 451 S.W. 2d 898, 902 (Tex. Crim. App. 1970).

18. In re *Jerry L. Spivey, District Attorney,* 480 S.E. 2d 693 (1997).

19. This account of the incident is consistent with the account offered by the Supreme Court of North Carolina. See In re *Spivey,* at 695. Further details are provided in the transcript of the hearing presided over by the trial judge whose decision to remove District Attorney Spivey was reviewed by the Supreme Court. See In re *Spivey,* transcript volume 1, 32–34. Mr. Roger W. Smith, who represented Mr. Spivey, generously gave me a copy of the transcript, which is now available at the Harvard Law School Library. Mr. Asa L. Bell, who represented parties seeking the ouster of Mr. Spivey, also shared with me instructive material.

20. In re *Spivey,* transcript volume 2, 159–60.

21. Ibid., 161.

22. Ibid., 197.

23. 315 U.S. 568, 571–72 (1942).

24. In re *Spivey* at 699.

25. Ibid.

26. Wendy B. Reilly, "Fighting the Fighting Words Standard: A Call for Its Destruction," *Rutgers Law Review* 52 (2000): 947, 956. See also Kent Greenawalt, *Fighting Words: Individuals, Communities, and Liberties of Speech* (1995), 47–64.

27. Cf. Kathleen M. Sullivan, "The First Amendment Wars," *New Republic,* September 28, 1992, 40, in which the

author complains that fighting-words doctrine gives "more license to insult Mother Teresa than Sean Penn just because she is not likely to throw a punch."

28. *United States v. Alexander,* 471 F.2d 923, 941 n.48 (D.C. Cir. 1973).

29. In re *Spivey,* at 699.

30. See Howard Kurtz, "The Shot Heard Round the Media: Bush's Off-Mike Crack Could Cut Both Ways," *Washington Post,* September 6, 2000; Rob Hiaasen, "The Truth? Adults Use Bad Words," *Baltimore Sun,* September 6, 2000.

31. See, e.g., John A. Goldsmith, *Colleagues: Richard B. Russell and His Apprentice, Lyndon B. Johnson* (1998).

32. Cf. *Rankin v. McPherson,* 483 U.S. 378 (1986).

33. In Richard Wright, *Eight Men* (1961).

34. *Fisher v. United States,* 328 U.S. 463 (1946). For a useful and detailed description of this case, see David M. Siegel, "Felix Frankfurter, Charles Hamilton Houston and the 'N-word': A Case Study in the Evolution of Judicial Attitudes towards Race," *Southern California Interdisciplinary Law Journal* 7 (1998): 317.

35. Quoted in Siegel, "Felix Frankfurter, Charles Hamilton Houston and the N-word," 360.

36. Quoted ibid., 361.

37. See *United States v. Alexander*, 471 F.2d 923 (D.C. Cir. 1972).

38. A similar strategy would later fail another black man, who would be convicted of attempted murder in 1990 after seriously injuring a coworker who had repeatedly called him "nigger." See *Ohio v. Hall,* 1992 Ohio App. LEXIS 3915.

39. See *Boyd v. United States*, 732A.2d 854 (D.C. Ct. App. 1999).

40. 214 S.E. 2d 85 (1975).

41. Ibid. at 89.

42. See *State v. Tackett,* 8 N.C. 210 (1820).

43. Ibid., Id. at 217.

44. Among the works I have found useful on this question are Alan M. Dershowitz, *The Abuse Excuse and Other Cop-outs, Sob Stories, and Evasions of Responsibility* (1994); Victoria Nourse, "The New Normativity: The Abuse Excuse and the Resurgence of Judgment in Criminal Law," *Stanford Law Review* 50 (1998): 1435; idem, "Passion's Progress: Modern Law Reform and the Provocation Defense," *Yale Law Journal* 106 (1997): 1331; Joshua Dressler, "When 'Heterosexual' Men Kill 'Homosexual' Men: Reflections on Provocation Law, Sexual Advances, and the 'Reasonable Man' Standard," *Journal of Criminal Law & Criminology* 85 (1995): 726; Ann M. Coughlin, "Excusing Women," *California Law Review* 82 (1994).

45. Charles Lawrence III, "If He Hollers Let Him Go: Regulating Racist Speech on Campus," *Duke Law Journal,* 1990, 452.

46. See Richard Delgado, "Words That Wound: A Tort Action for Racial Insults, Epithets and Name-Calling," *Harvard Civil Rights–Civil Liberties Law Review* 17 (1982): 133.

47. Coughlin, "Excusing Women," 4.

48. Ralph Ellison, *Shadow and Act* (1964), 111. Ellison seems to have been quite interested in the phenomenon of provocation. At the beginning of his best-known novel, for example, we encounter the following episode:

One night I accidentally bumped into a man, and
perhaps because of the near darkness he saw me and
called me an insulting name. I sprang at him, seized his
coat lapels and demanded that he apologize. He was a
tall blond man, and as my face came close to his he
looked insolently out of his blue eyes and cursed me,
his breath hot in my face as he struggled. I pulled his
chin down sharp upon the crown of my head, butting
him as I had seen the West Indians do, and I felt his flesh
tear and the blood gush out, and I yelled, "Apologize!
Apologize!!" . . . And in my outrage I got out my knife
and prepared to slit his throat . . . when it occurred to
me that the man had not *seen* me. . . . I was both dis-
gusted and ashamed.

Invisible Man (1952), 4.

49. My main guide on this matter is Dressler, supra, note 44.

50. See generally Daniel Givelber, "The Right to Mini-
mum Social Decency and the Limits of Evenhandedness:
Intentional Infliction of Emotional Distress by Outrageous
Conduct," *Columbia Law Review* 82 (1982): 42.

51. See *Wilkinson v. Downton,* 2 Q.B.D. 57 (1897). According to William Prosser, *Wilkinson* was "the leading case which
first broke through the shackles of the older law" (*Prosser on
Torts* [1971], 60).

52. *Bielitski v. Obadick,* 61 Dom.L.Rep. 494 (1921). See
also Prosser, *Prosser on Torts,* 61.

53. *Wilson v. Wilkins,* 181 Ark. 137 (1930). See also *Ruiz v.
Bertolotti,* 236 N.Y.S. 2d 854 (1962).

54. *Moore v. Savage,* 359 S.W. 2d 95; 362 S.W. 2d 298.

55. 355 F. Supp. 206 (S.D. Fla. 1973).

56. 768 So. 2d 1198 (2000).

57. 355 F. Supp. at 208.

58. Ibid.

59. Ibid.

60. 768 So. 2d at 1199.

61. Ibid. at 1201.

62. Restatement (Second) of Torts, Section 46 (American Law Institute 1964).

63. Calvert Magruder, "Mental and Emotional Disturbance in the Law of Torts," *Harvard Law Review* 49 (1936): 1023, 1035.

64. 355 F. Supp. 206 at 211.

65. Ibid.

66. *Bradshaw v. Swagerty,* 563 P. 2d 513 (1977).

67. *Irving v. J. L. Marsh,* 360 N.E. 2d 983 (1977).

68. *Dawson v. Zayre Department Stores,* 499 A. 2d 648, 649 (1985).

69. *Jones v. City of Boston,* 738 F. Supp 604 (1990). See also *Caldor v. Bowden,* 625 A. 2d 959 (1993).

70. *Lay v. Roux Labs.,* 379 So. 2d 451 (1980).

71. *Paige v. Youngstown Bd. of Educ.,* 1994 Ohio App LEXIS 5942 (1994).

72. See *Parker v. DPCE,* 1992 U.S. Dist. LEXIS 16921.

73. My rendition of the facts in this case is based on the court of appeals' decision in *Brown v. East Mississippi Elec. Power Ass'n,* 989 F. 2d 858 (5th Cir. 1993), and the unpublished opinion of the trial court. It is also based upon the parties' briefs, which Alison Steiner, counsel for the plaintiff, was kind enough to send me.

74. 989 F. 2d at 861.

75. Ibid.

76. Ibid. at 862.

77. Ibid.

78. Ibid. at 861.

79. *Spriggs v. Diamond Auto Glass Co.*, 242 F. 3d 179 (4th Cir. 2001).

80. Ibid. at 182.

81. See *Harris v. Forklift Sys., Inc.*, 510 U.S. 17 (1993).

82. Ibid. at 21.

83. Ibid.

84. 242 F. 3d at 185 (quoting *Rodgers v. Western-Southern Life Ins. Co.*, 12 F. 3d 668, 675 [7th Cir. 1993]).

85. Ibid.

86. *Bolden v. PRC, Inc.*, 43 F. 3d 545 (10th Cir. 1994).

87. Ibid. at 551.

88. Ibid.

89. Ibid.

90. See Eric Schnapper, "Some of Them Still Don't Get It: Hostile Work Environment Litigation in the Lower Courts," *University of Chicago Legal Forum 1999*, 277. Some students of the hostile-workplace case law assert that courts tend to be more solicitous toward plaintiffs making racial-discrimination claims than toward those making gender-discrimination claims. See, e.g., Robert J. Gregory, "You Can Call Me a 'Bitch'—Just Don't Use the 'N-Word,' " *DePaul Law Review* 46 (1977): 741.

91. 116 F. 3d at 631.

92. *Jackson v. Quanex Corp.*, 191 F. 3d 647 (6th Cir. 1999).

93. Ibid. According to another version of the facts, the

supervisor stated that the sludge was "ass deep to a tall nigger" (191 F.3d at 652).

94. Ibid. at 659.

95. Ibid. at 662.

96. Cf. Steven Hetcher, "Creating Safe Social Norms In A Dangerous World," *Southern California Law Review* 73 (1999): 1.

97. *United States v. Magleby,* 241 F.3d 1306, 1318 (10th Cir. 2001).

98. *United States v. Tocco,* 200 F.3d 401, 420 (6th Cir. 2000).

99. Ibid.

100. *Robinson v. Runyon,* 149 F.3d 507 (6th Cir. 1998). See also *Heno v. Sprint/United Management Co.,* 208 F.3d 847 (10th Cir. 2000).

101. *Brown v. City of Hialeah,* 30 F.3d 1433, 1434 (11th Cir. 1994).

102. Ibid. at 1436.

103. See, e.g., Alan M. Dershowitz, *Reasonable Doubts: The Criminal Justice System and the O. J. Simpson Case* (1997); Vincent Bugliosi, *Outrage: The Five Reasons Why O. J. Simpson Got Away with Murder* (1996); Jeffrey Toobin, *Run of His Life: "The People v. O. J. Simpson"* (1996).

104. 1995 WL 15923 at 21–24 (California Superior Court transcript, January 13, 1995).

105. Ibid. at 25.

106. *Ross v. Douglas County, Neb.,* 234 F.3d 391, (8th Cir. 2000).

107. *Preston v. Preston,* 627 N.Y.S. 2d 518 (1995).

108. *Lee v. the Superior Court of Ventura County,* 11 Cal. Rptr. 2d 763 (Cal. Ct. App. 1992). Actually, Lee petitioned to change his name to "Misteri Nigger" but stated that he intended for the *i* at the end of the first name to be silent (ibid.).

109. Ibid. at 764.

110. Ibid.

3. Pitfalls in Fighting *Nigger*

1. Leon F. Litwack, *Been in the Storm So Long* (1979), 59.

2. See Charles Miller, "Constitutional Law and the Rhetoric of Race," in Paul Finkelman, ed., *African Americans and the Law* (1992), 416; Mencken, American Language, 379; Irving Lewis Allen, "Sly Slurs: Mispronunciation and Decapitalization of Group Names," *Names* 36 (1988): 217.

3. See Aljean Harmetz, *On the Road to Tara* (1996), 144; Leonard J. Leff, "*Gone With the Wind* and Hollywood's Racial Politics," *Atlantic Monthly,* December 1995.

4. Hugh Rawson, *Wicked Words* (1989), 270.

5. At the same time, Secretary Udall changed all "Jap" references to "Japanese." See Mark Monmonier, *Drawing the Line: Tales of Maps and Cartocontroversy* (1995), 52. See also Lois Thomas, "What's in a Name," *In These Times,* October 20, 1997; Richard Willing, "Cripple Creek, Squaw Tits, and Other Mapmaking No-Nos," *Washington Magazine,* June 1996.

6. See *Hamilton v. Alabama,* 376 U.S. 650 (1964). See also Petition for Writ of Certiorari to the Supreme Court of Alabama, No-793 (filed January 29, 1964).

7. William Bradford Huie, *Three Lives for Mississippi* (1965), 35.

8. See Robert McFadden et al., *Outrage: The Story Behind the Tawana Brawley Hoax* (1990); Grand Jury of the Supreme Court, State of New York, County of Dutchess, Report of the Grand Jury and Related Documents Concerning the Tawana Brawley Investigation (1988).

9. See Kathryn K. Russell, *The Color of Crime: Racial Hoaxes, White Fear, Black Protectionism, Police Harassment, and Other Micro-aggressions* (1998), 157; James Merolla, "Newport Woman Reports Getting More Racist Messages: Tisha Anderson Says She Is Afraid to Leave Her Apartment after Receiving Telephone Threats and a Note," *Providence Journal-Bulletin,* November 16, 1995; "Anonymous Donor Offers Reward in Racist Threat; Police Report No New Leads on Slurs Scrawled on Walls and Steps of the Newport Green Apartment Complex," *Providence Journal-Bulletin,* November 14, 1995. For a glimpse of the wasted effort, damaging confusion, and hurtful recrimination generated by this episode, see Celeste Katz, "Newport NAACP Branch Meets over Racist Attacks; They Question the Newport Police's Efforts and Demand Further Action in the Case of Tisha Anderson," *Providence Journal-Bulletin,* November 18, 1995. For a murky case that seems to have involved another racial hoax in Providence, see Marion Davis, "Charges against Clemente Dismissed; Garrick Clemente Was Accused of Hiring Someone to Paint a Racial Slur on His Front Door," *Providence Journal-Bulletin,* August 5, 1996.

10. Russell, *The Color of Crime,* 162; "Sentencing in False Report of Racism," *Seattle Times,* December 11, 1996.

11. Russell, *The Color of Crime,* 163; Caitlin Francke,

"Hate-Crime 'Victim' Pleads Guilty; Tenant Painted Slurs in her Townhouse," *Baltimore Sun,* January 16, 1997; Ed Heard, "Support Pours in for Targets of Racial Graffiti; North Laurel Family Gets Donations, Encouragement," *Baltimore Sun,* April 26, 1996.

12. Peter Applebombe, "Woman's Claim of Racial Crime Is Called a Hoax," *New York Times,* June 1, 1990; see also Russell, *The Color of Crime,* 160.

13. Applebombe, "Woman's Claim of Racial Crime Is Called a Hoax."

14. See Debra Dickerson, "The Last Plantation: The 'Niggardly' Scandal Should Teach Whites to Watch Their Language and Blacks to Toughen Up," *Salon,* February 5, 1999.

15. Julianne Malveaux, "Of N-Words and Race Men," *Black Issues in Higher Education,* February 18, 1999. See also Roy Riley, "David Howard Is History Because of Indiscretion," *Washington Times,* February 26, 1999: "Mr. Howard is history because he was not bright enough . . . not to utter the word 'niggardly' in a city that is predominately black."

16. See, e.g., Jonathan Yardley, "Cool Words Can Influence, So Drop Them," *Newsday,* February 4, 1999; Steven Pinker, "Racist Language, Real and Imagined," *New York Times,* February 2, 1999.

17. Dickerson, "The Last Plantation."

18. Courtland Milloy, "Some Words Just Taste Unpleasant on the Tongue," *Washington Post,* January 31, 1999.

19. Sam Fullwood III, "D.C. Mayor Under Fire in War of Words over Word Use," *Los Angeles Times*, January 29, 1999.

20. Barry Saunders, "That D.C. Style: A Kinte Cloth Man-

tle of Oppression," *News and Observer* (Raleigh, North Carolina), February 6, 1999.

21. Tony Snow, "Linguistic Lynching over 'Niggardly,' " *Des Moines Register,* February 3, 1999. See also editorial, "Obsessing over the N-Word," *Hartford Courant,* February 3, 1999 ("Talk about the excesses of political correctness: last week, an assistant to Washington's new Mayor lost his job for being literate. . . . A person shouldn't lose his job because others misunderstood proper word usage"); Lynda Hill, "A Word, a Hairtrigger Racial Sensitivity, a Job Lost," *Christian Science Monitor,* February 3, 1999; Ken Hamblin, "PC Police Strike Again," *Denver Post,* February 2, 1999; Cynthia Tucker, "The Blacker-Than-Thou Thing," *Denver Post,* February 2, 1999.

22. See Gwen Carleton, " 'Niggardly' Upsets UW Student," *Capitol Times* (Madison, Wisconsin), February 2, 1999.

23. Natalie Anderson, letter to the editor, *Boston Magazine,* May 1998.

24. Sandra B. Fleishman, letter to the editor, *Boston Magazine,* May 1998.

25. Craig Unger, "A Letter from the Editor," *Boston Magazine,* May 1998.

26. See Lawrence Otis Graham, "Head Nigger in Charge: Roles That Black Professionals Play in the Corporate World," *Business and Society Review,* June 22, 1995.

27. See, e.g., Stan Simpson, "In Defining the N-word, Let Meaning Be Very Clear," *Hartford Courant,* November 3, 1997: "What would happen if a white friend were to come up to me and say [as does my black brother], 'Hey, Nigger! How are you doing?' Well, excuse my ebonics, but we be fightin'."

28. Listen to Chris Rock, "Niggers vs. Black People," on *Roll with the New* (1997). For the video performance, see Chris Rock, *Bring the Pain* (1996).

29. Quoted in Kathleen Pfeiffer, introduction to Carl Van Vechten, *Nigger Heaven* (University of Illinois Press ed., 2000; orig. pub. 1926), xiv.

30. Quoted ibid.

31. Quoted ibid., xiv, xxx, xxxi.

32. Quoted ibid., xxx.

33. Quoted ibid., xxvii.

34. See Kevin Merida, "Spike Lee, Holding Court: The Director Talks Movies, Hollywood, Basketball and, Oh Yes, Controversy," *Washington Post,* May 1, 1998.

35. See Lynne K. Varner and Hugo Kugiya, "What's in a Name?—A Hated Racial Slur Finds New Currency—and Controversy—in Popular Culture," *Seattle Times*, July 6, 1998.

36. See Richard Corliss, "The Scheme of a Notion," *Time,* October 9, 2000; "Spike's Minstrel Show," *Newsweek,* October 2, 2000.

37. Delphine Abraham, "Changing Webster's Dictionary," *Essence,* March 1998.

38. Ibid.

39. "NAACP Leader Kweisi Mfume Says Merriam-Webster's Decision on Use of Racial Slurs Is 'Unacceptable,' " *Jet,* May 25, 1998.

40. See John M. Morse, "Sparing Sensitivities Isn't Dictionary's Job," *USA Today,* May 11, 1998.

41. Quoted in Jarvis DeBerry, "Keeping a Hateful Word inside a Dictionary," *New Orleans Times-Picayune,* June 23, 1998.

42. John H. Wallace, "The Case against *Huck Finn,*" in James S. Leonard, Thomas A. Tenney, and Thaddious M. Davis, eds., *Satire or Evasion: Black Perspectives on "Huckleberry Finn"* (1992), 16.

43. Mark Twain, *Adventures of Huckleberry Finn,* ed. Thomas Cooley, Norton critical ed., 3d ed. (1999).

44. Wallace, "The Case against *Huck Finn,*" 21.

45. See Shelley Fisher Fishkin, *Lighting Out for the Territory: Reflections on Mark Twain and American Culture* (1996), 73–74.

46. Quoted ibid., 82.

47. See, e.g., Jane Smiley, "Say It Ain't So, Huck: Second Thoughts on Mark Twain's 'Masterpiece,' " in *Adventures of Huckleberry Finn,* Norton critical ed.

48. See *United States v. J.H.H.,* 22 F.3d 821 (8th Cir. 1994).

49. See *Dambrot v. Central Mich. Univ.,* 55 F.3d 1177 (6th Cir. 1995). See also Michael P. Pompeo, "Constitutional Law—First Amendment—Athletic Coach's Locker Room Speech Is Not Protected under First Amendment, Even Though University Policy Is Found Unconstitutional—*Dambrot v. Central Michigan University,* 55 F.3d 1177 (6th Cir. 1995)," *Seton Hall Journal of Sport Law* 6 (1996): 277. My understanding of *Dambrot* has also been enriched by conversations with Professor Robert A. Sedler, who represented Coach Dambrot on appeal.

50. See First Brief of Plaintiffs-Appellants–Cross-Appellees in *Dambrot v. Central Mich. Univ.* at 6 (quoting Complaint of Keith Dambrot).

51. Ibid. Coach Dambrot had also said on one occasion prior to the locker-room incident that his players should not be "niggers in the classroom." Questioned later about that

comment, the coach explained that he had been trying to express his feeling that "you can't be aggressive, tough, hard-nosed in class, especially at a school like Central Michigan University where the faculty members don't understand a lot about black people or have many black people in class" (55 F.3rd at 1181).

52. First Brief of Plaintiffs-Appellants–Cross-Appelless, *Dambrot v. Central Mich. Univ.* at 10 n. 4.

53. Ibid. at 11–12 n. 7.

54. Ibid. at 12–13 n. 9.

55. Ibid. at 13 n. 11.

56. Other coaches have used *nigger* in the same way Dambrot did. For example, testifying on Dambrot's behalf, Adele Young, an African American basketball coach, explained that "a coach is around the players seven days a week, nine months of the year. The players are a part of the coach's family. A coach can pick up the players' language and speech patterns without being aware of a change. . . . My players, both African-American and White, use [*nigger*] freely as I do in the coach setting. When used in this way, 'nigger' means a tough, hard player. Coach Dambrot understood the way players use 'nigger' and when he used it, he used it the very same way they did" (Ibid. at 9).

57. Chris Colin, "The N-Word," Salon.com, November 8, 1999; Alison Schneider, "To Many Adjunct Professors, Academic Freedom Is a Myth," December 10, 1999. See also *Hardy v. Jefferson Community College,* 2001 FED App.0267P (6th Cir. 2001).

58. See "Black Students Forgive Teacher's Mistaken Slur," *New York Times,* October 17, 1988.

59. See Richard Delgado, "Words That Wound: A Tort Action for Racial Insults, Epithets and Name-Calling," *Harvard Civil Rights–Civil Liberties Law Review* 17 (1982): 133; idem, "Campus Antiracism Rules: Constitutional Narratives in Collision," *Northwestern University Law Review* 85 (1991): 343; Charles Lawrence III, "If He Hollers Let Him Go: Regulating Racist Speech on Campus," *Duke Law Journal,* 1990, 431; Mari J. Matsuda, "Public Response to Racist Speech: Considering the Victim's Story," *Michigan Law Review* 187 (1989): 2320.

60. See, e.g., *UWM Post, Inc., v. Bd. of Regents, 774* F. Supp. 1163 (E.D. Wis. 1991); *Doe v. Univ. of Michigan, 721* F. Supp. 852 (E.D. Mich. 1989).

61. For examples of this rhetoric, see Lawrence, "If He Hollers Let Him Go," 434, 449; Matsuda, "Public Response to Racist Speech," 2370 ("Marked rise of racial harassment, hate speech, and racially motivated violence marks our entry into the 1990s"). Even fervent opponents of speech codes accede without sufficient questioning to their antagonists' portrayal of rising waves of campus racism; see, e.g., Nadine Strossen, "Regulating Racist Speech on Campus: A Modest Proposal?," *Duke Law Journal,* 1990, 484, 488. For useful commentary on this point, see James B. Jacobs and Kimberly Potter, *Hate Crimes: Criminal Law and Identity Politics* (1998), 45–64; Richard Bernstein, *The Dictatorship of Virtue* (1994), 183–215.

62. Lawrence, "If He Hollers Let Him Go," 433.

63. Ibid., 432.

64. Ibid., 433.

65. Ibid., 434.

66. Henry Louis Gates Jr., "War of Words: Critical Race Theory and the First Amendment," in *Speaking of Race, Speaking of Sex: Hate Speech, Civil Rights, and Civil Liberties* (1994), 42.

67. Lawrence, "If He Hollers Let Him Go," 451.

68. See S. Douglas Murray, "The Demise of Campus Speech Codes," *Western State University Law Review* 24 (1997): 247, 266 n. 158. See also Handoff, "Chilling Codes," *Washington Post*, March 25, 1995.

69. Lawrence, "If He Hollers Let Him Go," 448.

70. Gates, "War of Words," 47.

71. See Strossen, "Regulating Racist Speech on Campus," 484.

72. *West Virginia State Bd. of Educ. v. Barnette,* 319 U.S. 624, 642 (1943). See also *Chicago Police Dept. v. Mosey,* 406 U.S. 92, (1972) (Justice Marshall: "Above all else, the First Amendment means that government has no power to restrict expression because of its message, its ideas, its subject matter, or its content").

73. See William Lee Miller, *Arguing about Slavery: The Great Battle in the United States Congress* (1996); Harry Kalven Jr., *The Negro and the First Amendment* (1965); Michael Kent Curtis, "The Curious History of Attempts to Suppress Antislavery Speech, Press, and Petitions in 1835–37," *Northwestern University Law Review* 89 (1995): 785.

74. Delgado, "Words That Wound," 180. Note, though, that Delgado adds yet another complication: if *nigger* "was intended and understood as demeaning, minority plaintiffs could sue other members of the same or another minority

group" (ibid.). He does not broach the question of whether it would be permissible under any circumstances—e.g., if done with affection—for a white person to call a black person "nigger."

75. Matsuda, "Public Response to Racist Speech," 2364.

76. Ibid.

77. Langston Hughes, *The Big Sea* (1940), 268.

78. Lucius Harper, managing editor of the Chicago *Defender,* observed in 1939 that *nigger* "is a common expression among the ordinary Negroes and is used frequently in conversation between them. It carries no odium or sting when used by themselves, but they object keenly to whites using it because it conveys the spirit of hate, discrimination and prejudice" (quoted in Mencken, *The American Language,* supplement 1, 626).

79. Halford H. Fairchild, "N Word Should Be Odious from Anyone," *Los Angeles Times,* September 16, 1987.

80. Ron Nelson, "The Word 'Nigga' Is Only for Slaves and Sambo," *Journal of Blacks in Higher Education,* autumn 1998.

81. E. R. Shipp, "N-Word Just as Vile When Uttered by Blacks," *New York Daily News,* January 21, 1998. See also idem, "There's No Excuse for N-Word, Now or Ever," *New York Daily News,* March 11, 2001; Mary A. Mitchell, "N-Word OK for Blacks but Not for Whites?," *Chicago Sun-Times,* December 28, 1997.

82. Quoted in Laura A. Randolph, "Life after the *Cosby Show,*" *Ebony,* May 1994.

83. See Melvin Patrick Ely, *"The Adventures of Amos 'n' Andy": A Social History of an American Phenomenon* (1991).

84. Ibid., 9.

85. Ibid., 171–73.

86. Ibid., 173–74. See also the photograph following page 82.

87. Ibid., 215–16.

88. I have focused in the text that follows on black defenders of *Amos 'n' Andy,* but the show also had countless white fans and a number of white champions, some of whom were undoubtedly profoundly racist. In August 1931, the editor of the *Sterling City* (Texas) *New Record*, for example, denounced Negro critics of *Amos 'n' Andy* as "a lot of fool Niggers" and opined that the series brought out "nigger characteristics true to Nigger nature just as it is among the denizens of the colored race in large cities" (quoted in Ely, "*The Adventures of Amos 'n' Andy*," 185).

89. Quoted ibid., 171.

90. Ibid., 181.

91. Quoted ibid., 182.

92. Quoted ibid.

93. Ibid., 222.

4. How Are We Doing with *Nigger*?

1. Susan Schmidt, "Sen. Byrd Apologizes for Racial Remarks," *Washington Post,* March 5, 2001.

2. See Annie Nakao, "N-Word Use Increasing, Not Without Protest; Use of the Racial Slur Among all Ethnicities Elic-

its a Variety of Emotions," *San Francisco Chronicle,* July 29, 2001.

3. For a biting critique of Tucker's humor, including his use of *nigger*, see Justin Driver, "The Mirth of a Nation: Black Comedy's Reactionary Hipness," *New Republic*, June 11, 2001.

ACKNOWLEDGMENTS

I would like to thank Gerhard Casper, who, during his tenure as president of Stanford University, invited me to give the Tanner Lectures at his great institution in the spring of 1999. Those lectures, "Who Can Say 'Nigger'? . . . and Other Related Questions," provided the initial impetus for this book. I would similarly like to thank Professor Richard McAdams, who made it possible for me to deliver "*Nigger!* As a Problem in the Law," the fall 2000 Davis C. Baum Lecture at the University of Illinois at Champaign School of Law.

Harvard Law School is a wonderful setting within which I have been privileged to work. Dean Robert C. Clark, an enthusiastic friend of scholarship, offers constant encouragement, while colleagues and students offer productive criticism. As always, the staff at the Harvard Law School Library provided invaluable assistance. Especially helpful were the reference librarians, Deanna Barmakian, Amy Brower, Joan Duckett, Michael Jimenez, Janet C. Katz, Josh Kantor, Naomi Ronen, and Terry L. Swanlund. Particularly noteworthy among Harvard Law School students and professors who have offered helpful comments are Eve Madison, Mathew Tollin, David Solet, Justin Driver, Zachary Price, Sapna Sadarangani, Richard Fallon, Duncan Kennedy, Todd Rakoff, Lloyd Weinreb, and David Wilkins.

Other colleagues who have given me much-appreciated encouragement, information, and advice include Yvedt Matory, Sanford Levinson, Kathleen Sullivan, Stephen Schulhofer, Joshua Dressler, Glenn C. Loury, Jennifer Hochschild, Fred Schauer, R. Richard Banks, Kevin Mumford, Richard Ford, George Packer, Anita Allen, Eric Foner, and Vicki Schultz.

Mr. Benjamin Sears carefully typed the manuscript and buoyed many a workday with his good cheer. Altie Karper managed the copyediting with her usual grace.

My literary agents, Andrew Wylie and Sarah Chalfant, and my editor, Erroll McDonald, teamed up to make sure that procrastination did not stall publication. I am grateful for their efforts on my behalf.

Finally, I want to acknowledge again the people to whom this book is dedicated, folks who have surrounded me with love throughout my life: the men and women who constitute the Spann Clan's Board, led by its Chairman for Life, Gary E. Bell.

INDEX

Aaron, Hank, 24–25
Abraham, Delphine, 133–37
academia, speech codes
    adopted in, 150–59
Africa, Pryor's visit to,
    185–86
African Americans, *see* blacks
AIDS, 29
Ali, Muhammad, 35–36
All God's Chillun (O'Neill),
    52
Amos 'n' Andy (TV), 163–70
Amsterdam News, 168

Anderson, Natalie, 126
Anderson, Tisha, 118
Andrews, William, 189
And Then There Were None
    (Christie), 115
antidiscrimination statutes,
    58, 88–104, 173
    accumulated totality of
        racist acts in, 102–4
    direct evidence under, 95
    hostile workplace
        environment under,
        96–104, 105–6, 110

antidiscrimination statutes
(*continued*)
overenforcement of, 95
racial discrimination
under, 88–96
rudeness vs. illegal abuse
in, 99–101
see also courtroom
procedures
antilynching bill, 9–10
antislavery politics, 25–26
Army, U.S., 16, 35
Associated Press, 134

Bamboozled (film), 132
Barkley, Alben, 10
Bates, Daisy, 17–18
Beloved (Morrison), 29
Bentsen, Cheryl, 124
Bicentennial Nigger (Pryor),
186
"black Republicans," 25–26
blacks:
cultural conflict among,
160–61
cultural turf of, 49–50,
127, 131–32
nigger used by, 34–35,

36–51, 127, 160–63,
174, 207
pain mastered and
contained by, 80, 154
self-hatred of, 45–49
terms of address, 113–16
Blease, Coleman Livingston,
9
Blyew v. United States, 33
Board on Geographic
Names, U.S., 116
Bolden, James L. Jr., 99–101
Bond, Julian, 122
Boston Magazine, 124–27
Brawley, Tawana, 117–18,
119
Brown, Claude, 37
Brown, Henry, 89–95
Brown, H. Rap, 61–62
Brown v. Board of Education, 52
Bruce, Lenny, 38–39, 111
Bullins, Ed, 141
Bush, George W., 60
Byrd, Robert C., 54, 173
Byrnes, James, 10

Cambridge, Godfrey, 39
censorship, 115–16, 128,

137–41, 151, 158–59,
173–75
Central Michigan University
(CMU), 142–47,
148
Chan, Jackie, 175
Chang, Iris, 29
Chaplinsky v. New Hampshire,
67–69
Chase, Chevy, 30–31
Chesnutt, Charles, 129
Chideya, Farai, 28
children's rhymes, 6–7
chink, 3
Christie, Agatha, 115
civil liberties, 150, 173–74
Civil Rights Act (1964),
Title VII cases,
88–104, 105–6, 110
civil rights revolution,
26–27, 35, 113
CNN, 134
Cochran, Johnny, 108–9
Cohn, Avern, 102, 103
Coleman, Rev. Louis, 148
Collins, Sabrina, 118–19
comedians, 30–31, 38–41,
45, 127, 162–71,
185–86

communities:
complexities of, 159–60
divisiveness in, 49
protection within, 160
Congress, U.S., 9–10, 62
Conrad, Joseph, 115, 133
Constitution, U.S., First
Amendment, 67–69,
85, 144–45, 158–59
content neutrality, doctrine
of, 158
Coolio, 43–44
Cosby, Bill, 162–63, 166,
169–70
Coughlin, Ann, 79
courtroom procedures,
32–34, 56–112
antidiscrimination
statutes in, 58,
88–104, 105–6, 110,
173
appellate courts in,
93–95, 111
categories of, 58
criminal law in, 80
diminished capacity in,
75
direct evidence in, 95
divorce case, 110–11

courtroom procedures
(continued)
Emmett Till case, 56–58
emotional distress as
claim in, 81–86, 88
fighting-words doctrine
in, 67–69, 111, 155
judicial review in, 72
jurors biased in, 58,
59–61, 104–9, 189
mere-words doctrine in,
69, 76–80
nigger as provocation in
murder cases, 58,
72–80
nigger used by officials in,
58, 61–72
nigger used in variety of
cases, 32–33, 110–12
partial responsibility in,
73–74
perils of leniency in,
79–80
playing the race card in,
108–9
"reasonable people" in,
97–98
relief obtained in, 81
Simpson case, 107–9

social meaning of, 32
speech codes tested in,
150–59
tort law in, 58, 81–88,
173
see also specific cases
cross-burning, 104–5, 140
Cullen, Countee, 128
cultural conflict, 160–61
cultural expression, 49–50,
127, 131–33, 157–58,
170–71
Cypress Hill, 43

Dambrot, Keith, 142–47,
150
Darden, Christopher, 28,
108
Davis, Benjamin Jefferson,
17
DeBerry, Jarvis, 37
Def Comedy Jam (HBO), 163,
166, 170
Delgado, Richard, 79, 150,
160, 207
Dellums, Ron, 133
Dickens, Charles, 133
Dickerson, Debra, 121

dictionaries, *nigger* defined
      in, 4–6, 133–37
Diggs, Charles C. Jr.,
      56–58
DMX, 43
Doctorow, E. L., 52
doctrine of content
      neutrality, 158
"Double Nigger" (Dumas),
      141
Douglass, Frederick, 12–13
Dr. Dre, 43
Dreiser, Theodore, 141
Duke, David, 117
Dumas, Henry, 141
Dyson, Michael Eric, 51

Easton, Hosea, 5
"Electronic Nigger, The"
      (Bullins), 141
Ellison, Ralph, 80, 193–94
EMEPA case, 89–95
Eminem, 50–51
Emory University, 118–19
eradicationists, 45–46, 141,
      159–71, 173
Ethics of Living Jim Crow, The
      (Wright), 13–16

Etowah County, Alabama,
      116

Fairchild, Halford H., 162
Federal Radio Commission,
      166
fighting-words doctrine,
      67–69, 111, 155
films, 114–15, 130–32,
      140, 175
First Amendment, 67–69,
      85, 144–45, 158–59
Fisher, Julius, 73–74, 75, 76
flag burning, 158–59
Foxx, Redd, 39
Frankfurter, Felix, 74
Franklin, John Hope, 66
freedom of expression,
      158–59, 173–74
freedom riders, 26–27
Fuhrman, Mark, 107–9

Gates, Henry Louis Jr.,
      124–27, 154, 157
Geto Boys, 43
Goffman, Erving, 187–88
Goldman, Ronald, 107

Gone With the Wind (film),
    114–15
Goodfarb, Stanley Z., 62
gook, 3, 32
Gould, Arkansas, High
    School, 148–49
Government Printing Office
    (GPO), U.S., 114
Green, Ely, 18
Greenberg, Jeff, 60–61
Gregory, Dick, 20–21, 39
Grisham, John, 52

Hacker, Andrew, 28
Hance, William Henry, 59,
    61, 62
Hardy, Ken, 147–48
Harlem Renaissance, 53, 129
Harper, Lucius, 207
Harris, Persey III, 118
Hartigan, John, 54–55
Hassan, Umar Bin, 48
Hastie, William, 169
hate speech, 150–59
Herndon, Angelo, 17
Hicks, James, 57, 58
Higginbotham, A. Leon, 52
hip-hop culture, 50–51
HNIC, use of term, 124–27

Holmes, Oliver Wendell, 55
Holocaust, 28–29, 158–59
Home Box Office, 163
honky:
    comparative damage of
        term, 28, 32
    in courtroom
        procedures, 32
    defining, 135
Houston, Charles Hamilton,
    73–74, 75
Howard, David, 120–22
Howard University, 11
Howells, William Dean, 52
Huckleberry Finn (Twain), 52,
    137–41
Hughes, Langston, 53–54,
    161

Ice Cube, 44, 51
Ice-T, 44
Imperative Duty, An
    (Howells), 52
Internet, 7–8, 134, 179
Ito, Lance, 107–9

Jackie Brown (film), 130
Jackson, Linda, 101–4

Jacobs, Bruce A., 49
Jacobs, Harriet, 12
Jacobs, Ray, 65–66, 70, 71
James, Sonia, 118
Jaz-Z, 43
Jefferson Community
        College, 147–48
Jews, and Holocaust, 29,
        158–59
Jim Crow, 13–16, 26, 35,
        36, 56, 114, 139, 159
Johnson, Charles S., 129
Johnson, James Weldon, 10,
        129
Johnson, Lyndon B., 11–12,
        52–53, 71
Johnson, Paul, 116–17
jokes, 7–8, 34–35, 36, 38,
        163
Jones, Ira, 9
Jordan, Michael, 22
Journal and Guide, 169

Kennedy, John F., 38
kike, 3, 32
King, Martin Luther Jr., 36,
        74–75
Kingsblood Royal (Lewis), 52
Kramer, Larry, 29

Lakoff, Robin Tolmach, 178
landmarks, names of, 115–16
Larsen, Nella, 129
Last Poets, 47–48
Lawrence, Charles, 79, 150,
        157
Lee, Helen Jackson, 37
Lee, Spike, 131–32, 133
Lee, Tom S., 91–92
Lee, William, 118
Lennon, John, 50
Lewis, Sinclair, 52
Lewis, Theophilus, 168–69
"Lift Ev'ry Voice and Sing,"
        129
Lincoln, Abraham, 25
linguistic expression, 173–74
literature, 13, 16–17, 29,
        52, 115, 128, 137–41,
        193–94
litigation, *see* courtroom
        procedures
Long, Huey P. "Kingfish,"
        10, 164
Lopez, Jennifer, 174–75
Lorde, Audre, 22

Mabley, Moms, 39
McKay, Claude, 141

McLaurin, Charles, 21–22
McReynolds, James Clark, 11
Magleby, Michael Brad, 104–5
Major, Clarence, 36
Malcolm X, 18
Malveaux, Julianne, 121
maps, names on, 115–16
Marsalis, Branford, 22–23
Marshall, Thurgood, 52–53, 73, 110, 169
Matsuda, Mari, 150, 157, 160
mere-words doctrine, 69, 76–80
Merriam-Webster's Collegiate Dictionary, 133–37
Mfume, Kweisi, 134–35
mick, 3
Milloy, Courtland, 121
Mississippi Burning (film), 140
Mitchell, Lansing L., 62
Mixon, Liza, 113
Montgomery, Robert, 33–34
Morrison, Toni, 29
Morse, John R., 134, 136
movies, 114–15, 130–32, 140, 175
Mulroy, J. Kevin, 63

murder, 58, 72–80, 189
Murdock, Benjamin, 75, 76

NAACP (National Association for the Advancement of Colored People), 10, 115, 117, 119, 122, 129, 134–35, 166–67, 169, 179
Nanking, Rape of, 29
National States Rights Party, 27
negritude traits, 45, 132
Negro, use of term, 114
"Negro National Anthem," 129
Nelson, Ron, 162
New York Times, The, 114
nigga, as distinguished from nigger, 5
niggardly, use of term, 120–23
nigger:
    ambiguity of use, 175
    automatic labeling of, 95
    blacks' use among blacks, 34–35, 36–51, 127, 160–63, 174, 207

and book censorship,
116–16, 128, 137–41
in book title, 128–30
celebrity controversy
about, 124–27
in court, *see* courtroom
procedures
and culture
protectiveness, 49–50,
132–33, 145–47
current practices, 172–76
and eradicationists,
45–46, 141, 159–71,
173
etymology of, 4–6, 66,
133–37
excessive punishment for
use of, 117, 122,
141–50
in film scripts, 114–15,
130–32, 140, 175
"good" vs. "bad," 63–64,
161–62
impact of, 4, 98
as incitement to murder,
58, 72–80
lying and silly defenses
against use of, 119–23
mistaken protest against,
137–50

as paradigmatic slur,
27–31, 98, 147, 174
pejorative meaning
attached to, 5–6, 178
and political correctness,
147–59, 170, 172–73
positive use of, 37, 48,
117, 146, 175–76
racist vs. nonracist uses
of, 160
and regulationists,
150–59
renovation of, 174
as rhetorical boomerang,
36
and speech codes,
150–59
stigmatization of,
117–19, 155, 161–62,
172–73
ubiquitous nature of, 6
variety of meanings of,
34–35, 37–38, 54, 95,
115
whites described as,
54–55
whites' use of word,
8–12, 70, 127, 174,
207
in wordplay, 160, 162

Nigger, The (Sheldon), 52
nigger eggs (bowling balls), 27
Nigger Factory, The (Scott-Heron), 141
nigger golf (craps), 27
nigger hams (watermelons), 27–28
Nigger Heaven (Van Vechten), 128–30, 161
Nigger in the Window (Lee), 37
"Nigger Jeff" (Dreiser), 141
nigger lover, 25–27
"Nigger Lover" (McKay), 141
"Nigger Lover" (Sandburg), 141
nigger luck (bad luck), 28
nigger news (gossip), 28
Nigger of the Narcissus, The (Conrad), 115
nigger rolls (one-dollar bills), 28
niggers of Europe (Irish), 27
niggers of the Middle East (Palestinians), 27
nigger stompers (heavy boots), 28
Nims v. Harrison, 81–83

Nixon, Richard M., 12
NWA, 44
N-word, as euphemism, 3

Oates, Joyce Carol, 52
O'Connor, Flannery, 12
O'Neill, Eugene, 52
Ono, Yoko, 50
Opportunity, 129
overbreadth doctrine, 157–59

Parker, Lonnae O'Neal, 23
Pittsburgh Courier, 165–66, 168–69
police, excessive force used by, 106–7
political correctness, 147–59, 170, 172–73
pornography, 158–59
Postal Service, U.S., 105–6
Powell, Adam Clayton, 11
Pryor, Richard, 30–31, 39–41, 185–86
Pulp Fiction (film), 130–31
Purdue University, 151
Pyszczynki, Tom, 60–61

racial epithets, 5, 27–34
  comparisons of, 27–31
  in Congress, 9–10
  context of use, 51–52,
    95–96, 126–27, 174
  in court, *see* courtroom
    procedures
  as fighting words, 67–69,
    111, 155
  lists of, 3, 32, 147,
    158–59
  as "mere insults," 86
  positive meanings of, 37,
    48, 146, 175–76
  as solidarity vs.
    disrespect, 50
  taboo status of, 38–39,
    147
  third parties affected by,
    60
  volatility of, 147
  see also specific slurs
racism:
  in colleges, 151–58
  internalization of, 45–46
  nonracist usage vs., 160
  in workplace, 93, 102–4
Ragtime (Doctorow), 52
rap, 43–45, 50

Rape of Nanking, 29
Rawlings, Marjorie Kinnan,
  115
Reardon, Catherine Cooper,
  73–74
regulationists, 150–59
Reinhardt, Stephen, 28
Reports from the Holocaust
  (Kramer), 29
Robeson, Paul, 18, 129
Robinson, Aleia, 105–6
Robinson, Jackie, 18–19
Rock, Chris, 41–43, 127
Rolfe, John, 4
Roosevelt, Eleanor, 164
Roosevelt, Theodore, 9
Ross, Otis, 110
Rowan, Carl, 19–20
Rush Hour (film), 175
Russell, Nipsey, 39
Russell, Richard, 9

Sahl, Mort, 39
Sandburg, Carl, 141
sand niggers (Arabs), 27
Saturday Night Live, 30–31
Saunders, Barry, 122
Schuyler, George S., 16–17

Scott-Heron, Gil, 141
Selling of Joseph, The (Sewall), 5
Selznick, David O., 114–15
Sewall, Samuel, 5
Shakur, Tupac, 44
Sheldon, Edward, 52
Shipp, E. R., 162
Sigel, Beanie, 44
Simpson, Nicole Brown, 107
Simpson, O. J., 107–9
slavery:
    fight against, 159
    as holocaust, 29
    lampooning of, 34
slaves, memoirs of, 12–13
Smalkin, Frederic N., 98
Smith, Lillian, 52
Smith, Otis, 119
Smith, Patti, 50
Smith, Tommie, 22
Smith College, 151
SNCC (Student Nonviolent Coordinating Committee), 21–22, 61
Snow, Tony, 122
song lyrics, blacks lampooned in, 6
Spears, Arthur K., 55

speech codes, 150–59
Spivey, Jerry L., 65–72, 149–50
Spriggs, James H., 96–98
Stanford University, 154–57
State of North Carolina v. Rufus Coley Watson, Jr., 76–78
Stickell, Ernest, 96–97
Stowe, Harriet Beecher, 52
Strange Fruit (Smith), 52
Sumner, Charles, 26
Supreme Court, U.S., 11, 33, 52–53, 68, 74, 97, 114, 116, 145, 158, 169
Swango, Curtis L., 57

Talmadge, Eugene, 10–11
Tarantino, Quentin, 128, 130–31, 133
Ten Little Niggers (Christie), 115
That Nigger's Crazy (Pryor), 39–41
Them (Oates), 52
Thurmond, Strom, 9
Till, Emmett, 56–58
Tillman, Benjamin, 9

Time to Kill, A (Grisham), 52

Title VII, Civil Rights Act
    (1964):
  express aim of, 104
  hostile environment
      cases, 96–104, 105–6,
      110
  racial discrimination
      cases, 88–96
  "reasonable people" in,
      97–98
Tocco, Jack William, 105
tort law, 58, 81–88, 173
  degrees of
      outrageousness in,
      86–88
  difficulties of, 83–86
  relief obtained in, 81, 84
  see also courtroom
      procedures
Tribe Called Quest, A, 43
True Romance (film), 130
Truman, Harry S, 11, 71
Tucker, Chris, 175, 209
Twain, Mark, 52, 133,
    137–38, 140

Udall, Stewart, 116
Uncle Tom's Cabin (Stowe), 52

Unger, Craig, 125
University of Michigan, 151
University of Wisconsin,
    123, 156

vagueness doctrine, 158
Vann, Robert L., 165–66
Van Vechten, Carl, 53–54,
    128–30, 161
Van Vechten, Charles
    Duane, 128
victim status, comparisons
    of, 28–32
Vietnam War, 35–36
vocabulary of indirection,
    157
voting rights, 20–21, 35

Wallace, John H., 138, 140
Walls, W. J., 165
Washington, Booker T., 9
Watkins, Mel, 40–41
Watson, Rufus Coley Jr.,
    76–78
Webster, Noah, 4–5
*Webster's Tenth New Collegiate
    Dictionary,* 135
wetback, 3, 32

White, Walter, 10, 115, 129
White Citizens Council, 11
white man's nigger, 190
white racism, internalization
    of, 45
whites:
    avoidance of *nigger* in
        usage by, 9, 51
    infringement of black
        culture by, 49–50,
        127, 131–32
    nigger used by, 8–12, 70,
        127, 174, 207
white supremacists, 9
white trash, 9
Whitfield, Stephen J., 57
Wiggs v. Courshon, 81–82,
    85–86
Wilkins, Roy, 10, 167–68,
    169
Williams, Anthony, 120,
    122–23
Wilson, August, 22
Wilson, Edmund, 12
Woodford, Brenda, 23–24

Woods, Tiger, 22
wop, 3
words:
    assaultive, 79, 152
    defining, 136–37
    fighting, 67–69, 111, 155
    freedom of expression
        with regard to,
        158–59, 173–74
    hypersensitivity to,
        120–23
    mere, 69, 76–79
    power of, 49, 147
    uses of term, 55
workplace:
    discrimination cases,
        88–96
    hostile environment,
        96–104, 105–6, 110
Wright, Richard, 13–16,
    72–73

Yearling, The (Rawlings), 115
Young, Adele, 204

ABOUT THE AUTHOR

RANDALL KENNEDY received his undergraduate degree from Princeton and his law degree from Yale. He served as a law clerk to Supreme Court Justice Thurgood Marshall before joining the faculty of the Harvard Law School. A member of the American Academy of Arts and Sciences, the American Philosophical Association, and the American Law Institute, Mr. Kennedy lives in Dedham, Massachusetts.